SIR JOSEPH CARRUTHERS

Founder of the New South Wales
Liberal Party

SIR JOSEPH CARRUTHERS

Founder of the New South Wales Liberal Party

Zachary Gorman

Connor Court Publishing

Connor Court Publishing Pty Ltd

PO Box 7257
Redlands Bay, Qld 4165
sales@connorcourt.com

www.connorcourtpublishing.com.au

ISBN: 9781925501766

Cover design by Renee Gorman

Printed in Australia

CONTENTS

INTRODUCTION

Liberalism is Australia's oldest political tradition. Indeed without the success of nineteenth-century liberalism in winning battles to end convict transportation, introduce responsible government and expand democracy, the very conditions under which all other Australian political disputes have been fought out would not have existed. Despite this, it is generally the Labor Party that boasts most proudly about its history. Its members frequently cite the fact that their party has existed since the 1890s, while Liberals seldom mention anyone further back than Menzies. There are obvious reasons for this. The Liberal Party lacks continuity in its existence. At the Federal level it started out as an uneasy alliance between Free Traders and Protectionists in opposition to a perceived socialist menace, before the twin disasters of the First World War and the Great Depression prompted further compromises for the sake of the nation. Such disconnection hides a story of evolution and transition, through which the present party of the centre-right emerges from the past.

Nowhere is this underlying continuity more visible or important than in New South Wales. The "Mother Colony" won responsible government for herself and for her daughters, and was home to the liberal titans who oversaw the birth of Australian democracy. While having the deepest of nineteenth-century roots, New South Wales also had the most resilient of twentieth-century Liberal Party structures. More so than anywhere else, the State's Nationalist Party and United Australia Party were simply their Liberal Party by another name.[1] That party had been founded in 1902 as the Liberal and Reform Association by the subject of this biography, Sir Joseph Carruthers.

Born in the quiet backwater of Jamberoo at the advent of responsible government, Carruthers' life encompassed the transition from a pervasive and loose culture of political liberalism to the partisan struggles between institutionalised Liberal and Labor parties that now dominate our elections and our parliaments. As an infant he was taken to see William Charles Wentworth, writer of the New South Wales Constitution, and by the time of Carruthers' death Menzies was just about to enter Federal

Parliament. In the meantime, Carruthers had been Premier of his State and a founding father of the Australian Federation, not to mention a prominent Minister under giants Henry Parkes and George Reid.

He climbed his way to the top through a mixture of belief, talent and ambition, maintaining an affable reputation while leaving numerous rivals in his wake. Once there he materially changed Australian history. Not only did he help to write the Federal Constitution but he also introduced comprehensive local government in New South Wales and won the fight to save the Legislative Council from abolition. He thus affected the composition of all three tiers of government. He instituted tremendous reforms in education and the administration of Crown lands, setting up thousands of farms that helped to facilitate Australia's continued emergence as an agricultural powerhouse. Perhaps most importantly of all, Carruthers set precedents for financial management and tax reform that future Liberals are still trying to emulate. Even in his sixties he was dictating political affairs in New South Wales, pulling the strings behind the Fuller Government.

Carruthers' greatest legacy is his New South Wales Liberal Party. This biography tells the story of how that organisation emerged from years of failed attempts by the Free Traders to create a permanent body to fight and win elections. It also tells the story of how the Liberal Party took the classical liberalism of nineteenth-century New South Wales and redirected it into a partisan stance aimed at defeating the Labor Party. Carruthers endured the political turmoil of the 1890s where a three-party system and minority governments fuelled instability. In response he came up with the idea of imposing clear "lines of cleavage" on the political landscape and making elections a clear choice between two competing philosophies of government.

These philosophies were the liberalism New South Wales had long supported, and the new big government interventionism that characterised a broad understanding of "socialism". Through a combination of fierce rhetoric, skilled campaigning and careful organisation, Carruthers would impose this dividing line on New South Wales politics, destroying the "Progressive" third-party and securing two election victories. This success would inspire George Reid to emulate Carruthers at a Federal level. His famed anti-socialist campaign borrowed heavily from Carruthers, and through it he would prompt the fusion of the Federal Free Trade and Protectionist parties into a broad anti-socialist Liberal Party, and thus the birth of the modern Australian political divide.

Carruthers' Liberal Party and the lines of cleavage thus helped determine the fact that Australian liberalism would sit on the centre-right of politics. An emulator of Gladstone, Carruthers believed in balanced budgets, free commerce and, as much as possible, letting people live their lives unmolested by government. At the same time, he was fundamentally a pragmatist, who defined his belief in individualism and enterprise broadly enough to attract a wide variety of liberal and conservative followers. Though he held sincere liberal views, Carruthers was a practical politician rather than a political philosopher. His skill lay in applying his beliefs to the concerns of the day and making them succeed in the electorate. He was particularly capable of establishing what he and his party stood for in relation to their opponents, and then conveying that message to the voters. Long before Menzies re-erected the banner of Australian liberalism, Carruthers had unfurled it in a remarkably modern form.

The story told by this biography is the story of the creation of Australia's political divide, but it does not stop there. By following Carruthers' life until its end it also explores how that divide was tested and transformed by the creation of the Nationalist and United Australia parties. In doing so it highlights the underlying continuity in Australian liberal thought and the continued centrality of anti-socialism in how the centre-right has defined itself.

Joseph (right) with his brother. From the National Library of Australia, Canberra.

CHAPTER ONE

A Liberal Upbringing

> The active influences that bear upon the fortunes of a human life reach backwards in point of time to a past as mysterious as the most distant future. The mental beginnings of each individual life are shrouded in a mystery which no expert in any science or art can explain.

This is how Joseph Carruthers' close friend and political ally George Reid began his reminiscences. The sentiment is certainly apt for Carruthers, whose own unfinished autobiography is riddled with the mistakes of an old man recalling his distant past. By the time of his death even the year of his birth had become murky, as newspaper obituaries contradicted the date given in Carruthers' autobiography.

Sir Joseph Hector McNeil Carruthers gave his date of birth as 21 December 1856. He was born in Kiama, where his family owned a property on the Minnamurra River at Jamberoo. Kiama at this time was a comparatively large regional centre, as before the building of a train line the town acted as an important port for the transport of South Coast goods to the Sydney market. There the Carruthers family occupied a modest weatherboard home that offered little creature comforts beyond keeping out the wind and the rain. Joseph recalled spending summer nights with the door open, watching flying foxes raid the orchard before his father peppered them with shot. Despite his spending only a few years on the Jamberoo property, the location had a lasting influence on Carruthers, who was ever after obsessed with regional development and land settlement.

Joseph was the youngest of nine children born to a poor but industrious immigrant couple. Joseph's father was John Carruthers, a Presbyterian Scot who had come to Australia around 1830.[2] Unbeknownst to his family, he had been sent over as a convict after a drunken and destructive binge which occurred while he was serving in the military in Ireland. He would struggle with alcoholism for much of his life, but eventually brought the problem under control. Through a combination of effort and good luck, John was able to successfully hide his convict history and save himself and his family from the associated social stigma.

Like a large number of convicts, upon completing his sentence John did not return to Britain but instead resolved to make his way in the Colony to which circumstance had brought him. In the 1830s New South Wales was undergoing a rapid economic expansion fuelled by booming wool prices and a large number of settlers flooding in from the British Isles. In these circumstances there were plenty of opportunities for any man willing to work his way up, and John was not shy of labour. At various times he worked as a house-painter, builder, contractor and a farmer and over several years he became a well-known personality not only in Kiama but in the heart of Colonial New South Wales, Sydney. He even developed a personal relationship with William Charles Wentworth, the most important political figure in the Colony. John was involved in the expansion of Vaucluse, the historic home of the writer of the New South Wales Constitution.

No doubt Joseph would have seen his father as a heroic "self-made man" of the type he would later encourage children to aspire to be. This idealised image was reinforced by stories of John, as a boy, diving into a ditch to save himself from dragoons during the infamous Bonny Muir "rising" of 1820. From a young age John had been attracted to politics and developed a fascination with the local agitations of the Scottish Reformers led by Andrew Hardie and Thomas McCulloch. The "rising" was a rally tied to their fight for increased political liberties, and also played off unrest caused by a general strike that was taking place at the time. Men "met to talk about the people's rights, and how they might be obtained through the three reforms of shorter Parliaments, manhood suffrage, and votes by ballot". Though Carruthers claimed the demonstration was largely peaceful, some of the protestors brought sharpened poles, and one a musket. This was enough to convince English administrators that the agitators were seeking to incite a violent rebellion. Troops were sent in to put down the rising and after a brief skirmish the men were rounded up and arrested. They were subsequently convicted of high treason, their leader was executed and the rest were sent to Australia.

John maintained that his emigration to Australia was forced by the rising, but it is now known that his hidden convict past had led him to the antipodes.[3] Regardless of the authenticity of his father's connection to the incident it is clear that it left a distinct impression upon Joseph and would have influenced his liberal outlook. Tales of English oppression of the Scots would have helped to shape the beliefs in liberty and political autonomy that would later be essential to Carruthers' politics. Scottish identity was an important part of Joseph's world view. From an early age at Jamberoo he was taught by Mrs McGillvray, an old Scottish schoolteacher, and between her and his father Joseph was left to wonder that he had not developed a Scottish accent. Both of them conveyed a great deal of Scottish history to the boy, and from an early age he developed a fascination with the past.

Though Scottish identity was important, Joseph developed a world view that was broadly British and colonial. His father was a staunch monarchist and a believer in the British Empire that protected and fostered the Australian colonies. New South Wales had started out as a penal colony and convict transportation continued for the first few decades of its existence. By the early 1800s however, free settlers had become the main driver of a booming population. Attracted by the promise of plentiful land and high wages, thousands of people left the industrial overcrowding of the British Isles and made their way to Sydney Harbour. Initially concerned primarily with administering convicts, colonial governments protected the common law property rights of the free, and British financial institutions were soon recreated, setting up a capitalist system in the Colony. Waves of intense migration fuelled financial booms and busts before a process of "recolonization" turned Australia into a major agricultural exporter to Britain in particular.[4] Australia was subsequently able to attract a large amount of British capital, which funded land speculation and public works construction, playing the central role in a rapid economic expansion.

The economic integration of New South Wales with Britain and its other settler colonies was matched by a cultural integration. New South Wales inherited the political, intellectual and religious values of the British countries that provided the vast majority of its settler population. Colonial educational institutions taught British history, book shops sold British books and newspapers reported extensively on British politics. Moreover, personal networks connected families, friends and businesses as letters and people travelled back and forth between the various parts of a wider British world.

This created a sense of shared identity that was crucial to Carruthers' outlook. Like most New South Welshmen at the time, Joseph was brought up to believe that he was British and that he was entitled to the individual and political liberties that an idealised "Britain", with its long history of extending and defending rights, was meant to embody. This was an overlapping identity that allowed him to still identify as "Australian" without any more contradiction than mixing national and state ties. To be a "Briton" was to be one of the exclusive inheritors of the liberty of the Magna Carta and functioning rather than demagogic democracy. The Australian Colonies often pre-empted Britain on issues such as the extension of the franchise and the introduction of the secret ballot, but these reforms were frequently advocated as a natural outgrowth of inherited British rights. In turn, colonial reforms often affected the turn of events in the Mother Country.

The overlap of British and Australian identity and politics was personified by John. Joseph's father maintained the passion of the Scottish Reformers and was heavily involved in political movements that encouraged individual initiative and independence. John was a member of the Anti-Transportation League which fought to end the oppressive and humiliating practice of forcibly bringing convicts to the Colony. He was also chairman of the Land Reform League, which fought to open up Crown land to industrious individuals. Campaigning heavily between 1854 and 1864, the League became "the motive force" behind the introduction of John Robertson's land laws. These aimed to give individuals the opportunity to own their own piece of land in the form of cheaply available plots. These plots were representative of a belief in the opportunities of a "new" land and while perhaps not as prevalent as in the United States the notion of individual opportunity still shaped the world-view of many colonials. A "progressive-liberal to the backbone", John taught Joseph that he should be concerned about the conditions of those around him. He placed a tremendous value in community, but that community was defined by families and individuals rather than by the government.

By the time of Carruthers' birth New South Wales was developing a distinct liberal political culture which his father exposed him to. Earlier in the Colony's history there had been attempts made to set up a conservative society based on the pillars of a landed gentry and an exclusively established Church of England.[5] Many great pioneer families were involved in this enterprise, but the effort ultimately failed. New South Wales, though almost exclusively Christian, was too religiously diverse to allow the establishment of a single state supported religion, while free selectors and liberals had undermined efforts to create a land holding aristocracy.

Without these pillars of Toryism, New South Wales did not end up emulating the political divide of Westminster. Instead, battles over democratic government, convict transportation and land distribution allowed liberals to develop a political hegemony over the Colony. The autocratic rule of all-powerful Governors had frequently been seen as arbitrary and oppressive, so when citizens won democratic control over the levers of government in 1856, there was a general sense that it must be used to foster freedom. Individualism, rationality, the concept of progress and a belief in self-help; these were the central tenets of the cultural faith that gripped New South Wales. The development was epitomised by the *Sydney Morning Herald*, the Colony's most important newspaper, which after a brief period of intense conservatism became a proponent of individual liberty and the political economy of Adam Smith.

At the apex of colonial liberalism was Henry Parkes. The son of a traditional English tenant farmer, Parkes' family had been displaced by the great social dislocations of the industrial revolution. Intensely poor, he tried making a go of it in Birmingham and London, before immigrating to Australia in desperation in 1839. At various points a stonebreaker, farm hand, ivory turner, toy shop owner, journalist and newspaper editor, Parkes embodied the search for financial independence that drove many immigrants. His political fame was due initially to his fight to extend democracy and kill a plan to reintroduce convict transportation to the Colony. The latter was a prototypically liberal issue as it involved a fight against an arbitrary government decision in England and sectional squatter interests who were happy to have cheap convict labour. Parkes became a prominent member of the Legislative Assembly, serving as Premier on five separate occasions. Though far from an ideological demagogue, he had clear beliefs encapsulating freedom, opportunity, democracy, education and unfettered commerce which helped to define the politics of his age. John was a partisan supporter of Parkes and he took Joseph to meetings and rallies. Joseph, at a very impressionable age, would have thus seen Parkes in his prime. It created a feeling of awe towards Sir Henry that Carruthers would maintain, to varying degrees, throughout his life.

Joseph's mother was born Charlotte Prince. Unlike her very Scottish husband, she was English and an Anglican. This English heritage would have tempered the Scottish radicalism Joseph may have been exposed to, helping to make him a liberal rather than a radical. Originally from London, Charlotte came to the antipodes as a bounty immigrant. Bounty immigration was a scheme whereby the government paid British recruiting agents to bring people to Australia to overcome an acute labour shortage during the great wool boom of the 1830s. The fact that Charlotte took part in such a scheme suggests that her situation was desperate enough for her to desire emigration, but also that she was deemed a valuable settler.

Upon arriving in Sydney Charlotte met John, who managed to woo her with the same charms that allowed him to climb the colonial social ladder. Records suggest that John may have already been married to an

estranged wife in Ireland, but after an extended courtship and the birth
of two children the pair tied the knot in 1838. Charlotte had little formal
education, she signed her marriage certificate with a cross, but she was
highly intelligent and matched her husband's capacity for hard work. She
was known to be a miser; Joseph described her as having "an English-
woman's sense of the value of thrift". For a family of little means such
penny-pinching was essential however, and as the family's finances gradually improved Charlotte expanded her horizons to become something of
a land speculator and small time mining investor. She even invested the
young Joseph's measly savings, achieving a significant return for her son
and in the process inspiring Joseph's later penchant for productive investment. It was Charlotte's thrift, financial experimentation and his parent's
sacrifices that would help to pay for Joseph's education. Any examination
of the five meticulously balanced budgets Carruthers presented as Treasurer clearly show that Charlotte's values rubbed off on her son.

Joseph inherited his mother's Anglican faith, not his father's Presbyte-
rianism, but from both sides he was resolutely a Protestant. His brother
James became a prominent reverend, but Joseph was not particularly
devout. An extremely active community member, he simply did not have
the time to spend on excessive worship or theological debates. He certainly believed in God, but his thoughts were with the world of the present and he was more-likely to fundraise for a church institution than
spend hours praying. Perhaps because of this slight detachment, Joseph
did not grow up to possess the sectarian prejudices common amongst
his peers. There are numerous examples of him having admiration for
and friendship with Catholics, and in 1927 he even made a donation
towards the construction and upkeep of St Mary's Cathedral in Sydney.[6]
The extent to which Carruthers' Protestantism later manifested itself in
"wowser" beliefs is also highly debatable. He would support "local option" control of the liquor trade but this had much to do with his father's
experience as a reformed alcoholic rather than Protestant moralism, and
Joseph himself was no teetotaller. He was also a keen fan of horserac-
ing, even helping to set up Kembla Grange racecourse in the Illawarra,
something that wowsers would not have supported.

While Carruthers was not an absolutist Protestant, Protestant culture pervaded his identity and beliefs. Liberalism had a deep attachment to the individual and particularly the free exercise of an individual conscience that had largely emerged from Protestant morality. Many strands of Protestantism were based around an individual's direct relationship with the scripture and with God, free from outside control. Moral choices had to be made on a daily basis and were not confined to a separate religious sphere; hence many Protestants were inherently suspicious of outside control of any aspect of their lives. Individual freedom was connected to personal responsibility and an imperative to utilise that freedom to do good. These beliefs bled into liberalism, and even when liberals were not consciously thinking as "Protestants", they inherited Protestantism's philosophic legacy.[7]

Though Carruthers developed a deep attachment to the Illawarra-South Coast area, he did not spend long in Jamberoo. In 1861 the family moved to Sydney so that John could take up a post as clerk of the Sydney markets. After only three years, Joseph moved again, this time to the Macleay River area on the North Coast of New South Wales. "For some good reason, probably to give me a chance to get better health in pure country air", Joseph had been sent north on a steamer in to the care of his sister Sarah. She was married to James Wood, who along with Joseph's brother Henry had selected a 1280 acre property in the fertile but underdeveloped region. As a small boy who would grow into a rather short man, Joseph had a history of ill health, and this would plague him throughout his life. Such was his parents' concern that at less than ten years of age they sent him to live on the practical frontier of colonial society.

As Carruthers' family were the only non-Indigenous people settled in their particular section of the Macleay area, Joseph spent much of his time playing with Aboriginal children. He would later recall that in "that in those days, when they had not been contaminated by the whites, the Aborigines, young and old, were outright decent people – clean in thought, in words, and in actions".[8] He also maintained that "Civilisation has much to answer for, in its ruthless indifference to the fate of native races not physically or mentally fitted for the first rude shocks of contact with the whites, who have invaded their homelands, bringing with them new diseases and vile habits, and sometimes unspeakable cruelties that have unnecessarily wiped out millions of so-called inferior and backward peoples". Joseph's notion that white settlement had been detrimental for Indigenous people was comparatively enlightened for the time, though his views were also laced with patronising paternalism. He called them Australia's "Peter Pans – boys that never grow up". This statement, uncomfortable to modern ears, reflects the fun that Joseph had as a seven-year-old fishing and hunting with his very own nulla nulla.

Carruthers became immersed in Aboriginal culture, even learning much of the native language. His best friend was a young man known as "Yellow George", who used to carry the small boy on his back for long journeys. More than fifty years later Carruthers would pay another visit to an aged Yellow George, arranging that he be given a small pension and a boat. Joseph's experience as a boy and his friendship with George influenced his attitude towards all native peoples. The origins of his later campaign for the rights of Samoans can be traced back not just to Carruthers' liberalism but also to his time on the Macleay River. Despite holding views that were often patronising, Carruthers' reflective summation of the Indigenous issue is frankly modern; "plainly, as an Australian, I feel shame for the way we have treated our native blacks".

Having gained some semblance of strength, Joseph returned to Sydney to be enrolled in school. He first went to William Street before finding a home at the Model Public School in Fort Street. There he began his education, discovering a passion for learning and analysis that would be an integral part of his life. Unfortunately, he perhaps showed too great an aptitude for learning, for his intelligence got him picked out to be recruited as a "cash boy" for a leading firm of Sydney merchants. His parents may have hoped that by agreeing to the offer they were setting their son up for a career and that he would make valuable connections, but the fact that they put him to work at such a young age suggests the family's finances remained somewhat strained. The gruelling job took Joseph out of school as he was forced to work ten and a half hours a day.

After experiencing a year of its trials the eleven-year-old's health broke down once more. Though we do not know exactly what illness he suffered, Carruthers would later trace his partial deafness to this incident. The family doctor, Sir Arthur Renwick, suggested that Joseph needed to get out of Sydney and hence he was sent to Goulburn to attend George Metcalfe's High School as a boarder.

Metcalfe's operation was one of only a handful of High Schools in the Colony at the time, and attendance was a great opportunity for young Joseph. Metcalfe encouraged a rounded education that included various sporting activities of which the sickly child was in dire need. He also cultivated his students' individuality while balancing this by imbuing in each of them a deep sense of personal responsibility. By the time Joseph arrived at the school he had fallen far behind his fellow students. Nevertheless, his teacher found him to be "intelligent, studious and above all anxious to learn" and soon took an "especial interest in developing his inherent ability".[9] Joseph showed an initial strength for algebra, but Metcalfe took the pains to teach him Latin and introduce him to the writings of Cicero. Soon he was also reading Greek and discovering a real passion for the classics.

It is indicative of the "small world" that colonial New South Wales was at this time that at Goulburn Joseph went to school with future Premier Thomas Waddell, after having spent much time in Jamberoo in the company of the family of George Fuller. Later at University Joseph would play cricket both with and against future Prime Ministers. Nineteenth-century liberals had a respect for individual opinions and a distrust of party politics, and part of the reason for this was the "small world" these educated men lived in. They often maintained personal relationships even with those politicians with whom they disagreed. The rapid increase in the size of New South Wales, as well as the introduction of the payment of members, which widened the pool of people from which politicians could be drawn, would gradually lead to the breakdown of this system of "personal" politics.

The boys were given a considerable amount of freedom to roam Goulburn and the surrounding bushland, though some supervision was required to guard against the very real threat of bushrangers. They frequently went hunting and fishing, much to the delight of Joseph whose inquisitive mind relished the chance to discover the native wildlife. School was their main priority however, and Joseph was given few breaks from it. One year his parents made the gut-wrenching decision to deny their son a Christmas trip home in order that he could take advantage of more time with Metcalfe. The hard work paid off, and by late 1872 his teacher thought that he was ready for university. Initially John was reluctant to cut his son's schooling short, but Metcalfe insisted that he "would work him hard, and save a year of his life". John and Metcalfe jointly decided that Joseph should enter the legal profession, one of the few careers in which the bright boy's talents might fully be utilised. Hence in March 1873 Joseph sat and passed the matriculation examination before being enrolled at the University of Sydney.

Founded in 1850 under the instigation of William Charles Wentworth, the University was a pillar of colonial New South Wales, and a vehicle for the transfer of British intellectual culture to the antipodes. Its creation was tied to the pending advent of responsible government and the need, acknowledged even by conservatives, to educate future leaders for a democracy. There Joseph studied classics under one of the more remarkable figures in the Colony, Charles Badham. Carruthers placed him alongside Sir Henry Parkes and General Booth of the Salvation Army as the three greatest men of his time. Badham had spent seven years studying in the great libraries of Germany, France and Italy and was one of the most qualified people to teach at the University in its early days. The many prominent students that he taught included many of the most promising young men in the Colony, and few were more enraptured with their teacher than Joseph. He would later recall that Badham's "value lay not alone in his worth as a classical scholar and teacher but in his broad grasp of the public duties both of the citizen and the state".[10]

From Badham Carruthers developed a historically aware world view that had perhaps been first awakened by his father's discussion of Scottish history. Badham's "daily lectures to the students were studded with brilliant flashes of rhetoric as he applied the force of the lessons of the past to the circumstances of today". During one lesson he delivered a forceful philippic against the abusive use of Pacific Islanders as labourers in Queensland and "urged his students to devote their talents to the service of the public". Badham had a huge influence on Carruthers' politics, as his teachings combined with readings of historians like Macaulay to imbue a Whig idea of a historical struggle for liberty that had been going on since the dawn of civilisation itself. When he later became a politician, Carruthers would often draw on precedents from Greek, Roman or British history. He had a deep respect for "the great empires which laid the foundation of our civil laws and nurtured even through the period of their decay, the germs of modern civilisation". Later in life he even tried his hand at being a historian himself, delivering lectures and publishing a book on Captain Cook.

Badham also taught Carruthers "that candour which strives to occupy a point of view from which an opponent is speaking and that courtesy which seeks to refute without insulting or degrading the holders of opposite opinions". This debating technique was very important to Carruthers' success as a politician, as he always took pains to understand his opponent's viewpoint in order that he might critique it more effectively. Continuing his education in debating, Carruthers was involved in the creation of the University of Sydney Union. At the time this organisation was essentially a debating club for the benefit of those wishing to enter the legal profession, rather than the heavily politicised body it would later become. The experience in public speaking would prove invaluable for the diminutive student, and he was soon making up in voice what he lacked in height. He even learned to use one of his major disadvantages, his partial-deafness, to his advantage. Feigning deafness could be used to buy time by making an opponent repeat themselves or even to ignore a tricky question all together. His deafness certainly did not affect his confidence, and the perspicacious speaker soon earned himself the label "cocky Carruthers", though many referred to him by the more depreciative "little Joey".

While at university Carruthers would often visit Parliament to listen on the political debates in the Legislative Assembly. His favourite speaker was the man his father had always supported, Henry Parkes. This was around the time of Parkes' first Ministry when he reduced tariffs and fought for Upper House reform, two issues the impressionable young observer would later pick up. Carruthers recalled that "it seemed to our young minds as if he [Parkes] were physically a product of those classical ages when Cicero and Demosthenes swayed the impulse of the people in great affairs of state".[11] This is a good example of the historical view of current events Carruthers developed under Badham, though it was not a unique perspective as others maintained a biblical image of Parkes as a Patriarch. He also recalled that "rightly or wrongly, I was a Parkesite because I felt that his was the master-mind and the master-hand that this state needed in those times". Parkes possessed a personal charisma that attracted many talented young men into his orbit. He was a very important early influence on Carruthers and helped to inspire his entry into politics. Once there however, Joseph's idealised image of the man would be severely battered, only to be rebuilt after Parkes' death and by the passing of time.

Carruthers' interest in politics led him to read widely. By the time he became a politician he had read John Stuart Mill and some of the other pillars of classical liberalism, helping to firm his romanticised notion of individual freedom. Most of his readings were of a more practical nature however, be they about past and present politics, as well as broader issues. He was able to deliver lectures on the works of Macaulay, while his earliest publication was an 1874 article on agricultural chemistry for *The Kiama Independent*. Michael Roe has highlighted the fact that many of the advanced "progressives" of Carruthers' era read Nietzsche and other high philosophers, and that this partly shaped their beliefs in the extensive use of the state to achieve ideals and quell unrest.[12] Carruthers' more grounded reading, particularly of political history, led him to the more sober conclusion that "the Millennium has to come more from the people themselves than from their lawmakers and that all that Parliament can do is strictly limited to removing disabilities and restricting privileges that deny equal opportunities to each man to work out his own salvation by his own good efforts".[13] One of his favourite quotes was attributed to Goldsmith, though it is said to have come from Samuel Johnson: "how small, of all that human hearts endure, that part which laws or kings can cause or cure".

Other interests Carruthers pursued while at university were cricket and football. He loved both games, but cricket was the overwhelming passion. Joseph played for the university team for many years and would later become a stalwart of the parliamentary team. He was a bowler for both sides while Edmund "Toby" Barton often kept wickets. Eventually Carruthers came to occupy the presidency of the New South Wales Cricket Association. He held the post for many years, and played the central role in destroying a scheme to make South Africa a part of the Ashes. He was a perennial observer of England tours and intercolonial matches, and his memoirs are filled with anecdotes about the best and most eccentric cricketers of his day.

Joseph's involvement in sporting clubs would continue throughout his life, perhaps as a respectable alternative to the rowdy social clubs in which other prominent men were involved. In Sydney the best known of these was the Athenaeum Club, which followed Barton's financial policy of trying to "drink itself out of debt".[14] Carruthers was not a teetotaller and would later become an early advocate of Australian wine, but revelling in binge drinking was something out of step with his Protestant sensibilities. In his spare time he would also attend the theatre, developing a passion for both the arts and the nineteenth-century equivalent of "popular" culture. This would bleed into his speech writing, as his addresses were often laced with references that offered humorous illustrations to prove a particular point.

It was while playing cricket that Carruthers would meet a man who would play an integral part in his political career. He described him as a "neat and dapper fellow, not so portly as he was in after years, but with his blue eyes, light flaxen hair and moustache, and fair complexion, rather a good looking dandy".[15] It was the future Premier and Prime Minister, George Houstoun Reid.

A fellow Scotsman, Reid had been born in Renfrewshire before moving to Australia when his father, a Presbyterian Minister, took up a post preaching in Melbourne. The family later moved to Sydney so that the father could work alongside radical firebrand John Dunmore Lang. At the time Carruthers met him Reid was working as a public servant in the Colonial Treasury, but he already had a keen interest in politics and particularly the tariff issue that would lead him enter the Legislative Assembly in 1880. He was something of a jovial figure, an impression exaggerated by his obese belly and decisive wit, but he was also a man of great intelligence and principle.

When they met Carruthers and Reid were opponents, as the latter did not play for the university team. During their next meeting they would also be opponents, for at the School of Arts Debating Club they argued over the comparative merit of Dickens (Reid) and Thackeray (Carruthers). These incidents began a friendship which endured until Reid's death. With matching moustaches and contrasting heights and girths, the two friends formed quite a striking pair, the political equivalent of Asterix and Obelix. Though in their initial meetings they had fought against one another, in politics they were almost always to be found on the same side. Independent minded nineteenth-century liberals, they did not agree with anyone on every single issue, but each man's politics was arguably closer to the other's than it was to anyone else's. They shared a classic liberal free-trade ideology that emphasised individual freedom and democracy and which was laced with a heavy dose of pragmatism. It was this formulation that made them both successful.

According to Carruthers, "Reid was a man of fine qualities, consistent in his liberal principles, a great advocate of Free Trade, an upholder of the best features of the system of responsible government". In 1918 he would fondly recall Reid's "very noticeable habit of going off to sleep at any odd moment, or in any place". During a fishing trip the two men went on this habit became the source of much humour. As Reid tried to call over Carruthers' hunting dog Ponto, the former fell asleep. Upon reaching the slumbering man the dog then wandered off again. Consequently, when Reid woke up he had to call for Ponto only to once again fall asleep before he arrived. The whole process was repeated several times and brought the rest of the party to hysterics. On another occasion Carruthers recalled, Reid fell asleep and began to snore loudly when an opposition member was speaking in the Legislative Assembly. The member raised a point of order over the interruption but the Speaker ruled that there was no order against it. Reading Carruthers' anecdotes one gets a clear sense of the warmth and affection he felt towards his friend.

Given both men's profession of a close friendship and their respective historical importance, it is odd that their relationship has received almost no attention from historians. While not a great deal of correspondence between the two of them survives, what has clearly tells us that they were close friends. Even their wives were close, and would go out of their way to visit each other when sick.

To truly understand either man as a political figure, the importance of their influence on one another must be taken into account. Michael Hogan has argued that "there is no indication that he [Carruthers] admired Reid as he admired Parkes".[16] This is essentially true but it is missing the point. Carruthers had an idealised image of Parkes from his father and his time at university. He was the "grand old man" of New South Wales politics when Carruthers entered Parliament as quite a young gentleman. Reid on the other hand was someone Carruthers had played cricket against and casually debated. Despite an age gap of more than ten years they were equals and friends and in that, as will be seen later, there lay a relationship where they could reciprocate in the passing of ideas and by helping each other to reach prominent positions.

Reid never idolised Parkes like Carruthers did, but the two friends did share an admiration for another grand old man, William Gladstone. As was the case with Parkes, Carruthers' young adulthood corresponded with the height of Gladstone's career and the young colonial liberal would have followed newspaper accounts of the great British political battles over electoral reform, free trade and retrenchment. Reid would even go so far as to take a sort of pilgrimage to visit the aged Gladstone in the late 1890s and while Carruthers never had that opportunity his frequent quotations offer ample evidence of his admiration. Such was Carruthers' penchant for citing Gladstone that in 1905 an *Evening News* cartoonist would even draw an impression of the short Premier trying to fill the great statesman's famous collar.[17]

The importance of Gladstone for Carruthers' liberal ideology and the New South Wales free trade tradition in general is difficult to overstate. The liberalism of Carruthers was essentially Gladstonian liberalism with a colonial bent. Some tenets the former borrowed from the latter included an emphasis on liberty, a community not defined by government, and individual initiative as the driving force of progress.[18] "Progress" in this sense had a historic undertone, suggesting the improvement of humanity through the exercise of individual freedom. True progress could only be achieved by unshackling people from the oppressive demands of the government and letting them make their own decisions. This had moral and philosophical undertones, both of which tied into Gladstone's strong Protestant beliefs. On a practical level freedom exercised through enterprise was seen as the essential source of economic advancement. Taxation inhibited the main vehicle of material progress, therefore spending needed to be kept low for the good of all. In this vein free trade and the "free breakfast table" of cheap goods unencumbered by tariffs were meant to benefit poor people most, for they not only had the least money to waste on taxes but also the greatest need for the opportunities that unencumbered enterprise was supposed to provide.[19]

As a Homeric scholar Gladstone like Carruthers had a historical view of politics, and saw liberty as being grounded not only in relatively small government but also in the long standing institutions of the British system. Both men shared a belief in the extension of democracy, but a democracy founded on liberty and which avoided the excesses of mob rule. Perhaps most important of all, Gladstone turned classical liberalism into practical rhetoric and policies that could win elections and boast legislative achievements. Abstracted ideology is of little value until it is adapted to the political circumstances in which it needs to operate and it was in this process of pragmatically putting beliefs into practice tactically, organisationally and legislatively that Carruthers would excel throughout his career.

On the day that Carruthers graduated from the University of Sydney, Charles Badham told his former pupil "you came here too young". It may have been a fair comment. Carruthers later recalled that he had taken his Bachelor of Arts degree before he was eighteen and before he was twenty-one passed the exam for admission as a solicitor. He had been articled to the lawyer-politician A.H. McCulloch, and quickly forged connections within the beating heart of Sydney's legal and political superstructure. After passing his examination, Carruthers began to practise law and tutor pupils for matriculation. Though he was accepted as a solicitor for the Supreme Court, he soon found that his hearing made him unsuitable for the role. Instead he decided to focus on conveyancing and set up his own firm.

Carruthers inherited his parents' capacity for hard work, and burned the candle at both ends to make his business a success. In his prime he was known for his encyclopaedic memory and the ability to dissect even the most complicated contract or piece of legislation. It was a trait that would serve him well both in law and in politics. His firm "had success from the outset, and with a few wise or lucky investments I soon found my feet".[20] As might be expected from a conveyancer, these investments generally came in the form of property. They would be important for his political career, as though he would continue to practise law the income from these would allow him the freedom to spend less time earning a living and more time attending Parliament.

On 10 December 1879 Joseph Carruthers married Louise Marion, the youngest daughter of successful lawyer William Roberts. The two moved into a house at Woolahra, but they did not stay long. Joseph was offered a part in a promising land purchase at Kogarah, then on the far outskirts of Sydney. This was the very beginning of the suburban age when good economic times combined with improvements in transport, namely the growth of train and tram lines, to make it increasingly possible for ordinary people to buy their own home. Home ownership did not reach the heights that it later would in the 1950s, but in many ways this was the beginning of the transference of the Australian dream from owning a farm to owning a smaller but more centrally located piece of land. The purchase Carruthers was involved in was intended for profitable subdivision aimed at satisfying this growing appetite for houses.

Appreciative of the beauty of the St George area, Joseph also obtained a plot nearby for himself and his young family.

Over the next few years Louise would give birth to three children, Elsie in 1880, Ida in 1882 and Jack in 1883. Though he was very busy with work Joseph became, by nineteenth-century standards, something of a doting father. He placed tremendous value in his children, and in providing for them a loving home and a solid education. One of Carruthers' great strengths as a politician would be his humanity and the extent to which his experiences were grounded in the family life shared by many of his constituents. His relationship with Louise would often be strained, but Joseph maintained an emotional attachment to the concept of the family home and the independence that land ownership gave an individual.

Joseph was a tremendously civic-minded man. The late nineteenth-century was a time of great community projects and individual charity, and Carruthers immersed himself in the goings-on of the emerging Kogarah community. He lobbied hard for the creation of an Illawarra railway line to service the area. He also led the successful fight for the incorporation of Kogarah as a Municipal Council, eventually serving briefly as an alderman. His community roots were laid still deeper with involvement in the creation of Kogarah School of Arts and the foundation of St George Cottage Hospital. The latter was probably his proudest local achievement. Built on the back of a great deal of public philanthropy and a comparatively small government grant, the hospital symbolised both community spirit and the fact that individuals would willingly look after one another without the need for compulsion. Like most community projects at the time, it was funded through personal subscriptions and seized upon the naturally charitable temperament of hard-working people.

Behind Carruthers' efforts lay a genuine altruism, but also a restlessness that pointed the way for a career devoted to serving the public. Part of the reason he was successful as a lobbyist for his local area was because of the network of political connections he inherited from his father, and it certainly appeared as though Joseph harboured political ambitions of his own. In the late 1870s he became involved in his first political campaigns. During the 1877 Sydney City Council elections Joseph spoke at election meetings for Samuel Lees. Lees, a prominent Orangeman and Freemason, was standing for election in the Macquarie ward. While there is no evidence to suggest Carruthers was influenced by sectarian prejudices, some members of the circles in which he mixed evidently were. Lees would later become a Free Trade politician and would institute a policy of substantial economies when Mayor in 1895. The campaign was a failure but it gave Carruthers his first taste of electoral public speaking.

In 1879 Joseph was appointed honorary secretary for Sir Arthur Renwick's election campaign for the University of Sydney seat in the Legislative Assembly. Renwick was an old family friend and had been the doctor who had recommended Joseph leave Sydney after his year as a "cash boy". The fact that such a man was a friend shows the political circles in which the family mixed, for he would go on to be twice a Minister. As honorary secretary Carruthers was responsible for the organisational side of the admittedly small campaign. Renwick's opponent was the young Toby Barton who was a heavy favourite to take the seat. This is what eventuated, with Barton winning by 58 votes to 38.

Both of Carruthers' early political undertakings had been failures. Even so, they would prove to be invaluable experience for the young man. The speeches given in support of Lees were a step beyond the relaxed addresses Carruthers would have been able to give at the School of Arts Debating Club. At just twenty-one he was learning how to sway the crowd. Perhaps even more important was Carruthers' time as honorary secretary for Renwick. This exposed him to the organisational side of campaigning, an essential, though frequently under-appreciated, aspect of securing electoral success. Good extra-parliamentary organisation would be a hallmark of Carruthers' political career, as he never lost an election when standing as a candidate or even as the leader of a party. These experiences would be built upon with campaigning in Kiama, Woollahra and Canterbury. In the days before party machines gave a clear path of advancement to apparatchiks our young subject would enter politics with a level of experience few of his contemporaries could match.

CHAPTER TWO

Parkesite Politics

Carruthers would spend the early half of the 1880s focusing on his legal career and on his young family. Meanwhile the political situation in the Colony was undergoing a rapid shift. When Joseph had seen Henry Parkes speak in the Legislative Assembly and campaigned for Arthur Renwick, New South Wales politics was in its "factional era" which had emerged from the early days of responsible government. When a fully elected Legislative Assembly had been inaugurated in 1856, passionate liberal and conservative groups had fought over the political issues of the day. After the resounding defeat of the latter, this ideological division faded away and politicians were left to find a new way to form majorities and ultimately governments. The method developed was that of factional alignment, as prestige, personal loyalties and common interests were used to cobble together votes in the Lower House. This era was characterised by largely independent members, who though they may have been loosely connected to factional leaders were not bound by party or extra-parliamentary organisations. These members were supposedly elected on their merit as the "best" men of their area, and were fiercely defensive of their right to individual opinions.

Once early conservatism faded, liberalism was left with nothing to define itself against and became less of a clear agenda and more of a pervasive political culture reflected in the individualistic way of parliamentary life. Bede Nairn has described the presence of a set of "traditional social values … derived from an exaggerated view of individual freedom".[21] Most members believed in keeping taxation low and encouraging commerce. Fierce debates raged over land laws, public education and where to spend significant public works investment, but the idea that government should become a significant and controlling part of citizens' lives was seldom contemplated. In the middle of the decade the coming of the "fiscal issue" heralded the beginning of the end for this system, as ideology began to rival personality as the driving force behind politics.

The "fiscal issue" was a debate over tariffs between Protectionists and Free Traders. Protectionists believed that high tariffs could protect native industries from foreign competition and lead to more work and higher wages for the lower classes. Free Traders believed that high tariffs artificially raised prices, taxing all of society to help manufacturers with the burden being particularly acute for working people. They also argued that the high costs of production created by protection hurt the economy by encouraging inefficiency and making exports uncompetitive. Underpinning these practical beliefs was a moralistic belief in goodwill. In the eyes of many of its devotees free trade was a Christian policy for it relied on generous reciprocation rather than the retaliation of protection. This moralism even stretched to the point of utopianism, for some hoped that by fostering international trade relations and co-dependency free trade could help bring an end to war. Free trade was also emblematic of an underlying belief in fostering a free society, and encouraging individuality in thought, speech and action.

The intellectual roots of free trade ideology stretched back to men like Adam Smith, whose intellectual justification for commerce and free enterprise held great value for Carruthers and many other liberals. Smith's idea that trade fuelled the expansion of an economy and ultimately the wealth of a nation, acted as a counterpoint to the protectionist argument that local industries needed to be sheltered. Perhaps the greatest practical hero of the philosophy was Richard Cobden, who had successfully fought against the Corn Law tariffs that artificially raised the price of grain in Britain. Because these Corn Laws hurt poor people for the benefit of landowners, Cobden was a popular democratic as well as liberal figure. A "Cobden Club" was set up in his honour, an organisation that offered honorary membership to those who greatly contributed to the propagation of free trade theory. One recipient was George Reid, whose 1875 work *Five Free Trade Essays* offered both a local and international critique of protectionism. Carruthers undoubtedly read this work, which likely strengthened a belief in tariff freedom that was already well associated with his liberal political outlook.

Traditionally New South Wales, with an economy that relied heavily on trade and exports, had been relatively committed to free trade. Some small duties were maintained but it was generally acknowledged that the Colony specialised in agricultural production and mining, and that it made logical sense to exploit overseas markets while importing those goods that were impractical to produce in a fledgling economy. Sydney was very much a merchant city. The wealth of the Colony emanated out from her docks and her merchants had long been strong backers of the Colony's classically liberal politicians. In contrast Victoria, with an economy that had been artificially inflated by the gold rush, looked to tariff protection to foster industries to replace the jobs once created by the now-depleted mineral. Many Victorians became enamoured by the possibilities of a tariff-protected manufacturing industry, and began to sell the idea to their fellow colonists. In response, in 1885 Carruthers' future political colleagues William McMillan and Bernhard Wise set up a Free Trade Association to promote tariff reduction and counter the perceived protectionist threat coming from Victoria.

It was a problem of finance that led to the "fiscal issue" becoming front and centre of New South Wales political debate. Alexander Stuart won the 1882 election with a promise to end the indiscriminate sale of Crown lands, which had led to the creation of large estates that were seen as alienating the land without settling the people. The problem was that the sale of Crown lands had become an essential part of the Colony's income that had allowed governments, Parkes' in particular, to spend lavishly on public works while still amassing budgetary surpluses. When Stuart came to power the effective suspension of auctions of Crown land led to a big drop in revenue and the quick accumulation of a large debt. Stuart's Treasurer George Dibbs was unable to solve the dilemma, largely because the Government's supporters refused to agree to a property tax.

The situation continued to get worse while a large loan delayed the inevitable. In 1886 the Jennings Government was forced to bite the bullet. It proposed direct taxation and 5% ad valorem duties in order to raise revenue. Protectionists outside of Parliament hailed the new tariff as the "thin end of the wedge" that would ultimately lead to trade barriers.[22] Free Traders were quick to buy into this conspiracy, and denounced the duty as an unwarranted attack on the Colony's economic system. Adding fuel to the free trade fire, the direct taxation measures were rejected by the unelected Legislative Council, increasing the pressure to make tariffs the main source of revenue.

Henry Parkes seized upon the discontent as a chance to get back into power. Then in his early seventies, Parkes' best days were behind him, but his ambition had not dimmed even after three successful stints as Premier. He presented himself as the natural leader of those holding free trade beliefs and moved a censure motion with the hope of dislodging some of Jennings' factional support. The Government was initially able to survive the turmoil until a split in Cabinet over a grant of reprieve for those convicted in the Mount Rennie rape case finally proved Jennings' undoing. He was forced to resign and the Governor called upon Parkes to form a government. The latter accepted on the condition that the Parliament was dissolved, a request that the Governor readily agreed to.

Thus in 1887 New South Wales headed towards an election which would ostensibly be fought over the fiscal issue. The Protectionists and Free Trade Association began to organise in earnest, as most candidates were forced to declare on which side they stood. With a clear ideological issue at stake and extra-parliamentary organisations helping to run campaigns, the election would bring about a "decisive and permanent break" with the old factional system, beginning the process of party development.[23]

It was in this watershed election that Joseph Carruthers would enter New South Wales politics. He had already been approached to represent his native district of Kiama, but at the time the young lawyer had declined. In 1886 his circumstances would change. In this year his daughter Elsie died suddenly from a bout of scarlet fever. Joseph was deeply attached to his first-born child and in the midst of the family tragedy he fell into a deep melancholy, withdrawing from both business and public life. As his depression wore on to the point of being disruptive, Carruthers' friend Mark Hammond delicately chided him "on the folly of giving way to misfortune".[24] Hammond had just retired as one of the four members for the seat of Canterbury and suggested that Carruthers should take his place:

> For a week or more I hesitated, and then one Saturday morning late in January 1887 I suddenly made up my mind. Within half-an-hour I drafted an announcement of my candidature for publication on the following Monday, and walked down to the *Sydney Morning Herald* office, handed it in to the advertising clerk, paid for it, and walked back to my office. As soon as I got back, I repented my decision and so hurried down to the *Herald* offices to withdraw my announcement. But the office was closed, and would not open again until the Monday, and so the die was cast.

It is difficult to determine whether Carruthers' profession of reluctance was sincere or just a matter of form. Hammond was a devout Catholic and "defiantly independent of party".[25] He was also a fierce believer in liberal economics, and it was this shared faith that led him to ignite the career of a Protestant Parkesite.

Carruthers publicly declared that he was a believer in free trade and a supporter of Parkes, but he was not preselected in the free trade "bunch" to contest the Canterbury electorate. Preselection was relatively new in New South Wales, an innovation brought about by the fiscal election and an early move towards the binding of members to extra-parliamentary organisations. Those receiving endorsement were meant to advocate the fiscal principle of the supporting organisation in Parliament, hence their individual actions were theoretically constrained and mild though this may have been it was the first step towards the modern party system. The Free Trade Association, which originally had not been involved in party politics, introduced preselection in a bid to ensure the electoral unity that would be needed to defeat their Protectionist opponents. It was Orangeman Francis Abigail who was responsible for preselection in Canterbury and, perhaps because of the Hammond association, he decided to leave the young Carruthers out. Consequently, while prominent Parkesites would speak for the other Free Trade candidates the courtesy would not be extended to the effective interloper.

Already a skilled public speaker, Carruthers took to campaigning quickly and was surprised to discover just how passionate he could be. His first speeches were given in his local St George area. There he was still known more as a sportsman, rather than a budding politician, but he found the crowds willing to give him a good hearing. At Kogarah he was introduced by the Mayor and told an assembly of 300 people that competition was the key to prosperity, that they needed to foster a better understanding between labour and capital, and that "the true destiny of the colony [was] as the Queen of the Southern Seas, with a mercantile marine carrying her products throughout the world".[26] While perhaps an appeal for the support of the powerful mercantile interest, this was a popular vision. The nineteenth century was a time of great optimism, growth and material progress, and the youthful figure emotively captured a widespread belief that New South Wales was on a path to greatness.

While St George formed the centre of his support, Carruthers was keen to ensure a breadth of appeal and therefore went to considerable effort to tour the electorate. When nominations opened he was given the chance to give the first speech from the Ashfield hustings. To the raucous and mostly working-class crowd that had assembled for the occasion, he proclaimed:

> Freetrade was a policy which meant the greatest good for the greatest number. This could only be achieved by opening their ports to the commerce of the world. Protection sought to restrict importation and to raise prices for the benefit of manufacturers, and would pauperise the bone and sinew of the colony. Their wages would not be increased by the manufacturer. They would have to work the same time for the same wages, and then would not be able to obtain the same quantity of goods for their money.[27]

It was an attack on the direct hip-pocket effect of tax increases and a dismissal of their highly theoretical flow on benefits. It made the fiscal issue tangible for the audience. Carruthers had pitched his address perfectly for the crowd, and despite having to wait anxiously as the numerous rival candidates gave their speeches, he won the show of hands that concluded the meeting.

Free trade and the other issues Carruthers brought up during his inaugural campaign show that there was a great deal of continuity throughout his career. He argued that the laws relating to the alienation of Crown land needed reform to give easy access to those that wanted to start farms and to prevent abuses from those that wanted to monopolise the land. He also urged the introduction of a comprehensive system of local government. At this time a community needed to voluntarily submit to becoming a municipality, something that many people were reluctant to do because it involved levying greater taxation upon themselves. Because little of the Colony had been incorporated into municipalities basic administrative tasks fell upon the Colonial Government in a manner that was both inefficient and unrepresentative. Carruthers hoped to fix this by extending local government across the entirety of the populated areas of New South Wales, thereby spreading local democratic representation and eliminating the tax discrepancies. In the midst of the budget crisis that had precipitated the coming of the fiscal issue, Carruthers also advocated retrenchment by means of public service wage cuts, but in a manner by which higher officials were "made to give up their luxuries before the poorly-paid class were made to give up their daily bread".[28]

While free trade, retrenchment and decentralisation via local government were all small government policies, he did support some measures involving government intervention. Carruthers argued for the establishment of a national bank to lower interest rates and thereby encourage private enterprise. He also advocated a scheme of industrial conciliation and arbitration that the *Sydney Morning Herald* supported because it believed that strikes were hurting industry as much as protection.[29] This formulation whereby Carruthers was generally inclined towards keeping government small and out of people's lives, but not dogmatically and with occasional exceptions, would be a hallmark of the pragmatic liberal's career.

Joseph Carruthers was elected top of the poll for Canterbury, a remarkable feat considering his youth and lack of party support. He remained the member for Canterbury and later the single member electorate of St George continuously until his retirement in 1907. He often fought on local issues, as a member for such an outer-suburban seat had to. These local issues will not be a focus of this biography, but it is important to remember that behind Carruthers' success as a Minister and Premier there lay strong local support that allowed him to have the electoral security to focus on broader issues.

The Free Trade Association's attempt to organise for the 1887 election was dogged by teething problems, particularly vote splitting which before the introduction of preferences would continue to be the bane of liberal parties. Still, with the help of the prestige of Henry Parkes, the FTA proved to be much more successful than their Protectionist counterparts and the Free Traders won the election in a landslide. The political polarisation created by the fiscal issue meant that Parkes would have one of the clearest parliamentary majorities since the first days of responsible government. This big majority was made up of some of Parkes' old factional supporters and a large group of newly elected and fiercely dedicated Free Traders. This group included William Mc-Millan, Bernhard Wise and Carruthers himself. After the 1889 election they would be joined by Bruce Smith. Loveday and Martin describe the group as being "associated with and in many respects the products of the Freetrade Association" but given that Carruthers had not been endorsed by that organisation it may be more accurate to refer to them simply as Free Trade Young Turks.[30] Their politics varied widely but they shared an almost insatiable appetite for free trade that Parkes would find difficult to satisfy.

The Young Turks were an incredibly talented group of budding politicians who all emerged at roughly the same time. Bruce Smith and Bernhard Wise were ambitious political theorists, both having produced books that offered contrasting views of liberal politics. Smith was a businessman and barrister who had spent a considerable amount of time in Victoria and developed an aversion to the interventionist politics, particularly protectionism, that were then gaining prominence in the southern Colony. His 1887 book *Liberty and Liberalism* acted as a protest at what he saw as undue interference with individuals, enterprise and property. Central to Smith's idea of liberalism was the concept of liberty, something he defined as "the freedom to do as one wishes; freedom from restraint – subject to the same or equal freedom in our fellows". He argued that liberty should be maintained through limited government, not only because freedom was inherently valuable but also because the energy latent in the pursuit of individual goals would ultimately benefit society as a whole.

Wise was a barrister who had been educated in England and was greatly influenced by the radical politics he had been exposed to as President of the Oxford Union. In 1884 he had produced *Free Trade and Wages*, a published lecture that sharply contrasted with the views of Smith for it embraced paternalism and encouraged government intervention for societal and humanitarian ends. While still advocating free trade, Wise put forward "labour views" in support of government regulation, common wages, union preference and compulsory arbitration, all of which were quite out of tune with traditional liberal views on freedom of contract and association. Wise's views reflected his interest in the philosophy of T.H. Green, an influential Oxford professor who had dismissed the idea that individual liberty was an end in itself and advocated the use of government to enforce the "general will".[31] Wise was in this sense a "new liberal" whereas his Young Turk compatriots, though they themselves were often innovative, built their beliefs on a more classical base. The ideological creativity shown by men like Smith and Wise laid the groundwork for a transformation of the pervading liberal consensus into a new agenda, even before the rise of protectionism shook that culture from its lofty position.

The skills of Carruthers and McMillan lay not in abstract political theory but in the practical work of political organisation. They were concerned with achievable goals that, while they were inspired by classical liberal ideology, were not restricted by utopian dogmatism. The group was perhaps too talented for their own good as over the years there would be numerous conflicts between them, often based on personality as much as policy. Carruthers would be the only one to stay within the Free Trade Party throughout the whole of the 1890s. Despite this group's importance to Parkes' majority, he effectively snubbed them by maintaining a Ministry formed largely out of old factional supporters with the exception of Wise who became Attorney-General only after William Foster resigned.

Joseph Carruthers delivered his maiden speech in the Legislative Assembly on 22 March 1887. It was far from a genteel affair. In the preceding speech, Protectionist James Fletcher had made some spurious allegations of corruption relating to the building of a tramway from Kogarah to Sans Souci. Carruthers had been a member of the Sans Souci Tramway League which had successfully lobbied for the construction, and he was forced to defend himself and the others involved. He argued that the tramway was necessary as the Sans Souci area had been neglected by the Western route chosen for the earlier railway line and dismissed allegations of personal interest by showing that he had already sold his property near the route.

It seems that Fletcher had his own personal interest in the matter, and was trying to delay the construction for the financial benefit of a pre-existing tramway. Whatever the case, Carruthers was able to fight off his political assailant. His reaction was swift and firm:

> the constant reiteration of charges is never held in any community to be a justification, or proof of those charges; the mere insinuation of corruption is never held to warrant the assumption of corruption, and prejudice, evidenced by prejudgment of a case, is sufficient in all assemblages to debar a person showing that prejudice from sitting in judgment in the matter.[32]

Drawing on all his legalistic skill, Carruthers' speech was a tour de force. Afterwards he was approached by William Teece, the Government Whip, who told him "the Old Man is wonderfully pleased with the way you fought those Kilkenny cats".[33] Ironically, the attacks he had been exposed to had helped to place Carruthers above the pack and draw the attention of Henry Parkes.

Carruthers would continue to grab Parkes' attention, though for less positive reasons. During the committee stage for the Custom Duties Bill, he introduced an amendment to add a 5% ad valorem duty on the importation of luxuries and jewellery in particular. Carruthers was always keen on balanced budgets and he saw this as a form of revenue raising that caused as little harm as possible to people and business. The amendment caused a storm amongst the Free Traders. For a Government supporter to move an amendment to a Bill without consulting his colleagues went against even embryonic notions of party solidarity. The young member gave way to the pressure that was mounted upon him, dropping the amendment and learning a valuable lesson on the importance of unity.

This incident made some people question Carruthers' attachment to free trade, but such a query seems misplaced. Carruthers was deeply committed to the principle of tariff reduction and the most emotive speeches he gave during this period all revolved around the fiscal issue. It was more than a simple coincidence that Carruthers entered New South Wales politics during the fiscal election after rejecting earlier overtures to do so; he firmly believed that people were better off under free trade than under protection. However, as in all his sincerely held political beliefs, Carruthers laced ideology with pragmatism. Duties on luxuries that were revenue raising and not protective had none of the negative consequences free traders associated with protection. They would not hurt ordinary people or increase production costs by raising the price of anything necessary or even useful. At the same time, because these duties were not protective, they would not eliminate competition for locally produced luxuries, thereby allowing prices to rise and making local products un-exportable. All of this was completely compatible with free trade beliefs and even small government beliefs that held that some revenue raising was a necessary evil and that it should be done in a manner that interfered with people as little as possible.

Though Parkes castigated the young member for his attempted amendment, such a rebuke was more about the gall of the action rather than any betrayal of free trade. The Premier arguably had less of an attachment to that principle, and his "free trade tariff" was a disappointment. While increases in rent from Crown land leases had improved the financial situation, the reduced revenues of full free trade would require direct taxation and Parkes was not prepared to tackle such a difficult issue. Instead he put it off, claiming that local government would have to come first. In the meantime Parkes introduced moderate tariff reductions, with the aim of achieving free trade in a staggered and therefore economically "safe" way. For the idealistic Young Turks who had been whisked into the political sphere by their vehement views on the fiscal issue, such a move was an evasion. The tension thus created would simmer behind the scenes a play a significant role in the course of the Ministry's life.

In June 1887 Carruthers tried to introduce his pet project, the Trades Arbitration Bill, but was forced to delay his speech because the refreshment hour had arrived. Events in the Legislative Assembly took their course and the speech was never given. In April 1888 the Bill was read a second time as the Trades Conciliation Bill. Based on a French precedent, the Bill was designed as much as possible to eliminate strikes that Carruthers felt were harmful to both the business community and working men. It proposed to create an "impartial" board that could deliberate over trade disputes, resolving them in as timely a manner as possible. After Carruthers gave a forceful speech advocating the Bill, it was moved to the select committee for consideration where it was eventually dropped.

Later picked up by others, industrial arbitration would go on to become a defining feature of the Australian political and industrial system for most of the twentieth century. It is important to note however, that the Bill Carruthers introduced in 1887 was fundamentally different to the system that became a central pillar of the "Australian settlement" and that he later denounced for herding people into unions and damaging freedom of contract. There were two main differences between Carruthers' Bill and the later system. Firstly, arbitration would not be compulsory; "I recognise this fact – I think its recognition will be found imprinted in this bill – that you cannot and dare not make arbitration compulsory – that if you attempt in any way to forcibly interfere in the relations existing between labour and capital, and endeavour to force the parties to go before a tribunal, you interfere in an improper manner between labour and capital".[34] Instead of directly forcing parties to abide by arbitration, Carruthers looked to "the court of public opinion – that court which will show the masters that if the verdict of the board of arbitration is against them, the public will not assist them in resisting the verdict of the tribunal".

The second way in which Carruthers' Bill was different was that individual workers could go before the tribunal. There would be no forcing men to join unions in order to appear, and therefore no impetus for forced association. These two differences meant that the Bill respected the old liberal ideal of the freedom of contract, something that Carruthers would later describe as "just as essential to mankind as freedom of conscience, freedom of speech and free exercise of the franchise".[35] The time and effort Carruthers dedicated to his Bill shows that he was genuinely concerned about the negative consequences of strikes. His attempt to alleviate this evil, though mildly interventionist, was still influenced by his classical liberal beliefs that generally held that individual freedom should be maintained where possible.

During his first term as a member Carruthers kept up his campaign for the extension of local government. He went to numerous municipality meetings throughout his electorate in order to gauge local issues, and never failed to express his views on the urgency of the issue. While efforts to introduce an extended system of local government were frustrated, Carruthers was keen to protect existing municipalities. When a Land Tax Bill was proposed in the House, he objected that by taxing those who paid council rates and those who did not equally, the Bill would effectively double tax those who lived in municipalities. He was also concerned that existing municipalities would have enough funding, hence Carruthers lobbied for larger municipal endowments. Parkes was left to remark that "the honourable member excelled every honourable member in finding ways to the public treasury".[36]

It was not that Carruthers was naturally inclined towards greater public spending, but as someone who had served on a Council himself he was not willing to leave municipalities to bear the negative consequences of the Parliament's own lack of initiative. Rather than being inclined to lavishness, the young member held an almost self-righteous belief that the spending of other people's money was not something that should be taken lightly. When a Bill establishing the payment of MLAs was introduced to the Assembly, he gave an impassioned speech that argued that such a move should not be taken without a referendum. Though the case for direct democratic approval was based on the specific circumstance of members of Parliament appropriating public funds for themselves, the reluctance to abuse the public purse foreshadowed his later diatribes against "extravagance".

At this early stage in Carruthers' political career it is difficult to chart the personal relationships he was developing. The collection we have of his correspondence does not really begin until 1889, and even then what has survived has been sporadic. Worse still for the historian, his early career corresponds with the rise of the telephone and this quickly became a central means of communication for younger members. Carruthers had a phone by 1893 at the latest and probably much earlier. This meant that many important conversations that would have survived as letters have been lost. Despite the deficiencies of the sources, it is possible to ascertain by events that at this time Carruthers was developing a personal relationship with William McMillan.

McMillan was a successful merchant with a personal interest in free trade and a reputation for conservatism that was only partially warranted. He had entered Parliament at the same time as Carruthers; however he did so as a founder of the Free Trade Association and had been given the honour of moving the address in reply as his maiden speech. These auspicious circumstances meant that he and not Carruthers appeared to be the coming light in New South Wales politics. McMillan had been a frequenter of the School of Arts Debating Club, and would have known Carruthers was an adept and powerful speaker even before he saw his forceful performances in Parliament. Such talents were a great asset to the free trade cause, and the two men struck up a friendship based on their shared enthusiasm. Although Carruthers had won his seat without the backing of the FTA, he soon became a prominent member of Mc-Millan's organisation.

A prominent organisational role was not the only thing Carruthers received from McMillan. When the Parkes Government first introduced its version of "free trade" that left over thirty tariff duties, Carruthers had seen little awry and had even tried to introduce a duty on luxuries. By late 1888 however he began speaking in increasingly ideological terms about free trade, suggesting that he had gone over to that group of Free Trade members, led by McMillan, who were growing frustrated at Parkes for not using his majority to institute "real" tariff reduction.

In November Opposition member Henry Copeland put forward a soap-box motion in favour of protection. Carruthers led the Government's response with a long and vitriolic speech. He attacked protection as "at the very best … the policy of the producer *versus* consumer", whereby despite the fact that "every man is a consumer" the government weighs in on the side of the numerically inferior producers to the detriment of the majority.[37] He then, as he would do many times afterwards, began a long and detailed comparison between protectionist Victoria and America against free trade New South Wales and Great Britain. Using official records Carruthers tried to show that wages were actually far lower in America, and that the benefits of the protectionist taxation flowed not to the working man but to "monopolists". He even went so far as to label protection "slavery" for trying to dictate to people who they could trade with, noting that "the last country to give up dragging the souls out of human beings by slavery was Protectionist America". Finally, he summed up by arguing that "with our vast mining, pastoral, and other resources, we have here avenues of employment sufficient to give employment to ten times the population that we have at present, and that without having recourse to this artificial policy of scarcity, this barrier against trade which will give employment only by fostering maudlin industries to compete with those which are sound and natural to the country".

The speech marked Carruthers' political coming of age. No longer was he just another backbencher pursuing pet projects. He was now a prominent supporter of the Government delivering the main speech on the most important issue of the day. It is no coincidence that Carruthers' break out speech was also his most rhetorically-loaded up to that point. At this time New South Wales politics was becoming increasingly ideological as it moved away from the old faction system into the new party era. Indeed with the writings of Reid, Bruce Smith, and Wise it was arguably a golden age for free trade and liberal theorising. Carruthers was not particularly theoretical, but he possessed the ability to maintain sincere beliefs without being too doctrinaire, and to translate those beliefs into emotive yet rational language which would resonate with the electorate. It was this that made him a success.

Not long after Carruthers' break out speech, an event was to occur that would be a crucial turning point in the development of party politics. A debate was held over press accusations criticising appointments Parkes had made to the Railway Commission. This resulted in an impromptu division in a thin House where eight nominal Free Traders crossed the floor in protest at the arrogant way in which Parkes had handled the matter. Carruthers did not cross the floor but Parkes was defeated in the vote and resigned. Opposition leader Dibbs formed a new Government, but when it introduced a Supply Bill McMillan, who had also stayed put during the division, proposed an amendment telling the Governor that the Ministry did not have the confidence of the House. In the debate that followed McMillan went on to argue that the earlier vote "was to a certain extent a vote against the personal actions of the Premier, and not against the broad policy of the Government".[38] Essentially he was arguing that the Government was not the Premier but the party with a majority in the Legislative Assembly.

Perhaps wisely, Carruthers did not participate in the contentious debate except to defend himself when he was accused by Ninian Melville of having effectively been a slave to the Government's wishes after an initial showing of independence over the duty on luxuries. Carruthers voted with McMillan and most of the other Free Traders for the amendment, which passed despite the fact that Parkes voted with the Protectionists against it. Although the Free Trade Party had thus demonstrated that they had control of the Assembly even without Parkes, after seeing two governments fall in a very short space of time the Governor decided to dissolve Parliament.

The Free Traders went to the election as a party without a clear leader, a situation that had been almost unthinkable previously as during the factional era the leader had effectively been the party. It was untrodden ground for the Free Traders who had achieved so much success at the last election because they had been able to combine their new organisation with Parkes' prestige and old factional support. Although he staked no claim to the leadership of the Opposition, as founder of the FTA McMillan would be de facto leader for the election. In his task he would need assistance from men like Bruce Smith, George Reid and Carruthers. The latter, who had only recently come to the Free Trade foreground, would thus be heavily involved in the campaign and cement his position within the Party.

At this time in New South Wales history elections were held over an extended period of time with different electorates going to the polls on different days. Carruthers' Canterbury poll was relatively early in the schedule and would help set the tone for the wider election. This time Carruthers would be campaigning not just for himself but for a Free Trade "bunch" of four candidates, of whom he was the most prominent. He began a vigorous speaking tour, reiterating his strong support for free trade along with direct taxation and the extension of local government. The stagnation in Parliament over issues like local government and land reform meant that over his career many of Carruthers' election speeches were almost monotonously repetitive, as issues from previous elections refused to resolve themselves. This tendency was exacerbated by the new ideological party division in Parliament. Every election for the foreseeable future would be a fiscal election, as even if Carruthers had felt that "free trade" had been achieved under Parkes, that achievement would need to be perpetually defended against Protectionist opposition that showed little sign of disappearing.

One of the few innovations was given in a speech at St Peters where Carruthers proposed an extensive program of decentralisation that went beyond just the extension of local government. He brainstormed that "the colony be divided into five provinces", with subservient local boards and a parliament to deal with national issues.[39] Carruthers had a long standing interest in decentralisation; something he believed would both reduce spending and facilitate democratic autonomy. This was one of the more radical expressions of those beliefs, which would later re-emerge in his fight for States' rights. Ironically the provincial proposal was meant to "act as a forerunner of a united Australia", which would have had these smaller provinces in lieu of States. He would soon give up this radical proposal in favour of the more popular federation cause, but it is interesting to note that he was already juggling a national outlook and a view towards local independence.

During the Canterbury campaign Carruthers' old friend George Reid came to the electorate to speak in favour of Free Trade. Reid had held an anomalous position in the late Parliament. Although his views generally mirrored those of Free Trade Young Turks, Reid had refused to be a part of Parkes' Ministry when offered a position. He seems to have been sceptical of Parkes' commitment to free trade, and worried about the dangers of subjecting himself to such an overbearing factional leader.[40] Reid had remained relatively independent throughout the Parliament, a staunch Free Trader but no clear supporter of the Government.

The fact that Parkes was not the official leader of the Free Trade Party at the 1889 election gave Reid greater room to ingratiate himself with his colleagues and campaign outside his electorate. Nevertheless, his relations with some Government supporters were strained and the fact that he campaigned for Carruthers and the Canterbury Free Trade "bunch" suggests the two were still close, particularly as Reid spoke in Canterbury the night before his own East Sydney poll. Carruthers recalled that while Reid was a fine speaker in the House, "outside he was the darling of the gods, as he could sway a political meeting by his oratory and make it roar with laughter by his quips and sallies of wit".[41]

The Canterbury poll was held on Saturday 2 February. The *Sydney Morning Herald*'s vivid description of the day offers a unique insight into electoral organisation at the time:

> In the early morning the organisations of each party were brought into action, and throughout the day they did yeoman's service. Voters indolent required to be incited, voters recalcitrant needed to be brought back to the fold and voters irresolute had to be cajoled into decision. That was the work in which the various committees, assisted by a host of individual partisans, were engaged during the

day. The candidates themselves showed no lukewarmness in the cause to which they were aligned. Had they been gifted the power of ubiquity they could scarce have more visits; they were everywhere and nowhere. The Canterbury electorate is one of the most extensive in the Colony, and the 17 polling places where separated by considerable distances. As the afternoon advanced excitement at the various centres increased. At Ashfield especially, as the headquarters, was the interest magnified and intensified. Many were the outward and visible signs of the battle which was being so earnestly waged. Walls and fences were botched with mural literature, cabs and carts and vehicles of hybrid descriptions were about in all directions, and at the polling places gathered many hundreds of persons. These were some of the signs of activity.[42]

What is remarkable about all this is how closely it mirrors the chaos of modern elections. The fledgling party organisations had to do all the work that their better funded modern counterparts have to. The passage shows what a feat it was for Carruthers to come top of the poll in 1887 without the help of the Free Trade Association and how invaluable his experience campaigning for people like Arthur Renwick must have been. It also explains why so many politicians in this era saw the creation of a permanent extra-parliamentary organisation as imperative. The Free Traders won all four Canterbury seats in the 1889 poll, with all four men attracting more than double the votes of their Protectionist opponents. It was a victory not just for Carruthers and the Free Trade "bunch", but for the numerous volunteers who had made the success possible.

Despite the tremendous success achieved in Canterbury, Colony-wide it was clear that the 1889 election would be much closer than that of two years previous. No doubt the loss of Parkes as leader and the internal divisions thus revealed had taken their toll. With the country electorates that polled later than their city counterparts likely to favour protection, Carruthers was sent out to preach the free trade gospel. He addressed electors in the Illawarra, attacking Protectionist opposition to his Trade Conciliation Bill in a bid to appeal to working men. In the Hawkesbury electorate Carruthers not only gave speeches but also stayed to help out on election day, no doubt offering his experience at organisation. Free

Trade supporters in Hawkesbury gave the Sydneysider a pair of carved emu eggs to thank him for his help. Carruthers' efforts paid off. The Free Traders won all the seats in these two electorates, despite an overall swing to Protection that was more pronounced in rural areas.

The Free Traders managed to win the 1889 election with a reduced majority. They now had only 71 seats to the Protectionists' 66.[43] Notably Bernhard Wise had lost his South Sydney seat. In spite of the narrow result, the Free Traders celebrated in lavish style with a cruise around Sydney Harbour. Although the Free Traders had won the election largely without Parkes (who had campaigned outside his electorate so could claim some credit for the victory), they held a meeting where they elected him as their leader. The young Free Trade members still looked up to Parkes and given their electoral setbacks it was difficult to imagine governing stably without his experience and prestige. Even McMillan, who had so recently argued that the Government was the party and not the man, was at heart a Parkesite.

Although Parkes remained as leader, his biographer notes that "his position had nevertheless, subtly changed".[44] He had been *elected by the Party*, at a meeting that he did not attend. The balance of power had shifted ever so slightly towards the party apparatus and away from Parkes. After the Free Traders used their majority to get rid of the Dibbs Government, it was clear that Parkes would have to construct a Ministry that gave due representation to the men to whom he at least partially owed his leadership.

Now the Young Turks would utilise their new political leverage. Rather than allow one or two of themselves to be promoted to lesser Ministries while the others were left in the wilderness of the back bench, Carruthers, McMillan and Bruce Smith put their heads together and "agreed that we should each work for the same purpose, that the three of us were to be included, otherwise we would not join".[45] Parkes, who needed at least McMillan in his Ministry, quietly acquiesced. In what was a major coup for the Young Turks, McMillan was made Treasurer, Bruce Smith became Secretary of Public Works and Carruthers was made Minister for Public Instruction.

It is noteworthy that Carruthers made an alliance with these men. Both were known for their hard-line views, particularly on economic issues. Though a pragmatist who was thought of as being sympathetic to the working man, even at this early stage Carruthers' liberalism had more in common with these "right" small government politicians than the "left" interventionism of people like Wise.

The final Parkes Ministry. Included are Brunker (far left), McMillan (second from the left) and Smith (arms crossed, third on the right). From the New South Wales State Library, Sydney.

Carruthers, Reid and a large group of companions on a picnic.
From the Mitchell Library, Sydney.

CHAPTER THREE

Minister for Public Instruction

Before the new Ministry could get down to business some organisational issues brought up by the recent election had to be dealt with. McMillan had been disturbed by the recent near-defeat and decided that for the Party to succeed it could no longer be based on a "single issue". Hence in March 1889 meetings were held to form a Liberal Political Association. The name encapsulated a desire to turn liberalism into a broad agenda that contained free trade but was not limited to it. This would then both inform and inspire a parliamentary and extra-parliamentary Free Trade Liberal Party. The fact was tacitly accepted that in an age of party liberalism would have to be the property of a party and the Free Traders were trying to take ownership of what they felt was their political inheritance. Ideology was important in shaping beliefs, but it was also a rhetorical tool which could be used to justify and sell the acquisition of power. The popularity of a loose concept of "liberalism" in colonial New South Wales made the title "liberal" a grand prize for those who could take possession it. The pervading liberal consensus in the Colony had long accepted free trade, hence the Free Traders felt justified in their claim to both the ideology and the past.

The task for the LPA meetings was to solidify the Free Traders' claim to the title "liberal", and construct a liberal agenda suited the concerns of the day. Carruthers, along McMillan, James Brunker and others formed a six member committee which wrote the confidential platform for New South Wales first comprehensive "Liberal Party". On 26 March the platform was revealed for consideration at a meeting that Parkes did not attend. Its points included freedom of trade, direct taxation including a tax on the unimproved value of land, economy in public expenditure, efficient and economical control of the public services, reforms to the land laws, local self-government, the establishment of agricultural schools, the extension of technical education, electoral and parliamentary reform, and the "encouragement of local industries by any legitimate means not imposing a tax upon the many to benefit the few".[46] Several of these points were intertwined as the direct taxation would make up for lost tariff revenue while the economies in expenditure would ensure that overall taxation remained low. The platform clearly reflected Carruthers' ideology but it also represented beliefs common to many Free Trade liberals. A point in favour of federation was originally included but was removed as it was not part of the Government's policy at this time.[47]

It is noteworthy that the LPA platform was the product of McMillan and Carruthers rather than Wise or Smith. Because of this it was more practical. It defended individualism and limited government, but not in the absolutes of *Liberty and Liberalism*. It allowed for some small government intervention, but not in the extensive and fetishized "new liberal" way of *Free Trade and Wages*. Through pragmatic minds liberalism was adapted into a broad agenda which took it out of the abstract and gave it a clarity that in the factional era the pervasive ideal had often lacked. A philosophy was being distilled into a set and sellable program, a process that was inherently restrictive and put limits on interpretations that many might disagree with. Nevertheless, the role of liberalism in New South Wales politics was being revolutionised. In an emerging age of party liberalism would no longer be a property of the pervading culture, it would be the inspiration for a *partisan* legislative agenda.

In order for liberalism to be truly partisan it required opposition, something that is difficult to establish considering the Protectionists were not far removed from the erstwhile reigning political culture. However, the attempts of the Protectionists to restrict "commercial freedom" and the vestigial elements of rural conservatism prominent in the Legislative Council were sufficiently removed from classical liberalism to allow for a rhetorical differentiation between them and the Free Trade liberals. Over the next few years Carruthers and others would exploit this, facilitating a potential crystallisation of "liberal" views in the minds of the electorate. This was a process in its infancy that would not mature until the Labor Party was firmly established, but the LPA can still be seen as an important step in the creation of party-liberalism.

Though the LPA reflected liberal beliefs, its broad scope required a greater sacrifice of absolute individualism than the FTA had. In this sense the LPA was a far greater step away from the old factional era than the fiscal organisations that came before it. Many of its structural elements remained similar. The organisation would be made up of branches, and these would be involved in the election of delegates to a central conference. There was also to be a central association with half-yearly meetings and members would be required to pay an annual membership fee which would fund campaigning. The radical change was that members would have to pledge to support the far-reaching platform. This would not be enforced in the rigid way that the later Labor caucus pledge would and the liberal roots of the organisation meant that it still held its members' right to individual opinions in high regard. Even so, this still represented a significant innovation in the way MLAs were envisaged increasingly as party members as well as individuals.

This complex new organisation did not last long until it merged with the Free Trade Association to form the Free Trade and Liberal Political Association. This retained the innovations of the new organisation while absorbing the extensive membership of its predecessor. In late August the FTLA held a week long convention to promote the association and iron out any issues with the platform that it had inherited from the LPA. Carruthers was to be one of the main speakers along with George Reid and a less than enthusiastic Henry Parkes. It is testimony to how far Carruthers had climbed that he was given such a prominent place in proceedings. During his speech he argued that "by the policy of free trade a Government does not interfere with taxation except to carry on the Government, and protect the lives and property of the people".[48] He also suggested that free trade was a "divine policy" as it worked with "goodwill amongst all men" rather than through the selfishness of retaliatory protection.

During the debates at the conference Carruthers positioned himself alongside Reid in opposition to the demagogic followers of Henry George. George was an American social reformer whose 1879 book *Progress and Poverty* offered a utopian solution to the unequal distribution of wealth through the implementation of a "single tax" on the unimproved value of land.[49] This tax was meant to replace all other forms of taxation, and would attack the institutionalised wealth of property owners while leaving others free from the burden of the costs of government. The fact that the tax was on the "unimproved" value was meant to encourage people to continue to develop their land while punishing those who lived off the unearned increment that was derived through ownership and inflation rather than work. The tax was therefore meant to curb speculation and tax city properties, whose value was derived from their location, more than rural farm properties whose value was derived from what was produced on them. George wanted to use the tax to "appropriate rent"; hence land taxation was a roundabout way of achieving a pseudo nationalisation of land.

George's beliefs were influential in the early Australian Labor movement, and despite their socialist undertones they were also picked up by many Free Traders.[50] There were several reasons for this. The fact that the "single tax" would replace all other forms of taxation meant that it could be used as a method of achieving free trade. The tax on the unimproved value tapped into a hatred of the inherited wealth of land owners, while leaving most forms of commerce relatively free from taxation in a manner conducive to capitalism. George's implication that a lack of taxation would go a long way to improving the situation for poor people also echoed arguments about the "free breakfast table". Meanwhile, the fact that the nationalisation of land was implicit rather than real meant that, to some extent at least, property rights would be preserved. Most Free Traders picked up the notion that a tax on the unimproved value of land was a relatively harmless way of achieving necessary taxation, without accepting George's theory as a whole.

This was the way Carruthers treated it. He had often quoted George in support of his attacks on Protectionist America, but he felt that "in New South Wales the application of his theory was impracticable".[51] Above all the "single tax" was an absolute policy that the pragmatism of Carruthers could not accept. To embrace the single tax would have meant abandoning the flexibility that had seen him to try to introduce a revenue raising tariff on luxuries. There were a significant number of more doctrinaire "single taxers" at the FTLA meeting, and they maintained that the platform should require absolute free trade and also that "no local government measure should be countenanced if it did not involve rates on unimproved land values".[52] Although Carruthers believed in those rates, he was not prepared to put up artificial barriers in the way of a local government bill he felt had already been delayed far too long. Carruthers and Reid made their views clear to the meeting, and the two friends won the day. The conference gave unconditional support to local government, while also agreeing to revise but not arbitrarily abolish the tariff. The coming together of Carruthers and Reid in the important internal party debate marked a crucial point in their burgeoning political relationship.

The FTLA conference marked the zenith of early attempts to create a permanent Free Trade Liberal Party with external organisation. Peter Gunnar has argued that "it already had the 'model party' structure soon to be 'invented' by Labor".[53] It did not live up to this early promise however and after a poor showing in the 1891 election it faded out of existence. Joseph Carruthers had played an important role in the creation of the first comprehensive New South Wales Liberal Party. He learnt much from its early success and would learn even more from its ultimate failure.

There were two main reasons for that failure: the reluctance of Parkes to get behind an extra-parliamentary organisation that acted as a check on his power, and also deep internal divisions. The conference had already revealed ideological cracks over the "single tax", and afterwards many of the more devout followers of Henry George decided to invest their energy in the separate "Single Tax League". This internal conflict would only grow with the rise of the federation issue and the debate over whether it should be prioritised over free trade. These divisions were exacerbated by bad timing. The organisation came into existence when the Free Traders had already been in office for two years and there were already cracks showing. It is much harder to get a party united behind bold policies in a period of stagnation than it is to unite them in ideological opposition to something. Parkes had seen this when he skilfully used the fiscal issue to catapult himself back into power.

Carruthers played a central role in the policy positioning and structural formation of the FTLA, but throughout this period he was also playing a more practical organisational role. This was as the Party's main by-election campaigner. At the time campaigning was a rough experience. Open air meetings were prone to interruptions and to be a good speaker one had to be able to dispose of interjectors swiftly and soundly. Carruthers certainly possessed this ability. On one occasion when an interjector persistently asked him if it was necessary to have an Upper House in Parliament, Carruthers held his hand up to his deaf ear and replied "my friend wants to know if I think it is necessary to have two Chambers. I can tell him that if I needed two chambers I would get a kerosene tin". It was not uncommon to be pelted with rotten eggs, vegetables, bags of flour or even pieces of the so called "blue metal", which were broken stones used for road making. Country districts had their own peculiarities, and Carruthers had to deal with meetings being accosted and broken up by partisan horsemen.

In many ways Carruthers' electoral experience became self-perpetuating as he was given new tasks and responsibilities because of the knowledge he already possessed. At one contest in the Manning River district Carruthers was given the novel responsibility of finding a suitable candidate and then successfully securing his victory. He chose Walter Vivian, a Sydney real estate agent, who won the contest only to lose at the general election the next year. At another by-election in Monaro, he gave outdoor addresses alongside Reid and O'Connor to large and rather rowdy crowds. When the strong Free Trade presence failed to yield a positive result the Protectionist press dismissed Carruthers as little more than "a Domain howler", one of the populist and often socialist or atheist orators that were then frequently seen trying to whip up sentiment in Sydney's major parks. As a University student Carruthers had been morbidly-fascinated by these fomenters of discontent. They may indeed have influenced his early speaking style, though such a label offered little acknowledgement of his underlying eloquence and grasp of the English language. A contrasting report suggested Carruthers was second only to Reid as the Party's greatest platform orator, and the amount of people who asked him to speak seems to corroborate such a fact. In 1890 Carruthers also campaigned against John Norton in the Lithgow area, earning himself the eternal enmity of the infamous *Truth* editor.

While all this was happening Carruthers was getting used to his new elevated position as Minister for Public Instruction. It was a job to which the youthful politician, brimming with enthusiasm and energy, was particularly suited. He had already set out the main points of his educational agenda when helping to write the platform of the LPA. Since this platform was written without Parkes, it appears that Carruthers was given at least some autonomy by the Premier who was notoriously overbearing with his Ministers. Carruthers recalled that when he was a Minister Parkes "insisted on being consulted" but "rarely interfered with me".[54] This appears to have only been partially true. When Carruthers tried to improve juvenile correction facilities by replacing the old ship on which delinquent boys were then housed, he managed to offend his chief by appealing directly to the Governor for help. The Governor offered the use of a far larger British battleship, but Parkes blocked the move as overly expensive. A cheaper ship was subsequently obtained, but the eager Minister had been taught who was really in charge.

Outside of this incident Carruthers was able to rack up a considerable list of ministerial achievements. His first significant act was the creation of a Women's College at the University of Sydney. It was to be a non-sectarian establishment to "give the same advantages to women who desire university education as are now possessed by the male portion of the community".[55] In justifying the move, Carruthers pointed out that England, France, Italy and Switzerland had made facilities available for the higher education of women and that the Colony could profit both economically and socially by copying the experience of these older countries. The college was to be given a £5,000 Government grant to be matched by private donors. Like many nineteenth century liberals the young Minister saw education as one of the few areas in which increased public spending could be justified, though the partnership of government and philanthropy certainly smoothed the process.

This cooperation did not mean that the Bill enabling the endowment was uncontroversial. The redoubtable Paddy Crick fiercely attacked women's tertiary education as a waste of public money. Carruthers had to fight off his assailant by insisting that there were jobs open to women that required specialist education, specifically medicine and teaching, and that even in their traditional role as mothers the enlightenment of women was beneficial. He insisted that "the better the understanding of our women the better will be the understanding of their children" and that knowledge and learning were both an essential part of the human experience and of achieving happiness. The latter points were tied subconsciously to Protestant notions of moral enlightenment and self-advancement, helping to imbue Carruthers' words with a persuasive fervour:

> There is no doubt that we can increase the happiness of every human being by increasing his knowledge. Knowledge is not merely a thing which teaches certain facts; but it is imparted in the form of education to bring out all the powers of the mind; so that persons may be able to create knowledge for themselves, to think better, and to act better. Being able to think better and to act better, they can live with more happiness to themselves. We ought not to deprive them of one iota of those rights which are acknowledged as a good thing for humanity.[56]

This was not enough to convince Crick, who pointed to Helen of Troy and Cleopatra to suggest that highly educated women would pose a threat to society. Crick's views proved to be something of an outlier, and after a number of members did their best to dismantle his arguments the Bill passed with a broad range of support.

Carruthers' main ministerial task was to oversee the administration of the public education system in the Colony. The system provided for compulsory primary education and had been largely set up by Henry Parkes. It had proven to be a major flash-point for colonial politics, particularly over the sectarian issue. While some wanted public education to be completely secular, Carruthers held to the common ideal that the basics of religion should be taught, but that this must be done in a non-denominational fashion. Most Catholics objected to either option, insisting that education was pervasively religious and fearing that non-denominational Christianity was essentially a guise for Protestantism. For that reason most Catholics opted out of the public education system and were resentful that they were taxed to pay for it while their independent schools received no funding. Carruthers defended a single non-secular public education system, arguing that "religion, being as it is interwoven with our political, social and family life is a thing which cannot be left out of account; that to profess to ignore it is absurd".[57] Such opinion was controversial, but on the whole sectarian disputes seem to have remained relatively dormant during his time as Minister.

To build on Parkes' system of education, Carruthers overhauled the training of teachers to ensure that education standards were lifted. Against "bureaucratic resistance" he increased the length and scope of teacher training.[58] He also pushed for the erection of a Teachers' College at the University of Sydney. Prior to this, teachers had been trained at the Model Public School at Fort Street, and while they already attended some lectures at the University Carruthers was directly linking teaching with a university education in a new and ambitious way. This meant a broader education for teachers, who would now study not just pedagogy, but also physics, mathematics and the classics.

Knowledge of the classics is not something that would now be seen as essential for a teacher, but for nineteenth century liberals and particularly for Carruthers as a pupil of Badham, it was not something that could be left out. Long before the birth of historical relativism, the lessons of the distant past were seen as tangibly beneficial knowledge for future generations to possess. Around this time Carruthers was sending copies of Badham's lectures as gifts to McMillan and Bruce Smith, thus his old teacher clearly still had an intellectual hold over him.[59] The need for classical education was also underpinned by how liberals understood education conceptually. State funding for education was directly connected to universal manhood suffrage and a need to ensure an educated public which could exercise their vote with care. For that reason education needed not only to train students in practical skills, but also teach them the values which would make them good citizens. Unfortunately, due to circumstances beyond the Minister's control, the erection of a Sydney University Teacher's College would be long delayed, but Carruthers' vision for university educated teachers would eventually be realised.

As important as improvements to teacher training was the extension of technical education dictated by the LPA platform. In the burgeoning age of electricity and with Australia gradually developing manufacturing industries, it was more important than ever before that the youth of the Colony be given the educational background necessary to become skilled-workers. Moreover, technical education was linked to free trade ideology and the necessity of ensuring New South Wales businesses would be competitive in the global market in which they would have to compete. [60] Carruthers' method of improving technical education began with a move to abolish the Board of Technical Education and transfer its responsibilities to his Ministry. With direct control he was then able to dictate to those below him to ensure that technical subjects were given a greater role in the system of public education, and that new schools were built with that in mind. Along with technical schools, agricultural colleges were also set up, and a significant building program ensured that both industrial development and rural development were given full encouragement. By 1891 the money allocated to school buildings in the Colony's budget had doubled. Carruthers also took control of the Sydney Technical College, then highly neglected, investing it with resources that saw a great jump in student numbers.

There was a nation building motive behind these moves. Carruthers argued that education might be justified as "State enterprise" because it could be used to increase "the efficiency of labour, the economy of its production, and the power of its people to compete with the labour of other countries".[61] Hence the policy fell under the category of the "encouragement of local industries by any legitimate means not imposing a tax upon the many to benefit the few" set out in the LPA platform.

Carruthers believed that education was a worthy vehicle for industrial development as it encouraged individual effort while protection was not as it essentially worked through compulsion.

At a time when the Australian Colonies were feeling increasingly vulnerable to a foreign incursion, Carruthers went to considerable effort to reinvigorate the Public School Cadets Corps. The corps already existed, but its numbers had fallen as low as 1400 participating students. Carruthers, who had been a cadet himself during his days in Goulburn, reorganised the force and held large military reviews to increase the cadets' prestige and encourage participation. At one review, 1100 country cadets were brought into the city and camped at Moore Park. With so many boys away from their parents for the first time, Carruthers had to issue a memorandum to ensure that no "intoxicating beverages" were available on the grounds. The cadets reviewed with full military grandeur in front of the Governor Lord Carrington. Many of the lads were dressed up in the ceremonial garb of lancers, while there was even a cadet artillery consisting of four six pound guns. It was not all quite so serious however, for the students were given a chance to blow off some steam with a highly competitive sack-race. At a toast with the officers a proud Carruthers boasted that:

> to train the youth of the Colony in the habits of obedience and respect to those set over them, to discipline them, to accustom them to the use of arms and military drill, would be the broadest and safest basis upon which to build up our Australian standing army of civilians. Please God, the day would never come when the citizen soldiers of Australia would be called upon to fire a shot at the enemy; but if unhappily that evil day should come, Australia's best defence would be that army of sturdy sons which she was now rearing.[62]

It is significant that when speaking about defence Carruthers referred to Australia and not New South Wales. Colonial divisions were of little weight when it came to the stern matter of protecting the Empire.

Carruthers' other innovation in public schooling was the introduction of Arbor Day. Based on a South Australian public holiday, this was to be a day for the planting of trees and shrubs in public schools. In a circular issued to head teachers throughout the Colony Carruthers explained that it was hoped that "an interest in nature will be stimulated and a love for the beautiful encouraged among the pupils".[63] Clearly he wanted to inspire the same passion for flora and fauna which explorations of the Macleay River and Goulburn had ignited in him. He also felt that the trees would help improve the climate of schools by providing shade for the students. One of Carruthers' more quirky policies, Arbor Day would go on to become an institution in New South Wales schools for decades.

George Reid paid particular attention to Carruthers' actions as Minister for Public Instruction. It was a post that he had formerly held, and he was keen to ensure that his achievements were built upon. He played a key role in defeating Crick's attack on the Women's College Endowment Bill. Impressed by the totality Carruthers' efforts, in July 1890 Reid approached him with the suggestion that he introduce a Bill to prevent cruelty to children. Reid had been contemplating introducing such a Bill himself, but having heard Carruthers was thinking about it felt that such an important piece of legislation should be introduced by a Minister.[64] It is testament to Reid's humility that he was more concerned about the Bill getting the greatest possible support than receiving credit for it. Carruthers was unable to draft such a Bill before he left office, but shortly thereafter an Infants Protection Bill was introduced and passed by fellow Free Trader John Neild.

Carruthers' achievements during his first stint as a Minister are all the more remarkable because he was working in an Assembly that was largely stagnant. Indeed the Parliament elected in 1889 was rather famous for its small legislative output.[65] Admittedly one of the reasons Carruthers was able to achieve so much was that, provided he did not stir up sectarian animosity, he had a relatively uncontroversial portfolio. Michael Hogan and Ken Turner have argued that during this period "Carruthers was to be significant, not so much in government, but rather as a political tactician and electoral manager for the party".[66] While Carruthers' organisational role was vital, it is unfair to dismiss the achievements of one of the most productive Ministers in Parkes' last Government. It was only really in education that the ambitious LPA platform received enactment. Meanwhile the rest of the innovative liberal agenda was allowed to stagnate as a reluctant Premier stood in the way of any radical reform.

N.S.W PUBLIC INSTRUCTION – *Vide "Plain English"*
"One of the most renowned of Australian explorers was a Captain Stuart."
"Snakes are not numerous, nor is the arid soil of the continent favourable to their development."
"The kangaroo which is peculiar to Australia and some adjacent islands has a pouch under its neck"

Hop pokes fun at Carruthers for ordering some less than accurate textbooks on Australia from England. From the *Bulletin.*

Carruthers poses with his team after a cricket match.
From the Mitchell Library, Sydney.

CHAPTER FOUR

Combustion and Betrayal

One of Carruthers' duties as Minister was to deliver addresses to numerous schoolchildren and other youths throughout the Colony. At one such lecture to a group of disadvantaged youths known as the Boys' Brigade, Carruthers outlined his belief in individual opportunity that was central to his liberal outlook:

> Poverty arose from different sources, and much resulted from the vices of mankind; but its origin, no matter what it might be, should not stand in the way of alleviating suffering, and the people should never think of visiting on the heads of children any misfortunes brought about by the faults of parents. In spite of all difficulties, it was at the will of every boy and girl, no matter how poor, to achieve some meed of fame in the world, for the Almighty had designed it so that its good things could be shared by those who in early life had been deprived of their fair share of it. One in this country could combine words of hope with practical encouragement, for in our system of education, and under our form of government and social life, no great barriers were offered to any lad, no matter how humble, from going step by step from the lowest to the highest place in the community. In this country there were scores of instances of men who had risen by their own industry and perseverance to high, honourable, and dignified positions … In conclusion he told them not to be ashamed of poverty – it was a noble sign they would bear in after successes – but to take advantage of the great educational facilities at their command, and never to forget the grand principles of self-respect, self-reliance and self-help.[67]

This belief was fundamental to Carruthers' politics. His own heroes whether they were Sir Henry Parkes or Captain Cook were all self-made men and Carruthers listed to the Boys' Brigade examples as diverse as Homer, Abraham Lincoln and Lord Nelson. As the son of a convict he was arguably a shining example for this cult of opportunity. He had been privileged enough to go to university but only through the hard work and large sacrifices of his parents and as Minister he increased the number of merit-based university scholarships to try to ensure that those with the ability and the drive to climb the ladder were not denied access to it. To understand his politics one must understand that the principles of opportunity and freedom underpinned almost everything Carruthers did. While he saw that there were certainly problems that needed alleviation, Carruthers believed that New South Wales political, social and economic system was fundamentally sound because it had allowed him and others to achieve so much. His belief in the existing system was actually stronger because he had to climb to the top rather than be born there and hence felt that with hard work and perseverance others could do the same. Throughout his career Carruthers would reject highly interventionist policies of both protectionist and socialist inspiration because they were a threat to the individual freedom and opportunity that he saw as not only the source of progress and prosperity but also as essential to human existence.

In 1890 an event was to take place that would have lasting ramifications for the political and economic system that Carruthers believed in. This was the great maritime strike that acted as the catalyst for the birth of the Labor Party. Of the three Young Turks who had leveraged their way into Parkes' last Ministry, Carruthers was the only one to get through this incident politically unscathed.

During the strike Carruthers was sent by Parkes to investigate a gathering at Millers Point that looked like it could escalate into a riot. On arrival he was led safely through the crowd by the strike committee, who complained to him that hoodlums who were not representative of the strikers were threatening to escalate the situation. After a discussion with the committee, Carruthers returned peaceably, content that the situation had not got out of hand. Reflecting on the strike, Carruthers wrote:

> No man has a greater hatred of strikes than I. My experience has shown me that not only do they bring suffering to all classes and especially to women and children, but above all they strain the

whole machinery of government almost to breaking point. On the one hand you have an infuriated section of men sacrificing their livelihood for a cause which rightly or wrongly they feel bound to stand by; on the other hand you have the employers and the public who are anxious for work to be resumed, clamouring for the Government to act with a strong hand and to put down the strikers and their methods. Speaking as one who has held responsibility, I can only say that in a big strike, it is essential not only that a Government should be firm, but that it must keep its cool.[68]

Rightly or wrongly, McMillan and Bruce Smith were viewed as not having kept their cool during the maritime strike. It was alleged by some that during the strike Bruce Smith had said that the Government would "shoot down" the strikers "like bloody dogs", a hearsay allegation that he vigorously denied but which nevertheless stuck. Carruthers defended his colleague, describing the allegation in uncharacteristic language as being "as false as hell".[69] Though infuriating, the accusations levelled against Bruce Smith mattered little as his doctrinaire small government beliefs, admirable to many, meant that he was unlikely to ever reach the position of party leader. McMillan on the other hand was the Treasurer and the founder of the extra-parliamentary organisation of the Party. It looked like he would definitely be a future leader before the events of the strike cast a shadow over his career.

At the height of the strike Parkes was resting at home having recently been ill, when a deputation from the chamber of commerce came to Parliament House to discuss the situation. As the leading representative of the Government, McMillan received the deputation. After hearing reports of "acts of violence and disorder" and being shown a driver with a bleeding head, McMillan denounced the strike leaders, organised as the Labour Defence Committee, as a "semi-revolutionary government" that threatened to create "disorder and anarchy".[70] He then spoke for "the whole of the government" and threatened to take "steps to secure the liberty of the subjects of the country". When Parkes was approached for comment he publicly rebuked his Treasurer's bold statements. McMillan was inclined to resign before his ministerial colleagues pushed for reconciliation between the Premier and the Treasurer and Parkes gave McMillan a qualified public apology.

Whether McMillan's actions were justified and who was at fault are questions that are open to debate. What matters here is not whether the incident *should* have damaged McMillan's career but that it *did* damage it. Although he had always been seen as a representative of the mercantile interest, after the strike McMillan became the unions' number one enemy. There would be violent demonstrations at his 1891 election meetings disrupting his ability to campaign, and when the Labor Party was born its members would be openly hostile towards him. His public rebuke and near resignation had also greatly dented McMillan's prestige, hurting him in circles that paid no heed to the attitudes of the union movement. He would remain an important figure within the Government, debatably second only to Parkes, but he was no longer head and shoulders above Carruthers as he once was. The strike thus propelled the stocks of the Free Traders' youngest Minister, for he had demonstrated a propensity to avoid political land mines.

Carruthers believed that the maritime strike and subsequent rise of the Labor Party ultimately destroyed the last Parkes Ministry.[71] While this is partly true, the divisive federation issue also played a central role in the fall of Parkes. Federation was an idea that had lingered in the background of colonial politics for years. There was a clear need for the independent Colonies to coordinate their defence and immigration policy, and to end what amounted to a destructive intercolonial competition for trade. In the mid-1880s a Federal Council had been established with the hope of alleviating these problems, but New South Wales, fearful of undue Victorian influence within the Council, had wrecked the project by refusing join it.

In 1889 Parkes, urged on by Governor Carrington, breathed new life into the federation ideal. He delivered a famous oration at Tenterfield near the Queensland border urging the issue and placing it squarely on the Government's agenda. Parkes had several reasons for doing this, not least of which was the desire to cap off a long career with the crowning achievement of the birth of a new nation, but he may also have been trying to offer a diversion for a Cabinet that was growing increasingly frustrated by his lack of action on free trade. Federation was not the liberal agenda of the LPA; it was a distraction from it. It thus acted as a brake on the partisan evolution of politics as Parkes tried to find a new disposable issue through which to hold onto power in what was an old factional manner. The various Ministries that preceded the party era generally had a stock cause to unite them, and this is what Parkes may have been trying to replicate. He was initially able to hoodwink the Young Turks into allowing this to happen, but over time federation would become a source of frustration within the Party.

Parkes' abrupt manner of bringing up the federation issue was enough to cause some early furore. Members of the Cabinet were angry that they had not been consulted before the Tenterfield speech, and they were even more furious that the Premier had discussed the issue with members of the Opposition.[72] The main person he had discussed it with was Edmund Barton. Then in the Legislative Council, Barton had refused an offer to join the Parkes Ministry because he was inclined towards tariff protection. Nevertheless, he remained close to Parkes and over the coming years the two men would jointly lead the Federal crusade in New South Wales. Barton was a patriotic Australian, but there was also an element of vanity in his attachment to federation. He wanted to be associated with the birth of a nation and was willing to make considerable sacrifices in order to achieve this. He projected an aristocratic air and did not hold strong political views on most issues. When he eventually achieved the honour of becoming Australia's first Prime Minister he would not make the effort of facing a second election.

McMillan, Bruce Smith and James Brunker had a tense meeting with Parkes over his indiscretion, but they were unable to assert their will. It is noteworthy that Carruthers was not in this group that angrily approached the Premier. His place in the Young Turk triumvirate had been taken by the "Old Turk" Brunker. A businessman with eclectic interests ranging from butchery to life insurance, Brunker would play an important role in Carruthers' career. A supporter of Parkes since the 1860s, he had built up considerable personal power, but generally utilised it for the benefit of the Free Trade Party as a whole rather than for destructive self-interest. Entering Parliament in 1880 as the member for East Maitland, he would be a pillar of stability, both within the Party and in the minds of the electorate, until his death in 1910.

Carruthers' absence from this group signified a slight drift away from McMillan that would have far-reaching consequences. It has been said that after placing themselves in Parkes' shadow McMillan, Wise and Carruthers "never really recovered to redeem the promise that some contemporary observers and some later historians detected in them".[73] This is certainly not true for Carruthers, whose later achievements should not be underestimated simply because they took place in a State Parliament that had not yet been robbed of many of its constitutional powers. One of the reasons that Carruthers would go on to succeed was that during this crucial period when the Free Trade Party was increasingly divided, he did not attach himself too closely to anyone. McMillan and Bruce Smith were practically joined at the hip during this period and they maintained a strong sentimental attachment to Parkes despite their frequent run-ins with him. Carruthers on the other hand kept close to Parkes, McMillan and the Free Trade dark horse George Reid, without growing too reliant on any of them. Despite his Parkesite upbringing, when the time came to jump ship from Sir Henry, Carruthers would be more willing than McMillan or Bruce Smith to take a leap into the unknown.

A couple of days before Parkes had given his Tenterfield speech Carruthers had coincidentally given an address at Burwood on federation and nationalism. After a long diatribe against Protection, he had insisted that freedom of trade must be the basis of any union and that "they would never shake hands with an enemy".[74] That enemy was Protectionist Victoria, and though Carruthers praised federation as "the true theory of Australian nationalism accomplished", he warned his audience not to "allow the dark trail of protection to be drawn across the path to a great fame which was ours". All national sentiment aside, Carruthers seemingly wanted his neighbours to convert to his fiscal faith before any union would be acceptable.

Just a couple of weeks later, Carruthers had noticeably softened his attitude to Protectionists in the federation movement. In November 1889, he appeared on a platform with Parkes and Barton to speak in favour of federation under the auspices of the Australian Natives' Association. Practically rubbing salt into the wounds of those who were concerned about what federation would mean for free trade, Carruthers lauded the attendance of "men of all shades of political influence". He went on to say that:

> One of the best and most noble things was the spirit of patriotism. He hoped that there would be a common feeling throughout the colonies, and amongst all political parties, and that they would realise the words of Macaulay, "that men would show themselves that none were for the party and all were for the state". However they might differ there was a common love of Australia which animated nearly all public men, and that common love in the face of a common aspiration would rouse the Australians to stand shoulder to shoulder and to help Sir Henry Parkes to realise federation; and that there would yet arise a greater Britain in a new land.[75]

Carruthers' inconsistency is disconcerting. At first glance it may appear that he was simply falling into line behind Parkes. While Parkes' actions no doubt influenced him, a slavish reaction was uncharacteristic of a man who had been quite independent as a backbencher and had asserted his power in negotiations surrounding the formation of the Ministry. Perhaps he was just trying to brush over the internal divisions within the Party by standing behind the Premier. Another reason may be that he simply did not buy into the idea that federation was inherently a threat to free trade. While at Burwood he was eager to use federation to attack Protectionists, Carruthers felt that the Free Traders could win a fiscal fight in a Federal parliament just as they had done in New South Wales. He was not alone in his change of heart. McMillan, who had publicly insisted that federation would be intolerable without free trade, would follow Carruthers' lead in softening his attitude to the fiscal necessities of a union.

Parkes' federation campaign quickly gained momentum. A meeting of Premiers was held in Melbourne in 1890 to discuss the idea before a National Australasian Convention was organised to take place in Sydney in March 1891. At the first of these meetings Parkes and McMillan represented New South Wales. For the convention a much larger delegation was sent that again included McMillan but excluded Carruthers. The fact that McMillan was chosen for both these conventions points to his continued prominence in the Free Trade Party even after the maritime strike. Despite coming over to Parkes' campaign much faster than the Treasurer, Carruthers was still not quite important enough to warrant inclusion in the delegation.

The convention agreed to a draft Constitution Bill that would need to be approved by the Colonial Parliaments before it could be sent to London for approval. As the Mother Colony, New South Wales was expected to take the lead in passing the Bill. The Bill was controversial as it proposed a Senate with equal representation for the States regardless of population that for the largest Colony seemed like a threat to both their sovereignty and to the principles of democracy. The newspapers were rife with rumours of a split in Cabinet over it. George Reid, still a relatively independent member and under no obligations to defend Parkes, came out as one of the leading opponents of the Bill. He attacked the Senate compromise that did not completely exclude that House from touching money bills and he also criticised a failure to prescribe the responsibility of the executive and thus make it clear that the new constitution would operate under a system of responsible government that as British people they were familiar with.[76] More brashly, he personally attacked the New South Wales delegates, in particular Parkes and McMillan, for giving up so much. While Parkes had often crossed swords with Reid, the remarks deeply hurt McMillan who consequently had a falling out with his East Sydney counterpart.

While reaffirming his support for federation, Carruthers initially publicly reserved his judgment on the details of the Bill. One paper reported him to be taking Parkes' side in a Parkes-McMillan Cabinet split over it and its place in the Government's program, while another had him taking the opposite course.[77] On 22 April Parkes wrote in his diary that Carruthers and Gould "seemed to think that they could improve the bill".[78]

Carruthers would have also been perturbed that the Federation Bill had pushed the Local Government Bill to a lower place in the Government's agenda, but it does not seem that his reservations were grave enough to cause a split with Sir Henry. In a speech at Burwood on "Union or Disunion" Carruthers argued that "each state was entitled to equal representation" in the Senate but also that New South Wales should be given the capital.[79] Even here he appeared to be side-stepping the crucial issue of what powers a Senate with equal representation should have. His main concern seems to have been not to alienate himself from any section of the Party. He firmly believed in federation, but he also shared some of his colleagues' concerns that other important legislation was being sidelined in pursuit of union.

After a long adjournment Parliament resumed on 19 May. In an attempt to accommodate his Cabinet dissidents, Parkes intimated that Parliament would have the right to amend the Federation Bill, not simply to pass it. Not content with this compromise, Reid moved an amendment attacking the Bill on the grounds previously described but also as a threat to free trade. The amendment failed but Parkes was pressured into dropping the Bill to third place in the Government's legislative agenda. Dibbs then moved a censure motion which only failed on the Speaker's vote and Parliament was dissolved a week later. Carruthers once again kept his head down, voting with Parkes but not speaking in the debate.

With a divided Free Trade Party preparing to face an election effectively on the federation issue, organisation was thrown into disarray. The FTLA had already made it clear that it still believed that free trade should come before federation. Since the organisation would not buy into Parkes' federation dream, the Premier declared it "moribund" and formed a new "Free Trade and Federation Committee", much to the consternation of McMillan.[80] It is likely that in making this move Parkes was concerned not only about federation but also about narrowing the party organisation so that he could control it more directly. Since McMillan, the Party's main organiser, was still closely associated with the FTLA, Parkes chose Carruthers, who up until that point had still been active within the old organisation, to chair the usurping committee. It appears that Carruthers was not purposefully abandoning the FTLA but since that organisation had candidly critiqued the Government it became difficult for a Minister to defend it, particularly against the urgings of the Premier.

Carruthers was left with the almost impossible task of running a winning election campaign with a divided party that had little to show for the past two years in Government. To make matters worse the power of the free trade cry, generally a winner in New South Wales, had been greatly reduced by Parkes' emphasis on federation above all else. Economic conditions had also declined, with strikes and depression deeply hurting the Government. Carruthers had started organising before the new committee had even been formed. In March he had written to Parkes advising him on candidates for several rural seats.[81] The local knowledge that would have been required to make good preselection recommendations for distant seats hints at the amount of work that Carruthers put into running the campaign.

Connected to these meticulous preselections was an overall campaign strategy to focus on rural seats. Carruthers had written not only to Parkes but also to Bruce Smith on this issue.[82] He felt that the strike would inevitably lose the Free Traders seats in the city, a prescient prediction about the success of the new Labor Party, and that they therefore needed to pick up the slack in rural districts. The country had become the bastion of Protectionist support in New South Wales. This was largely because border territories and large farmsteads had felt the sting of their neighbour's tariffs more acutely than their city counterparts, as they were denied access to logical export markets whilst facing free competition from imports. This made many rural colonials support tariff reciprocation. In later years farmers would grow sceptical of tariff protection which increased the cost of farming equipment, but before large scale mechanisation such concerns mattered less than prefederation squabbles.

In spite of this sentiment Carruthers clearly felt that the Free Traders could make inroads in the bush. His own rural upbringing had shown him that country people were not automatically inclined towards protection. The Illawarra-Kiama district in which he had been born showed more support for free trade than many other rural areas. To secure success in the country Carruthers proposed a two-pronged approach. Bitter opponents should be ousted at all costs, and Ministers and materials should be sent to help campaign against them. Men needed to speak at every corner on which people congregated so that the crowds could be educated "in the policy of freedom". Softer enemies however could be offered help and conciliation in the hope of inducing them to change sides. Factional tactics were not dead yet.

Carruthers' first speech for the campaign was delivered in rural West Maitland. In a telling sign he declared that "the great question to be put before the people of this Colony was federation".[83] He spoke at length on the fiscal question, but it was federation that was given pride of place at the top of the speech. Understanding that the details of the Federation Bill were unpopular, he used the little leeway Parkes had given him by stating that "the Government did not ask them to swallow holus-bolus the bill passed by the Convention, but to suggest amendments in it as would carry out their desire for the federation of these grand Australian colonies and to make the whole of the colonies into a grand federated nation". It was an awkward compromise. Carruthers was asking the people to vote for federation but not for the Convention's Bill, an option he seems to have wished he had himself.

The Government agenda Carruthers outlined also included electoral reform, water conservation, coal mines regulation and local government. To complement coal mines regulation, Carruthers proposed to reintroduce a Conciliation Bill to deal with industrial disputes. The maritime strike was still fresh in everyone's mind, and Carruthers was trying to use his record to capitalise on the issue. He blamed Protectionists Melville and Dibbs for his earlier Bill's failure to get through the committee stage. His proposal to reintroduce it, delivered more as a private member than as a representative of the Government, fell on deaf ears. People concerned about the strike were more likely to vote for the new Labor Party than for the Government that had been in power when the whole mess occurred. That party had emerged from the recent strike, as union representatives frustrated with the failure of industrial action had decided to pursue their goals in Parliament.

Vote splitting would be a particularly difficult problem for the Free Traders at the 1891 election. Before a more rigid party structure evolved this issue would always be the bane of Liberal Parties, but in 1891 internal divisions made the situation much worse. While Carruthers was trying to organise preselections for the FTFC, the FTLA and Single Tax League all threatened to undermine his work. In Canterbury alone there were rumoured to be seven men who wished to run as Free Traders in addition to the four sitting members. The situation was so bad that it was even suggested that the popular Carruthers should run in the Redfern electorate to free up space in Canterbury. In Camden, telegrams between Carruthers and the local committee were published in the local paper, with candidates refusing to withdraw after Carruthers' adjudication.[84] The FTLA council had been meant to act as an arbiter in preselection disputes, but without a well-developed local branch system Carruthers' FTFC selections were often resented or ignored. Despite Carruthers' best efforts, Parkes' decision to abandon the innovative FTLA was coming back to bite the Free Traders.

After the first round of elections were held the Free Traders had a lead over their Protectionist opponents of 28 seats to 7. These numbers were deceptive however, as the polls for the Protectionist-dominated country electorates were yet to come. The great shock was the election of 18 so-called "independent" candidates that included Reid and 17 Labor men. The Free Traders could take solace from the fact that Dibbs had been defeated and would now have to seek re-election in a safer rural seat. Carruthers, who had been re-elected with more votes than any other candidate in the Colony, went to the country in a last ditch effort to save the Government. His itinerary included visits to Marulan, Braidwood, Bungendore, Bulli, Wollongong, Raymond Terrace, Dungog, Clarencetown, Stroud and Bourke. Other Ministers were sent to all corners of the Colony.

When the dust had settled, the Free Traders had won 47 seats, Protectionists 51, Labor 36, with 7 independents.[85] These are somewhat rough estimations, as party affiliations were still relatively loose. Carruthers' efforts had made the best of a bad situation. Despite holding the most seats, the Protectionists had actually gone backwards at the election, their having secured 66 seats in 1889. Most of the seats the Free Traders lost went to the new and therefore "clean" Labor Party, many of whom had declared that they believed in free trade on the hustings. This points to strong continuing support for the policy of free trade within New South Wales, despite the fact that a Protectionist government would soon hold power. One may argue that Labor's great victory was due in large part to the weakness and divisions of the Free Trade Party. In 1894, under a leader far more dedicated to fiscal principles, the Free Traders would win back some of the seats they lost to Labor in 1891. Carruthers would again play a central organisational role in that victory, so his running of the campaign should not be blamed for this defeat. His focus on country areas had paid little dividends. An election fought on federation was not the time to convince rural Protectionists of the merits of free trade, while the Federation Bill itself was too unpopular to be a vote winner. Although he did not manage to win many new country seats, the retention of 47 seats represented a reasonably successful sandbagging effort given the circumstances.

When the election was over McMillan urged Parkes to resign rather than face the ignominy of trying to continue only to be defeated. Parkes declined the suggestion and decided to carry on as Premier for as long as he could. A frustrated McMillan, who was also concerned about the time he was spending away from his business interests, resigned his post as Treasurer to be replaced by Bruce Smith. Carruthers did not follow McMillan's course of action but it is likely that he too was frustrated. His father had passed away a few weeks before the election and he had been forced to soldier on in spite of the emotional burden. By abandoning the FTLA and focusing on an unpopular Federation Bill, Parkes had made Carruthers' thankless task even more difficult. In the new Parliament he may have looked forward to the passing of a long awaited Local Government Bill, but the political situation made success on this front seem further away than ever.

In September Carruthers hinted at his frustration in a letter he wrote to Lord Carrington, the former-Governor and confidant of many a politician. In it he confessed that he felt that Parkes' federation seed had been "planted out of season" and was "destined ere long to be the downfall of his ministry".[86] Carruthers sympathised with Sir Henry because "he has his heart set on this scheme", but the letter gives the impression that he was growing disillusioned with his chief.

This growing disillusionment with Parkes and his policy priorities marked a crucial turning point in Carruthers' career. Parkes had been his political hero ever since his father took him to rallies as a boy. He believed in Parkes' federation dream, but was not prepared to see him wreck the Free Trade Government over it. Divisions between Parkes, McMillan, Reid and others that had badly hurt the Party at the 1891 election showed no sign abating while the flawed Federation Bill remained in the Government's program. Meanwhile free trade and the direct taxation it required remained unrealised, while local government seemed to go up and down the agenda at the political whims of the Premier. Carruthers had not yet abandoned Parkes, but doubts over the Premier's waning leadership abilities festered in his mind. He wrote to Carrington that Parkes was tired, his health was failing and that "feebleness is supervening his usual vigour".

While the letter to Carrington shows Carruthers slowly drifting away from Parkes, it also suggests that he may have been moving closer to George Reid. The 1889 election campaign, FTLA debates and his time as Minister for Public instruction had all drawn him closer to his old cricket and debating chum. The only thing they really disagreed on at this point was the campaign for federation. With Carruthers now believing that federation needed to be put on the back burner, the way was open for these two skilled politicians to unite. Political circumstances had prevented them from campaigning together in 1891, but Carruthers noticeably refrained from criticising Reid in any significant manner during the campaign. This was in contrast to Parkes and McMillan, who both attacked the man whose actions had precipitated the election. All of this suggests that not only were Reid and Carruthers rekindling their friendship, but that the latter may have already started considering the former a future leadership option.

Though the party system had been developing for several years, the coming of the Labor Party represented a new and sharp turn. There had been Assembly members associated with business interests and less frequently the unions before but most of those, outwardly at least, professed to govern for the whole community. The new Labor Party unashamedly represented one section of the community and so was quite foreign to the liberal political culture that reigned in New South Wales. In the 1850s liberals had fought off conservative attempts to create a hierarchical society based on class and sectional interests and this historical legacy made them sceptical of anyone who viewed society through this lens. It was a matter of perspective as to what section of society Labor represented, whether the working class or the unions alone, but any such representation went against beliefs in individualism and governing for all. A rejection of class representation is one of the unifying traits of Australian liberalism that has crossed both time periods and provincial divides, hence Labor's very *raison d'être* immediately placed it outside the individualist philosophic boundaries of its future enemy.

This foreignness would grow over the next few years as the Party developed its caucus pledge that restricted the ability of individual members to express their own opinions. At this point its platform was still relatively mild. It had much that Carruthers already supported like local government and electoral reform, but its overall tone stressed government intervention. Bede Nairn has described early Labor as accepting "the best of socialism" while rejecting "a policy of organising a socialist state".[87] Later the adoption of the socialist objective would suggest that Labor may have prepared to organise such a state, but as the Party intended on pushing its agenda through parliamentary means revolutionary socialists were always ostracised from it. Labor fundamentally accepted much of the pre-existing political and social system, but it wanted to use government to reshape it at the edges. It aimed at "civilising" capitalism, but in doing so its enemies feared that it would restrict freedom, and destroy the economic system that had allowed the prosperous Colony to expand so rapidly. Carruthers later recalled that the early Labor members thought that they could fix anything with an act of Parliament and this rash interventionism did not endear them to him.[88]

Shortly before Parliament resumed Parkes mulled over the upcoming problems of a three-party House in his diary, writing that "with the exception of Carruthers I don't think any of the Ministers comprehend the difficulties before the Government, and whenever they express themselves their views are so puny that they provoke me to inward laughter".[89] Clearly the young Minister had a great deal of political realism, if not a lingering melancholy as well. Carruthers assessed that in the new session Reid and a number of other theoretical Free Traders would remain opposed to the Ministry while "there are many members even on our side ready to trim at a moment's notice if they see the tide set against us and the general feeling now is one of wavering on account of an assumed decay in the popularity of the Ministry and the principles it upholds".[90] He told Parkes that the only way the Government could hope to survive was to prove its worth by passing local government and a new electoral bill evening out the electorates to ensure votes had equal weighting.

When Parliament resumed on 14 July, Parkes proposed a program similar to that suggested by Carruthers, but with added "reformist" measures to grant a temporary stay of execution from the Labor Party. The controversial Federation Bill was not to be dealt with until late October. The Government would not last that long, Parkes having resigned by mid-way through the month. This left Carruthers with little time to build on his achievements as Minister for Public Instruction.

His main contribution before the Government's fall was his attempt to guide the hotly debated Representation of the People Bill through the divided House. At one point in the debate on the various electoral reforms contained within the Bill, the issue of Aboriginal franchise was brought up. Protectionist William Traill, who wanted to remove the right of indigenous people to vote, claimed that "there is no conceivable possibility that he [an Aborigine] can ever rise to that scope of perception that will enable him to have any idea of what his vote actually means".[91]

At this Carruthers rose up to defend the people who had partially raised him on the Macleay River:

> I have a better opportunity than most members of the house to see the state in which the Aborigines are, and the state to which they can be brought. We have established schools for the Aboriginal children, and we have learnt by the experience of these schools that the Aborigines are not devoid of perception to any greater extent than the white population of the colony … It is not of their own choice that blackfellows are in a country where they are liable to be denied the privileges enjoyed by other people. Considering the manner in which the Aborigines of the colony were treated in days gone by, it would have been a good thing if they had not only had a vote, but if one of their number had been here to voice their sufferings and their wrongs. I am sure the Committee will not deprive the Aborigines of the vote which they have had in the past. Nothing has been shown to indicate that the vote has been abused in any way, and it is consonance with the principle of one man one vote to allow these persons to possess the privilege which they have enjoyed in the past.

It was a heartfelt and truly liberal speech. Dibbs responded by claiming that Europeans of the Colony would be insulted at being compared with Aborigines, and that Indigenous people should not possess the vote "on account of their low type of brain power". While Carruthers would betray his liberal principles by taking up a populist line on issues like Chinese immigration, he would stand strong when it came to Aborigines. As far as he was concerned immigrants were at liberty to come to the country, but Indigenous people had not been given a choice and hence he was more willing to stick his neck out to have their freedom preserved. In this instance he won the day. The Bill being debated had not intended to disenfranchise Aboriginals and the debate moved on swiftly to other issues.

It was the Coal Mines Regulation Bill, one of the legislative acts that had been intended to woo Labor support, which finally brought down the Parkes Government. McMillan tried to recommit the Bill in order to get an eight hour maximum workday clause removed. It was late in the night, so Barton moved that the debate be adjourned. Parkes agreed but the Labor Party, excepting Joseph Cook who voted for adjournment, managed to defeat the motion. Parkes took the vote as a defeat of the Government and resigned from the Premiership. Utterly exhausted, he also resigned from the leadership of the Free Trade Party and moved to the crossbenches. Parkes had a long history of performing such stunts, so the permanency of the move was questionable. Sir Henry privately assumed that if he did not come back the leadership would go to either McMillan or Brunker.[92]

Shortly after Parkes' resignation Carruthers wrote him a letter thanking him for his leadership over the past few years. In it he gave the earliest glimpse we have of his real opinion of the Labor Party. He prophesied that "an awakening must come from this dream of socialism which has frenzied the people and a little hardship will restore common sense".[93] Interestingly the letter seems to be quite accepting of the fact that Parkes had resigned and, though hopeful of an eventual return to the public sphere, Carruthers did not implore him to take up the leadership once more. It appears that unlike many of his colleagues he had accepted the fact that the Party needed new blood in order for new successes to be achieved.

What happened next is a matter of some controversy. A meeting to discuss the leadership was held on 17 November. Prior to it, Wise had privately warned McMillan and Bruce Smith that they were unpopular with the Labor Party and told them that they should not put their hands up for the leadership because to do so would entrench the Protectionists.[94] The meeting opened with the reading of a letter from Parkes. This repeated his earlier declaration that he was withdrawing from public life, leaving the meeting to find a new candidate. After some discussion it was put forward that George Reid should become leader. "A rather awkward silence" ensued before Bruce Smith suggested that a deputation be sent to Parkes to ascertain his views. Wise felt that Smith may have been buying time to sound out support for McMillan, but the meeting agreed that the grand old man should be approached.

Wise and Smith led the delegation that went off to speak to Parkes.

He found them to be unenthusiastic suitors. Fully expecting to be asked back, Parkes was surprised that his guests showed "an anxiety not to succeed" in convincing him to return.[95] In response to the cold reception he reiterated his disinclination to take up "any position that would cast upon me any responsibility other than that of a simple member of Parliament". Wise later claimed that the deputation failed because it had not been authorised to give a clear offer of leadership to Parkes.[96]

The account just presented is largely that of Wise, but it is somewhat contradicted by the Free Trade member for Paddington John Neild. He maintained that Smith's suggestion was a genuine offer to get Parkes to take up the leadership but in response:

> Mr. Carruthers made an almost violent speech in opposition to Sir Henry, and as a result the committee that had been all but appointed, to wait on the ex-Premier to invite him to retain the leadership was altered into a committee to ascertain his views on the political situation, which of course was and was intended to be, a more or less polite way of shunting the aged statesman.[97]

At first glance Carruthers' action seems hard to believe, but given the concerns he had voiced to Lord Carrington and even the tone of his correspondence with Parkes, Neild's account is arguably well-corroborated by contemporary evidence. Both Wise and Neild agree that the wording of the deputation's task was the decisive factor in determining Parkes' response; hence *Carruthers played the key role in dispatching Parkes* so that there could be an injection of new blood into the leadership of the Party. Wise may have left out Carruthers' actions on purpose, as in his account he tries to claim responsibility for Reid's ascension and such an inclusion would have fundamentally weakened that claim. It may also be that Wise felt duty bound not to reveal Carruthers' betrayal of Parkes, for he would later suggest he knew a secret about Carruthers but never revealed it.

Given that Reid's name had already been mentioned before the member for Canterbury made his attack, the latter was clearly acting in support of Reid's candidacy. By choosing Reid over Parkes Carruthers was essentially pushing for free trade and the partisan liberal agenda to take precedence over federation. Though not a Young Turk himself, Reid embodied many of their ideals and could be expected to push the ideological line they supported. Under Reid the transformation of liberalism could be expected to accelerate in a way that Parkes would never allow. Parkes' federation distraction had failed and this had ultimately proved his downfall. Whether Carruthers' fateful speech was a predetermined set-piece is difficult to gauge, though both Neild's account and Parkes' diary seem to suggest that the campaign for Reid's election began before the first meeting.

With Parkes ruled out, a second meeting to determine the leadership was held on 19 November. Unfortunately for the historian, everyone who attended this meeting seems to have recollected its events differently. Carruthers recalled that he was nominated by McMillan to oppose Reid. He declined the nomination due to his young age and partial deafness but also because "*I personally favoured Reid*, as I had a great liking for him and much admiration for his great abilities as a politician".[98] Consequently Reid was elected unopposed. Wise gives two contradictory accounts of the meeting. In *The Making of The Australian Commonwealth* he recollected that he nominated Reid, James Inglis nominated Bruce Smith and Jacob Garrard nominated Wise, but the latter two declined to stand and once again Reid was duly elected. Inglis was a merchant on the right of the Party; hence his nomination of Bruce Smith likely reflected the wishes of the more powerful McMillan. In an earlier article in *The Catholic Press* Wise claimed that Varney Parkes nominated Reid and he seconded the motion, while James Brunker not Bruce Smith was also nominated and declined. Wise did not specify who nominated Brunker and said that Wise was nominated by Inglis, though this seems unlikely and may just be Wise trying to show that he had the broad support that would have been required to win if he had run. Here Wise also claimed that Carruthers mistakenly thought that the nomination of Brunker was actually directed at him and so declined despite never being nominated. Other accounts have McMillan and Want also being nominated but refusing to stand.[99]

When the contradictory and confusing accounts are compared it appears that McMillan may have been making a last-ditch attempt to find an alternative to Reid. This was less of an ideological dispute and more of a clash of personalities. Earlier in the month Parkes had had a conversation with McMillan and noted that "he was very strong in repudiating the suggested leadership of G.H. Reid".[100] Reid and McMillan fought the 1891 East Sydney election on different tickets and when the former won the leadership the latter would refuse to serve under him. In the meeting McMillan, who had been warned not to stand and remained concerned about his business interests, tried to get either Carruthers, Bruce Smith or Brunker to run in his place. Brunker seems the most likely candidate and if Wise's story about Carruthers' error is true then McMillan, who Carruthers believed had nominated him, would have actually nominated Brunker. When this failed McMillan may have been tempted to stand himself in spite of everything, as Bruce Smith was urging him to, but instead he gave up the fight, possibly because Carruthers had come out strongly in favour of Reid.[101] Correspondence surrounding the next leadership contest certainly seems to imply that Reid owed Carruthers above his other supporters, possibly for what happened during this and the previous meetings.[102]

The likelihood of the Reid-McMillan divide scenario put forward here is reinforced by the fact that it was Wise, who afterwards was no big fan of the new Opposition Leader, who nominated or seconded the nomination of Reid. The left-leaning Wise saw Reid as the only real alternative to the supposed "Tories" McMillan and Bruce Smith and was under the impression that Labor would support a censure motion if moved by Reid.[103] Wise later claimed that he was responsible for Reid's election as he refused his own nomination and lobbied in favour of the successful candidate. His actions mattered less than he claims however. Wise was already on the leftward fringes of a party that he would leave in a few years. Carruthers on the other hand represented the bulk of the Party. He was not interventionist like Wise, not doctrinaire like Bruce Smith and had not yet antagonised Labor like McMillan. Importantly he also had the organisational expertise that would otherwise be lost without McMillan and this helped to reinforce the influence of his support.

The voting in the leadership contest makes it clear how important Carruthers' support for Reid was. According to Wise, Reid received 14 votes in favour and 8 against with 18 abstaining, though again Wise contradicts himself in *The Catholic Press* where he claims Reid received 16 votes in favour with everyone else leaving the room. Reid, who had spent his whole career in opposition to Parkes, was clearly not a popular choice. With Carruthers onside McMillan would have been able to get whatever candidate he wanted elected, hence the evidence suggests that Carruthers' support was the determining factor in the election. His support would prove even more important over the coming years as Carruthers stuck by his friend through Parkes' numerous attempts to destabilise Reid's leadership. Meanwhile McMillan, Bruce Smith and Wise would all abandon their new leader.

Reid's biographer W.G. McMinn argues that his subject's election to the leadership marked a clear break from Parkes, as Reid would remain leader of the New South Wales then Commonwealth Free Trade Party until his retirement seventeen years later.[104] The irony McMinn does not acknowledge is that it was Joseph Carruthers, someone who was quite literally *born a Parkesite* who played the central role in enabling this to happen. Though he had been involved with the FTLA and had been widely acknowledged as a leader of the free trade movement, Reid remained aloof from the Parliamentary Party who, despite internal conflict, generally stayed loyal to Parkes. Reid could easily captivate an audience with his wit and speaking ability but personal relationships were his political Achilles heel. Throughout his career he managed to antagonise Parkes, Deakin, Wise, McMillan and Bruce Smith to name just a few. His relationship with Deakin in particular was so bad that it delayed the fusion of the Federal non-Labor Parties until after Reid's retirement. At this crucial moment however, his friendship with Carruthers gave him an opening into the heart of the Free Trade Party, allowing Reid to achieve the position that his political skill deserved.

By supporting Parkes' enemy, Carruthers was effectively choosing his friend over his old hero, a decision that irrevocably changed New South

Wales and indeed Australian history. Parkes was indignant at this perceived betrayal:

> Poor little Carruthers, the injury I did in making him a Minister! He says he will fight under Reid right gladly. It is to be hoped he will be more loyal to his new Leader than he was to his old.[105]

BALLASTING THE BOAT.

Carruthers helping to bail out Reid's sinking Free Trade boat.
From the *Bulletin*.

Not everyone thought Carruthers' coastal labour settlements were a good idea. From the *Bulletin*.

CHAPTER FIVE

Reid's Lieutenant

Ever after that Reid and I were close friends and in agreement in most matters except federation. Moreover, I may claim to have been his closest friend, acting as his legal adviser in his affairs and as his lieutenant in his political campaigns.[106]

This is how Carruthers described his relationship with Reid after the latter had been elected Free Trade Party leader. Though he had clearly won Carruthers' support, Reid did not have long to consolidate his new position before facing Parliament. Dibbs had been called upon to form a Ministry which would need to secure the support of the Labor Party if it were to survive. The most conspicuous appointment was Edmund Barton as Attorney-General. Barton had secured a Lower House seat in 1891 as a Federalist and had been giving Parkes nominal support before his fall. The fact that he now accepted a Protectionist portfolio suggests that even he understood that the federation movement had paused for the moment.

When the members filed into the Assembly, Reid, Carruthers, Wise, Brunker, Bruce Smith, Sydney Smith, Albert Gould, and James Young occupied the Opposition front bench. Parkes was noticeably absent and McMillan took up a conspicuous position below the gangway on the Opposition side. Though he did not follow McMillan's lead in sitting on the crossbenches, Bruce Smith would have a markedly poor attendance record throughout the rest of the session. With three of the most prominent members of the late Government thus abandoning Reid, Carruthers was left to pick up the slack and take on a more central role than ever before. J. A. Ryan has argued that, initially at least, the Free Trade Party was a hastily assembled group that was only able to stay together through Parkes' leadership.[107] With Parkes now gone, only the loyalty and dedication of men like Carruthers could keep the Free Trade ship afloat.

His first act in his new prominent role was to implore the Government to take up the electoral reforms he had been guiding through Parliament. These were meant to end plural voting, redistribute the seats of the Colony on a single member basis and reduce greatly the discrepancy between the high number of votes required to elect a city member and the comparatively low number of votes that were required to elect a country member. They embodied the oft professed "one man, one vote" principle and Carruthers would later cite their introduction as Parkes' last great liberal act. Dibbs, whose Protectionist Party benefitted greatly from the rural electoral bias, declined his appeal to pass the reforms as they currently stood. Instead a motion moved by Barton to reconsider the whole issue in committee was passed and Carruthers was left to fight for as democratic a Bill as possible clause by clause. It was a long and tedious process. The frustrated member for Canterbury maintained that by the time the Parkes Government fell the old Bill had reached the stage where it could "be passed through the Assembly in one night" but instead it had been replaced by an "abortion of the system of one man one vote" that allowed existing inequalities to continue.[108]

It was not long before the new Protectionist Government brought up the fiscal issue that would inevitably lead to a make or break division. On 1 December the new Treasurer John See moved a motion to introduce some "revenue" duties, citing a large public debt as the justification. These were inevitably seen by the Free Traders as protection and two days later Reid moved a censure motion. According to Wise's testimony, one of the main reasons Reid had been elected was because it was believed that the Labor Party would support a censure motion if it was moved by him. This belief turned out to be mistaken. Reid's motion did not attack protection per se, but it censured the Government for bringing up the contentious fiscal issue when there were "a large number of pressing subjects" which were "ripe for settlement".[109] In doing this he may have been trying to ensure he did not divide the Labor Party by making it about the fiscal issue and the "pressing subjects" he cited in his speech were those "reformist" measures that that party was meant to be concerned with. He argued that the Colony's fiscal policy should not be changed until the people's views had been ascertained on the basis of "one man, one vote".

The debate was a long one, and it was not until 9 December that Carruthers gave his main speech on the censure motion. He followed Reid's line, arguing that "whilst these fiscal proposals might be made and fairly receive consideration in an ordinary session, it is preposterous for the Government to ask the House, in so short a space of time as nineteen days, to alter the fiscal and financial constitution under which the colony existed".[110] With an eye to Labor support, he also attacked the attitude of Dibbs and even McMillan to the Coal-Mines Regulation Bill. Carruthers was particularly scathing when it came to the budgetary justification for the duties, suggesting that the Government had effectively cooked the books:

> This deficit is entitled to be called, fairly and truly, a bogus deficit. It has been shown that moneys have been charged to the revenue of 1891 that are fairly chargeable to the trust account. It has been shown too, that moneys have been charged to the expenditure of 1891, not one penny of which has been, or will be, expended in that year. And the strongest and best argument against this proposed alteration is that almost the whole of the deficit is created by supplementary estimates, which cannot be justified as proper estimates to be placed before the country ... the supplementary estimates of the Department of Public Instruction are not mine at all, although they are submitted by the Government as the estimates of their predecessors. I repudiate that statement.

It was one of Carruthers' first financial speeches, a watershed moment for a man whose Premiership would be centred on sound finance. Debt was a touchy subject for Carruthers. He was not willing to sit back and let the Dibbs Government charge his administration of the Department of Public Instruction with expenses that it had not made. He did not take the spending of public money lightly, as his speech on the Payment of Members Bill had shown. By making their justification for protection a personal attack on the members of the previous Government, the Dibbs Government had provided solidarity to a party that had been largely divided since the loss of Parkes. Even the crossbencher McMillan, on having his administration of the Treasury abused, was forced to vote with the rest of his former colleagues.

This new Free Trade solidarity would not be enough. The Labor leader James McGowen was sympathetic towards Reid's push to have the fiscal issue decided on the basis of 'one man one vote', and tried to insert a plebiscite into the motion in order to achieve this. The Speaker ruled him out of order. After this amendment failed the Labor Party was left with the difficult decision of picking a side in a fiscal debate they had wanted to avoid. Since it was the Government who had raised the contentious tariff issue the "probable correct choice was to vote for the [censure] motion" but the Party split and except for McGowen "they voted as their fiscal faith guided them".[111] The final division was 63 ayes, 71 noes.

The vote would be a turning point in the history of the Labor Party, who in response to the split would introduce radical measures to ensure party unity. It would also mark a clear break in Carruthers' career. His actions in the meetings to determine the leadership had remained largely obscure, but he now firmly and publicly broke with Parkes. His former chief had conspicuously abstained from voting in the crucial division when his support had been sorely needed. Perhaps worse than this, Sir Henry's main speech on the censure had "virtually ignored the motion and launched into a diatribe against Reid's behaviour over federation and against the Party which after he himself had been forced to retire as master of the ship had elected a 'pirate' in his place".[112]

Carruthers responded to Parkes' actions in an address he gave to his Canterbury constituents in January. In it he claimed that "Sir Henry Parkes had run away from the leadership of the Free Trade Party" and that he was now "right glad to fight under his [Reid's] leadership".[113] He criticised Reid's actions in undermining the late Parkes Government, but maintained that Parkes' reciprocation in the present circumstances was even more reprehensible. Urging the Party to stand united behind their new leader, Carruthers argued that "once Mr. Reid was elected leader of the Opposition no man could attack him without attacking the Party".

This was a crucial statement considering the whole idea of an elected Free Trade leader had only existed since 1889, and shows Carruthers' developing sense of party loyalty. He also described Reid as "the man who came forward in a crisis, and had volunteered and taken up the leadership which had for some time been sacrificed by Sir Henry Parkes". He was clearly rebuking his former leader and positioning himself firmly behind Reid. It was this speech that prompted Parkes' "poor little Carruthers" response quoted in the last chapter.

As a clear repudiation by one of Parkes' former Ministers and close allies, the speech caused a stir in the newspapers. The *Newcastle Morning Herald and Miner's Advocate* was particularly virulent in its response. It printed that "Joseph's political coat is of many colours, and, like the chameleon, he changes his hue according to his company".[114] It also published a "parable" of Joseph, a man who forsook Parkes and started worshipping Reid. This Joseph went preaching to the Georgites (followers of Henry George) and after a run in with the Protectionists, all that remained of Reid was his glass eye and "Joseph was seen and heard no more in the land, and all was happiness and peace". It was not the last time that Carruthers' biblical first name would be utilised by the pressmen.

Accusations of disloyalty levelled against him had some merit. After all the man he had shunted was not only his childhood hero but also the person who gave him his first ministerial position at a very young age. Shortly before he died Parkes is said to have described Carruthers as exceedingly talented but also untrustworthy and Machiavellian.[115] The latter was probably a fair description, at least in this case, for he had been willing to do what he felt necessary with little regard for sentimentality. Nevertheless there was a silver lining. Carruthers had been loyal, not so much to his chief but to the principles of free trade and the wider liberal agenda. Time would demonstrate that Reid would be a much stronger advocate of the new partisan incarnation of liberal politics than Sir Henry had been. Even if Carruthers' switch to Reid was motivated by purely personal considerations, it was the right decision. Reid would go on to win the next election and hold power for the longest consecutive period of time up to that point in New South Wales history, while the aging Parkes would languish as his political skill eluded him. Ironically Reid's success was due in part to Carruthers' continuing loyalty and it appears that a combination of practical, ideological and sentimental considerations endeared him to his new leader in a manner that had no parallel in his career.

Personally at least, Carruthers' break with Parkes would not be permanent. Within a few months the two men were writing letters to each other once more, though Carruthers still seems to have been more distant from his old chief than either Wise or McMillan were. In contrast to Reid who had a habit of rubbing people the wrong way, Carruthers appears to have been quite amenable. His only personality conflict as Minister of Public Instruction was a brief disagreement with McMillan who he refused to acknowledge as having any seniority over him. A tetchy letter to Parkes attests to some ruffled feathers, but even this seems to have sorted itself out rather quickly. Though he now stuck closely to Reid, Carruthers remained friends with Parkes, Wise, McMillan and Bruce Smith despite the fact that they were often drifting apart politically. This ability to foster friendships was one of Carruthers' defining character traits. He seldom cut people off and because of this he was able to stay as informed as possible about individual sentiments and developing political events. This strategic advantage combined with the more direct benefits of affability to ensure Carruthers was well-liked and well-connected whenever the opportunity for advancement came his way.

Having lost the censure division, Carruthers and the Free Trade Party refocused their efforts on disrupting the implementation of Dibbs' tariff. At the end of his speech on the censure motion Carruthers had boldly proclaimed that "any attempt to sneak that tariff in … any such attempt, I say, would be an ignominious failure even if there were only 'the last of the Mohicans', the last Free Trader, to stand up in this house and fight until the very end".[116] The Free Traders tried to give effect to that proclamation using a tactic known as "stonewalling", effectively a filibuster whereby they would try to force a vote on every item in the

Customs Duties Bill to ensure it took as long as possible to get through the House. Carruthers would play a central role in implementing this tactic, delivering numerous speeches in sessions that lasted up to 37 hours.

He took particular delight in quoting to the House a statement made by Barton in which he had said that the implementation of protection would be an obstacle in the way of federation.[117] Federation was a stick with which Carruthers could beat the Government that Reid would have found difficult to wield without him. He also turned the argument that a fledgling nation's industries required protection on its head, pointing out that production required consumers and therefore a large population and "the more you attempt to force production in the face of a want of consumers, you will have production on unprofitable lines, and you will hinder people in other industries". Carruthers was aware of the "invisible hand" of Adam Smith, and this was a strong rebuke of the inevitable inefficiencies caused by any government manipulation of a free market. Mixing parochialism with emotive language, he maintained that since the Protectionists did not possess a majority in the House the people should be consulted before the fiscal policy was altered; "when the people are called upon to give their verdict I am sure they will be in favour of that policy of freedom under which New South Wales has progressed and become, not merely the oldest, but the strongest and most prosperous of the Australian colonies".

His other main action during the session was to contribute heavily to the debate surrounding the Trades Disputes Conciliation and Arbitration Bill. As with electoral reform, the late Parkes Government had introduced a Bill on this issue that was dropped by Dibbs only for a very similar Bill to be introduced in its place. One of its few differences was that the president of the arbitration board was to be appointed by the Governor for a period of ten years instead of elected by the board's members without a fixed term. Carruthers felt this would prejudice the ability of that person to fulfil their role, as there was a public presumption that the Executive Council that advised the Governor favoured the big end of town and even though that may not be the case the suspicion would be enough to undermine public confidence in the board.[118] Though he may have been playing up to the Labor Party, Carruthers' system would have allowed the board to be more flexible in electing a different president for different disputes. He clearly had a personal interest in the success of a Bill that was still largely the same as the one he had first introduced.

After a marathon sitting the House finally divided on 1 April. Dibbs was taking a controversial trip to England in the hope of attracting investment capital to prop up the Colony's struggling economy. His absence meant that Parliament would not sit again until August. The Free Traders would try to use this time to consolidate their organisation. They formed an organising committee made up of Carruthers, Reid, Wise, Neild, Brunker and Sydney Smith. The committee did its best to make preparations for the next election but without a solid branch structure or the funding it provided efforts were inevitably limited. It was arranged that Reid would deliver a manifesto and that committee members would use the break to campaign in regional centres.

While country areas would again be a focus, it appears that Carruthers was also making a conscious effort to ingratiate himself with some of the more moderate Labor Party members. In March he had visited Lithgow and delivered a lecture in the School of Arts alongside Joseph Cook. Born amongst the coalfields of England, Cook was an intelligent and balanced representative of the working class. Like Carruthers, he had clawed his way up from modest beginnings and this had imbued in him a sense of the opportunities that emerge from hard-work. When Cook entered Parliament he and Carruthers quickly became close friends. In many ways Cook was a natural liberal, for though he was a dedicated member of the union movement he believed in individual conscience and the benefits of relatively free enterprise.

In May Carruthers delivered a supposedly non-political address on "Industrial Evolution" under the auspices of the Ashfield branch of the Labour Electoral League. In it he traced the history of machinery from ancient Rome and Egypt up until the present day. It was an anti-luddite speech that argued that "those countries destitute of machinery are the most impoverished".[119] Carruthers maintained that in "New South Wales it could be seen that science and invention, applied to certain industries, were developing them to the increased wealth of the community, and to the advantage of the workers engaged in them". He cited examples such as dairying, meat exporting and mining to show that technology created many jobs while it made few redundant. Finally, he shook off his non-political garb and proclaimed that "we should encourage commerce in its freest sense". In essence Carruthers' speech was a defence of capitalistic growth and efficiency, a surprising topic to present to the LEL. Perhaps he still felt that he could influence the economic views of individual Labor Party members.

Carruthers was involved in some more by-election campaigning before Parliament resumed on 30 August. The situation was not bright for the Government. The depression that had begun under Parkes had got much worse under Dibbs, a boon for Free Traders who immediately blamed the tariff for the deterioration. Admittedly the depression of the 1890s was not isolated to New South Wales, so it was difficult to pin the blame entirely on the Government's policies. Then again, the other Colonies who were suffering also had high tariffs, so it was easy to offer free trade as a possible solution to the economic woes. Adding to the problems of an exceedingly high unemployment rate, a long and bitter strike had broken out in Broken Hill. Given the situation one may have expected the Labor Party to side with the Opposition but since that party had split over the fiscal issue Reid would have a difficult time in convincing its Protectionist members to vote with him. Nevertheless, he and his Free Traders would leave no stone unturned in trying to unseat the Government.

As was traditional, the fight began in the debate over the address in reply to the Governor's speech. Censuring Dibbs' long absence, Carruthers attacked it as "the speech of a cabinet without its head".[120] He defended the stonewalling tactics used in the last session as fair debate and consideration of measures. He also suggested that the Government was using its supporters in the Legislative Council to block electoral reform. It was a valuable if hardly original contribution to the Opposition's attack on a still Dibbs-less Government.

The main motion of censure came once Dibbs finally returned. It was not over the address in reply but over the Government's handling of the Broken Hill strike. The strike leaders had been arrested in controversial circumstances and Reid moved a general censure motion in the hope of capitalising on Labor discontent. Carruthers delivered another valuable speech contrasting the attitude of the Protectionists during the maritime strike with the present. While defending the Government's firm defence of law and order he castigated it for not having formed boards of conciliation and arbitration to prevent such strikes in the six months since that Act had been passed. Labor tried to amend the censure motion to make it explicitly about the strike, but the Opposition refused to give them support lest they be seen as beholden to the third party. In the end the censure motion was defeated by four votes.

Though the whole purpose of the censure debate for the Free Traders had been to try to move members of the Labor Party to come over to their side, Carruthers took exception to a statement by the member for Balmain William Murphy, which implied that Labor were the only friends of the masses. In response he gave an honest rebuke of Labor's self-righteousness and paid tribute to his former chief:

> The records show that, after an existence of 100 years, the people of this country possess a degree of liberty and freedom which is not excelled by that of any other nation. We have amongst us on my left an hon. member who, although men may differ with his political principles, has been a hero of many a fight on behalf of the masses of this country; who has earned for himself a reputation amongst the people of this country for having fought and won nearly every liberty they possess. When this colony was a convict settlement, when an attempt was subsequently made to land crowds of undesirable persons on these shores, he was the man who raised his voice successfully against the reintroduction of that system; he saved the colony from that blight. When the battle was fought for responsible government, when Wentworth fought within these walls the battle which won the Constitution under which we exist, the hon. member stood side by side with him, and fought the battle, not only here, but all through this country. The battle of manhood suffrage – the privilege which we prize so

dearly, and which we are seeking still more to purify – was fought by the hon. member and by many other men who occupy today eminent positions in the community. These privileges were fought and won long before the hon. member for Balmain was heard of, long before his party came into existence, and the people of this country are not yet so forgetful of past history that they cannot speak with some respect and gratitude of those who, in days gone by, earned for themselves honourably and truly the title of friends of the people.[121]

He went on to cite public education as another of Parkes' many liberal and democratic achievements. Coming shortly after his public break with Sir Henry, the speech is probably our most accurate picture of Carruthers' image of Parkes. It shows that he was still his hero, even if in recent years he had failed to live up to his own legend. It also shows that the historically-minded Carruthers felt a connection to what he saw as a liberal tradition that was as old as New South Wales politics itself.

The speech was a refreshing dose of honesty in a time when some Free Trade members, including Carruthers, manipulated some of their views in order to appease the Labor Party. This was a delicate balancing act as many Free Traders disliked Labor more than they did the Government. The impression we get of Carruthers is that he was probably one of them, but he hoped that Labor could be utilised to achieve free trade policy goals. On the occasions that he tried to woo them he manipulated his emphasis rather than compromise his beliefs. For example when speaking on a platform with Cook Carruthers stressed his belief in state-owned railways, a view that he had always held but that would not normally appear prominently in his addresses.[122] He was still his own man however, and in that same address he dismissed socialism while on other occasions he put forward his liberal economic views without regard for Labor reactions. The relationship with Labor was a difficult issue for a party that still contained men with views as diverse as Wise's and Bruce Smith's, and Reid was careful to avoid courting it too openly.

After the disappointment of the failed censure motion it was the victory of Grover Cleveland in the American Presidential election that brought the Free Traders together. Cleveland was a free trade Democrat and a fiscal victory in America, that bastion of protection, was a great boon to local Free Traders. Carruthers had always paid close attention to the political happenings in what might today be termed the "Anglosphere". Back in 1889 he had delivered a speech in which he proudly proclaimed that the Free Traders "would work side by side with the Democrats of America and the Liberals of England until the time should arrive when 'peace on earth and goodwill among men' should rule over the whole of the British dominions".[123] America's Democratic Party has greatly evolved since 1892, so one should avoid drawing allusions to the present day particularly as the 1892 election had a third party known as the Populists or People's Party that took up what might be dubbed the "left" position. Cleveland was known as a classical liberal but in 1896 the Democrats would take a sharp turn to the left when they adopted the Populists' presidential candidate William Jennings Bryan.

After Cleveland's victory a large demonstration was organised where Reid, Parkes, McMillan, Wise and Carruthers would all appear on the same platform. Reid delivered a speech where he announced that the triumph of American free trade had silenced any doubts in his mind that federation would lead to protection. Carruthers' address bellowed that it had been a victory not just for free trade but for good government throughout the world. Desperate to recapture the limelight from Reid, Parkes was even more hyperbolic. He suggested that the victory was the greatest American event since the abolition of slavery.

The Free Traders would need this new found unity as Parliament produced yet another censure attempt. In December the Government delivered a financial statement in which it revealed that there was a deficit of £1,152,772.[124] At this Reid rose up and charged the Treasurer See with "leaving the country practically in the dark as to the fact of the deficit which they were to wipe off being almost doubled".[125] Carruthers, who was ever to be the custodian of a balanced budget, raised his voice in the debate far earlier than in the other censures. The normally restrained member for Canterbury declared the financial statement "a disgrace to the honourable and learned member who uttered it" and was promptly ruled out of order. In the long and frequently interrupted speech that followed he attacked the Government for its neglect of local government and coal mines legislation and urged an election on the grounds that "until confidence is restored the British investor will not invest his money in this country, that business here will not revive". In a newspaper interview given a couple of days later Carruthers revealed that he believed the Government would be defeated in the division since the vote was over the estimates, which had directly paid Dibbs and two other members, hence those three would not be able to vote. His predictions proved wrong. Dibbs was able to vote and the Government held on by a majority of 7.

Another adverse motion relating to the Colony's finances was moved by Parkes in February 1893. Although it began with the preface that "I have not the slightest desire or intention to interfere with the honourable and learned member at the head of the opposition", Sir Henry may have been making his first moves in an attempt to recapture the leadership.[126] Reid does not seem to have seen it as a threat, as he voted for the motion that failed by only three votes. With all these censures the Parliament was struggling to do its job. Under the strain of a depression and a three-party Parliament, the system of responsible government was cracking. It is testament to the ability of those who had fleshed out Wentworth's bare-bones constitution that it managed to hold together, but the situation was far from ideal.

Though when See had initially given his disastrous financial statement he had proposed no new taxation, by February the Government had introduced an Income-Tax Bill. Carruthers was not opposed to the proposition of an income tax but he censured the Government for introducing this Bill before a land tax. In doing so he gave a revealing address, which shows that his motivations for supporting direct taxation as the source of necessary revenue were based on liberal economic principles:

> I do not consider that wealth is a detriment to the community, or that a person who possesses wealth should be treated as an outcast. The man who has wealth, and puts that wealth to good use, so as to get the greatest amount of production, and the greatest income,

is not altogether an enemy to his fellows. He employs labour, and benefits the community by an increase in production, and an increase of the goods of the community. But the man who possesses the sources of wealth, and who buries them as the man of old buried talents in the ground – the man who possesses those sources of wealth and yet refuses to make income by them, who locks up his land against production, who locks up the wealth he owns against toil and against industry, and who looks not to a return in the shape of interest, but to an increase in his capital – such a man is an enemy, and a hindrance to the progress of the community.[127]

This sentiment must be kept in mind through all that was to happen in the subsequent Reid Government that could easily be misconstrued as left-wing simply because it received the support of Labor. Direct taxation was not to be introduced for revolutionary or redistributive purposes. For Carruthers taxation was a necessary evil. Since Free Trade ideology restricted the use of tariffs as a source of income and land sales and debt were neither preferable nor sustainable options, direct taxation had to be used to pay for the running of government. The running of government was meant in a somewhat minimalist sense. Government was to be relatively small, not laissez-faire as there was to be a role for the state but people were still generally best left to their own devices.

This small government had to be paid for in the least intrusive way possible. People should be encouraged not discouraged to work and engage in enterprise hence a high income tax was not the preferred option. The ideal option was a tax on the unimproved value of land that would encourage people to improve their land and discourage people from leaving it idle. One of the main functions of government was to protect property under the law, thus those with property had a responsibility to pay some of the costs of government. This meant that for Carruthers there was a social justice motivation partly behind the move towards direct taxation but given that there would be no increase in the size of government there was a huge difference between making the rich bear a large portion of the burdens of taxation and using taxation as a means of redistributing wealth.

Though a land tax was to be the main form of taxation Carruthers was pragmatic enough to realise that other sources of government income would be necessary, particularly as too high a land tax would have its own negative consequences. The more the government spent the more revenue would need to be drawn from other sources, like an income tax, which were seen as being more disruptive to individuals and commerce. For that reason expenditure should be kept low, but again under certain circumstances Carruthers' pragmatism prevailed. Notable exceptions to limited government spending were public works, but only those works that were meant to recoup their costs, and education, which was essential to liberal progress.

Reid would display his pragmatism in April when the banking crisis hit. The depression had worsened, a number of Melbourne banks had collapsed, and it looked like those in Sydney were in serious danger of following suit. In order to prevent a full scale implosion of the New South Wales economy, Dibbs moved a Bank Issue Bill "to make bank-notes a first charge on bank assets; and to temporarily enable the Governor to authorise in certain cases an increased issue and circulation of the notes of any bank; and to declare bank-notes to be a legal tender".[128] Essentially the Government was proposing to guarantee bank-notes in order to prevent a panic that would see everyone withdraw their money and the banks collapse. The emergency Bill had been prepared in consultation with Reid and McMillan but it was highly controversial. Men with as diverse opinions as Wise, Parkes, Paddy Crick and Edward O'Sullivan all came out in opposition to it. Despite this opposition, the Bill was passed with the help of Reid and the majority of the Free Trade Party.

Carruthers appears to have had reservations about it. He was initially in favour of the Government's course of action and voted for the standing orders to be suspended in order that the measure could be rushed through the House, but he was also critical of the Government's methods in trying to avoid debate and implored the Assembly to give due consideration to Wise's critiques of the Bill. The latter amounted to a defence of pure currency and a warning against the dangers of paper money. When the vote on the Bill itself was taken Carruthers was conspicuously absent. It may be that he was simply protesting at the Government's attempts to stifle debate. It does not seem that he would have been opposed ideologically to interfering with the banking system as he had already proposed the establishment of a state bank to make credit more easily available. Perhaps he was not prepared to accept the costs of the Bill when the budget was already so far in deficit. Whatever his possible objections, the fact that he absented himself from the vote rather than going against his leader on such an important issue shows that he displayed more loyalty to Reid than either Wise or Parkes. In the next session when a Bank Notes Bill was introduced he would vote for it despite having some "misgivings" about relieving one class of the community and not the rest.[129]

In 1893 Carruthers sponsored a Birds Protection Bill. He had long had an interest in wildlife and a passion for hunting which for him was not contradictory. In fact, it was his experiences hunting which had exposed him to the depletion of a number of native species which he wanted to protect from extinction. The Bill imposed a fine of up to five pounds for anyone caught killing, capturing or injuring a number of native and imported birds including lyrebirds, pheasants, kingfishers and emus. It was hoped to simultaneously protect those native birds whose numbers had dropped alarmingly while allowing introduced game-birds a chance to establish significant populations which could then be hunted. For that reason the protections of the Bill were limited to a period of five years after which time they could be reassessed. The Bill was unpopular amongst less scrupulous hunters than Carruthers, who were unhappy to see any restrictions placed on their sport. The inclusion of emus was particularly controversial as many people were incredulous towards the suggestion that the numbers of the large and often destructive birds were dwindling. Despite this opposition, Carruthers was able to secure the passage of the Bill essentially as it had been introduced; striking an early victory for practical conservation which stabilised bird numbers while keeping hunting viable.

Despite the success of the Birds Protection Bill and the coming together of the two leaders over the Bank Issue Bill, the session had still been a dismal failure with very little in the way of meaningful legislation being passed. One of the drawbacks of the party system, particularly a three-party system, was that it created deep divisions that made even practical legislation difficult to pass. The Labor Party's class-based ideology made these divisions more acute and though the Party's members were flexible in their voting compared with how they were to be after the introduction of the caucus pledge, they could still be doctrinaire on many issues. These circumstances combined with the heightened tensions of one of the worst economic downturns in the Colony's history to largely cripple the Parliament.

Emotionally the session had wrecked Carruthers. In September he wrote candidly to McMillan that:

> I feel horrible things towards these socialistic roughs for their ruffianism and not less contempt for the so called respectable class who elect a man to represent them and then quietly stay at home whilst their representative is being crucified by the minority of roughs … Altho' I am a native of this country I have no pride left in me for her people and if I had my own way and the means I should leave it tomorrow rather than let my children face the misery which is surely coming upon their country.[130]

The latter sentence was in reference to the economic as well as the political situation. This early sentiment against the influence of a "minority of roughs" is the acorn from which the oak of his later belief in the necessity of "clear lines of cleavage" for the functioning of parliamentary democracy would grow. Much of the historiography surrounding the fusion between the Free Traders and the Protectionists focuses on the three-party House of the early Federal period, but it is important to note that the three-party confusion began in New South Wales much earlier. Carruthers was already beginning to come round to the view that it was Labor and not the Protectionists who were the greater threat to his classical liberal views and this would ultimately lead him to the conclusion that Labor and Liberal were the logical sides of what, in order to function, needed to be a two-party system.

While the state of affairs had taken a personal toll on him, it had also taken a toll on his Free Trade Party. Dealings with the Labor Party were creating new divisions in a party that was already split over the Parkes-Reid leadership question. A partially-dated letter from Wise appears to be from this time period. In it Wise warned Carruthers to beware of supposed "Tories" within the Free Trade Party who would be willing to support the Protectionists out of a fear of Labor.[131] Little did Wise know that Carruthers, given his private opinions of Labor, was probably sympathetic to the views of these men. The warning was surely about the fate of the Government, as party members were still independent enough to be able to vote as they liked on Bills and Free Traders had voted with Protectionists on many occasions. Despite his developing misgivings about Labor, with socialism far beyond the horizon and free trade a seemingly achievable goal, Carruthers was not yet willing to shake hands with the fiscal enemy.

Continuing to add to these internal party divisions was the federation issue. It was customary by now that the break between sessions would be used for political organisation and in 1893 this included federation organisation as well as party organisation. With Labor unenthusiastic about federation, the Dibbs Government had let the issue stay dormant. Barton had largely accepted that this would be the case when he took a spot in the Ministry, but in order to keep the embers of the movement alive he formed a new "Federation League". Initially the Free Traders (apart from McMillan) stood aloof from this organisation which they felt had Protectionist Party goals, but after radical republicans tried to take it over they changed their minds. Keen to fight off the radicalisation, Carruthers and Bruce Smith joined the League and were appointed to its central council.

The fact that Reid did not join the League led some newspapers to speculate that Carruthers' actions showed that he did not have much confidence in the Opposition leader. The speculation was unwarranted as Reid's main rivals Parkes and Wise both stood aloof from the new organisation as well. Subsequent events would prove Carruthers was not being disloyal as he would stick by Reid when Barton later attempted to make a federation party. It may well be that Reid, who has been described as a "critical friend" of the League, wanted Carruthers in it to help to control its direction.[132] A couple of weeks earlier Carruthers had written to McMillan to warn him not to associate himself with Barton and the new League, hence he must have had a sudden change of approach after this that may have been tactically motivated.[133] Carruthers would later claim that if the 'unificationists' had been in control of the federation movement the whole scheme would have been wrecked, perhaps a nod to an earlier attempt to keep the movement going down a practical path.[134]

On the party front, Wise had set up a Free Trade and Land Reform Electoral Committee. Having learnt the power that an organisation could give its chief organiser, Wise had himself appointed chairman. Reid was to be involved in the organisation but it was Wise's beast and it also gave a prominent role to Sir Henry Parkes. At a much publicised meeting of the FTLRC Carruthers moved a motion to establish branches throughout the Colony, but the organisation would never be successful enough for this to really eventuate. Its main problem was that it had too doctrinaire an approach to the land tax issue. The Committee's manifesto left little room for flexibility on either tariffs or an income tax and largely embodied the hard line stance that Carruthers and Reid had fought off within the FTLA. In the Canterbury electorate and elsewhere there was a lot of tension surrounding attempts to establish branches of the new organisation. Some branches of the FTLA still existed and were reluctant to associate themselves with what they saw as an organisation of "single taxers". Carruthers managed to get the two organisations to unite in his electorate and agreed that Free Trade candidates for the next election should agree to a tax on land, but he was also somewhat reluctant to commit himself to an FTLRC platform.[135]

Though he initially gave it his full support, Reid would slowly distance himself from Wise's organisation and in a split between doctrinism and pragmatism Carruthers naturally took Reid's side again. Wise seems to have been at the heart of all the party divisions and factional scheming that was going on behind the scenes during this difficult period. An intriguer but not a subtle one, he earned H.V. Evatt's summation that

"Wise, though never quite succeeding in getting what he wanted, always seemed to be detected in trying to do so".[136] Carruthers would later describe him as having "every good quality except consistency to party and to principle".[137]

Through the years of the Dibbs Government Wise would gradually try to usurp his leader, either personally or as king maker. His motivation for doing so is somewhat obscure. There was certainly an element of the Machiavellian in Wise, and after his prediction that Labor would immediately support Reid proved false he had no intention of sticking by a leader that he had backed on a misapprehension. In policy terms his main frustration with Reid over the coming years would be his leader's refusal to be drawn towards a more doctrinaire position on the land tax. This is in spite of the fact that Wise would have known Reid's pragmatic attitude before he had played such a prominent role in getting him elected Opposition leader. Bizarrely, through 1893-4 he started to treat Parkes and even McMillan as potential alternatives to Reid, despite the fact that they were arguably both less committed to a land tax than the current leader.[138] This suggests that he may have been motivated more by personal jealousy and animosity than any political principle. In November 1891 Reid had married Flora Ann Brumby, a woman that Wise was rumoured to have once courted, and it appears that a feeling of bitterness and regret slowly overcame him.

It is unfortunate that in their memoirs neither Carruthers nor Reid reveal much about what was going on within the Party during this time. Carruthers' incomplete memoirs do not say much at all about the period between his early career under Parkes and his election to the Premiership except for matters concerning federation, while Reid's memoirs were written with a hazy memory when many of his former colleagues were still alive, hence even if he had remembered something worthy of revelation he may have been reluctant to commit it to paper. Reid does however hint at the difficulties that he faced during this and other periods as leader. In defending his conduct when Parkes was Premier, he wrote that "*imperium in imperio* is never so objectionable in any form, I think, as in the ranks of a parliamentary party. It is very suggestive of divided counsels, unacknowledged ambitions, and internal dangers".[139] In another part of his memoirs Reid described Carruthers as not just his friend but his "ally" as well. Such a term may simply refer to their allegiance during the public political battles of the day, but given the circumstances of backroom intrigue it does seem that the label had a deeper meaning. Our greatest sources of information for the intrigues are the papers of Henry Parkes. It is these that reveal Wise's attempts to replace Reid and if Carruthers had any doubts about his leader he would likely have relayed them to his former chief. Rather than hint at intrigue however, all of Carruthers' letters to Parkes from this time stress the need for unity and lament the damage internal fragmentation was doing to the Party's reputation.[140] The evidence, however limited, thus suggests that Carruthers was fighting on Reid's side within the Party, as we might expect him to have done considering his role in Reid's ascension.

With an election looming under the new electoral laws, Carruthers had to decide which of the new single-member seats he would stand for. He had initially been highly critical of the appointment of a commission to conduct the redistribution of seats but in the end the Free Traders were not overly upset with its outcome. Canterbury had been one of the safest Sydney electorates for the Free Trade Party under the old system, and as in 1891 there were many people urging the personally popular Carruthers to stand for a more difficult seat. When he ignored these suggestions nobody was going to push him. Hence in October, with no clear election date yet known, he announced that he would be running for his local St George seat.

The move was as shrewd as it was safe. He was able to boast that at the 1891 election, with a general swing against the Free Traders, only twenty people had voted against him at the Kogarah polling station.[141] The decision was shrewd because the safeness of his seat would allow him to play the central organisational role that his party needed from him. He had always been a good local member, attending council meetings and bringing up local issues in Parliament and the goodwill he had built up over his six years in office meant that if he stayed in St George he could spend most of his time campaigning outside his electorate for the Party rather than simply for himself. Carruthers used the occasion of his announcement to reject attempts to sink the fiscal issue that was "like a cork, always bobbing up" and to condemn "the direct representation of any particular class, either labour, squatters, selectors, capitalists or any others". The latter statement was a clear dig at the very premise of the Labor Party, the first of many times that Carruthers would make this a campaign issue.

His already negative view of the Labor Party would deteriorate still further when it held its unity conference in November. A response to the tumultuous split that had saved Dibbs, the conference committed party members to voting as a solid block "on all the planks of the labour platform and on all questions affecting the life of the government".[142] Commitment to the platform was nothing new; it had been included in the Liberal Political Association rules though in practice it probably would not have been implemented strictly. It was the commitment to voting together on matters affecting the life of the Government which was the shocking turn. Platforms were made in advance and committed to on the hustings, but decisions affecting the fate of the Government had to be made as they cropped up. The only way a uniform vote could be enforced was by spontaneous decisions of caucus. This meant the removal of the parliamentary conscience of individual members, an aberration to nineteenth century liberals. It also meant that Labor members would be held to account by their party as much as their electors, a practice also seen as a threat by liberals. In response to the unity conference Carruthers' friend Joseph Cook left the Party, and much of what respect Carruthers had for that organisation left with him.

Labor's collectivist outlook had already seen it represent a specific group in Parliament, now it was used to justify the restriction of the liberty of that group's representatives and eventually it would reach its logical conclusion with the proposal for collective group control of much of the economy via extensive state enterprises and the theoretical goal of the socialist objective. All three points sat in philosophical obverse to Carruthers' liberalism and its emphasis on individualism. It is in this fundamental divide that the origins of Carruthers' antipathy towards the Labor Party lay. The fact that the three points developed over time helps explain why Carruthers' animosity evolved and became a more prominent part of his rhetoric over the years. There were other objections to Labor policy which helped to supplement his distaste, including Carruthers' belief in the necessity of a pragmatism that he felt early Labor members lacked. He also believed in the benefits of free enterprise, though in essence that was the economic outgrowth of individualism, it still emanated from the underlying philosophical divide.

Parliament resumed on 26 September and Carruthers not Reid led the Opposition's response to the address in reply. It was quite mild, saying that while the Opposition would fulfil their duty in holding the Government to account in this short session they would "endeavour to do all those things necessary to be done by this dying Parliament so as to prepare the way at the earliest date possible for an appeal to the people under the new electoral system".[143] His hopes were not realised and Parliament was prorogued on 8 December to resume on 17 January. When it returned the prospect of a more conciliatory attitude raised at the beginning of the last session was quickly dashed. The reason Parliament had been prorogued was because the Government had been defeated in a snap vote which attacked Barton and Richard O'Connor, the Minister for Justice, for accepting private legal briefs in a dispute involving the Railway Commissioners. Both men were forced to resign for the alleged impropriety, but Dibbs refused to take the negative vote as the will of the Parliament and quickly rushed through a prorogation to stifle debate. When Parliament resumed Reid tried to censure Dibbs for his action but was defeated by one vote. Carruthers wryly remarked that the Government "had been strong only in the tenacity with which they clung to office".[144]

During the prorogation Parkes and Wise had been lobbying for support to replace Reid. In the circumstances of clear disunity Carruthers sent a letter to Parkes in January 1894 to urge a public coming together with Reid. W.G. McMinn uses this as evidence that "Carruthers was not by any means deeply committed" to his leader.[145] This is simply not true. Carruthers had been and would continue to be Reid's most loyal ally throughout this testing time and politically Reid would probably not have survived it without him. It was Carruthers and Wise who had helped Reid become leader and we have no evidence that the former shared the latter's regret about the move. Carruthers' suggestion about the coming together of Parkes and Reid was based on concerns about the fate of the Party. As its main organiser, he had his finger on the pulse of the electorate and knew that the Party's less than secret intrigues had hurt the public's opinion of it. He believed that the public saw it as divided into Reid, Parkes and Wise factions and that a show of unity was needed in order to make successful organisation possible.[146] The letter made no mention of the leadership and when it later became a choice between having Reid or Parkes as leader Carruthers unflinchingly chose Reid. It is notable that the proposed show of unity would not involve Wise, the main intriguer and the person with the most unfulfilled ambitions. This suggests that Carruthers, however naively, may have hoped that he could get Parkes to lend the gravitas of his support to Reid without ever bringing up the leadership question.

On 9 May the Opposition met to establish a Free Trade Council to act as a court of appeal for preselection disputes for the coming elections. It was essentially a reincarnation of the FTLA council but without the clear branch mandate. Reid was to chair the council, and Carruthers, Parkes, McMillan and several other members of Parliament were to sit on it as well as an equal number of other prominent Free Traders to be elected at a later date. Wise was noticeably absent from the council, a sign that the FTLRC had split off from the main body of Free Traders.

A few weeks after the meeting Reid, as head of the council, sent a letter to Free Traders explaining the process of preselection arbitration. Firstly candidates were to meet together and settle their differences amongst themselves. Secondly if that failed they should try to get mutual friends or local arbiters to arbitrate for them. Thirdly the council offered its services. "Failing the acceptance and successful operation of one of these three courses, we see no alternative, in the interests of the party as a whole, but that of taking independent steps to ascertain in each case the name of the freetrade candidate who commands the best prospect of success: and to publish the result of our inquiries for the information of all those by whom, at this serious juncture of our history, the cause of freetrade and good government is more esteemed than individual rivalries and personal ambition".[147] The last phrase was the most telling; "individual rivalries and personal ambition" were and are essential to politics, yet they were ever to be detrimental to political parties.

With this organisational framework in place, Parliament was dissolved in June. Although Reid was the president of the council, Carruthers would play the central role in running the campaign and dealing with preselection disputes. He was not optimistic about the Party's prospects. He wrote to Parkes that "we are in greater trouble than ever before and I will require all the skill, all the hard work and all the power of the party to pull through".[148] Reid, perhaps in anticipation of the important role Carruthers was about to play, wrote to him to stress the importance he had always attached to his support.[149] Carruthers had missed a party meeting, and informed his leader of the circumstances which caused the indiscretion. In response Reid wrote that he completely understood and that Carruthers' support was a source of "genuine satisfaction". It was rare for Reid to write to Carruthers as the two men generally communicated in person or on the telephone, so the fact that Reid wanted to put this in writing ads weight to his sentiment. McMinn cites this letter as evidence of a change of heart by Carruthers "who earlier in the year had been prepared to consider Parkes' reinstatement".[150] However, as has already been shown, there is no evidence that Carruthers actually contemplated reinstating Parkes.

Carruthers' lack of optimism was somewhat understandable. The internal party divisions that had distressed him during the year had not gone away, though at least the FTLRC and FTC usually agreed on endorsements despite issuing separate lists.[151] Nevertheless preselection arbitration proved extremely difficult. The situation in the new single member Canterbury electorate was fairly typical of the problem. Varney Parkes and a Mr. T. W. Taylor had both wanted to run for the seat. Carruthers tried to negotiate the latter's withdrawal, writing him a letter where he said that he "would earn the gratitude and the esteem of the freetrade party if he came to some arrangement whereby only one member should be nominated".[152] Initially it seemed the intervention had worked but bad blood between the two candidates spilled over into a very public dispute that hurt the Party's reputation. Carruthers felt that "an arbiter's lot is not a happy one" and that he had never before "realised the selfishness which rules many aspirants for parliamentary honours".[153] His task was not entirely thankless however and he managed to get his decisions abided by in several electorates. In some ways the Free Trade Council held so many inquiries and meetings that it detracted from the Party's ability to campaign. The fact that they were willing to do this shows the high importance they placed on split vote prevention.

One prominent feature of the new electoral system was that elections were now to be held on the same day for all electorates. This limited the ability of leading members to campaign in the country electorates that used to have elections several days after they had secured their city seats. Despite this, Carruthers managed to give several addresses outside St George in places like Bathurst and West Maitland. The Opposition's policy rested on the anchors of "true" free trade and a land tax. J. A. Ryan has argued that in 1894 the direct taxation proposals represented the influence of Wise's liberalism.[154] This is difficult to maintain considering they were in the LPA platform written without Wise and the FTC's interpretation of them maintained the flexibility characteristic of both Reid and Carruthers. In reality direct taxation still represented necessary taxation and was not inherently tied to interventionist "new liberal" views. Adding to free trade and direct taxation were issues such as land reform, a throwback to the debate over free selections that was as old as New South Wales politics itself. Finances were also an important issue and in January Carruthers had declared that "the time had come when borrowing had to cease and when [extravagant] public expenditure had to cease".[155]

It was an agenda that was likely to win some Labor support but it was fundamentally a liberal free trade agenda with main planks that could be found in the LPA platform. By salvaging that innovative platform the Free Traders were continuing the adaptation of liberalism from a pervasive culture into something both crystallised and partisan. On the organisational front the Party no doubt had gone backwards, but by utilising some of the political creativity of 1889 Reid was able to gain an advantage over his Protectionist opponents. That advantage was not just the breadth of the Free Trade program but also the fact that its disparate points were tied together by an underlying liberal ideology and that this lent itself to electoral rhetoric. Carruthers was able to succinctly tell his audiences that while the Free Traders would promote freedom "protection took away the liberty of the individual and what was bad for the individual was bad for the country".[156] The ultimate success of the liberal agenda, even when unsupported by the structure of the FTLA, is testament to the value of the document that Carruthers had played a central role in writing. Though the FTLA's legacy would thus be consolidated, innovations remained gradual and after 1895 a liberal electoral platform of the same scope would not be repeated until Carruthers himself took the reins.

The election was held on Tuesday 17 July. The combination of economic depression and large budgetary deficits took their toll on the Government, and the Free Traders were able maintain enough unity to secure a great victory. They had effectively won 62 seats (12 of those being independent free traders) out of an Assembly of 125.[157] This meant that Reid would need only one vote from the 8 independent Labor members that included people like Joseph Cook to get a majority, though the inconsistencies of the Free Traders meant that in practice he would need more. What was crucial was that, unless there was a major split, he would not have to rely on the votes of the caucus-committed Labor members. Some minor legislative concessions were offered to Labor ensure Reid extra stability, but the fact that the new Ministry was not entirely reliant on them would allow it to keep its integrity and allow Reid some degree of independence.

The controversial decision to elect Reid Party leader, which Carruthers had firmly backed, had paid off immensely. Loveday, Martin and Weller argue that the election "confirmed the strength of the party's moderate 'centre' under Reid's leadership".[158] They position this "centre" between radicals like Wise who fetishized a land tax and conservatives who disliked direct taxation. This formulation is a fairly accurate representation of some (though not all) of the ideological divisions within the Party that stood hand in hand with the personality divisions, hence the election was as much a victory for Carruthers' pragmatic liberal beliefs as it was a vindication of his support for Reid's leadership.

Before the new Government could get down to business, the leadership question would rear its head one last time. In what was a sad indignity for Parkes, he had spent election day travelling round Sydney in a carriage desperately trying to claim credit for the victory. The attempt failed. When Dibbs resigned the Governor called on Reid to form a Ministry. Wise would later argue that the Governor's commission had unfairly removed the Party's chance to decide on the leadership, but given Reid had clearly led the Party at the election and had the greatest chance of maintaining a stable government the decision was entirely justifiable.[159] With the Governor already calling for Reid, a party meeting was held during which the members unanimously endorsed his leadership. The motion was put forward by McMillan, who had now somewhat reconciled himself with the leader. Carruthers needed no reconciliation. He had stood solidly behind his leader during the difficulties of the late Parliament and now, as Reid's lieutenant, he looked towards the coming battle for reform.

CHAPTER SIX

Minister for Lands

The extent to which the Free Trade Party had been divided in the preceding period may be partly a reflection of the teething pains of the party system. Wise's plotting would perhaps have been considered less insidious during the factional era, particularly considering he was in opposition. The same could be said of those, occasionally including Wise, who wanted to reinstate Parkes to the top job. In earlier days scheming and forming alliances was one of the main ways to get out of opposition. Now in the emerging party era, permanent groupings meant that unity was required even when out of government. Allegiance to a leader was also necessary, even when that leader was not the Premier. At this early stage Carruthers seems to have accepted these facts to a greater extent than many of his colleagues. Shortly before the election he had declared that the "recognised leader of the party, who occupies that position by virtue of an election made in the only recognised fashion, that is, at a caucus of the members of the party during the last parliament, is G.H. Reid".[160] Such a statement was not just an endorsement of Reid, but also of the Party's ability to elect a leader and the members' obligation to respect that election.

In the upcoming Government Carruthers would continue to be a force for unity. In doing so he would seek to protect the Free Traders' liberal legislative program, even if that meant making further sacrifices of the independence of MLAs. The old liberal way of parliamentary life was slowly dying off, but our pragmatic subject was more concerned with results than mourning the loss of a culture which long predated him.

With internal party divisions still raw, Reid faced the hard task of constructing a stable Cabinet to undertake his ambitious agenda. Carruthers was to be heavily involved in the confidential discussions which would precede any announcement by the Premier. Initially it was widely speculated that the new Ministry would be a reconstruction of the old Parkes Ministry minus the former leader, with McMillan as Treasurer, Wise as Attorney-General, Brunker as Minister for Lands and Carruthers as Minister for Public Instruction. It soon became clear however that this would not be the case. While promising to fully support the Government, McMillan declined to accept a ministerial position because of his business commitments. Less convincingly Wise, who had been reported as having said that Parkes was the "natural leader" of the Free Trade Party, also declined to serve under Reid on the pretext of needing to focus on his profession.[161] Bruce Smith, who also had a difficult relationship with Reid, was not considered for a position as he had retired from politics and had not contested the recent election. It was rumoured that he would be nominated for the Legislative Council, but this did not eventuate. All of this meant that the new Ministry would be robbed of several of the most prominent members of Parkes' last Cabinet. This was to ultimately be a blessing in disguise, as their exclusion would allow Reid to have a more united if less experienced team.

Having failed to recruit either McMillan or Wise, Reid put in a strong effort to convince James Brunker to join him. A "good grandmotherly administrator" with the "confidence of the public", Brunker was needed to add a veneer of experience to what would be a relatively green Ministry.[162] Reid eventually succeeded by offering Brunker his choice of positions. He chose Colonial Secretary, traditionally the post of the leader since Premier was not yet a paid ministerial position. This left Brunker's old post as Minister for Lands vacant. Given the Government's agenda it was reported that the strength of the Ministry would be determined by who were its Treasurer and Minister for Lands. In the absence of Brunker it was thought that James Young would be given the latter position, but Reid left him as Secretary of Public Works and gave the important lands portfolio to his ally Carruthers. It was essentially a promotion, perhaps a reward for his support during the tumultuous last session. Newspapers voiced concerns that Carruthers "had never shown any aptitude for administering the crown lands of the colony" but tempered their consternation at his appointment by pointing to his good record as a Minister.[163]

Carruthers' promotion was not the only surprising ministerial choice. With the experienced McMillan declining to serve, Reid had appointed himself Treasurer. This involved a £500 pay cut compared to the Premier's traditional position of Colonial Secretary, but it would allow him to directly oversee the financial proposals that were central to a free trade land tax program. Since the roles of Premier and Treasurer had been combined, this left Carruthers as arguably the second most important member of Cabinet. The other surprise appointment was Joseph Cook as Postmaster General. Given that he and Carruthers had got along well in the last Parliament, the latter Joseph would have probably been pleased with this decision and may have even helped to convince Reid to choose Cook over other possible independent Labor inclusions. Cook's appointment seems to suggest that Reid was more concerned about the support of these independent Labor members rather than caucus Labor, as the latter were antagonised by the move to include a "rat", though it may be that he simply misread what their reaction would be.

The Labour Electoral Leagues promised to contest Cook's electorate, as well as those of several other Ministers. At this time an archaic law, which was a remnant of a time when the Crown directly chose Ministers, required those accepting office to seek re-election before taking up their posts. Reid had lost one of these elections when appointed Minister under Stuart, and in 1894 several Free Trade Ministry seats were marginal enough to be of concern. Carruthers' was not one of them. He was to be one of only two Ministers whose re-election was not contested. The *Sydney Morning Herald* wrote that "the ridiculous minority in which his [Carruthers'] opponent found himself as the result of the last election is regarded as indicating the hopelessness of any opposition, and even the most sanguine officers of the LEL seem inclined to allow the honourable member an uncontested return".[164]

After his unopposed re-election Carruthers delivered a speech to his constituents at Kogarah. He claimed that he would have preferred to have remained Minister for Public Instruction but that his colleagues unanimously pressured him into taking up the lands position. Responding to the leadership speculation that had surrounded the election result, he defended his support for Reid over Parkes. Carruthers professed that Reid "having been pressed into the service, or having volunteered into it, had led the party nobly and well in circumstances of adversity" and that in supporting him "I must be forgiven if I desired to be loyal rather than chivalrous, and to be just rather than to be generous".[165] He went on to compliment the new Premier, citing his refusal of offices under Parkes as evidence that he was not hungry for power.

Reid returned the compliment a month later in a banquet given in Carruthers' honour. Reid and Carruthers were the only two to receive such banquets after the election, perhaps an acknowledgement of the latter's growing importance. Reid said that Carruthers "has fought his way from humble beginnings, and elevation after elevation, instead of contracting, has added warmth and breadth to the humanity of his sympathy".[166] These sickly panegyrics show that the new Government was trying to project an air of unity and positivity in response to the negativity of Parkes. When the latter had been invited to Reid's victory banquet organised by McMillan, Parkes had written a letter of response in which he explained that the invitation was an insult and then relentlessly attacked the Premier. He was pleased enough with how this piece of vitriol had turned out that he then got it published in the press, an act which deeply offended the original recipient. Later in a newspaper interview Parkes, with a probable eye towards Carruthers, had also claimed that members of the Ministry "have acted towards me in a most treacherous way on many occasions".[167]

Reid was as keen to distance himself from Parkes' overbearing leadership style as he was to distance himself from these attacks. As was discussed earlier, Parkes had had several conflicts with his Ministers and his party when he was last Premier. In order to avoid these divisions and perhaps in acknowledgement of the fact that the new party system had changed the nature of political leadership, Reid stressed his equality with his colleagues and his intention to consult with them before making decisions. It was a long-term strategy since Reid had written to Carruthers before the election promising him earnest consultation.[168] The evidence we have is that Reid fulfilled his promise, for Carruthers' papers contain a folder of information on subjects outside his portfolio forwarded to him during the Reid Ministry that has no equivalent from his time under Parkes.[169] Reid's change of approach is an important development in the fledgling party system that has received little attention from historians. In terms that Carruthers would have no doubt appreciated, Parkes the *rex* had been replaced by Reid the *princeps*. It appears that the approach worked as there were less obvious rifts in Cabinet during Reid's Premiership than there had been before.

Carruthers played an integral part in Cabinet discussions. He had a reputation for being bookish and was ever ready to offer an informed opinion. Between his position as Minister for Lands, experience in education and reading of economic literature, there was scarcely a topic on which Carruthers could not claim some authority. *The Catholic Press* described him as:

> perhaps, the most interesting member of Cabinet. He is feared even by those with whom he is intimately associated, he is brainy and mysterious, and he has youth on his side ... Mr. Carruthers is not much to look at, and he would probably be like a wet blanket to a jovial companion, but he has rare intelligence and dogged perseverance, and a mind ready at all times to receive ideas.[170]

If Carruthers was indeed feared this was perhaps a reflection of a lingering reputation for ruthlessness after his role in the dispatch of Parkes. It also likely reflected an animosity amongst fellow Cabinet members jealous of his exclusive relationship with the Premier. Reid respected Carruthers both as a personal friend and a potential rival, and was careful always to keep him close by his side.

Land reform was to be one of the first of the Government's main election promises to be implemented. The land question had been at the heart of New South Wales politics since its inception. *Terra Nullius* had turned all of the land of the Colony into Crown land, the question was how that land should be divided and sold to accommodate the burgeoning settler population. Arguably the main difference between nineteenth century Australian liberalism and its twentieth century counterpart was the importance of this land issue. Liberals had two concurrent concerns; that the land was to be settled and improved but also that a rural aristocracy be prevented from forming. They had learnt from their European counterparts that large estates were the antithesis of liberalism as they symbolised inherited rather than created wealth and they threatened the principle of equality of opportunity. At the same time, liberals also believed that small free holdings could be a vehicle for national development based on individual initiative. For these reasons liberals had opposed the emergence of large estates, whether they had been created through squatting, land grants or auction sales. The land question was bigger than these basic liberal concerns and also encompassed issues of freehold versus leasehold and pastoralist versus free selector.

The greatest liberal land reform had been the introduction of John Robertson's Land Bills in 1861. These hoped to open up the land by introducing the principle of "free selection before survey" on the conditions of residence and cultivation. These selections were to be freehold purchases at £1 per acre given out in 320 acre lots. Initially these reforms were hailed but gradually their deficiencies became apparent. Through a process known as "dummying" the 320 acre lots were being combined to create the large estates that the legislation had explicitly tried to avoid. Dummying involved the use of false selectors to claim multiple lots or reserve prime land, which was then consolidated into a larger holding. This abuse of the system had allegedly grown widespread, undermining the democratisation of land ownership. Moreover the residency qualification, which had not required perpetual residency anyway, was largely being ignored and many people were living in the city while reaping the profits of their large estates. Part of the problem was that geographically and climatically Australia was more suited to large pastoral estates than the agricultural freeholds preferred by liberals. Adding to all these difficulties, the land was badly administered and there were frequently disputes between squatters and free selectors over leases.

There had been many adjustments to the land laws between 1861 and 1894, but Carruthers would still have to deal with these same basic issues. One advantage he did possess was that as someone who had lived their whole adult live in the city he did not have any personal attachment to the various disputes beyond his liberal beliefs. Before he could get down to business and draft his land reforms, Carruthers had some legal technicalities to sort out. A number of leases given in the central division of New South Wales were due to expire in 1895. According to the Land Act of 1884 if these leases were not to be extended the tenants were required to be notified two years prior to expiration. They had been notified in time by the *Gazette*, but the lease holders had argued that the Land Act of 1889 had implicitly repealed the 1884 Act. A test case was brought before the Supreme Court which ultimately decided in favour of the lease holders. The legally minded Carruthers respected the decision of the court and framed his land laws so that they would not overturn existing leases. Though the *Freeman's Journal* was to compare him rather unfavourably to the younger Gracchus, he was anything but a revolutionary.

On 28 August the new Assembly sat and the Governor's speech declared that "the most pressing subject of legislation is an amendment of the land laws".[171] Two weeks later Carruthers introduced his Crown Lands Bill. He began by citing figures showing that since the introduction of Robertson's land laws the proportion of the population in the city had actually increased and hence he argued the attempt to settle the land had failed. He also showed that the amount of alienated land per head of population and therefore the average size of a holding had also increased since 1861. He connected the failure of the land laws to the depression in the city as "thousands of idle hands" were wanting work while the Colony had "a sparsely settled country with lands waiting and pining for willing workers, large producing interests languishing from want of justice, for want of proper methods with dealing with the soil, and the very foundation of the national prosperity sapped because of the absence of a recognition of that sound principle which should regulate the acquisition of and occupation of lands by the people".[172]

It is noteworthy that Carruthers spoke of regulation, since H.V. Evatt has connected liberalism's response to the land question with the downfall of "laissez-faire" beliefs.[173] While regulation of the acquisition of Crown lands might be contrary to an absolute interpretation of laissez-faire, for generally small government liberals like Carruthers *state involvement* in the parcelling out of *state lands* was necessary by definition rather than being an overtly interventionist act. Australia's youth gave liberals a chance to create a more ideal spread of land ownership without disrupting property rights that were seen as essential to the smooth running of society and government. They were not being left wing; they were taking advantage of a unique opportunity. It is important to note that this more ideal spread of land ownership had more to do with increasing production and opportunities for enterprising people and also avoiding land being left idle, than it did with any notions of "social justice". As John Ward has remarked, the liberalism embodied in the various land reforms was essentially "right-wing" as it aimed at increasing the number and prosperity of property owners.[174]

The urgency of Carruthers' criticisms of the current system of Crown land distribution shows that he felt that this opportunity was being lost. His solutions to the problems he had outlined were multi-faceted. Free selection before survey was to be replaced with extensive survey and classification to try to ensure that land was put to its best possible use, and flexibility was introduced to allow for the great variance of land quality throughout the Colony. Poor quality land could be given out in larger improvement leaseholds, while good land was reserved for individual plots. The latter were given out as homestead selections. Based on precedents that Carruthers insisted had built up the greatness of America and Canada, a man would be able to acquire a homestead "on terms which will not cripple his resources in his early stages".[175]

In order to encourage small primary producers already in occupation of Crown lands, security of tenure would be granted with perpetual leasehold in perpetual rent. For these leaseholders rent was to be kept low but permanent residence would be a strict requirement. To free up good land that had already been partially alienated for settlement, those pastoralists with large leaseholds were liable to have up to half their property confiscated, but they were to be fully compensated with an extended lease on the rest of their property. These leaseholders also had a right to the improvements they had made on their confiscated land.

Most radically of all, the Government was proposing to buy back large freehold estates for the purpose of land settlement. Even this radical move recognised the property rights of the owners, though Carruthers was keen to stress in his legalistic way that the Crown was effectively a landlord even for those who owned freehold.

In the debate that followed Carruthers' speech, the main critique came from Wise. He did not have any real problems with the Bill itself but he was critical of the fact that it had been put to the Assembly before the fiscal and direct taxation proposals. He warned the Ministry that members of the Opposition were pushing the Land Bill in order that they might later censure the Government for pushing back other legislation. Wise's thinly veiled attack overlooked the fact that during the last Parliament the Free Traders had criticised the Government for bringing up the fiscal question when other less contentious pieces of legislation were waiting to be passed, so they were only being true to that sentiment in putting the Land Bill first. The great divisions that were about to be stirred up over Reid's main proposals show that it was a practical move. Practicality did not hold much importance for Wise, whose "scheming" would not end just because the Free Traders now held office.

In introducing his Bill, Carruthers had appealed to the members of the Assembly to look beyond party differences. For once the appeal seems to have worked, at least to some degree. A large majority were in favour of it, with some members of the Opposition more concerned about claiming credit for what the previous Government had done to facilitate the land reforms than debating the proposals themselves. Some criticisms inevitably came however. Copeland, the previous Minister for Lands, argued that the Bill would encourage dummying in spite of the strict permanent residency requirements and finality of selection that had been designed to prevent such an eventuality. Most critiques came from the various interested parties, who were quick to allege that the Bill favoured new homestead selectors over pastoralists and even old free selectors, ignoring the fact that the security of tenure that both of these groups had been pining for was to be granted. Despite these criticisms, most still agreed that Carruthers had done a good job of balancing competing interests. After lengthy discussions in committee, the Bill eventually passed with a reasonable majority. It was a great start for the Reid Government and suggested that it might be able to end the parliamentary stagnation that had dogged the two previous administrations.

In a very short space of time Carruthers' land reforms proved to be highly successful. Land settlement historian Stephen Roberts has shown that cultivation increased 35% within two years of the Bill being passed.[176] This is quite an astounding outcome, though the rate of land settlement would have been increased by the depression in the city. This was intentional, as Carruthers had cited the depression as a motivation for introducing the Bill; hence the figure suggests he was somewhat successful in achieving this socially ameliorative goal. Despite this success, the population discrepancy between the country and the city that he had cited to suggest the failure of the previous system ultimately continued largely unabated. Like most historical processes, this was not something that could be overturned by an Act of Parliament.

One of Carruthers' responsibilities as Minister for Lands was to oversee the administration of labour settlements. These were a form of relief for people struggling to find work that had been introduced by the previous Government. They involved placing people in state-run work camps along with their families. Carruthers was not entirely sold on the idea but with the depression still in effect, he tried to increase the money that was allocated to these camps so that the experiment could be carried out to its conclusion whether that be a success or failure. In moving this he argued that it was not a large risk as the value of the improvements to the land created by the workers would outstrip the costs of running the camps.[177] This was about as far as Carruthers would go with government intervention and the notion that this form of welfare, provided it was carried out on a limited scale, would be remunerative was a central part of the reason he was willing to support it. He proposed that any new settlements should be built on coastal areas so with fishing and agriculture they could be as self-sustaining as possible.

Carruthers' insistence on keeping costs low was not born out of callousness. He appears to have been genuinely concerned about the welfare of the unemployed and his Crown Lands Act had been designed with the specific intention of making land available to those with little money. However, small scale examples of municipalities who had spent money they did not have in order to "create" jobs had suggested to him that the debt involved could do more harm than good. Ultimately he believed that private employment was the main avenue out of the depression, and though the Government should offer what relief it could, its main task was to get out of the way.

In November Reid made his first financial statement as Treasurer. He proposed some rather radical measures to adjust the Government's bookkeeping on account of the three million pound deficit that Dibbs had left him with, but on the important measures of direct taxation he acted with caution. These were to be delayed until he could get a clearer view of the financial situation. The Free Trade proposals which they were to fund were to be delayed also, with local government to effectively leapfrog both on the agenda. This was necessary as the success or failure of local government would essentially determine how much money the Government would need to raise from direct taxation.

At the end of Reid's speech Wise rose up to attack him for postponing the fulfilment of his main election promises. Carruthers, who by now was fast becoming Reid's right hand man, jumped to the defence of the Premier. He began by declaring his hope "that before this debate closes the Government will know its friends from its foes".[178] He attacked Wise for never having supported the Government after he had promised Reid he would do so, and quoted a speech in which Wise had advocated the course of action Reid was taking. Carruthers claimed that "there is only one government which it is possible for him [Wise] to support, and that is a government led by himself". He also labelled Wise ignorant for arguing that a land tax should be rushed through before the land and income assessment that the Government was proposing had ascertained the value of the properties that were to be taxed. Carruthers was more concerned that the machinery be in place to ensure that direct taxation ran smoothly than with any loss of face caused by a slight delay in its introduction.

The debate on the financial statement continued intermittently over the next couple of weeks. On 21 November Henry Parkes took his opportunity to lay into Reid, dragging up in vivid detail the history of 1891 and how Reid had personally destroyed his Ministry on the pretence that Parkes was delaying free trade, only to now repeat the process. He was particularly aggrieved that Reid had suggested the State's financial problems had begun before the advent of the Dibbs Government, arguing that if the Premier thought that the previous Parkes Ministry was so bad he would not have endeavoured to enlist so many of its members. With an air of hypocrisy, Parkes attacked the Premier's ego, how he had dismissed the achievements of his predecessors and cobbled together a Ministry out of friends and personal followers. The speech was particularly acrimonious, levelling personal insult after personal insult with only tokenistic regard for the issue at hand.

Once again it was Carruthers who gave the Government's reply. He regretted "that the grand old man of Australia today – I do not know why, no one can tell why – after having left his party, to be driven as it were to the four corners of the earth by the winds of Heaven, now when this party has to some extent concentrated its forces, and when it has to some extent got the capacity and the power to give the country what it is crying for, should do his utmost to thwart it in the accomplishment of its purpose".[179] He went on to censure Parkes for not having passed a local government bill when he had the chance and for having tried to sink the fiscal question at the election only to attack the Government for being slow to introduce free trade. He also pointed out how Parkes had done little to achieve free trade in his own time in office.

At one point Wise began interjecting, threatening Carruthers "not to encourage me to say what I know of him", a threat that in the context of a debate on party loyalty appears to refer to the shunting of Parkes. The member for St George implored Wise to "get all those things off his political chest which are weighing him down", but the latter fell silent. If Wise's threatened secret was indeed about the shunting of Parkes, the fact that he bit his tongue even when tempers were frayed explains why he would omit it from his later accounts of the leadership election.

Though Carruthers and Wise frequently clashed politically they maintained a personal friendship, and whatever the secret was, he was clearly unwilling to betray his friend's trust.

The speeches showed Carruthers' deep sense of loyalty to party, something that perhaps could not have been present in any member elected before 1887 who had not politically grown up in the party system. Even his betrayal of Parkes, probably the most "disloyal" act of his career, had ultimately been about the success of the Party to which he remained faithful. Carruthers argued that "party government is only possible by a combination of men who are prepared to sink to some extent their strong individual opinion in order that some common purpose may be achieved" and he attacked the "faddists" and "extremists" who could not accept that. It was this understanding of the need for compromise and unity that would allow Carruthers to go on to found the more permanent New South Wales Liberal Party.

For now however, he was acting as Reid's attack dog, more important than any Government whip, tearing to shreds anyone who openly tried to undermine the Party in order to ensure that others were warned off doing the same. His motivation for doing this was largely altruistic, as he honestly believed that it was necessary in order to pass legislation for the benefit of the Colony. This echoed his later justification of a two-party system and given that disunity on all sides had led to a highly stagnated Parliament for most of his time in office, it is easy to understand why he felt this way. The unity that Carruthers desired was certainly not as strict as caucus Labor and left liberal room for individual opinions. It was more concerned with the scheming that had been going on behind the scenes and in Parliament than imposing uniform views, but it still represented an important evolution in liberal politics. The debate left both Parkes and to a greater extent Wise isolated within Free Trade circles, hence Carruthers achieved his purpose.

As was to be expected, Carruthers was involved in the committee debates surrounding Reid's Local Government Bill. He spoke fiercely against a proposal to increase the amount that municipalities could borrow particularly in light of recent attempts to use borrowed money to relieve the unemployed. He argued that even productive works, if paid for by debt, could ultimately cripple a municipality's ability to function. He cited Penrith Council's recent financial difficulties, which had forced them to practically suspend payments before coming begging "cap in hand to the Government", as evidence for his claim.[180]

The Bill was ultimately scuttled when the Protectionists and Labor combined over an amendment to remove plural voting. Reid and Carruthers may have been inclined to accept the amendment were it not for the fact that plural voting was necessary to secure support in the Legislative Council. Without it there was no point going on with a Bill that was doomed to fail. Comprehensive local government was recognised by all parties as an urgent necessity, but as had been the case several times before, politicking got in the way of compromise. Labor were aware of the likely consequences of the amendment but were unwilling to sacrifice a point of principle. Protectionists cared little about the detail but wanted to score a political point over the Government. This was a major defeat for both Reid and the reforming spirit that lay behind the Free Trade Liberal program. Carruthers condemned the "unholy combination" that had destroyed the Bill, and in particular the Protectionists who did not even believe in the amendment but had used it to thwart the Government.[181] Attacking Labor's dogmatism, he claimed that:

> no government can attempt to pass legislation if at every point it is met, first of all by those who in a hundred points desire to see their conscientious scruples respected, who desire to have the whole of their principles affirmed, sacrificing ninety-nine points gained for the sake of one they cannot gain, and who, at the same time, are so unsuspecting and inexperienced as to allow themselves to be used as plastic material in the hands of a skilful Opposition.

The incident was to be a turning point in the souring of relations between the Free Traders and Labor. For Carruthers, who privately had been one of the first to turn against that party, had been the strongest advocate of local government and for whom pragmatism was a guiding political principle, the experience was particularly galling.

The failure threw out the Government's carefully thought out financial proposals which had been predicated on the passing of the Local Government Bill. Reid delivered another financial statement in May, proposing a land tax of a penny in the pound above £475 and an income tax of sixpence in the pound above £300, as well as the introduction of the shortest tariff schedule in the world. Henry Parkes, who had made a secret alliance with Dibbs, used the occasion to move a motion of censure against the Government for delaying federation in favour of its radical financial proposals. Wise joined in to make what was essentially the opposite attack on Reid, criticising the long delay in introducing direct taxation. Predictably Carruthers interjected to point out that the Government had introduced the legislative machinery to lay the groundwork for direct taxation six months earlier.[182]

As the debate wore on Wise's contrary support for a censure that went against the grain of his critique became something of an embarrassment. In the end he lost his nerve and was paired against the motion with the censure ultimately failing by a huge majority of 28 votes. This put a premature end to the Parkes-Dibbs combination and killed off what little influence Wise had left in the Party. It was a sad day for Carruthers, who had to see his old hero Parkes go through yet another indignity as he struggled to wrest back power. In a newspaper interview during the prolonged censure debate he had lamented that "having always regarded him [Parkes] as a staunch opponent of the restrictionists, I am not only surprised, but very much pained to find that he is about to throw himself into the arms of those who will use him as a tool – strong man as he is – and throw him away as soon as they have done with him".[183] Sir Henry's response was bitter; "that gentleman [Carruthers] is also pleased to say he very much admires my character! In reply to that, I say that I admire very little in his".[184]

The Government was now safe but it would still have to face the obstructionist tactics of its opponents as it tried to get its financial reforms passed. With his opinions in favour of direct taxation and free trade a matter of considerable public record, Carruthers spoke little in these debates except occasionally to use his legal skills to debate points of order. He also spoke against a Conditional Purchases Bill that aimed at meddling with his recent reforms, which was introduced by Protectionist Thomas Rose partly to delay debate on the financial proposals. If anything Government supporters were encouraged to speak as little as possible as the Opposition was attempting to filibuster by giving long and largely pointless speeches in order to hinder the passing of measures. When pushed, the Government occasionally resorted to using controversial powers to gag the debate. In these difficult circumstances, the direct taxation reforms slowly made their way through the Legislative Assembly.

With opposition to the Government's financial program quelled in the Assembly, all eyes turned towards the Legislative Council as the last obstacle in the way of reform. At the time the Legislative Council was made up of members appointed by the Governor to serve for life. Though selections were generally made on the advice of the Premier, the House was deliberately undemocratic and meant to act as a necessary check on legislation and populist impulses. It played an important role in improving legislation and blocking ill-thought ideas, but it was far from impartial. The life-long terms combined with premise that "distinguished men" were appointed to ensure that the majority of the Council's often quite elderly members were inclined towards conservatism. Many Councillors also owned large landed estates and this personal interest also came to bear on their decisions. Governors had the ability to "swamp" the Council with new members if it became too intractable and refused to recognise the democratic will, though this was something that they were reluctant to do outside of exceptional circumstances. This combination of inherent conservatism with bend rather break flexibility was one of the defining aspects of Wentworth's carefully balanced Constitution.

Carruthers' changes to the Labour Settlements Act had already been thrown out by the Council, though it had acted with restraint when dealing with his Crown Lands Bill, sending down just three mild amendments. After a brief period of negotiation one of these amendments was accepted and the Bill was finally passed shortly before the failure of the local government reforms. There was little hope of such a conciliatory approach when it came to the direct taxation measures that would personally affect the members of the Council. In June their opposition to these measures came to a head when they threw out Reid's Income Tax Assessment Bill. Reid painted the rejection as a constitutional issue since parliamentary tradition theoretically gave the elected House exclusive control over finance. He managed to convince the Governor to dissolve Parliament and call an election which would be fought as a battle over the supremacy of the democratic Legislative Assembly.

Along with the constitutional issue, Reid raised the prospect of Upper House reform. He proposed to replace lifelong appointments with five year terms and to emasculate the Council's powers, freeing it from the control of anything to do with finances and introducing plebiscites that could overturn the Council's rejection of ordinary bills if at least 100,000 votes were cast. Carruthers, who again would play an important part in the campaign, was more than happy to pick up the issue of Council reform that he had been advocating since 1887. He was also happy to pick up the popular rhetoric that this constitutional election gave him as a weapon. He painted the contest as a question of "who was to rule?" and a choice between "government by the people and for the people or misgovernment by a body out of touch with the people and defying the people".[185] He attacked the nominee Council as a product of Parkes and Dibbs that was still obeying its masters. He also claimed that in the negotiations over the Crown Lands Bill Councillors had revealed that they were primarily concerned with their own vested interests by openly referring to "our runs", "our leases" and "our rights".

While Carruthers certainly held some sincere beliefs when it came to Legislative Council reform, he was being at least partly opportunistic in utilising language that was more radical than his long held position on the issue. His statement that the Government was doing all it could "to save this colony from the turmoil and distress of a bloodless revolution fomented by the usurpers of power who represented wealth and property alone" may have been informed by his knowledge of history, but it probably went too far. It is likely that this hyperbole was a deliberate tactic meant to pressure the Council more than it was meant to win votes and once the election was over Carruthers, like Reid, would throw off his radical garb and remain the pragmatic liberal he had always been. Indeed, since the Free Traders already had a workable majority in the Assembly, the whole election had been designed to put pressure on the Council and the campaign's ideological eccentricities should be seen in the context of these hard fought "negotiations" rather than as a regular poll.

While the election objective was to influence the Council, the best way of doing this was to pick up seats so regular electioneering would be required. Any new seats the Free Traders won would have to come from the Protectionists or lapsed Free Traders as the Government Party had decided not to contest seats of Labor members. Labor only sporadically returned the favour. The LEL would not contest St George, but this had as much to do with the futility of such an effort as any sympathy for the member. Carruthers saw the election as an opportunity to "purify" the Free Trade Party and so it was decided by the Free Trade Council to contest the seats of those like Wise who had been causing so much trouble during the last Parliament.[186] The decision to oppose Parkes was taken out of the Party's hands as he decided to square off directly against George Reid in the Sydney-King electorate. Since the Free Trade Party was too loose an entity to really enforce expulsion, contesting elections was the Party leader's main weapon in enforcing discipline and giving practical effect to Carruthers' attempts to isolate internal foes during the last session. Free Trade "discipline" was still more about loyalty than removing a liberal's freedom of thought, hence while the disloyal land taxer Wise was opposed, the largely loyal Philip Morton, who was denied party endorsement because he did not support a land tax, was not opposed by the Party in the Shoalhaven.

During the election Carruthers took up his usual role as travelling salesman for Free Trade. He visited Albury, Kiama, Jamberoo, Robertson, Campbelltown, Darlington and Paddington. He made great publicity out of receiving a deputation of Victorians at Albury who were preparing to move to New South Wales to take advantage of the new Land Act. Carruthers was keen to stress that the Act was not his alone but that "it was owing to the loyalty of Mr. Reid and his colleagues that the bill was now law, and also the loyalty of their supporters".[187] This stress on loyalty was a clear swipe at the "disloyal" Free Traders whom the Party was now trying to unseat. Carruthers attacked the "variety troupe" opposition faced by the Government, loosely made up of Dibbs, Parkes, Wise and Labor-cum-Protectionist member William Schey.[188] Responding to Parkes' use of federation as an election issue, he claimed that federation was "as dead as Julius Caesar" as long as it was in "the hands of those who put it to the base use of stifling the honest aspirations of democracy for domestic reforms".[189]

Most of the areas he visited had sitting Protectionist members hence Carruthers' campaigning was offensive rather than defensive. Considering he was attempting the difficult task of unseating people he was quite successful. In Camden where he had been involved in the selection of the candidate the Free Traders stole a narrow victory while they did the same more convincingly in Albury. In Darlington they were only defeated because the Labor Party split the reform vote allowing the Protectionist to scrape through. Much to Carruthers' consternation the Protectionist held on in his "native district" of Kiama as was also the case in Robertson.

The election resulted in several personal victories for the Free Traders. Dibbs lost his seat and Parkes' grand struggle against Reid ended in failure. Both were never to return. Wise too lost Sydney-Flinders, though the split in Free Trade support caused by the contest allowed a Protectionist member to take his place. Of Carruthers' "variety troupe" only William Schey, by far the least important member, would remain in Parliament. Copeland, the ex-Minister for Lands who had been one of Carruthers' leading opponents was also defeated. Overall the Party Free Traders won 59 seats by modern counts, a significant improvement from the year before; though both Carruthers and Reid claimed there was an absolute majority of 63 Free Traders based on their interpretation of party loyalties.[190]

This result certainly put pressure on the Legislative Council, but within the Assembly the Free Traders' true position may have actually worsened. The fiercely partisan election had seen the defeat of many independents who had previously shown themselves willing to work with the Government. These losses outweighed the Free Trade Party gains; hence the Government was now more reliant on the support of caucus Labor. Bede Nairn has suggested that "in 1894 Reid was not completely dependent on the Labor Party" but "in 1895 he was virtually dependent on it".[191] This statement is only partially true. Provided the Free Trade Party stayed solid which following its "purification" it was now far more likely to do, the Government (again according to modern figures) needed only four votes from the seven remaining independent Labor and Free Trade members to have a majority. The statement also ignores the fact that the Protectionists were not yet in any position to try to call on the support of Labor, so for now Reid could still act independently in pursuing his liberal free trade program.

Carruthers spent election night riding around the city with Reid and Attorney- General John Want, as crowds of people "in pure playfulness" threw flour on them. The party then retired to the Oxford Hotel to thank their volunteers. To Carruthers' delight, the election had been a victory for "party" Free Traders, but there was one last act of "purification" necessary before the Government could get down to business. McMillan had been over in England when the Parliament was dissolved and returned with his pre-existing grudge against Reid inflamed by being forced to seek re-election in absentia. When Parliament reconvened he delivered an attack on the details of the Government's Land and Income Tax Assessment Bill, arguing against the proposed exemptions for people owning or earning under £475 and £300 respectively. Their removal would broaden the base of the tax and reduce the level of taxation needed, and it was the course favoured by Henry George himself. Nevertheless, the withdrawal of exemptions would also have removed the idea of making those with property pay a large proportion of the costs of running a relatively small government whose main role was to protect property, and thus have hurt the populist aspect of the Free Traders' appeal.

In advocating this McMillan pointed out that he was speaking as an "independent member" as Reid had done when Parkes was Premier.[192]

Times had changed since then however and the Free Trade Party had learnt its lesson from the damage that absolute independence had wrought. When McMillan sat down Carruthers got up and proceeded to accuse his former colleague of either having gone through a "Rip Van Winkle sleep" or having spent too much time mixing with Tories in the old country. McMillan protested that he supported the Government's policy entirely apart from the exemptions to which Carruthers replied that "if anything were needed ... to assure the honourable member that he was on the wrong track, it would be the cheers with which he was greeted from the Opposition benches".

This was the crux of the matter. It was not just that McMillan's proposals would have fundamentally changed the Bill; it was that he delivered a public attack on the Government's main policy that might threaten its whole existence. A clear parallel could be drawn with Carruthers' own amendment to Parkes' Custom Duties Bill that did him "good to learn party methods so early". The lesson he learnt was that a liberal's right to their own opinion, which would continue to be a self-defining difference between them and Labor members, had to be constrained *to some extent* in order for party government to work. Most of the problems the Free Traders had in the first half of the 1890s revolved around learning that lesson and putting it into practice. It was a lesson learned relatively independently of Labor, as the Free Traders' divisions stretched back before that party existed, and their solution to the problem still allowed more freedom than caucus. By late 1895, with Parkes and Wise gone and McMillan now an "independent" Free Trader, the goal had largely been achieved.

Carruthers and Reid had reshaped the Party in their own image. It still contained a "broad church" of opinions, as Australian Liberal Parties always would, but some small measure of pragmatism, practicality and above all loyalty was now a prerequisite for those who wanted to hold important positions within it. None of this was yet fully set in stone and party discipline would remain a problem, but arguably a much smaller problem. The reward Carruthers and Reid got for undertaking the painful task of introducing party discipline would be an unparalleled legislative success rate and the ability easily to survive censure motions even when much of caucus Labor abstained from voting.

As an aside it is worth mentioning that McMillan and Bruce Smith were eventually reconciled with the Free Trade Party when they entered Federal politics. For them it was the demand for stricter loyalty combined with personality disputes that was the problem. For Wise, who never re-joined the Free Traders, the problem ran deeper. His interventionist beliefs, though he certainly had his followers within the Party, were fundamentally out of step with the views of most of its members. This tendency would be exaggerated over time as the rise of Labor slowly made the Free Traders shed their leftward fringe.

If Wise embodied the left of the Free Trade Party, one might tentatively place Carruthers in the "centre' of it. This centre was still a relatively small government "centre-right". Its fundamental emphasis was on individual and commercial liberty, even when allowing for occasional exceptions like the Coal Mines Regulation Bill and the Factories and Shops Bill that the Reid Government attempted to pass during this period. While hard-line believers in laissez-faire opposed these Bills, Carruthers was accepting of them. To him they were relatively mild forms of regulation which would hopefully improve conditions for working people without placing unreasonable restrictions on their employers or on the freedom to negotiate contracts. This was a reflection of his pragmatic approach to government, and he remained generally opposed to interfering with the interaction of free individuals.

When historians have assessed the philosophy of the Reid Government too much emphasis has often placed on these ancillary policies. This is particularly the case with John Ward, who labels Carruthers, Reid and Wise "new liberals" in juxtaposition to the "conservatives" McMillan and Bruce Smith.[193] The term "new liberals" has been used by Ward and others to imply a belief in government intervention similar to that of Alfred Deakin, but the label is inappropriate for the more Gladstonian liberalism of Carruthers and Reid. One need only read the latter's *My Reminiscences* to see that he placed far greater importance on the classical liberal achievements of free trade, land reform and sound public finance than the small instances of practical intervention brought about by the social circumstances of the depression. By the mid-1890s New South Wales liberalism had evolved, but the germ of that evolution lay in the broad policy of the LPA and not some sudden push for intervention which for these limited-government liberals, who still emphasised freedom as the hallmark of their beliefs, remained the exception and not the rule.

After the election victory Reid had requested nine nominees be appointed to the Legislative Council. It was a moderate number given the circumstances and the Governor obliged. Nine new members were not nearly enough to change the balance of power, and when the Government sent up its Land and Income Tax Assessment Bill the Council amended most of its clauses. The two most crucial of these amendments were to the exemptions, with the income tax exemption to be reduced to £160 and the land tax exemption to be removed entirely. These changes were too much for even those as pragmatic as Carruthers and Reid to take. It was arranged that a conference between the two Houses would take place in order to break the deadlock and Carruthers was elected as one of the representatives of the Legislative Assembly. Initially the Council's representatives proved to be as stubborn as ever but after Reid had a less than secret chat with the acting Governor that hinted that the Council might be swamped with new members, they began to give ground. The fact that this threat of swamping was taken seriously was one of the main advantages the Government had gained from going to an election to strengthen its mandate.

An agreement was reached that the exemption levels would be £200 for income tax and £240 for the land tax. The Government had achieved the essence of what it wanted in what was one of the most remarkable political victories in New South Wales history. With the Colony's finances now sorted out the Government was also able to pass the free trade tariff that had been the motivation behind its whole campaign for direct taxation.

It is testament to how small government was in 1895 that someone with an income of £400 a year was liable to pay just £5 tax, while a person owning £5000 worth of land (on unimproved values) owed the Government less than £20 a year.[194] One of the measures Reid introduced to make government even smaller was the creation of an independent Public Service Board. This board was designed to increase efficiency by introducing competitive examinations and merit based promotions to replace the patronage that had long dogged the appointment of government employees. This significant reform was the forerunner of Carruthers' later efforts to ensure public service efficiency and reduce costs while refraining from indulging in arbitrary retrenchments.

The victory over the financial reforms had essentially proved that the present Constitution, whatever its flaws, was still workable. Consequently when the proposed changes to the Legislative Council were rejected by that body the pragmatic Reid and Carruthers were willing to let them die. McMinn argues that Reid was "satisfied with the substance of victory" and was "not prepared to disrupt public business for the sake of winning a theoretical point".[195] Carruthers did not speak on the proposed changes when they were introduced in the Assembly and while in an ideal world he still desired to see a more democratic Upper House he appears to have shared Reid's practical position. The fact that the Government was able to get away with letting these distracting and less than urgent reforms go by the wayside is clear evidence that Reid was not being dictated to by the Labor Party to any great extent, despite frequent speculation to the contrary.

With the Government's main policies now in the statute books, Carruthers' concerns returned to his Lands portfolio. In September he had introduced a Selectors' Relief Bill to reduce the annual payments and rate of interest to be paid by those who had conditionally purchased or conditionally leased land from the Crown. This mainly affected those who had selected land before the introduction of homestead selections, many of whom were struggling to pay the Government the money they owed. Failure to make these payments and the consequent loss of the selection was a major obstacle to Carruthers' overall goal of promoting closer settlement. He believed that the "best way to solve the unemployed difficulty was to make more men their own employers" by settling them on the land and thus he felt that kicking out those who had already settled on the land was a step backwards.[196] He also argued that settlement was a much better solution to unemployment than public works because the latter only provided temporary employment. The fact that he was able to offer this relief was predicated on the success of the financial reforms that had freed the Government from needing land sales and rent as a major source of revenue. The Selector's Relief Bill was eventually defeated in the Council which still represented squatter interests in the residual squatter-selector conflict.

Carruthers' role as Minister for Lands caused him to take on some strange responsibilities. One was to show Mark Twain, then visiting Australia on a speaking tour, around the National Park at Port Hacking where the Minister was holidaying. Carruthers even caught the humourist lunch, though he was quite disappointed that their fare would only be a jewfish after he had hoped to secure a schnapper. Accompanied by his wife and daughter, Twain got on well with Carruthers as the two men spent a day discussing literature and fishing. Keen to show off Australian literary culture, the host read some lines of Banjo Paterson from a collection of his works. Twain became so engrossed that he missed the tour of the park in order to read the book front to back.

A more serious responsibility was given directly to Carruthers by the Governor Lord Hampden. This was the commission to oversee the administration of Norfolk Island; a small community largely descended from the offspring of white sailors and Tahitians. It had been a convict settlement but after the ending of transportation its governance had decayed. Carruthers was informed of one particular incident when a man had been given just a £4 fine after indecently assaulting a girl. He embarked on the task of improving the Island's justice system, finances and land laws as well as writing up a draft constitution. It was a delicate task as thorough consultation with the populace and the Imperial Government was required. The new Constitution placed the administration of the Island in the hands of a Government appointed Chief Magistrate and an elected twelve member Council. The new system thoroughly defended the rule of law and the rights of citizens, while also allowing for the imposition of new criminal laws more in line with moral and ethical standards.

As with his liberal views on Aborigines, there was nothing overtly racist about Carruthers' dealings with the ethnic Norfolk Islanders. He felt that they were worthy of the rights and freedoms of any British subject and set up their Constitution accordingly. This contrasted strongly with the arbitrary administration of Western Samoa soon to be pursued by the New Zealand Government. Though he clung to some of the assumptions of his day, Carruthers was not "racist" in an aggressive sense. He supported anti-Chinese legislation pursued by both Parkes and Reid, but it appears that this was due more to concerns about the threat of racial and ethnic tensions that had revealed themselves on the goldfields, rather than a Social Darwinism that saw non-white races as inherently inferior. Even this prejudice would be reconsidered in time.

Late in 1895 Joseph Carruthers divorced Louise Marion. At the time the divorce case which was heard behind closed doors received little media attention. He was granted custody of the two surviving children as it was later revealed that she had committed adultery. The lifestyle of a nineteenth-century politician took its toll on marriages and Carruthers was not the only one to get divorced. For men who were not yet full time politicians long hours at work were followed by long nights in Parliament. For someone in Carruthers' position these difficulties were added to by frequent regional tours, particularly after he became Minister for Lands. The evidence we have for Carruthers suggests that he was a devoted family man who made an effort to spend time with his children. His correspondence with Parkes shows that he made an honest effort to try to balance Cabinet meetings and family commitments.[197] Unlike many of his colleagues he was not a frequenter of social clubs, though he did attend the cricket religiously. His relationship with Louise had long been strained, and there are reports of heated arguments overheard by their neighbours. Joseph was evidently unable to keep his wife happy and their divorce was for him a personal tragedy eclipsed only by the deaths of his children.

Emotionally wrecked, Carruthers went on a fishing trip during the parliamentary recess in order to re-gather himself. This did not prove enough and his health gave way forcing him to cancel a proposed trip to Broken Hill in January. There could be no long break for someone in his position and he was soon back at work administering the huge Lands portfolio. He spent April touring the Riverina district advocating the Government's policy and gathering information on irrigation. It was only a couple of days after Carruthers returned from this trip when his old hero Parkes passed away. He solemnly attended the funeral along with many former and current colleagues.

When in June a Bill was introduced to offer a grant to Parkes' family who had been left in poverty the normally spending-averse member for St George spoke out strongly in favour of it against the opposition of the Labor Party. After castigating that party for being so irreverent to the man who he believed had done more than any other for the cause of working people he reflected that "we had in him a man who stood pre-eminent in the history of the colony; he rose from the ranks, never forgetting the source from which he sprang; he was always in touch with the people, and was always working for them by leading in the path of legislation tending to make our institutions more free and our lives more liberal".[198]

In 1889 *The Bulletin* had described Carruthers' relationship with Parkes thus:

> never having seen the sun, he worships the biggest light which has dazzled his eyes, just as the puppy in the fable, having while in the blind stage of existence, been entertained by stories of elephants, on emerging to daylight turned its stomach upwards and its legs in the air, as a slight expression of its awe and admiration of the mighty beast, on meeting a porker.[199]

To a "native" born New South Welshman and a colonial liberal Sir Henry Parkes was the sun. His gravitas was such that he inevitably drew young talent like Carruthers, Wise, McMillan and Bruce Smith into his orbit. One of the shrewdest moves of Carruthers' career was to break free of Parkes' pull, but he never lost sight of the light of the fading sun even after he had hitched his fortunes to a new and rising political star.

In his autobiography Carruthers maintained that Reid and Parkes had had a poignant reconciliation shortly before the latter passed away. Like all deathbed anecdotes this is difficult to verify, though A. B. Piddington presents the same story with Parkes' fateful line said to have been "I have very much misunderstood him".[200] Whether or not the two giants did patch up their differences matters less here than the fact that *Carruthers wanted them to have done so*. For a man who was no political theorist there was no "Parkesite" liberalism or "Reidite" liberalism there was just liberalism, a political tradition that connected the struggles of the 1840s with the battles of the 1890s. Accordingly he felt it was only right and proper that these two great liberal leaders should put aside their personal differences and come together. Carruthers had a belief that, despite a great deal of evolution which as a Young Turk he had been a part of, there was a more or less continuous tradition of liberalism that spanned the political history of the Colony of New South Wales. His Liberal and Reform Association would later substantiate this by consciously connecting itself to the political triumphs of the past and thus bridging the gap between nineteenth and twentieth century New South Wales liberalism.

CHAPTER SEVEN

Federation

When Parkes passed away his federation dream had yet to be realised. The momentum created by the Tenterfield speech practically ground to a halt when the first Draft Constitution Bill was critically examined by Reid and others. That Bill was already largely dead in the water by the time the Parkes Government fell. Despite the presence of Barton, much of the Dibbs Government was lukewarm on federation and progress stagnated during its existence. Nevertheless, the Federation League made slow but steady progress in drumming up support. As a member of the League's Council, Carruthers continued to advocate federation, though it appeared to be low on his list of priorities. Shortly before Reid's election the movement had been given a new breath of life by Victorian politician John Quick, who proposed a new convention of elected delegates to consider and adopt a revised Federal Constitution. This democratic idea allowed the movement to somewhat distance itself from the unpopular 1891 draft and quickly attracted support.

Joseph Carruthers' important role in federation has been almost universally under estimated. Even Beverley Earnshaw, who wrote a book called *One Flag, One Hope, One Destiny: Sir Joseph Carruthers and Australian Federation*, has failed to acknowledge his deepest significance as an invaluable ally for George Reid. That book was published by the Kogarah Historical Society and focuses more on connecting that locality to the formation of a nation, rather than reinterpreting the limited existing historiography surrounding Carruthers' Federal role. A large part of the reason why he is overlooked is because he is given little attention in the seminal accounts of federation written by Bernhard Wise and more importantly Alfred Deakin. Both of these men sought to portray Reid as a traitor to the Federal cause, hence they had little time for his right hand man. Deakin was particularly dismissive of Carruthers, describing him as "a little man with a great voice, [who] was overshadowed by his chief with whom he was not always in harmony".[201] Deakin's voice has arguably been the most imposing in the narrative of federation, hence historians have tended to regurgitate his opinion of Carruthers as a man of "little figure" in the federation debates. While the work of W.G. McMinn and L.F. Crisp has managed to salvage the significance of Reid from the condemnation of Deakin and Wise, Carruthers has yet to be offered similar redemption. He deserves to be given the same historiographical treatment as his chief, for few of Reid's much hailed federation successes would have been possible without the help, advice and loyalty of the member for St George.

In his autobiography, Carruthers maintained that after the Free Traders had won the 1894 election he had made it a condition of his joining Cabinet that the federation issue be pursued by the Government.[202] If he did indeed insist on this to Reid, it was of debatable consequence. Reid had already committed himself to federation after Cleveland's presidential victory had supposedly convinced him that it would not be a threat to free trade. On the other side of the coin, Carruthers agreed with Reid's policy prioritisation which put the liberal agenda and domestic concerns ahead of federation against the criticisms of the movement's most ardent supporters. Once most of the central tenets of that agenda had been fulfilled however, Carruthers' support was important in prompting Reid to pursue federation against the concerns of some of his other Cabinet colleagues. Those concerns, most of which Reid himself had previously elaborated, were very real and opinion in Sydney was far from universally in favour of a union.

At a Premiers' conference held in Hobart in 1895, Reid was able to convince most of his inter-colonial counterparts to agree to a new series of Federal conventions to be made up of elected delegates along the lines of Quick's proposals. In October 1895 the Australasian Federation Enabling Bill was introduced in the Legislative Assembly to facilitate this end. As a Federalist who was unhappy with the 1891 draft, Carruthers came out firmly in favour of the new Bill. He implored his parliamentary colleagues to treat it as a non-party issue and praised the elected nature of the proposed convention for trusting the people. Carruthers' speech was frequently interrupted by William Lyne, who had taken over as Opposition Leader after Dibbs' electoral defeat. Lyne was a large-scale sheep grazier who had been lured into supporting protection by a desire to reciprocate border duties. He held a hesitant attitude towards federation that had seen him keep his distance from Dibbs' attempt to combine with Parkes, and following Lyne's ascension Carruthers was quick to exploit this.

The Enabling Act passed the Legislative Assembly with relative ease. Despite this success, Reid did not call the convention as soon as was possible. Instead he delayed, hoping to use the extra time to convince Queensland to join in. This was an important strategic move as Queensland's presence would be essential not only to a successful federation, but also to New South Wales' prospects of winning out in the coming negotiations.[203] Another calculation of Reid's was his decision to try to bring Henry Parkes on board. By early 1896 Reid saw the aged statesman as little political threat and he was keen to utilise Parkes' gravitas to reinforce the legitimacy of the new convention. Cabinet agreed that Parkes be approached, and Carruthers was sent to convince his old leader. Two or three months before Parkes passed away, the two men dined together and Carruthers asked his host if he would consent to being put forward as a delegate for the Federal convention with a view towards making him the convention's president.[204] Parkes was gratified at the request, and left the matter in Carruthers' hands. Carruthers also approached Barton with the suggestion and was able to win his acceptance. Parkes' death meant the whole idea fell through, but it is still an important incident in showing how Carruthers was used by Reid as a go between in negotiations.

With Parkes gone, the Government had to decide who they would put up for the election of delegates. There was a widespread insistence that the process should be free from partisan taint and that the best men be chosen regardless of their political affiliations. Consequently only three members of Cabinet were nominated, despite the fact that there were ten New South Wales positions up for grabs. This Free Trade team would have the Government Whip help organise their nominations, and was made up of Reid, Carruthers and the ever present James Brunker. It was a well selected group. Reid's presence was clearly necessary and requires no comment. The inclusion of Carruthers, who had the best Federalist credentials in the Government, gave the group a connection to Parkes and the Federation League. He was pragmatic enough to be useful in negotiations but principled enough not to agree to federation at any cost. Brunker was the most senior member of Cabinet and gave the grouping some of the weight it had lost without Parkes. He had a reputation for being somewhat tentative towards federation, and when balanced with Reid and Carruthers he appeared a safe option for those who were in favour of federation but were not willing to make too many sacrifices for it. Though Brunker would not be very active at the conventions, this skilful team would prove incredibly successful in winning amendments disproportionate to their voting strength.

Carruthers was the first of these three men to deliver an election oration, effectively opening the ministerial campaign early in February 1897. He appealed for "caution and cool judgement" against the "sanguine and almost reckless enthusiasm of the ardent federalists" who were willing to sacrifice all for federation.[205] Some sacrifices would be necessary, as federation was a worthwhile goal which would help make a stronger Australia. The benefit on which Carruthers laid the greatest emphasis was internal free trade and the economic benefits that would be derived from that. He insisted that Federal Parliament should be limited to well defined areas of expenditure in order to prevent extravagance. He also maintained that federation would be unpopular if it meant an "increase in the burdens of the people". This point is crucial. For a man whose political career oversaw the evolution of government from one tier to three, none of these new levels were meant to increase the overall level of taxation or the size of government. If anything, through efficiency (Federal) and proximity (local) it was hoped that spending could actually be decreased.

While Carruthers was essentially running as a member of Reid's team, he put forward his own distinct opinions on several of the more contentious issues the convention would have to deal with. He opposed the ending of appeals to the Privy Council, at least until a greater population allowed a choice of jurors completely free from vested interests. Though Carruthers generally insisted that the Federal Government be given as few powers as necessary, he supported a Federal takeover of State railways against many of his peers. This was because he feared that preferential railway rates would keep up the costly provincial trade disputes even after internal free trade had been established. He supported the Norwegian principle of joint sittings to determine deadlocks between the Houses. He also insisted that the capital should be in New South Wales, preferably in Sydney, grandly claiming that "the records of the earliest achievement here of the Anglo-Saxon race are engraved on every hand in our midst, and it will be but fitting that she who was the first capital of Australia shall not be dethroned by one of her children".

Sectarianism was prominently brought into the campaign when Catholic Cardinal Patrick Moran sought election as one of the delegates. This provoked bitter reaction from Orangemen and the more militant Protestants. Carruthers steered clear of sectarianism in his speeches, lamenting its entry into the campaign. Despite this, the Orange institution nominated him as one of its bunch along with Reid, Barton, Lyne and just about every other non-Catholic leading man. When a group of Protestant Ministers came together to discuss their reaction to the Cardinal's campaign, Joseph's brother the Reverend J. E. Carruthers strongly opposed Moran's candidature but insisted that the group should not support anyone else in particular.[206] The group ignored his advice and put forward a bunch which included Carruthers and even Catholic R. E. O'Connor. O'Connor repudiated the honour.

Carruthers also rejected the nominations of the two groups. Though he acknowledged that he was closely associated with Reid and Brunker, Carruthers denied being part of any bunch. He fiercely attacked the Labor Party for nominating a full bunch of ten against the prevailing liberal ideal that the contest should be non-party. He described the nomination of this bunch as "the greatest blunder of the campaign so far" as it tried to suggest to the Colony that "wisdom and intelligence and patriotism" were centred entirely within the Labour Leagues.[207] Giving force to his professed indignation, he claimed that he would gladly vote for William Lyne and anyone else who possessed ability.

These anti-partisan concerns echoed the sentiment of the old factional era, and while Carruthers and Reid had done much to consolidate a united Free Trade Party, it is important to note that the transition towards modern party politics was far from complete. The ideology and youth of the Labor Party meant that they were unencumbered by the concerns of the past, but the Free Traders who accepted a liberal inheritance still had to accommodate older individualist ideals. These ideals appear to have resonated with the electorate, as not a single Labor member was elected for the conventions. By insisting on a full bunch, the Labor Party probably cost itself the votes of the more radical supporters of both the Free Traders and the Protectionists while at the same time it appears that Reid and Carruthers were still able to pick up votes from moderate Labor men who ignored the rigid instructions of their party.

The notion that the "best men" should be chosen regardless of political affiliation brought some interesting candidates into the field. McMillan, who by now could have little authority in a regular election, was one of the first to put his hand up. Wise and Bruce Smith, who were both out of Parliament at the time, also stood for election. These candidates suggest that although the Party had nominated only three men, there was still a possibility that there could be a Free Trade majority among the New South Wales delegates. Whether Reid or Carruthers wanted their former colleagues to get up is another matter. Politically, the radical Wise was poles apart from these pragmatic liberals on many issues and he was even starting to lose his attachment to free trade itself. McMillan's sense of independence had become self-righteous by this point and his animosity to Reid did not bode well as far as support in the upcoming negotiations was concerned. In the event, neither man would be of much help to Reid or Carruthers. Both Alfred Deakin's account and statistical voting analysis concur that during the conventions McMillan and Wise were more likely to vote with the Protectionist Barton than with the Free Trade Ministers.[208]

Welcome or unwelcome, McMillan and Wise were both successful in their election bids. McMillan came a respectable fourth whilst Wise sneaked in in tenth position. Bruce Smith was the only former Free Trade Young Turk to miss out, but even he polled higher than Labor Leader McGowen. Carruthers came third after Barton and Reid, a remarkable feat for someone who was still one of the youngest candidates in the field. Gratifyingly Brunker, who many predicted would not be elected because of his dubious support for federation came sixth, highlighting the overall strength of the Free Trade Party team. Protectionists Lyne, O'Connor and Abbott filled up three more spots while banker James Walker was the only non-politician to be elected.

The elected delegates met in Adelaide for what was dubbed the National Australasian Convention. The convention debates were held inside South Australia's Parliament House which had been specially renovated for the grand occasion. Even with these improvements, there was great difficulty fitting the various journalists that had gathered from around the continent into the inadequate press gallery. The influx of pressmen, secretaries and public servants, not to mention the delegates themselves, added to the great excitement that gripped the city. There was a tangible sense that the participants were about to make history and that the various "lions in the path" of a union of the Colonies could be overcome.

Carruthers' performance at Adelaide would be disappointing. It was not his eloquence or ideas that let him down, but an uncharacteristic lack of tact. His first action was to attack the appointment of select committees who would carry out their functions in "secret", insisting that transparency was key to the conference's success. Such committees were largely necessary for the efficient running of the convention; hence Carruthers' contrary objection did not make the best first impression on his inter-colonial counterparts. Impressions got worse when on more than one occasion Carruthers patronisingly described New South Wales' desire to gather up its "wandering brood that once owed allegiance to and formed part of the colony".[209] Later when discussing financial proposals he launched into an attack on American protectionism with little regard for the fiscal beliefs of his fellow delegates. So many toes were stepped on that one wonders if Carruthers was performing a set piece intended to make Reid look reasonable by contrast.

Whether the offence Carruthers caused was intentional or not, it undercut his important contribution to the debates. As a member of the "constitutional committee" his contribution was felt most in the debates surrounding the powers of the Senate and deadlock provisions. In light of their recent conflict with the Legislative Council, both Carruthers and Reid were acutely interested in the powers that the non-population representative and therefore questionably-democratic Upper House would have. Carruthers insisted that a Senate that gave equal representation to each State regardless of population could not claim any right to interfere with money bills unless each of those States made an equal financial contribution to the Commonwealth. Since this was impracticable, he fought hard to keep the Senate from having the power to either amend or veto money bills. He was unsuccessful, and the "money-bills compromise", which stopped the Senate from amending taxation and annual appropriation bills, but left it free to amend other appropriation bills and block either, remained in place. This would make the Australian Senate one of the most powerful upper houses in the Westminster responsible government tradition.

Carruthers was part of the generation who had grown up with the American Civil War and its massive loss of life. Because of this he was keenly concerned about how disputes over the role of the Federal Government would be resolved. The idea that each State may have the right to secede was briefly raised but quickly dismissed. Without this, Carruthers felt that the Constitution needed to be made amendable so that disagreements could be overcome without escalating into conflict. Though he was not on the "finance committee" Carruthers also offered his opinion on the cost of federation. Citing Australasia's soon to be seven governments and multiplicity of officials, he advocated that federation be used as an opportunity to decrease the machinery of government. He proposed a reduction in the number of Agents-General from seven to one as a small measure to help achieve this.

Carruthers returned from Adelaide disappointed. In a newspaper interview he lamented that the powers of the proposed Federal Government had been "unnecessarily enlarged" and that the Senate remained far too powerful.[210] Perhaps because Carruthers shared many of his cautious misgivings about the proposed constitution yet retained a desire to see federation achieved, Reid left him in charge of steering the draft constitution through the Legislative Assembly while the Premier visited England to take part in celebrations marking Queen Victoria's long reign. Following Reid's instructions, Carruthers was not to force through the draft constitution as it currently stood but to allow amendments that would be considered by another convention.

The member for St George introduced the Bill on 12 May, 1897. In a long and occasionally interrupted speech, he detailed the history of the federation movement and defended most of the provisions of the Constitution. He advocated the grafting of the principles of responsible government "which we, as members of the British Empire know and understand" onto federation, rather than utilising an American system of executive government largely independent of the legislature.[211] He also justified a bicameral Parliament as integral to a federation rather than a unification of States. Nevertheless, he insisted upon a "supreme recognition of the rights of the people once they come in conflict with the states", and thereby flagged a fight for Lower House supremacy. Carruthers felt this was particularly important as, against his wishes, the proposed constitution gave the Federal Government powers not only over what he saw as national concerns such as defence and inter-colonial trade but also over individual concerns like taxation, marriage and parental rights. It followed logically that for every power that was taken away from the States, those States became less able to give full representation their individual citizens and therefore the Federal Government needed to be made more democratic so that individuals' rights were not diminished.

Many of the amendments made by the Assembly to the proposed constitution followed Carruthers' line of weakening and democratising the Senate. In his introductory speech Carruthers had argued that the Senate's six year terms and inability to be dissolved by the Governor-General meant that it was destined to be "the strong house of the commonwealth". Labor member J. C. Watson picked up these points and moved amendments that reduced Senator's terms to three years and allowed the Governor-General to dissolve it. The former amendment failed as Carruthers abandoned it, but the latter succeeded. Watson also successfully introduced a procedure whereby a referendum could be used to pass a law that had succeeded in one House but had been blocked by the other, something that Carruthers had advocated at the Adelaide Convention. More controversial than Watson's amendments was the removal of the principle of equal State representation in the Senate. This was replaced with a system of proportional representation with the provision that each State was to have no fewer than three Senators. Sensing the overwhelming view of the House, Carruthers somewhat reluctantly voted for the removal of equal representation, though he still maintained that in matters of State concern it should be ceded.

Carruthers knew that most of these amendments were highly unlikely to succeed at the next convention, but he voted for them because he felt that "the convention could make no radical amendments unless it was suggested by the various legislatures or one of them". He was thus giving himself and Reid the ammunition with which to fight for a more democratic constitution. If even one of the amendments succeeded at the next convention, both men would find it easier to recommend the Constitution to their electors. The yes-no balance of how many grievances could be accepted was already being weighed up, and Carruthers was hopeful of tipping the scales.

Reid returned in late August, shortly before the second convention which was to be held in Sydney. The Government had endured a rough time in his absence. Brunker, who had been left as acting Premier, did not prove to be a great leader and received considerable newspaper criticism. Bogged down with his responsibilities as Minister for Lands and pilot of the Draft Constitution Bill, Carruthers had been able to offer little help to his temporary chief. Still out of Parliament, Wise had also been up to his old tricks in launching an attack on the Government's administration of the land tax. Despite these difficulties the Government's majority had held firm against a disruptive censure motion, and the administration had been able to pass a number of non-contentious Bills in Reid's absence.

The Sydney Convention would prove to be the arena in which Carruthers would firmly imprint his mark upon the Constitution. He entered the convention determined to fight for the amendments moved by the New South Wales Parliament. This went against the grain of New South Wales delegate opinion, as many of the State's delegates were dismissive of even those amendments that had received overwhelming support in both Houses. Bernhard Wise's opinion was typical when he intimated that those amendments had been made by the enemies of federation.[212] Carruthers did not agree and even fought for the highly contentious removal of equal State representation in the Senate. In one of his first speeches at the Sydney Convention he argued that Australian history had revolved around a long "struggle for equal manhood suffrage" and that the Senate's composition required the people "to give up that which they have been successfully battling for years and years past, and to adopt the retrograde stage of distinguishing between the voting power of the various individual members of the states".[213] He insisted that he would only support equal representation if there were adequate safety valves in the Constitution, and since the vote on the Senate clauses came before the vote on the deadlock provisions, Carruthers was one of only five members to vote against the six members clause.

Having established the democratic line he would maintain throughout the convention, Carruthers went on to fight for the referendum deadlock provision introduced by the Legislative Assembly. Though he believed that ideology and not geography would inevitably prove to be the dividing line of Australian politics, and also that a Senate elected by an entire State as one electorate would likely prove the more radical chamber, Carruthers argued that deadlock provisions were required to ensure that the will of the majority was felt no matter what divided the Houses. He was dismissive of a Victorian proposal for a "dual referendum" that required a majority of States as well as of people, but as the convention wore on he became convinced that his chances of passing an amendment allowing for a "mass referendum" to democratically solve deadlocks were negligible.[214]

This realisation led him to make a pragmatic change of approach. He introduced an amendment that, on the failure of a double dissolution to resolve a deadlock, allowed for a joint sitting of both Houses where a vote with a three fifths majority would succeed. With a "nexus provision" ensuring the House of Representatives would be double the size of the Senate, the Lower Chamber would dominate any such decision. To further supplement the ability of the democratic majority to assert its will, Carruthers also introduced provisions that allowed the defeated party in the joint sitting to petition the Governor-General for a referendum on the disputed piece of legislation and also for a simple majority in the joint sitting to be able to force its own referendum. These latter democratic additions failed, but the crux of Carruthers' amendment was carried, forever changing the Australian Constitution.

The successful fight for democratic constitutional provisions like the joint sitting is something that is often attributed to George Reid. L.F. Crisp, who barely mentions Carruthers, is typical when he argues that "it is to Reid in particular that Australia owes the more democratic, and also in some ways the more truly national and more viable constitution of 1900".[215] It is true that in September 1897 the battle over the Constitution still had a while to go and that Carruthers' contribution may have reached its high-water mark, nevertheless his role in tandem with Reid is something that deserves greater acknowledgement. The "Norwegian principle" of joint sittings was something that Carruthers had proposed when he first sought election as a convention delegate, and while this foreign transplant was by definition not an entirely original idea, Carruthers still deserves the credit for wording the amendment and helping to win its approval.

Though seldom mentioned in modern histories, Carruthers' important role in framing this aspect of the Constitution is something that has not always been overlooked. Quick and Garran's definitive 1901 work described the deadlock provisions that emerged from Sydney as the "Wise-Carruthers scheme" because Carruthers' joint sitting amendment "came to the rescue" of an earlier proposal by Wise for a simultaneous double dissolution that would have otherwise failed.[216] It is noteworthy that in this and other instances Carruthers' role in the Federal story, already minimalised by Deakin, has decreased in prominence over time. This is not because of a reappraisal of history that has proven him to be less important, but rather it is symptomatic of the fact that he is not a relative household name like Reid and Barton and is therefore less "interesting" to the casual and even the academic observer.

After the Sydney Convention, there was to be an extended break before the Federal delegates concluded their work in Melbourne. In the meantime Carruthers was to undergo considerable personal and political turmoil. The cause of this turmoil was two letters published in the notorious *Truth* newspaper that made scandalous accusations about the Minister for Lands. He was accused of taking part in a dubious land exchange, whereby 220 good acres of land were swapped for the same quantity of less fertile farmland. It was alleged that this was done as a favour for Carruthers' friend but though the swap was controversial the Local Survey Department had approved it and no evidence was ever found of corruption. Combined with this political accusation, *Truth* also printed a personal attack which accused the Minister of engaging in some morally questionable actions with women. This prompted Carruthers to launch a criminal libel suit against those responsible for the unfounded allegations, the dedicated Protectionist George Lonsdale and the newspaper's proprietor John Norton. Norton, who used a "sensational formula of abuse" to sell his papers, was also a Protectionist and a former associate of Carruthers' long-time adversary Paddy Crick.[217] It seems that these commercial and personal considerations lay behind his attack.

The libel case was heard at Armidale near the site of the contested exchange and dragged on for weeks. Its events were given considerable newspaper coverage from which an understanding of the sensational farce can be garnered. Norton, who was no stranger to having libel cases hurled against him, used innuendo and character witnesses in a bid to undermine Carruthers' case. He accused the Minister of having engaged in illicit behaviour with a woman on the Goulburn railway in 1891, and while no evidence was produced and a quick denial ensued the idea was nevertheless placed in the Jury's minds. After this Susan Blackburn, a prostitute, was brought to the stand to testify that she had pursued an affair with Carruthers, though again no corroborating evidence was found. In the end the numerous allegations forced him to reveal the details of his in camera divorce. This publicly exposed his ex-wife's infidelity, and a letter was read to the court in which Louise supported her former husband but declared that she could not bear to appear in person. Carruthers brought forth his own character witnesses, including Reid, in order to defend his good name but in the end Norton's tactic of focusing on Carruthers' character, rather than the unprovable allegations of corruption worked. The jury returned divided and the defendants were thus discharged.

The attacks and the trial greatly injured Carruthers. He was particularly aggrieved that his children had to deal not only with the allegations hurled at their father but also with the revelation of their mother's improprieties. This would exacerbate the teasing and heartache of those already going through the social stigma of their parent's divorce. Carruthers had signed himself up for a public life and the abuse that went with it, but that does not mean he was particularly thick-skinned. He had faced his first public abuse during the campaign to incorporate Kogarah. Angry at the prospect of breaking up the larger West Botany Council, a Mr. P.F. Smyth had attacked Carruthers as "a little man sometimes known as the stump orator or bush lawyer". In response, Carruthers went to the effort of writing a letter to the *Herald* defending his height, his oratory and his legal accreditation.[218] In later years he would learn that such efforts were futile, but in letters to friends he would frequently complain of the emotional torment of public life. In later years he would conclude that a man wanted a "cast iron constitution and a pachydermatous hide" to remain in a leading public position, but while Carruthers undoubtedly had the constitution he was too proud for his hide to be impervious.

The circus at Armidale ended not long before the final convention in Melbourne began. During the delegate elections Carruthers had opposed the removal of appeals to the Privy Council on the grounds that the distant court would be freer from local bias, and it is likely that his experience at the regional courthouse strengthened his resolve on this issue. In Melbourne he combined with Joseph Abbott to pass an amendment that, following a Canadian precedent, allowed appeals from the High Court to the Privy Council based on "any right that Her Majesty may be pleased to exercise by virtue of her Royal Prerogative".[219] Though successful, this amendment prompted a negative reaction from some quarters and opposition to appeals to the Privy Council shifted focus from private cases to the interpretation of the Constitution. Carruthers fiercely defended the right of appeal in constitutional cases. He envisaged the Privy Council as the "bulwark of the constitution", free from local influences and able to give decisions based on evidence alone.[220] He dismissed the sentimental argument that an Australian court should interpret the Constitution on the grounds of self-reliance, pointing out that the convention had already accepted that legislation passed by the proposed Federal Parliament would need to receive Royal Assent before it became law.

Carruthers' spirited defence was unsuccessful. The Constitution Bill that emerged from Melbourne stated that "no appeal shall be permitted to the Queen in Council in any matter involving the interpretation of this Constitution or the Constitution of a State, unless the public interests of some part of Her Majesty's Dominions, other than the Commonwealth or State, are involved".[221] As Premier, Carruthers would feel the wire netting affair justified his argument about the effect of local influences on decisions of the High Court. As was the case in the wire netting decision the Federal High Court, with judges nominated on the advice of the Federal Government, has often found in favour of the Federal Government over the States when interpreting the Constitution. The autonomous powers of the States, which Carruthers fought so hard to protect, have thus arguably been eroded. Whether Privy Council appeals would have prevented this imbalance is impossible to tell. The prestige of the Federal Government may still have given it more influence over constitutional decisions even when those decisions were made in England. Regardless of the viability of Carruthers' argument, the fact that the debate over Privy Council appeals involved more issues than a simple choice between greater independence and strong attachment to Britain is important, and it is something that is often overlooked by historians who are more concerned with the debates of their own times.

In his fight for Privy Council appeals Carruthers did not receive the support of his chief but in the fight over control of inland rivers the two men worked hand in hand. The fight revolved around the waters of the Murray-Darling Basin. New South Wales wanted to defend its existing right to this water, which the local pastoral industry depended upon. South Australia on the other hand was seeking a guarantee that the navigability of rivers would be protected from what was happening upstream. As Minister for Lands Carruthers had been pursuing a closer settlement scheme which relied on accessible water, hence he had a personal political interest in ensuring his Colony won the argument.

He began by pointing out that the value of New South Wales western lands would be greatly reduced without a guaranteed water supply, and that placing the issue in the hands of the Federal Government left too much uncertainty which would drive settlers away. Acknowledging the treacherous climate of the lands in question, Carruthers supported water conservation, by which he meant making the water available for pastoralists, over wasteful irrigation. Asserting that this right of water conservation was greater than the right of navigation, he questioned "what is the use of having a splendid water-way for ships to ply upon if the people alongside that water-way are deprived of the means of using their land to the best purposes – of employing it for the production of that which the ships are intended to carry?"[222] To reinforce his argument that New South Wales had a right to her waters, he even procured a large map that showed the watershed of the Murray-Darling system and hung it in the vestibule of the convention.

Having established his case, Carruthers moved an amendment giving water conservation precedence over navigation. A division on the amendment was not immediately taken and after some private discussions Carruthers dropped it in order to allow a compromise amendment that gave the Federal Government control over the Murray-Darling system with the provision that no State would be denied use of the waters for conservation or irrigation. Josiah Symon inserted the word "reasonable" before use, which for Reid was not a compromise but an "absolute surrender" as it left the whole issue open to the discretion of the High Court.[223] While he was undoubtedly also frustrated with Symon's amendment, Carruthers begrudgingly conceded the point.

After the Melbourne Convention, Carruthers returned to Sydney to campaign for the referendum to adopt or reject the Federal Constitution. Despite the numerous objections to various clauses Carruthers had made during the conventions, he came out strongly in favour of a yes vote. Given his track record this was not surprising. After all, despite private misgivings revealed in Parkes' diary, Carruthers had come out in favour of the 1891 Bill which addressed far fewer of his concerns than its 1898 counterpart. While the shape of the Constitution was still malleable he had been prepared to fight tooth and nail for the amendments he desired, but once it became a yes-or-no question he firmly backed a document that, crucially, contained his joint sitting provision.

Though this provision represented a compromise rather than Carruthers' democratic ideal, he still used it as his main weapon in arguing the yes case. He was careful to point out to concerned voters that in the event of a joint sitting the combined representatives of New South Wales and Victoria would possess two votes more than necessary for a three-fifths majority.[224] This meant that despite equal representation in the Senate the will of the democratic majority could bring itself to bear on any important issue if it either had universal support in the two large States, or majority support in the large states and minority support in the smaller States. Carruthers' calculations were based on Queensland not being a part of the Commonwealth; hence her possible admission could undermine the ability of the democratic majority to assert its will. This helps explain Reid's reluctance to accept the two-thirds provision, though the regional interests Queensland shared with New South Wales would somewhat mitigate against the cohesion of the smaller States. The deadlock provisions were not the only thing Carruthers argued made the Constitution democratic as he also pointed out that in spite of equal representation a Senate elected by universal manhood suffrage was still a vast improvement on the nominee Legislative Council.

Apart from the defending the democratic nature of the Constitution, Carruthers also had to rebuff the charge that if New South Wales joined a federation with her protectionist neighbours it would destroy the free trade cause. He did this with a four point argument:

1. That the constitution gives us a guarantee for freetrade practically for nearly one-half of our total trade

2. That our intercolonial export trade must and will increase with the removal of heavy border duties.

3. That for the remainder of our trade (about one half of the total) there will be either a revenue tariff or a protective tariff, according to the views of the majority in a House of Representatives in which New South Wales has the largest representation.

4. That with the abolition of border duties there will be less inducement for the farming districts in any colony to advocate a protection which will not benefit them.

He also rejected the argument, common in free trade circles, that the Braddon clause would necessitate protection. This financial clause was a product of circumstance. Many of the other Colonies relied on tariffs as an essential source of government revenue. These would now be handed over to the Federal Government, so something had to be done to prevent a fiscal crisis. The Braddon clause aimed to solve this problem by requiring that three quarters of Federal customs revenue would have to be either returned to the States or used to pay off interest on State debts taken over by the Commonwealth. Many felt that this would force the Federal Government to set duties far higher than would otherwise be the case. Far from guaranteeing protection, Carruthers argued that this made customs duties such an inefficient way of raising revenue that Federal Governments might be persuaded to look elsewhere for money.

The defensive nature of Carruthers' arguments for a yes vote was a reflection of the strong opposition to federation and to the proposed constitution prevalent in New South Wales. Both Protectionist leader William Lyne and the Labor Party declared in favour of a no vote. The Reid Cabinet was given a largely free hand to campaign for either side.

The Attorney-General John Want resigned his post to lead the no campaign, while Carruthers was debatably the only Minister to give his full backing to the yes campaign. Reid initially kept his cards close to his chest, but eventually he made a statement that would go down in history as the Yes-No speech. In it Reid examined both the good and bad aspects of the proposed constitution before equivocally endorsing a yes vote. The negative aspects raised by Reid included the money-bills compromise, the three-fifths majority rather than a simple majority in joint sittings, the Braddon clause and the "reasonable" right to water. Many of Reid's concerns were shared by Carruthers, but the latter was able to overlook them. It may be that a vestigial attachment to Parkes meant Carruthers was more willing to compromise to see his former hero's dream fulfilled.

For his honesty with the electors, Reid earned the eternal enmity of the Federalist ultras. Wise was particularly vitriolic claiming that "Federalists, reading Mr. Reid's unsparing condemnation of all the clauses in the Bill to which objections had been raised, and his half-hearted approbation of the few others, about which there was no difference of opinion, could conclude only that, under the specious guise of judicial fairness, he had marshalled nearly every argument which told against the Bill; and that his faint praise was intended to be more damning than the most acute criticism".[225] Though he too was a dedicated Federalist, Carruthers' opinion of the Yes-No speech could not have been more different. He felt Reid's honesty was a principled action of self-sacrifice that earned the Premier no favours. Years later Carruthers recalled that "Reid was actuated by an undue sense of personal responsibility to act impartially and not as an advocate of the bill".[226] He maintained that were it not for the sacrifices Reid made to fulfil this personal responsibility and an unfortunate snoring incident during the Adelaide Convention, Reid would have been Australia's first Prime Minister.

When the Federal referendum was held in New South Wales the yes vote received a narrow majority but did not reach the minimum 80,000 votes required for the Bill to pass. This failure was probably due more to the public concerns underlying the Yes-No speech than the speech itself, as the division between the pro-Federal *Sydney Morning Herald* and the anti-Federal *Daily Telegraph* showed that Sydney's opinion of the Bill was already very mixed before Reid even spoke. Despite this, many Federalists were quick to blame Reid for the failure of the Bill. Carruthers defended the Premier, insisting that he had been consistent in his views throughout the conventions and beyond. The member for St George's own electorate had voted against the Bill and he blamed the financial provisions, rather than Reid, for the failure to reach the quota. The anti-billites had argued that these financial provisions took away more revenue from the States than the Federal Government would take away in governing costs, hence a "net deficiency" would be created that would undermine State finances.[227] The simpler argument that federation would lead to an increase in the size of government that would necessitate higher taxation was also an important concern.

Almost immediately after the failure of the referendum, Reid sign-posted negotiations with the other Premiers in the hope of achieving an "alteration in the terms of the bill that would make it more amenable to the people of New South Wales". An election was looming in the Colony and the timing required that Reid win a new mandate before he was able to meet with his inter-colonial counterparts. Barton himself wanted the opportunity to lead the negotiations; hence he directed the Federal Association to set up an election committee, effectively turning it into a political party. Barton thus usurped a large part of Lyne's power, and the election, far from being a traditional fiscal fight, was turned into a contest between the Federalist ultras and the Reid Government. Though Reid was fighting for a more "liberal" constitution, the thrust of the election was a step away from the ideological conflicts of 1894 and 1895. Instead the poll was to be a question of leadership and loyalty to the federation cause, an echo of the personal battles of the factional era.

Under the circumstances there was some idle newspaper speculation that Carruthers might follow Barton. This was never a real possibility. Carruthers relished the opportunity to further improve the Constitution Bill and was not about to make an alliance with Protectionists and the disloyal Free Traders Wise, McMillan and Bruce Smith only to weaken

New South Wales' hand at the negotiating table. Carruthers' continuing support would prove vital for Reid, as it shored up his Federalist credentials and prevented the unequivocal Federalists from presenting a united front against the Premier. It also helped to stem the flow of Federalist Free Traders into Barton's camp. This latter point is seldom mentioned in the historiography surrounding federation, but it is of the utmost importance. It was not just the already "independent" Free Traders like Wise who went over to Barton, but some genuine party-men as well. The most notable of these was Dugald Thomson, who would go on to become the Federal Free Trade Party's deputy leader and a Minister in the Reid-McLean Government. Had Carruthers, as the leading Federalist Free Trader, made the same decision the Party would have been torn asunder. Despite Deakin's suggestion of disharmony between Carruthers and his chief, it was this crucial show of loyalty that saved Reid and saved his party.

As the contest developed issues of personality quickly superseded those of policy. Both leaders wanted federation and even Barton admitted that some changes to the Constitutional Bill were necessary in order to win its acceptance in New South Wales, hence the question became whether Reid or Barton should be the one to negotiate those changes. Carruthers' speeches thus focused on the respective qualities of each leader. Though he was careful not to be too hateful towards Barton, Carruthers described him as being "a little bit prone" and "a little bit pliant" to the representatives of the other Colonies.[228] Reid on the other hand he praised as the man who "since taking office ... had brought federation from a thing in the clouds to a stern reality". To overcome the financial problems Carruthers blamed for the Bill's failure, he proposed cost saving exercises including reducing the size of State Parliaments, doing away with superfluous officers and pooling debts in order to be able to negotiate lower interest rates.

Throughout the campaign the *Sydney Morning Herald* continued to subtly help Barton's "National Federal Party", listing their candidates before those of "Liberal Federal Party"(which is what the Free Traders were calling themselves), even though the latter group was not only in Government but also came first alphabetically. In spite of the paper's efforts, the Government held on to power, but only just. Reid personally defeated Barton in the King electorate. Wise succeeded in clawing his way back into Parliament but both McMillan and Bruce Smith's National Federal campaigns ended in failure. Carruthers received almost 75% of the vote in St George and was carried through Rockdale on the shoulders of his enthusiastic supporters. Elsewhere the Free Traders fared less well. The Government's majority was reduced and three Ministers lost their seats. For the first time Reid would be truly reliant on Labor support.

THE FLY IN THE OINTMENT
"N.S.W Attorney-General Want will uncompromisingly oppose the Federation Bill"
LITTLE BROTHER JOEY CARRUTHERS: "I'll tell George when he comes back!"
BROTHER JACK WANT: "I'm 'fraid it'll be too late then. We'll see what's in it, anyway!"

While Carruthers was firmly in favour of Federation the Reid Ministry was divided over the issue. From the *Bulletin*.

158

CHAPTER EIGHT

Personal and Political Tragedy

The loss of three Ministers at the election necessitated a Cabinet reshuffle in order to fill the recently vacated spaces. It was widely reported that Carruthers had grown tired of his position as Minister for Lands and would ask the Premier to move him to a different office. For the moment however, Reid left him where he was and promoted Varney Parkes, James Hogue, and Charles Lee from the backbench. Later Carruthers' name was frequently mentioned in relation to the vacant position of Agent-General for New South Wales in London. Carruthers declined to seek the position because his health was not amenable to English weather, but also because his new wife did not want to relocate.

Ignoring the turmoil of the Norton libel case, Joseph Carruthers had married Alice Burnett at the start of the year and had used the Melbourne Convention as a honeymoon. Alice was the 21-year-old daughter of Scottish immigrant and telegraph officer Alexander Burnett. That Scottish heritage gave her an immediate connection to Joseph, whom she met as a rising political star. Perhaps this knowledge that she was marrying into a political lifestyle made her more accepting of its burdens. She certainly became a rock for Joseph, offering emotional support while also charming the Sydney social circles in which the pair mixed. In that sphere she became highly engaged in charitable activities. She was also quite the savvy investor. Following the custom of the day she had been given a marriage settlement involving a number of financial assets and she was intelligent enough to put the money to work. It was said that Alice's love for horse races may have exceeded even her husband's and that she invested greatly in racing tracks (which were a far sounder prospect than individual thoroughbreds).

While she had something of limited a public persona, Alice's main interests remained the home and the family that she maintained with her husband. She would give birth to six children, first three sons Joseph, Douglas and Wallace, then three daughters Alice, Evelyn and Thelma (known as Peg or Peggy). Joseph was at heart a family man and appreciated the caring mother that Alice became. She taught her children to read and write from an early age and they were always proud to show off with letters, sent with "love and kisses", to their father. The children were inculcated in the middle class values of hard work and moral virtue, but in a caring rather than draconian manner. During the height of Carruthers' political career the family occupied "Ellesmere", a grand house at Sans Souci. It featured a bowling green and a music room, as well as a boating jetty that could be used to take the children out fishing on Kogarah Bay. The home was a warm place filled as much with games and laughter as judicious study. Joseph firmly believed that play was an integral part of Sunday rest, and was ever eager to join in the fun. He also maintained "an abiding love of a good dog", which meant the house was generally filled with pets.

If the loss of three Ministers had left the Free Traders in a mess, then their Opposition was in disarray. Having lost the King contest, Barton was desperately seeking another seat in Parliament but was having a hard time convincing any of his colleagues to give way. Without Barton, the National Federalists were forced to leave Lyne as Opposition Leader even though his Federalist credentials were far weaker than Reid's. Lyne had outwardly opposed the Federation Bill at the recent referendum and his leadership exposed the hypocrisy of the National Federalist "Free Traders" who sat behind him.

In his first major speech of the session Carruthers made great use of the whole situation, quoting Barton's previous denunciation of Lyne on Federal grounds, much to the delight of the Ministerialists. He was also keen to point out that the person who had moved the amendment requiring a minimum number of yes votes for the referendum to succeed was sitting in the ranks of the Opposition. The whole speech was marked by frequent exchanges with the recently-returned Wise. A noticeably aggravated Carruthers suggested that his opponent's "querulous criticism" had more to do with an animosity towards Reid than any principle.[229]

Carruthers delivered his speech on 23 August. The next day an incident occurred that shook the member for St George to his core. His son Jack was cycling home that night when he collided with a cart. The shaft of the vehicle struck him on the chest and he was thrown a considerable distance. Passengers in a passing tram stumbled upon the incident but help was slow in reaching him. Initial reports told that Jack had fractured a rib and was suffering from bruises and shock. It was expected that he would stay a while at his father's house and would ultimately recover. These reports proved wrong however, and Jack passed away at St George Cottage Hospital on the morning of the 26th. He was almost fifteen. An inquest into the death was heard, but as some of Jack's last words had intimated that the collision was his fault the incident was ruled accidental.

Joseph had been in Parliament the night of the accident and was distraught at the news. His divorce had brought him closer to both of his children, and while he adored Ida, Jack was in many respects the apple of his eye. Joseph saw himself in Jack. Jack was named Hector after his father, and the two males looked eerily similar to one another. They particularly shared deep, soulful eyes that gave both of them a captivating if somewhat mournful gaze. Like Joseph, Jack was an incredibly bright child and had already ascended to the top of Sydney Grammar School. Jack however possessed none of his delicate father's frailties, and naturally thrived on the sports field to a degree that Joseph, who despite his enthusiasm always struggled to make the first eleven for his cricket team, was exceedingly proud of.

A funeral was organised and Reid and many other colleagues attended. The burial service was said to be one of the largest and most solemn events ever witnessed in St George, with at least 2000 people turning out. Jack was laid to rest beside his sister Elsie, whose death in 1886 had proved the catalyst for Joseph's political career and whom the young boy would have barely known. Dozens of wreaths were laid to rest on Jack's grave, but the most poignant was his father's which was made of deep violets and shaped like a cradle.

Jack's death was reported in papers the length and breadth of Australia. Joseph received a huge quantity of condolence letters from all manner of political friends and adversaries. In spite of his overwhelming grief, Carruthers could take little time to mourn. The Government held only a tiny majority in the Assembly, and his voice as much as his vote was needed to fend off the various censure motions that would inevitably be coming Reid's way. Carruthers had always been a family man, repeatedly willing to sacrifice his social life to spend time with his children. He felt a duty towards the public as well however, and in this case it took precedence over his emotional torment.

By 6 September Carruthers was back in Parliament. By the 13th he was again berating Wise as the Government fought off a censure motion over the federation issue. Reid was seeking parliamentary approval of a list of amendments to the proposed constitution which he was about to negotiate with the other Premiers over. The points included a simple majority in joint sittings or else a referendum to break deadlocks, removal of the Braddon clause, protection from the alteration of State boundaries without consent, that the capital be in New South Wales, a clearer safeguard for water conservation and irrigation, that the Senate be prevented from amending all money bills and that Privy Council appeals be allowed in all cases or no cases.[230] Apart from the Privy Council provision, Carruthers was largely in favour of all of these amendments. He could take heart from the capital point in particular, as this had been his pet issue. Though Reid had always thought it desirable to have the capital in the Mother Colony he had frequently given the issue a low priority. Carruthers' arguments combined with the clear popular appeal of the issue eventually won the Premier over.

In hindsight it is easy to dismiss the capital site issue as pure provincialism, but in the days when transport was slow and arduous it would vitally affect the nature of Federal politics. Carruthers was ultimately unable or unwilling to enter Federal politics because Melbourne became the temporary capital site and as Federal Opposition Leader Reid's efforts would be compromised by his inability to attend Parliament on a constant basis. In an age before national media the local papers of the capital were also likely to influence Federal politicians, and many New South Welshmen would later blame David Syme's *The Age* for the success of Protectionism. As the largest State and the State that would make the greatest financial sacrifices for federation, both Carruthers and Reid felt that New South Wales had a right to the capital and thus to have the largest population be unaffected by the tyranny of distance. In accepting that the temporary capital be in Melbourne in order that the permanent capital be in New South Wales, Reid would ultimately sacrifice his own career for the sake of future generations of New South Welshmen.

Lyne's censure motion was directed at Reid's list, which he complained placed conditions on the negotiations. In reality it was just an excuse to test the strength of the House, something that the Opposition had been delaying in the absence of Barton but had evidently decided they could delay no longer. The division was tight, with the Government holding on by only four votes. Though he argued strongly for the Government during the censure debate, Carruthers was unable to attend the actual division and would have been amply relieved when the Government scraped through.

Two more censure motions would have to be overcome before the final federation negotiations could begin. The first involved a by-election campaign fought between Barton and defeated Minister Sydney Smith. The Opposition claimed that during the campaign the Secretary for Public Works J. H. Young had acted improperly by receiving a deputation on some local works while also canvassing for the candidate. The censure was defeated by six votes. A second censure involved the introduction of some small tariffs as a temporary revenue raising device. This was of course highly unpalatable for the Free Traders, but other measures to improve the Colony's finances had been blocked by the Legislative Council hence Reid was left with little choice. The upcoming federation would almost inevitably result in a far more substantial tariff, at least until the fiscal fight was fought out, so the Government could console itself that it was merely jumping the gun. Barton's censure of the Government for bringing up the tariff while federation was yet to be settled failed by the large margin of twenty-three votes.

In late January 1899 Reid finally met with the other Premiers to try to iron out the perceived problems in the Federal Bill. He was pleasantly surprised at their ameliorative attitude. He wrote confidentially to Carruthers that the meeting had so far been a success and that he was having pieces of "butter" crammed down his throat by the other Premiers:

> I am very sanguine that we will do some good at the conference. I will aim at imitating that quiet, thorough, practical way of working out things which is characteristic of you, and to which I am so often indebted for good advice.[231]

The fact that Reid was keeping Carruthers informed while the secret negotiations took place in Melbourne is highly significant. There is a sense that Reid felt that the whole Federal escapade was something that he had undertaken with the member for St George and that at this critical juncture it would have been wrong to leave him out of the loop. Through the entire Federal campaign Reid had been isolated except for Carruthers. He was isolated in a Cabinet that shared even greater concerns about federation than he did. He was isolated as one of only three members of the Government in the New South Wales delegation. He was also isolated as one of the few delegates who fought hard for democratic principles with scant regard for their reputation as "Federalists". Carruthers and Reid had differed slightly over the referendum campaign, but even then Reid had still received the support of his friend. It was this support, along with Carruthers' good advice that made Reid's principled Federal fight possible. It is a shame that we are not informed what the advice Carruthers had been giving Reid was, but Carruthers' influence is clearly visible in the amendments that Reid fought for and ultimately in the document that became the Australian Constitution.

This influence can be seen in the results of the Premier's Conference. The three-fifths majority in joint sittings was changed to an absolute majority. Though he had defended it during the referendum campaign, the three-fifths principle had never been something Carruthers was entirely satisfied with. His original proposal had included referendum provisions to overcome the democratic deficiencies of the three-fifths majority; hence the absolute majority was more faithful to the thrust of his amendment. This was reinforced by another change adopted by the Premier's

Conference that allowed a referendum on a constitutional amendment to be held if it was passed twice by one House but blocked by the other. The capital was to be in New South Wales, though disappointingly it was to be at least a hundred miles from Sydney. The Braddon Clause was limited to ten years while the boundaries of a State were protected against being altered without that State's permission. This last amendment would have satisfied Carruthers' belief in State autonomy. Unfortunately the inland rivers, money bills and judicial appeals clauses were left the same but for a pragmatist these were sacrifices worth making.

The amended Enabling Bill passed through the Legislative Assembly with relative ease, but encountered problems in the Legislative Council. It moved that there should be a minimum referendum vote required for adoption, that a minimum of three months should elapse between the passing of the Bill and the holding of the referendum and that New South Wales should not join the federation until Queensland had. A conference between the two Houses was organised to sort out these issues, and Carruthers was elected as one of the representatives of the Assembly. On the suggestion of Carruthers, Reid argued that instead of having a minimum vote the election should be held over several days to give people a greater opportunity to vote. The Council would not agree and the conference failed to resolve the deadlock. Instead Reid got the Governor to appoint twelve new members to the Council and that body eventually gave way. The only amendment it carried was that there should be an eight week delay between the passing of the Bill and the referendum.

Carruthers played an important but subtle role in the second referendum campaign. He was on the organising committee of the United Federal Executive, an amalgamation of the existing Federal organisations that managed to briefly unite Reid and Barton. He gave a few prominent speeches in Sydney, but his main task was preaching the yes case in the countryside. He toured the South Coast and the Western districts, and also spoke at Newcastle and in the Southern Highlands. With the improvements to the Constitution and considerable bipartisan support, the second referendum succeeded in New South Wales and was soon successful in most of the other colonies. Parkes' dream had been carried through by Reid, and Carruthers could be satisfied that, posthumous though it was, his two chiefs were finally in accord.

Carruthers had been balancing his time between the Federal campaign and the Lands Office, and though the former often took precedence the latter could not be ignored. By 1899 there had been a devastating drought in New South Wales that had lasted four years. Many claimed that it was the most severe drought in the Colony's history and its effects had been exacerbated by a rabbit plague which had swept through the West. In the circumstances many felt that some form of government intervention was necessary lest the closer settlement scheme would fail. Carruthers' generally small government instincts made him reluctant, and he controversially rejected a suggestion to give a blanket five year extension to all expiring Crown land leases. Eventually deteriorating circumstances forced the Minister's hand, and he introduced a Bill "to authorise the raising of a loan for the making of temporary advances to settlers and to provide for the making and repayment of such advances".[232] He justified the lending of taxpayer money to farmers whilst there were still unemployed in the city by pointing out that agriculture was at the heart of the New South Wales economy, and that its success was vital to the success of the Colony as a whole. It is important to point out that not only was this to be a loan not a hand-out but that it was to be lent out at an interest rate that would cover the rate of the initial loan and all costs incidental to the measure. Hence it was hoped that in the long run the State's finances would not be disturbed and the taxpayer would not have to foot any bill.

Carruthers introduced the Bill hoping that it would be a non-party measure. The rurally based Protectionists could not be expected to reject relief for their constituents, while it was also not something that the Labor Party would likely abandon the Government over. He was surprised then, when the House erupted as he tried to suspend the standing orders to rush the urgent Bill through. An argument broke out between two National Federalists. The rural member James Carroll supported the Bill, while the city representative Henry Copeland came out against it. The argument quickly deteriorated into threats of physical violence and Copeland had to be physically restrained as he attempted to attack Carroll. In spite of Copeland's agitation, the Bill was passed with an overwhelming majority. It was to be Carruthers' last significant act as Minister for Lands. In late June a Cabinet reshuffle promoted him to the Treasury, while Reid took up the less arduous position of Attorney-General. It seems that Reid forfeited the Treasury in order to give himself more time for political management in an increasingly treacherous House.[233] While this practical motive was paramount, Carruthers' promotion also suggests that, with federation looming, Reid may have been designating a successor. Reid's own ascension had established the elective leadership premise within the Free Trade Party, but the support of Reid and experience as Treasurer could only help Carruthers' chances in any internal ballot.

Despite the impression of a fresh start given by the Cabinet reshuffle, there were clearly troubled waters ahead for the Reid Ministry. The Government's success meant they had exhausted the partisan liberal agenda of 1889 and the distraction of federation had encumbered the formulation of anything to replace it. Even if a new agenda could be found, it was difficult to imagine how the long serving Ministry could gain the momentum to push in another direction. Since the 1898 election, federation had all but assured Reid's position since the democratic line he and Carruthers took on the Constitution had encouraged the support of the Labor Party. With that now off the table, interventionist National Federalists like Wise and Edward O'Sullivan could offer Labor far more concessions than the limited government liberalism of Reid and Carruthers could possibly countenance. The Free Traders did propose an Early Closing Bill, Navigation Amendment Bill and relief to the victims of mining accidents, but the mild nature of these reforms meant they were of little interest to Labor. With a fundamental respect for individual freedoms, Reid would not allow himself to be pushed beyond his own limits of government intervention. John Rickard has suggested that Reid "combined a strong advocacy of democratic principles with an orthodox view of political economy".[234] The Free Traders had built their alliance with Labor on the former while largely defining themselves by the latter. Now that the democratic battles over the land tax and federation had been won and the fight over the Legislative Council had petered out, they found themselves with little in common with a Labor Party that was increasingly focused on issues like compulsory arbitration. Having lowered tariffs and balanced the budget, the economic liberalism of the Free Traders still had a lot to offer the electors in the form of good administration, relatively small government and continued economic recovery. The election had not been fought over these issues however, and now the Government's fate lay in the hands of those who were least likely to buy such a sales pitch.

After a trip to Queensland to promote the adoption of the Federation Bill in the northern Colony, Carruthers returned to Sydney in time for the opening of the next session of Parliament. It became clear almost immediately how fractious the House had become. On 26 July he introduced a Bill seeking two months' supply for the Government. The debate quickly deteriorated into an attempt by the Opposition to prove that the Government had been misleading the public over the state of the finances. Their argument was that despite frequent assertions of budget surpluses, the independent report of the Auditor-General suggested that the Colony was actually in debt. Carruthers was quick to point out that the Government's claim that the budget had been balanced year to year was correct, but that some debt carried over from previous administrations still existed. He maintained that that debt was being paid off slowly, and that the Opposition were the ones who were misleading the public by suggesting that the deficit was a result of the current year's finances.[235] It was a baptism of fire for Carruthers' Treasury credentials and with the judicious help of Reid he was able to survive it, showing expert knowledge of the numbers despite having only held the position for a month.

Just two weeks later Carruthers delivered his first budget. Meticulously dissecting the Auditor-General's report, he was able to show a surplus in the accounts for the year just gone and predict a surplus of twenty thousand pounds for the ensuing year.[236] To further increase revenue, he proposed to increase probate duties but not to a level greater than that of Great Britain or any of her dependencies. He also proposed to force companies whose dividends were paid out of earnings from the soil of the Colony to register in the Colony so they could thus be taxed. Previously certain businesses registered in Victoria or elsewhere who operated in New South Wales only had to pay tax in the place where they were registered. These were minor changes that would not greatly increase the burdens of the people or hinder business. More radically, Carruthers flagged the creation of a State bank as a more permanent version of the Advances to Settlers Act. Though most certainly an interventionist creation, this bank was not aimed at competing with private banks but helping the nation-building project of closer settlement.

Though there was some continued wrangling over the Auditor-General's report and the declared surplus, the bulk of Carruthers' budget soon faded into the background as it was overshadowed by other events. The budget estimates had revealed that the member for Paddington J.C. Neild had been paid in advance of appropriation for a report on old age pension schemes he had written after conducting research in Europe. Though frowned upon, payments in advance of appropriation were not illegal and had been frequently resorted to by previous administrations. Members of Parliament receiving government fees was also viewed in a negative light, but again it was something that many members of both sides of the House were guilty of. Carruthers, who though the payment had been made before he was appointed to his current position was at the heart of the controversy because he was Treasurer, could show that Lyne, Barton and Wise had all received payments in the same manner in the past. Despite the hypocrisy of making criticisms given the situation, the Opposition were keen to use any opportunity they could to try to bring down the Government. Knowing that Neild was personally unpopular amongst Labor Members, the National Federalists launched an attack that led to a William Lyne censure motion which ultimately brought down Reid.

The censure motion was the culmination of weeks of scheming, at the heart of which was Bernhard Wise. Keen to bring down Reid by any means necessary, Wise had been pushing the claims of Barton amongst

Labor Party members. With memories of the Broken Hill strike that were still surprisingly fresh, Labor would not accept the aristocratic ultra-Federalist as Premier. Wise eventually realised this and began to move that Barton be replaced with Lyne. As a Protectionist who had opposed both the land tax and the Federation Bill, Lyne had almost nothing to recommend himself to Wise except the fact that he was not George Reid. Given the member for Ashfield's all-consuming hatred for the Premier, that was enough and Barton was convinced to step aside. He may have been promised a clear path to the Federal Prime Ministership as an incentive to go quietly.[237] With an intimation that the Opposition would not raise the fiscal issue once in office, Free Trade defector John Fegan was also roped into the plot. This "party of revenge", as it was described by Carruthers, began lobbying for Labor support both in the debate in the Assembly and in the corridors of the House. Fegan moved a critical amendment to the censure "that the present Government does not possess the confidence of the House", adding "and deserves censure for having made payments of public money to Mr. J.C. Neild, member for Paddington, without asking Parliament, and contrary to assurances given by the right hon. Premier".[238] This amendment was designed to be very difficult for the Labor Party to vote against, and if they voted for it they would effectively be censuring the Government.

Though Wise and Fegan helped to lay the groundwork for Reid's demise, it was the Labor Party that would decide the fate of the Government. Ironically it was the future Nationalist leaders William Hughes and William Holman who fought hardest against Reid. Hughes was able to gain an undertaking from Lyne that if made Premier he would introduce a number of measures that Labor desired, including an Early Closing Bill that went much further than Reid's. Hughes took that information into caucus and fought hard to convince his colleagues to abandon their partner of five years. After a long debate, it allegedly took the threat of resignation by an anti-Reid group known as the "solid six" to win the day for Lyne.[239]

The actions of the solid six are highly controversial. The account of their resignation threat comes from contemporary newspaper reports and Reid's autobiography, and is also backed up by a speech from Holman in which he bragged about being a member of the solid six and helping to bring down Reid.[240] Meanwhile Hughes' account of events denies that a threat of resignation was made and his biographer L.F. Fitzhardinge concurs with him.[241] Reid and Holman seem more reliable as not only do they back each other up but their testimonies were given far closer to the event than the one given by an aged Hughes more than forty years later. Authoritative Labor historian Bede Nairn has concluded that the "solid six" probably did threaten resignation, but that it was ultimately the legislative concessions offered by Lyne that proved the telling factor.[242] Whatever the exact circumstances, Labor cut its ties with Reid and in the final division the Government lost by 75 to 41.

Regardless of whether or not it was the "solid six" who really brought down the Government, Reid's account reveals there was an impression amongst the Free Traders that a threat of resignation had been successfully used to manipulate caucus, and this would have affected their views of the Labor Party. Carruthers was fully aware of who was responsible for the Government's fall. In his last utterance as a member of the Reid Ministry he discussed an earlier speech given by McGowen, who though bound by caucus to vote against Reid, had referred generously to the achievements of a Government he had helped support for five years. Carruthers described it as a "eulogy", the likes of which no outgoing government had ever been afforded in such glowing terms.[243] Despite this praise, he pointed out that McGowen "stands here as an opponent of the Government, voting as he intends to do to put us out of office".

His speech went on to attack Barton and Wise, but this hint at the hypocrisy forced upon members of the Labor Party by caucus solidarity is of lasting significance. The rumoured actions of the solid six in determining the will of caucus were already an open secret. Carruthers had been one of the first to turn against the Labor Party and he had always opposed the illiberal system of caucus solidarity that had seen the exit of his friend Joseph Cook. This perceived new precedent confirmed and exceeded his worst fears. Not only had men been openly forced to vote against their conscience, but the controlling will of the Labor caucus had not even been the enforced will of the majority. Instead a mere six men had allegedly been able to strong arm a caucus fearful of yet another Labor split into adopting their views. From the Free Traders' perspective this was a tyranny of the minority, absolutely abhorrent to liberalism and even to the democratic principles for which Carruthers and Reid had been fighting side by side with Labor. The jarring incident would be a telling factor in Carruthers' eventual decision never to work with the Labor Party again.

Carruthers was personally aggrieved at the loss of government, but he was more concerned about the blow to his friend and chief. He sent Reid a heartfelt note, to which Reid replied "your note received yesterday afternoon gives me greater satisfaction than I can well express".[244] Clearly he was touched by his friend's emotional outpour, which was made even more poignant by the knowledge that Joseph was still dealing with the lingering emotional torment of Jack's death. Reid stressed his continuing resolve and his eagerness to "fight together as staunchly and as successfully as in the past".

It was not long before the two men were fighting together as they were not about to let Wise's ministerial by-election go uncontested. Wise had been made Attorney-General in a Lyne Government which had also rewarded Fegan with the position of Secretary for Mines and Agriculture. In the Ashfield by-election both Carruthers and Reid gave strong speeches in favour of the Free Trade candidate Thomas Bavister. Carruthers declared that, though he was generally against contesting ministerial by-elections, Wise's political inconsistency meant that the electors deserved another choice. Speaking of the amendment to the censure motion that had been crafted by Wise but delivered by Fegan, he also claimed that he "very much more admired the man who fired off that shot than the man who loaded a gun and stood behind the hedge watching the effects of the discharge".[245] In the end Wise narrowly avoided getting kicked out of Parliament for a third time, holding onto his seat by a mere 21 votes.

When Lyne formed his Ministry he appointed himself Colonial Treasurer and promptly tried to denounce the previous Government by claiming that the coffers were bare. Carruthers was quick to refute their claims, citing the signed statements of two independent accountants to show that with trust funds and loan funds included there was £7,358,410 available in the Treasury when he left office, up from a deficit of £508,705 when Reid had entered it.[246] For a short while this rebuttal put an end to the accusations, but by early December Lyne released a budget where he again tried to show that Reid and Carruthers had manipulated the figures.

In his response Carruthers latched on to an assertion by the Premier that there was a £3,000,000 deficit. He was able to point to a statement signed by Treasury officials and even the current Treasurer himself which said that there was a surplus of £116,000 and also to a worst case reading of the Auditor-General's report that showed an overall deficit of only £781,000.[247] The vast bulk of the debt present in that report, £696,000 worth, was from two obligations undertaken eleven years earlier which the Reid Government evidently had nothing to do with. The remainder of the discrepancy between the Treasury and the Auditor-General he put down to an anomaly in the bookkeeping of the Bank of England requiring a deposit of government money to be in credit for 1 July. This money could be retrieved at a later date; hence it was not expenditure even though the Auditor-General took it as such. He thus asserted that the cash account system that Reid had brought in in 1895 had been working very successfully and suggested that the only way the £3,000,000 deficit could exist was if the Secretary for Works Edward O'Sullivan had spent the bulk of it since entering office.

The debate over the public debt was to rage throughout Lyne's short tenure as Premier, but in many ways Carruthers and Reid had already won the argument. Lyne commissioned a report by a number of bankers in the hope that they would prove his findings, but even they had to concede that the accounts showed a surplus if read according to the Audit (Amendment) Act and the Treasury Bills Deficiency Act. The report did criticise the policy of using Treasury Bills to cover the deficit left over from previous Governments, but as Treasurer Carruthers had already shown that this debt was not being swept under the carpet but was being paid off in steady £150,000 increments. The Free Traders would be further vindicated when Lyne released his next budget and declared a substantial surplus. This they argued showed not only that the Treasury had never been significantly in debt in the first place, but also that the Free Trade tariff which had yet to be abolished was creating economic growth. Carruthers boasted that "the Colonial Treasurer has had to stand up here to-night and admit that without one line of alteration in the financial policy of his predecessors, without one line of alteration to the fiscal policy of the country, we stand in that splendid position that, facing drought, disaster, plague expenditure, and military expenditure, we have a booming revenue and a substantial surplus".[248]

There was an inherent tension between the economic conservatism of the older members of the Protectionist Party that led Lyne to pursue budget surpluses and the economic radicalism of men like his spend-thrift Secretary for Works Edward O'Sullivan. A former journalist with strong ties to the union movement, O'Sullivan might have ended up in the Labor Party had the beginnings of his political career not predated that organisation. Drawn to protection by the hope that government intervention could help the working-man, he had little regard for economic orthodoxy, and was happy to spend as much taxpayer money as he could access in order to provide jobs for his various working-class supporters. While the economy continued to grow the tension between him and his chief could be kept in check, as increases in Public Works spending could be hidden behind a growing revenue stream, but once the economy soured differences between O'Sullivan and the main body of the Protectionists would be exaggerated.

Already the Government suffered from a fundamental lack of a co-herent ideology. It was a Protectionist ministry that had promised not to raise the fiscal issue and a National Federalist ministry that no longer had the federation issue to hold it together. In these circumstances a minority of radicals who possessed clear beliefs were slowly able to gain the upper hand. In the short term this strengthened the Government's alliance with the Labor Party, but in the long term it hurt them at the ballot box. After all, those who wanted radical policies were still going to vote for Labor, while those who preferred a more limited style of government would be left with little choice but to vote for the Free Trade Liberals.

Central to the Protectionist-Labor alliance were the commitments Lyne had made during the backroom negotiations which had brought him to power. It was not long before one of the more important of these commitments was fulfilled, as the Government introduced its Early-Closing Bill (No.2). This Bill introduced a strict six o'clock closing time for shops most days of the week, and even earlier closing on Saturdays. Carruthers objected to both the rigid nature of the Bill, and the fact that it would only affect the metropolitan and the Newcastle shopping district. He argued that if early closing were a good principle it should be good for the whole Colony and not just certain sections of it.[249] He did not highlight the fact that those areas to be affected were Labor districts, while the rural seats of many Protectionists were to be left alone, but he did suggest that early closing would be particularly problematic in suburban areas where people needed to shop after work.

Throughout the committee stages, Reid and Carruthers repeatedly tried to water down the Bill to ensure that it was less detrimental to individual freedoms. Such efforts would be to no avail, but the fact that they attempted it in the face of frequent assertions that they were trying to "kill the Bill" shows that the two men had moved on from trying to win Labor support and were gravitating towards an ever more independent position.

Soon after the introduction of the Early-Closing Bill, events in South Africa were to overshadow domestic politics. In October 1899 a conflict had broken out between the British Cape Colony which occupied the southern tip of the continent and the independent Boer Republics, made up of the descendants of earlier Dutch settlers, which sat to its North. Though initially confident of a swift victory, the British had suffered a number of setbacks and their colonial possessions had thus been endangered. The deteriorating military situation prompted a decision by the New South Wales Premier to equip and dispatch a force to South Africa. Like most of his parliamentary colleagues, Carruthers came out firmly in favour of the motion. He argued that such a response was the result of cool headed thinking, not jingoistic hysteria. He reasoned that the joint security of the Empire, which Australia relied on for her own defence, was at stake and might crumble if the series of disasters the British had endured continued.[250] He also pointed out that while Britain's navy was her great strength, her land forces were not as well accomplished and since this was a land war Australia's help was especially needed.

I hough he supported the Boer war, the member for St George was not reflexively militaristic. In July the next year Lyne proposed to send a contingent of troops to China to help put down the Boxer rebellion. The rebellion threatened a British "sphere of influence" rather than a Colony and Carruthers came out against it. He pointed out that no war had been declared, the Imperial Government had not asked for help and that the great powers of the world stood in line with Britain and hence there was no real danger. He went on to argue that "it is a very dangerous thing in these small and young countries to excite the warlike ardour of the people unless there is a great occasion for that stance to be taken", a reference to the ugly side of jingoism that had revealed itself with the outbreak of the Boer war.[251] An expedition would be wasteful both in terms of lives and money, to spend large sums of which "on un-called-for expeditions, is practically depriving the taxpayers of what they have a right to expect from the Parliament – a rigid protection of the revenues of the colony". Carruthers was isolated in his liberal stance and absented himself from the House as the question was resolved with an overwhelming majority.

The act of federation had not been completed with the success of the Federal referendum in New South Wales and elsewhere. For that to be achieved the Constitution still needed to pass the Imperial Parliament. This would not be a simple task for the Imperial Government had already expressed a number of concerns in secret memoranda given to Reid during his 1897 visit to England. Pre-empting some difficulties, a Premiers' Conference held in early 1900 appointed a delegation to travel to the Mother Country and urge the passage of the Bill. Each Colony was given only one representative, and inevitably Edmund Barton was appointed as the New South Wales delegate. The limited number of delegates meant that the multiplicity of views which had been a defining part of the Constitutional Conventions would not be represented in England. This would be most evident in the fight over clause 74, which dealt with appeals to the Privy Council.

The delegation arrived in England determined to have the Bill passed as it currently stood. The Imperial Government, chiefly represented by the Secretary of State for the Colonies Joseph Chamberlain, was equally determined to see some changes. The most controversial issue was clause 74, with the Crown Law Office determined to protect the Royal Prerogative to grant a special leave of appeal to Her Majesty in Council. This was substantially the same as the amendment Carruthers and Joseph Abbott had supported at the Melbourne Convention. The Imperial Government justified its position by arguing that a united Empire needed a single highest court of appeal and pointing to Canadian precedent.

In rejecting this amendment the delegation spoke as if the whole of Australia opposed any changes to the clause, ignoring the fact that the convention had been highly divided over this issue. This prompted Carruthers, who had been closely following events in England, to weigh in on the debate. He sent a letter to the *Times* in London, which declared that rejection of clause 74 would not offend Australian sensibilities, nor would it delay the accomplishment of federation.

Back at home he elaborated his position. He pointed to the fact that of the great many petitions the Federal Conventions had received not one had asked for removal of Privy Council appeals and that the convention itself had been contradictory on the issue, initially rejecting Privy Council appeals in all cases except interpretation of the Constitution and then entirely inverting its position. Beyond the constitutional interpretation issue, he argued that the Constitution as it currently stood left the Federal Parliament with the power to end Privy Council appeals altogether, something that could undermine the confidence of the British investors which Australia's economy relied upon. He maintained that it was a "shallow argument" that Australia should be able to interpret its own laws when the vast majority of its laws were British common law.[252] He summed up by quoting Edmund Burke, "change is an ill-omen to happy ears".

The Burke quote is highly revealing. Essentially Carruthers was contending that if the system was not broken it did not need fixing and that change for change's sake was both illogical and dangerous. Such sentiment is a central part of the melding of liberalism and conservatism in Australian politics. Carruthers saw traditional British institutions, which through long struggles had evolved to become more liberal over time, as a safeguard of the individual freedoms which were essential to his ideological outlook. As a liberal he felt that these institutions would and should continue to evolve, but to throw them away entirely would be to unnecessarily discard a safety net. As a student of history Carruthers also felt that freedom was not inevitable or innate, and rightly or wrongly he did not see the same level of liberty in countries which did not have the British institutions he was trying to protect. It is worth noting that Burke's writings also justified the creation of political parties based on shared principles, and it appears they influenced Carruthers considerably.

Carruthers' intervention in the last stage of the Federal battle would prove unsuccessful. In the end it was the Imperial Government and not the delegation which backed down. Despite creative suggestions of compromise such as appointing colonial members to the Privy Council, clause 74 was left as the Melbourne Convention had controversially shaped it. Barton won the day and would later receive his reward when he was elevated to the first bench of the High Court. With the last obstacle overcome, federation finally received Royal Assent on 9 July.

Preparations for the first Federal election had already begun. Early in 1900 an attempt was made to create a national free trade association to coordinate the upcoming fiscal fight. This saw a reuniting of McMillan and Bruce Smith with the main body of the Free Traders, but Bernhard Wise stayed aloof. As a member of what was essentially a Protectionist Government, he concocted the argument that a fiscal fight might wreck the Constitution in its early years of operation and hence he advocated a fiscal truce.[253] Though certainly no advocate of a fiscal truce, initially Reid also kept his distance from the attempt to create an extra-parliamentary organisation. It is likely that he did not want to appear to be presupposing a position of leadership in the national movement, and he was able to rely on Carruthers' presence to steer the organisation down his desired path. After a preliminary meeting which received the written support of the member for St George, an Australian Free Trade Conference was arranged to be held over several days in Sydney. Delegations from New South Wales, Victoria, Queensland and South Australia all attended, while Carruthers expressed regret at the absence of Tasmania.

Carruthers would play a prominent role throughout the conference. He successfully stressed unity as the meeting threatened to tear itself apart over whether it should advocate a low tariff or no tariff at all. In such circumstances the fringe single taxers once again reared their heads, but they were unsuccessful and the conference left its definition of free trade vague enough to appeal to both moderates and hardliners. Carruthers' most important action was to move a motion stating that the purpose of the organisation "shall be to ensure commercial freedom and the application of other liberal principles for the benefit of the people of the Australian Commonwealth".[254] The connection of commercial freedom to liberalism makes it clear that these "liberal principles" were intended to connote limited government, rather than the interventionist interpretation of liberalism prevalent in some of the other Colonies.

Carruthers' insistence that the organisation propagate a broad liberal philosophy as well as a fiscal position led to it being called the Australian Free Trade and Liberal Association, a reference to the defunct experiment of 1889. Though the specifics of a program had yet to be defined, Carruthers was trying to connect free trade to a wider liberal agenda as had been achieved in New South Wales. The problem was that on the national stage the distillation of a crystallised "liberalism" from loose theory would prove even more difficult than it had been in the Mother Colony. With regional and cultural differences further complicating what was already a controversial process, it would ultimately take years for circumstance and negotiation to produce a unified and stable "Liberal Party" in the new Parliament. The AFTLA would be successful in setting up divisions in most States of the Commonwealth, but an attempt to unify them through a National Council ultimately came to nothing.

Under the auspices of the AFTLA, a large demonstration was held in

December 1900 which saw Carruthers, Reid, McMillan and Bruce Smith stand united on the same platform for the first time in years. Carruthers used the occasion to launch an attack on the notion that the fiscal fight would endanger the Constitution. He argued that the presence of the ultra-Federalist McMillan proved these scare tactics false and assailed Wise "who won prominence on his espousal of free trade principles" for his absence from the Free Trade camp.[255] Led by the casual Protectionist Barton, the Protectionists had already begun downplaying their fiscal identity and had omitted any mention of it in the title of their Australian Liberal Association.

The federated Commonwealth of Australia was inaugurated on 1 January 1901 with a historic ceremony in Sydney. Grand arches were erected along the length of Pitt Street as representatives from every section of Australian society joined troops and dignitaries from all corners of the Empire in marching through the city. The procession led up to an impressive octagonal pavilion erected in the centre of Centennial Park. There the first Governor-General, Lord Hopetoun, and the first Federal Ministry were sworn in in front of a crowd the likes of which Sydney had never seen. That Ministry were to act as caretakers before the first Federal election could be held. Hopetoun had initially approached Lyne to be commissioned as Prime Minister but his former critiques of federation meant that he was unable to attract support. Instead Barton was chosen in his place. The preference for a New South Welshman made it clear that the position would have gone to Reid had he continued to be Premier, something that would only have been possible with further concessions to Labor that went beyond his liberal principles. As a former Federal delegate Carruthers took a central part in the celebratory proceedings, and beamed with pride at the show his city had put on for the world.

Less than two months later and with the Federal election fast approaching Carruthers announced his intentions regarding the contest. Up until that point it had been almost universally assumed that he would stand for a Federal seat. This logical assumption was based on the fact that he had been a Federal delegate, a founder of the AFTLA and appeared to have already begun his electioneering. Newspapers initially had him down for the theoretical seat of Cronulla, but when that entity did not eventuate he was said to be a certainty for the seat of Lang which included his stronghold of Kogarah. It would prove to be a very safe Free Trade seat which would not fall into Labor hands until 1928. Despite being assured of victory, Carruthers shocked the Australian political world by deciding not to stand.

This was one of the most important decisions of Carruthers' life and understanding the reasons why he made it is critical since it would forever change Australian and New South Wales political history. The explanation Carruthers gave reporters was that his private business commitments demanded too much of his attention to allow his taking part in political matters.[256] He had been able to juggle business and politics when it came to Colonial Parliament, so it was the capital site which New South Welshmen had temporarily sacrificed which forced this decision.

Business was likely only part of the reason why Carruthers gave up his Federal aspirations. After all, Reid was in a similar financial predicament and he was able to balance his commitments and head to Melbourne, even if these commitments did jeopardise his ultimate political success. There is some suggestion that Carruthers had his eye on the Premiership. This is certainly plausible. As someone who had fought hard for the autonomy of the States he would have been well aware that theoretically State Parliaments still had at least as many powers and responsibilities as their Federal counterpart. With Reid, Lyne and Barton exiting the stage Carruthers could be confident that his political acumen could bring him to the top of parliamentary ladder. On the other hand he would have known that the Federal leadership would inevitably come with more prestige and since he was more than a decade younger than Reid he could afford to wait it out behind his talented chief.

Beverley Earnshaw has suggested that it was Carruthers' poor health and young family that informed his decision.[257] Once again this is a likely scenario as Alice had already persuaded him not to become Agent-General because of a disinclination to move. The death of Jack would have also heightened his desire to spend as much time as possible with his family, something that long trips south would have surely hindered. It is intriguing how late Carruthers left the decision, making his announcement a little over a month out from the ballot after the election campaign had well and truly begun. In December a noticeably torn Carruthers had told Barton of his "hope" to be in the Federal Parliament but warned him that it may not be possible.[258] He clearly did not find the decision to be an easy one.

As with most important historical events it is likely that a number of factors, some of which we will never know, combined to determine Carruthers' choice. In many ways it was a choice which confined him to the historical footnotes, as though his important role had yet to reach its crescendo, the regional setting of the rest of his story has largely obscured it from academic view. This is in spite of the fact that the rest of his career would have a greater impact on national politics than those of many Federal ministers.

In the short to medium term the person who would be most affected by Carruthers' absence from Federal politics was George Reid. The value of Reid's first lieutenant in paving the way for the success of his Premiership is difficult to exaggerate. Though Reid was certainly the senior figure in the relationship, the two men had been partners in public and private politics since Parkes' exit in 1891. Their colleague A.B. Piddington once wrote:

> Reid was a man with hundreds of friends but no friendship. When it came to any crisis involving a profound choice, I doubt whether there was anyone to whom Reid would instinctively turn as a man does to an intimate friend for counsel. Yet no man needed intimate friendship more, because the singular thing about him was that, when isolated from immediate contact with affairs, he was apt to make egregious errors in judgment.[259]

If Reid ever experienced true friendship he experienced it with Carruthers. Unfortunately for the historian, the friends' relationship was so close that little formal correspondence between them survives for they generally spoke in person, over the telephone or through handwritten notes. A few of these notes survive and they are enough to glimpse the fact that Carruthers was Reid's counsel of the type Piddington described. Distance and busy lives meant that after federation they would steadily drift apart and the "egregious errors in judgment" notably absent for much of Reid's Premiership would increase. It would take Reid years to find a Federal political deputy who could come close to filling Carruthers' shoes. In 1906 he would settle on Joseph Cook but by that time the fiscal battle had already been lost.

Sir Joseph Carruthers, one of the Fathers of Federation.
From the Mitchell Library, Sydney.

Carruthers with some of his numerous animals.
From the Mitchell Library, Sydney.

CHAPTER NINE

The Political Wilderness

Carruthers' role in the first Federal election campaign did not end with his decision to remain in State politics. He continued to campaign hard in the seat of Lang, though now he advocated the election of the Free Trade candidate Francis McLean rather than himself. McLean was the State member for Marrickville who after Carruthers' withdrawal had seized upon the chance to represent his local constituency in Federal Parliament. Whether Carruthers' decision had been at all influenced by his colleague's desire to stand for Lang is difficult to tell, though it is certain that if the member for St George wanted the seat it would have been his. Carruthers' campaigning was not limited to his locality as he also delivered a speech at a mass rally the night before the election. In New South Wales the poll saw a great victory for the Free Traders, particularly in the Senate where they won five of the six seats on offer. Elsewhere, weak Free Trade organisations found it impossible to overcome the advantages given to the Protectionists by their unelected incumbency and Barton held on to the Prime Ministership despite failing to achieve a clear majority.

The election devastated the ranks of the New South Wales Parliament. Eighteen members ascended to the Federal Chambers, as all three major parties lost many of their leading men. The list included Barton, Reid, Lyne, Hughes, Watson, Cook and Dugald Thomson, to name just some of those whose absence would be noticeable. Not all who tried succeeded in moving up however. Two important failures were Labor leader James McGowen and Bernhard Wise. McGowen narrowly lost to the Free Trade candidate in South Sydney. Meanwhile, despite his prominence, Wise once again proved he was not personally popular amongst electors by comfortably losing the seat of Canobolas to the Labor candidate.

Not only had the ranks of the New South Wales Parliament been thinned, but that body's role had fundamentally changed. It lost the power to make laws on tariffs and defence, but it also had to contend with its new position "below" the national Parliament. Though it retained residual powers greater than its new counterpart, the State Parliament had undeniably lost some of its autonomy and prestige. The extent of these losses and how they would affect the nature of politics remained to be seen. Many departments and properties such as the post office had to be handed over, and the State Government was left with the expectation it would contract in size to reflect its newly reduced role. Despite some clear expectations much remained murky and a palpable sense of confusion gripped those whose actions would determine the practical workings of a bare-boned Constitution.

When Lyne left the Premiership he was replaced by John See in what was a relatively painless transfer of power. See was a long-time friend of Carruthers and despite their fiscal differences the two men had much in common both personally and politically. The son of a poor farm labourer, See was a self-made man of the type Carruthers admired. Such was the respect in which Carruthers held the new Premier that See's biographer, Keith Henry, decided to introduce his subject with a quote from the member for St George.[260]

The two men shared a rejection of class based politics and a belief that business was generally best left unregulated. Where they differed was over See's belief in "material progress", something that he felt could be achieved through government spending for national development purposes. Henry suggests that this belief was the defining principle of See's politics, and that See was willing to increase both debt and taxation in order to achieve it. Carruthers also believed in material progress as evidenced by his untiring support for closer settlement, but he felt that excessive debt and high taxation threatened rather than helped that progress. As Premier See would fail to exercise much control over his Ministers, and this meant that while spending would prove a hallmark of his Government, those principles which he shared with Carruthers would have little impact on ministerial policy.

See became Premier at a time when the fiscal issue had theoretically been removed from State politics and parliamentary talent had been greatly thinned. With these facts in mind, he came up with the idea of forming a coalition ministry out of the best men from each of the parties on the basis of an abstract principle of good government. The New South Wales Free Trade Party had yet to replace Reid as leader, so instead of broaching the idea with the Leader of the Opposition, See approached individual Free Trade members with the proposition. McGowen was also contacted, but due to the rules of his party he was never any chance of his accepting a portfolio.

One of the first people to be approached was Carruthers who was open to the idea of a coalition. He spoke to Reid about it, but the two men met in a crowded public place and the loud noise led to a fundamental misunderstanding.[261] When Carruthers told Reid that he had been approached from the other side, Reid took it that he had been approached about the Leadership of the Opposition not a coalition, hence he did not advise Carruthers to reject the overtures.

Assuming he had his leader's tacit support, Carruthers began to negotiate with See over the Easter long weekend. When he sought further advice, Reid was out of town and could not be reached. Carruthers then spoke to several Free Trade members including James Ashton and John Garland, most of whom intimated that a coalition was a good idea and worth pursuing. Carruthers finally heard from Reid on Easter Saturday, receiving a wire which said "prefer not to advise. Suggest consulting party, all leading members thereof".[262] It was later revealed that Reid was firmly against a coalition and it is likely that he only decided not to advise breaking off the negotiations since, due to the earlier misunderstanding, they had already progressed too far for him to directly intervene. After all he was now a Federal member who theoretically should not have been in control of the State party and was thus wary of being seen as pulling the strings. Reid had been backed into a corner by circumstance and at this critical moment he let his friend down. Carruthers would later lament the ambivalent response since Reid had "frequently in times of stress and trial sought my advice and got it freely".[263]

Having received Reid's reply Carruthers, who had already consulted all the leading Free Traders he could get hold of, continued his discussions with See and was able to get an agreement that four Free Trade members would be included in the prospective coalition cabinet. One of the Free Traders proposed was Brunker, who caught a train into Sydney and held discussions with Carruthers, Reid and Charles Lee. Reid showed consistency by not advising Brunker either way, and the latter made up his own mind and informed See that he could not accept a portfolio.[264] Brunker's decision wrecked the project and negotiations were broken off.

Throughout the discussions the *Daily Telegraph, Sydney Morning Herald* and *Evening News* had all come out against the coalition which they argued would unjustifiably prop up the existing Ministry and hurt the Federal Free Trade Party. There was a widespread argument that the fiscal issue should be kept alive in State politics so that State Parliament could act as a training ground for Federal politicians, something that the coalition would inherently inhibit. When the scheme fell through the press and aggravated Free Traders made Carruthers the scapegoat for the fact that it was attempted in the first place. He was forced to justify painstakingly his actions through the series of speeches and newspaper interviews which inform the account of events just given.

The public account is corroborated by a frantic telegram and letter from Reid which survive in Carruthers' papers. In these the misunderstanding is discussed, and it is clear that both men are aware that the recent events have gravely impacted on Carruthers' chances of inheriting the leadership. A regretful Reid wrote that he considered Carruthers "the most capable leader that the party could elect".[265] The debacle made it clear that the Free Trade Party needed to elect a new leader as soon as possible, but Reid made sure that his official retirement from the leadership and the subsequent election took place at separate meetings in order to give Carruthers a chance to regroup his position. The damage had already been done however, and Carruthers had no real hope of re-establishing himself in time. The leadership election took place on 16 April. According to one account Carruthers was nominated by Thomas

Jessop but knowing that he could not succeed refused to stand.[266] Ashton and Brunker also refused their nominations, and in the end Charles Lee, who had been one of the firmest opponents of the coalition, was elected unopposed.

Though See could hardly have planned the results, the abortive coalition could not have been more beneficial to the Protectionists or more detrimental to the Free Traders. The Free Trade Party had been torn asunder, with deep divisions exposed to the voting public. Worse still, Reid's logical replacement and one of the most talented politicians in the State Parliament had been barred from the leadership. Instead a mundane roads-and-bridges member had been elected in his place. A successful storekeeper from Tenterfield, Lee was a staunch believer in free trade but he was far from a political visionary. The only post he had held was Minister for Justice, and even then only for the brief period between the 1898 election and Reid's fall. The *Freeman's Journal* found him so uninspiring that they were left to speculate that Carruthers' supporters had elected Lee as a deliberate stop gap knowing that he would fail.[267] Carruthers would later recall that while he and Lee were "strong personal friends", his new leader was "not a fighter".[268] The Ministry's position, which should have been extremely tentative given the success of the State's Free Traders in the Federal election, was thus consolidated.

While the consequences of the attempt to form a coalition are relatively clear, one question is far more difficult to answer. That is why, regardless of Reid's advice, did Carruthers want to pursue a coalition? Any answer must be largely speculative as the man himself provides us with few clues. Certainly the abstract notion of good government which motivated See also helped to convince Carruthers. See was his friend, as was fellow Protectionist Thomas Waddell. Carruthers may have thought that with four Free Traders in cabinet the Protectionists could be steered down a limited government path and that their interventionist instincts could be curbed. Indeed, he may have hoped that in such a combination the undesirable elements of the Labor Party could be marginalised as could the big government and conservative wings of both fiscal parties, resulting in a more liberal Parliament than that which existed before the coalition. John Haynes and William Mahony later suggested that the co-alition was intended to "dish" both Labor and O'Sullivan, though their accounts are controversial and Carruthers denied them.[269] John Rickard has asserted that McMillan's support for the proposed coalition suggests that it was intended to be anti-Labor, but his support could easily be attributed to his position as a former National Federalist Free Trader.[270] It is likely that Carruthers' business commitments which had so recently kept him out of Federal politics also informed his decision, since he would have to spend less time in a coalition House provided that coalition continued to pursue his liberal goals.

What is clear is that, despite the fact that he would be a convinced Free Trader his entire life, Carruthers did not buy into the argument that the fiscal issue should arbitrarily be kept alive in State politics for the benefit of the Federal Parliament. For someone who believed in the continued importance of the States, the New South Wales Government still had far too many responsibilities to allow that distraction to get in the way of meaningful legislation.

If the abortive coalition was not intended to be anti-Labor, then it potentially represented the last gasp of the factional era. That era had been characterised by shifting alliances and broad coalitions of the kind a coming together of Carruthers and See would have represented. Throughout the negotiations it appears that Carruthers viewed himself primarily as an individual member with political friendships and alliances, rather than the committed representative of a party. This viewpoint was largely the product of the temporary death of his party's central premise, but it echoed the approach of an earlier pre-fiscal and pre-party age. As has already been discussed, Carruthers saw significant problems with the functioning of the three-party system during the 1890s and the grand coalition may have been intended to overcome these issues by overcoming the party system itself.

There were some major problems with this idea. Firstly the members of the Labor Party could not be expected to adhere to the liberal-indi-vidualist ideals of an earlier age, while socialist proposals also suggested the necessity of unified opposition. Secondly, the negative reaction of the press and the broader public to the coalition proposals showed that partisanship had progressed to a stage where broad concord would no longer be accepted by the electorate. For these reasons Carruthers' flirtation with the idea of a grand coalition was fleeting and he soon re-embraced partisanship and party which had otherwise been central to his political career.

When See's elaborate plans fell through he was forced to construct a Ministry out of his existing Protectionist supporters. In essence it would be a continuation of the Lyne Government, with the notable inclusion of Thomas Waddell as State Treasurer. A pastoralist with a keen interest in the business side of his enterprise, Waddell had long been friends with Carruthers and generally sympathised with his small-government outlook. Apart from the Premier and Treasurer the two most conspicuous members of the Ministry would be the Minister for Lands Paddy Crick and the Secretary for Public Works Edward O'Sullivan. The former was a notorious drunkard and gambler who, partly because of these traits, proved to be one of the most boisterous members to ever haunt the Macquarie Street bear garden. Slightly more tactful but nevertheless powerful, O'Sullivan had long occupied the leftward fringe of the Protectionist Party. During the Reid years that group had suffered from their party's association with the conservative Legislative Council, but the alliance with Labor had helped to re-energise them.

As already noted, O'Sullivan had begun a controversial spending program during the time of the Lyne Ministry. Under See this would accelerate, even in the face of drought and unemployment. The motivation for the program was proto-Keynesian, as O'Sullivan believed that public works day-labour could "promote economic activity and create employment".[271] Carruthers would take the opposite view that the effects of the debt involved in such a program, and the concerns it raised amongst private investors, harmed rather than helped the New South Wales economy. While Carruthers did not oppose putting the unemployed to productive work for humanitarian reasons temporarily, he believed that the continuous use of such a system would degrade people by making them entirely reliant on the Government. Hence, as a threat to individualism,

Carruthers had an ideological and to some extent moral objection to the program that went hand in hand with his financial objections. Over time the budgetary and economic consequences of the public works program would become one of the central issues of State politics and, because O'Sullivan was seen as a "Labor" influence within the Government, this debate would help to accelerate a Liberal-Labor political realignment.

The House had not sat since early December 1900, and the former and current Premiers were facing severe criticism for allegedly running the Government as their own personal dictatorship free from parliamentary responsibility. In the face of these attacks See flagged a June election for a July sitting, excusing the continued delay on account of a visit by the Duke of York to Sydney. The big question both fiscal Parties would have to face before the election was how were they going to restyle themselves now that their defining policy had been removed from State control.

Pushed on by the desire of the press not to let the fiscal issue die, Lee avoided a whole scale reconstruction of the Free Trade Party. He did pick up the liberal ideology that had long been attached to his side of politics and renamed the Opposition the Liberal Party, but he lacked a clear vision as to how to turn liberalism into the *raison d'être* for a political party. Carruthers was noticeably less faithful to his new leader than he had been to his old and part of the reason for this may have been Lee's failure to produce a crystallised liberal agenda. Reid himself had found it difficult to re-energise liberalism following his tremendous successes and New South Wales politics was in a bit of a holding pattern following federation, so it was perhaps the magnitude of the task rather than a personal failing of Lee which produced this stagnation. Nevertheless, there is a sense that Carruthers felt that he knew how to adapt liberalism into a convincing electoral position and wanted to be in charge at this pivotal juncture.

The Liberals were not the only party undergoing an existential crisis. The Protectionists also needed to create a post-fiscal identity. They decided to restyle themselves as the Progressives with the establishment of the Political Progressive Association. While the concept of liberalism was certainly open to interpretation, progressivism was almost entirely free of inherent ideological meaning. What was progress was entirely subjective, and See's "material progress" did not necessarily correlate with what O'Sullivan, who largely ran the PPA, meant by the word.

Though he had failed to capture the leadership, Carruthers was not prepared to take a back seat whilst Lee's free trade Liberals tried to rei-magine themselves. A little over a week after the leadership contest the member for St George took the initiative and delivered his own personal program as to what the Liberal Party should become. In a controversial speech at Rockdale he rejected the idea of using the fiscal issue to coast towards an easy election victory. Instead he proposed a fresh liberal agenda consisting of sound public finance, a comprehensive system of local government, Upper House reform, water conservation, the establishment of a State bank, the extension of technical education and the creation of mining schools.[272] He paid tribute to the way the Lyne-See Government had handled the Boer war and had instituted old age pensions, but he differentiated himself from them by attacking their extravagant spending. He argued that the revenue had been artificially inflated through the rents created by the resumption of Darling Harbour, while the interest due to those whose properties had been resumed had yet to be paid; hence the State was in a far worse financial situation than it initially appeared. He also questioned the creation of honorary Ministers without parliamentary approval, suggesting that it was unconstitutional.

While Carruthers was expected to make such attacks on the Government, he also called his own leader into question by suggesting that he was not committed to the reduction of State members. This was a popular issue which, following on from cost saving suggestions Carruthers had made during the federation campaign, sought a reduction in the members of the Legislative Assembly based on the fact that it now held fewer responsibilities. Carruthers was keen to use this opportunity for electoral reform to decrease the discrepancy between the number of electors in rural and city seats, but Lee, who represented a rural constituency, had made some statements defending the existing imbalance to which the former drew attention. Carruthers also questioned what he saw as Lee's condemnation of a seven shillings a day minimum wage on public works, a system which had been introduced by Reid Minister J.H. Young and extended by O'Sullivan. This was something that Carruthers supported, provided that it was ensured that each man receiving it did a full day's work and provided that the work was necessary and did not draw labourers required in the country into the city.

In response to the Rockdale speech Lee defended himself in the *Sydney Morning Herald* and suggested that "candid critics are generally admitted to be doubtful friends".[273] Many followed his lead and began to call Carruthers' loyalty into question. Rather than commit an act of simple disloyalty, it is likely that Carruthers was trying to make the tail wag the dog and control the direction his party was travelling from its rear ranks. For the moment he was not about to make the mistake of following Wise and McMillan's path of outright independence and he soon reconciled himself with his leader.

If Carruthers' intention was to shape the Liberal Party's platform then he largely succeeded in his goal. When Lee later delivered his election manifesto he committed himself to ending wasteful expenditure, reducing the number of members, municipal reform, the extension of technical education and water conservation.[274] While Lee's program resembled Carruthers', it was also almost identical to that delivered by See. With the fiscal issue gone both fiscal parties continued to search almost blindly for a unique agenda and while the financial issue that would be central to the next election was already there, it had not yet reached such a dire point as to allow Lee to define himself by it in the way that Carruthers later would. The similarities between "tweedle-See" and "tweedle-Lee" were exaggerated by the fact that they were both rural members, hence even the old city-country divide that had underpinned much of the fiscal division largely faded into the background. Many of those manifesto points which Lee had not borrowed from Carruthers focused on rural interests such as the appointment of a Minister for Agriculture. While the votes of powerful interest groups like the Farmers' and Settlers' Association were important, there was no underlying ideology that could connect these reforms to an overall "philosophy of government" to be conveyed to the electors.

In spite of their public spat, Carruthers was too important to Lee's election chances to be left out of the campaign. When a Liberal Executive Committee was formed to help select candidates, arbitrate disputes and preach the liberal message, Carruthers was given an important position on it. Reflecting the desire of the press and others to keep the fiscal issue alive in State politics, the LEC was directly tied to the AFTLA. The problems of preselection which had always proved a great difficulty for the party would be particularly acute in 1901. This was because of the great divisions amongst its supporters, including splits over the attempted coalition, the importance of the fiscal issue and the return of a number of anti-Reid Free Traders into the party fold. In these circumstances Lee simply did not command the respect required to enforce unity and despite the efforts of senior members like Carruthers, vote splitting would cost the Liberals more seats than ever before.

The organisational failings of the Liberals contrasted strongly with the Progressives who fought what was arguably their best run campaign. O'Sullivan's biographer Bruce Mansfield has argued that it was the organisational brilliance of his subject that won the Progressives the election in the face of fierce press opposition.[275] While O'Sullivan's role was important, the key to the election result was Lee's failure to inspire people enough to unseat incumbents. The Liberals lost a number of seats to vote splitting in the city, but it was their failure to make significant inroads in the country despite Lee's rural focus that ultimately cost them the election. Even Mansfield admits that O'Sullivan's quasi-socialist spending failed to win many votes in the city, so once again it was the over represented country seats that gave the Progressives their foothold. The Progressives did not have it all their own way in the country as many disillusioned Protectionists ended up voting for independents or Labor, but as long as these protest votes did not fall to the Liberals they were not going to affect the balance of power. "Tweedle-See" proved to be just as unimpressive as "tweedle-Lee", for despite holding onto Government the Progressive vote was significantly down on the National Federal vote of 1898.

The big winners from the election were the Labor Party who had capitalised on their opponents' lack of direction and poor leadership. Labor effectively won 24 seats, the Progressives 41 and the Liberals 37.[276] The weakness of the former fiscal parties also led to a large number of independents being elected. Despite holding fewer seats, the Liberals received 33.32% of the popular vote to the Progressives 22.08%, which to men like Carruthers was a clear indication of the need for further electoral reform. In St George, Carruthers once again received almost 70% of the vote. Significantly, for the first time in years his local opponent was not a Progressive candidate but a Labor Party man. This was a glimpse at the fact that in the city at least, elections were already on the road to becoming a Liberal-Labor contest.

In the election post-mortem some thought that the Liberals should have pushed Free Trade harder in order to achieve a victory. The *Evening News* held this opinion, and criticised Carruthers' role in the "sinking" the fiscal issue. Others thought the opposite, and suggested that Lee's free trade fight had failed proving that the fiscal issue was now dead in State politics. Carruthers himself was not about to fall back from his position, and immediately after the election he pointed to a new non-fiscal path by launching an attack on the disproportionate influence of the Labor Party who continued to hold the balance of power. Criticising the Ministerialists for letting Labor direct their agenda towards extensive regulation and expansionary spending even though most Progressive members were philosophically closer to the Liberals, he insisted that the parties:

> must fairly represent the opinions of the people according to well-defined lines of cleavage, because they will then ensure that all public questions shall be decided on the broad principles that underlie them, and not on the question of placating a minority in or out of Parliament … I believe in party government. I believe it is the true safeguard of the Constitution and of the liberties of the people, and the sooner we get back to a true system of party government the better for its future.[277]

In this important statement Carruthers was heralding the dawn of the fourth stage of the development of the Australian party system. First there had been factional politics based on personality more than ideology, then there had been the fiscal parties whose unifying principles had been limited to a specific area, and then there had been the birth of the FTLA and the Labor Party, both of which claimed to represent a broad ideology but had not yet managed to make an ideological gap the central dividing line in New South Wales or Australian politics. Now Carruthers was suggesting that the centrality of that ideological divide was essential to making parliamentary government work. In doing so he was breaking with the nineteenth-century idea which held that party government was the antithesis of individual liberty for it restricted the independence of members of Parliament. Instead he was arguing that an ideologically divided party system was the only way to ensure liberty for it was the only way to ensure the electors knew for what they were voting. The binary nature of the clear lines of cleavage would help to make a two-party system, ending the three-party turmoil that had hindered parliament and given disproportionate and therefore undemocratic influence to those holding the balance of power.

At the time Carruthers still envisaged this line of cleavage as that between liberals and conservatives to the exclusion of Labor, who he felt had no right to claim a monopoly over progressive legislation. This soon changed however, as the place of traditional conservatives in Carruthers' formulation was taken by an increasingly "socialist" Labor Party. This perceived socialism came first in support for extensive interventionist policies including those of O'Sullivan, and would culminate in a debate over nationalisation and a decision to place the "extension of the industrial and economic functions of the state" on the Labor platform. Once liberals began to feel that the most significant threat to individual liberty and enterprise came from the left and not the right, politicians were able to rhetorically position their liberal beliefs in opposition to socialism and the modern Australian political divide was born. Acceptance of the notion that liberalism once again had a clear enemy would be the final step in the process by which the ideology was adapted from a pervasive culture into a partisan agenda. Labor's foreignness to the preceding culture was perhaps the main impetus behind this transformation, but Carruthers would play a central role in facilitating and justifying the change.

Under Carruthers' "well-defined" lines of cleavage important questions like private enterprise or nationalisation, small government or big government, low-taxation or high spending and individualism or collectivism could be made the central choice at the ballot box in a Liberal-Labor party system. In practice other issues have inevitably dominated particular elections and even particular electorates, but over time these fundamental questions have continually reasserted themselves. The relative "philosophical positions" presented by the parties have been held flexibly rather than dogmatically, but a two-party system requires pragmatism in order to prevent the fracturing of the respective sides, and this was something that Carruthers himself showed. It could be argued that this flexibility has meant that at times the lines of cleavage have not been "well-defined", but the differences between Liberal and Labor have almost always been clearer than those between Liberal and Progressive in 1901. At times the Liberals have supported big government and regulation, while at the other end Labor has occasionally supported privatisation and deregulation, but though the political climate has constantly readjusted where the centre of politics sits, Liberals have almost always sat on the individualist and enterprising right of that centre while Labor have sat on the collectivist and interventionist left of it. The rest of Carruthers' career in the Legislative Assembly would be dedicated to establishing these lines of cleavage and reaping the legislative benefits of stable government.

Though Carruthers had already begun to set the agenda of realignment that would dominate the next decade of Australian politics, he still nominally owed allegiance to Lee. As Parliament prepared to sit on 23 July there were rumours that Carruthers and James Ashton were preparing to abandon their leader and form a new party with a number of independents. The son of Victorian coffee roasters, Ashton had left school aged ten and worked his way up through the printing business to become a regional newspaper proprietor. He was a tall, muscular man with a strong jaw and a steely resolve. Though self-educated, he was intelligent and optimistic and formed a good foil for Carruthers' bookish realism. The two men developed a close personal and political association. This was perhaps because Ashton, the member for Hay then Goulburn, had been one of the more informed and helpful rural Free Traders Carruthers dealt with as Minister for Lands. A common love of cricket also helped.

The member for St George did little to scotch the rumours of a split by sitting on the crossbenches, but it was soon revealed that his new found independence did not stretch to the point of creating a separate party. In the debate over the address in reply he declared that until the new lines of cleavage revealed themselves, he preferred "to remain with the old friends with whom I have worked in harmony for so many years".[278] While this implied a tacit support for the official Opposition, it was also quite a literal statement for Carruthers would be joined in his semi-independent stance by James Brunker. This left Lee, already outnumbered and outclassed in Parliament, without the help of his two most important colleagues.

Throughout the session Carruthers continually tried to capture the political initiative. He pushed hard for a royal commission into education to assess the viability of the reforms such as more rigorous teacher training and the reorganisation and extension of industrial education. The former Minister for Public Instruction even organised public meetings to press the Government on the issue, speaking side by side with Mc-Gowen at the Sydney Town Hall. He also fought for the construction of inner-city railways, a project that had stagnated despite the Government's inflated public works budget.

Carruthers' most important act was the introduction of his State Labour Selection Bill. This sought to end political patronage in the administration of day-labour by removing the responsibility of giving of contracts from the office of the Secretary for Public Works and placing it in the hands of an independent board. In introducing the Bill for its second reading Carruthers intimated that he hoped to end the evil:

> which tends to make working-men mere political hangers-on, in
> order to get a job, rather than independent men who obtain em-
> ployment by reason of their skill and ability to do the work they
> have to perform … the moment you commence to sap the in-

dependence of the working-classes and make them political crea-
tures, beholden for a day's work to the favour of some politician or
Minister, that moment you degrade labour more than anything else
could possibly do, and in connection with our system of government, introduce a corrupt system which may be just as fruitful of
evil results as the worst case of the contract system.[279]

This statement clearly shows how Carruthers saw the day-labour system as a potential threat to the individualism he held dear. Though he
insisted that he was not actuated by any ill-feelings towards the Secretary for Public Works, the Bill was part of his ongoing conflict with
O'Sullivan. It was O'Sullivan who had greatly increased the system of
day-labour with his proto-Keynesian public works program. For Carruthers, the fact that the Secretary himself was handing out jobs left,
right and centre had more than a hint of corruption about it and though
his Bill would not stop the continued expansion of day-labour it could
hopefully make it not only more independent but also more efficient by
ensuring employees were chosen based on their skill rather than their
political motives.

The Bill was initially met with the hostility to be expected of something that hinted at government corruption. Carruthers himself thought
that it would fail. The reasoned argument underpinning the Bill made it
difficult for the Government to ignore however, and in the end O'Sullivan
acquiesced. The State Labour Board began working in January 1902 and
while it did not completely remove the influence of the Trades Hall in
deciding contracts it was still a considerable improvement on the previous system.[280] It was a remarkable achievement for Carruthers. Very
few people succeed in changing the law while out of Government, let
alone changing a law that affected one of the Ministry's signature policies. The contrast was stark between the political skill of the member for
St George and the Leader of the Opposition, with the latter's censure
attempts continuing to fail miserably.

One the most significant Acts of the 1901 parliamentary session was
the passing of Bernhard Wise's Industrial Arbitration Bill. This had initially been introduced in the previous year under Lyne. The main dif-

ference between it and previous Arbitration Bills was that it introduced compulsory arbitration, something that Carruthers had previously opposed. When it was first introduced Carruthers made little comment. It is likely that he was weighing up whether he should support the Bill his name had been associated with since the Parkes Ministry or reject it since compulsory arbitration removed what he had seen as the fundamental right of freedom of contract. The premise was that a free adult had the right to enter into any contract they wished and that the government had no right to take that freedom away from them. In the end Carruthers sensed the way the winds were blowing and reluctantly accepted the compulsory nature of the Bill.

In the House he felt compelled to justify this position by giving a whole series of precedents as to where some form of "interference" in business had proved necessary and successful, the elaborate detail of which suggests that he may have been trying to convince himself as much as anyone else. In many ways the speech was the least small-government Carruthers ever gave in his career, for it argued that "our system of government, and our very system of civilisation exists for the very purpose of controlling the brute forces of our nature, and in regulating them in the common interests of society".[281] Such a statement went beyond the pragmatism and flexibility normally associated with his generally small-government liberalism, and could be used to discount many of the principles for which he had been fighting throughout his career. There is a sense that at times like this Carruthers could get caught up in the rhetoric of his argument and lose sight of his real beliefs. This explains but does not excuse his political inconsistency and in time he would back away from his support for compulsory arbitration and resume his usual stance.

While he accepted the Bill's central premise, this did not mean that Carruthers was prepared to swallow the Bill in its entirety. He opposed the provision that allowed the Arbitration Court to give unionists a preference over non-unionists, insisting that if compulsory unionism was to be imposed it should be done through Parliament and not through the back ally of the courts. Later he also condemned its provisions for forcing people into unions by insisting that only unions and not individual employees could appear before the Arbitration Court. In his memoirs Carruthers recalled that he had implored Wise to remove this requirement for it would remove an individual's freedom and "create a system of industrial slavery in which the union would be the slave-owner and the slave-driver".[282] This testimony is difficult to corroborate, and it is likely that Carruthers was speaking in hindsight for in later years he would come to reject much of what is now known as the "Australian Settlement".

Another important Bill introduced in this session was the Women's Franchise Bill that finally gave women the vote in New South Wales. Carruthers took an extremely conservative attitude towards this reform. Though he admitted that women were as good, courageous and intelligent as men, he argued that the granting of suffrage was a revolutionary step, hence the burden of proof was on those who advocated it to prove that it was necessary. He maintained that the case for it had yet to be proven and that the majority of women were not asking for the vote. He also suggested that to give a woman the franchise would degrade her by bringing "her down to the level of the ballot box".[283]

Carruthers' illiberal line was undoubtedly out of step with his long support for equal and universal franchise for men, though he did argue that if women were to be given the franchise they must be given voting rights entirely equal to those of men and that they must also be granted the right to sit in Parliament. Rejecting See's suggestion that the right to sit in Parliament would eventually be granted through natural evolution, he insisted that:

> of all the high grounds that have ever been put forward for enfranchising women, there is the superlative ground for giving women the right to come in here and be the law-makers that for over sixty years the great lawmaker of our empire has been, the noblest woman probably that we have any record of … Queen Victoria.

Carruthers was at least consistent in his argument, as when experience did prove the case for women's suffrage he repudiated his previous opposition to it. This was not mere political opportunism, for when out of Parliament in 1908 he would actively help the British suffragette movement. He did this by giving a detailed statement on the positive effects of women's suffrage in Australia for the paper of the National Union of Women's Suffrage Societies.[284]

Carruthers' illiberal floundering over compulsory arbitration and women's suffrage had taken away most of the leverage he could have got out of the State Labour Selection Bill. It would take the resurrection of the fiscal issue to click him back into gear. While the tariff was now a Federal issue, what to do with the tariff revenue New South Wales received under the Braddon clause was undoubtedly a State concern. When it was revealed that the See Government was spending that revenue in advance of receiving it and that there would be no remission of State taxation to make up for the increased burden of Barton's new tariff, Carruthers rose up in anger.

He was soon engaged in an extended debate with Wise conducted through a series of statements to the *Sydney Morning Herald*. His main argument was that New South Wales only accepted the tariffs associated with federation under the impression that other taxes would be lowered and that both Progressives and Protectionists had broken their earlier promises on the cost of federation. During the federation campaign Wise had famously claimed that federation would cost each person no more than the price of registering a dog, but now that assertion proved to be false. Excluding service charges and rents which still made up the bulk of the State's revenue, the new tariff would mean a proportionately huge rise in the burden of taxation in New South Wales. Carruthers estimated that a sixth of the average worker's wage would go to duties on essentials like sugar; hence a labourer would not start earning money until the Tuesday of the working week.[285] Such a tangible, if slightly exaggerated, demonstration of the effects of the tax increase was typical of Carruthers' ability to make such issues relatable to his audience of ordinary voters.

Apart from debating Wise, Carruthers also spoke at a mass rally at the Sydney Town Hall with Reid and Lee and held his own rallies in conjunction with Ashton. At first glance it may appear that the revival of the tariff issue in State politics was a step backwards, but the arguments Carruthers used against it were a glimpse into the future of Australian liberalism. He based his opposition on a rejection of high taxation, excessive spending and a belief in sound finances, all of which would form the core economic values of the Liberal Party. Many of these were old liberal beliefs, but in an age of expanding government they would be made a new partisan agenda. Carruthers pointed out that New South Wales expenditure was now £2,400,000 higher than in the final year of the Reid Government, but argued that the State had little to show for this excess.[286] He conceded that the small proportion of that money which had been spent on old age pensions had been well allocated, but insisted that the vast majority of it had been frittered away through extravagance and small grants of no consequence.

In many ways the tariff proved the first step in the inexorable growth of government under federation. It did not affect the other States nearly as much for most of them already had a tariff based system of taxation, but the New South Wales precedent had shown how reluctant governments would be to forgo any opportunity to expand. This was in spite of the fact that the majority of public opinion appeared to favour a reduction in the size of State government post federation, not its expansion.

Carruthers gained considerable traction out of the campaign against the tariff, more so than Lee who used most of the same arguments to less effect. Part of the reason for this was the gravitas Carruthers held as a member of the Constitutional Conventions which allowed him greater use of the cry that federation had gone awry. Adding to this was his consistency, for throughout the federation campaign he had repeatedly opposed anything that threatened to increase the burdens of the people. His claim that Australia was now "the most over-governed and over-taxed country in the world" rang more true now than when he had uttered a similar phrase some years earlier, but his hope that the Braddon clause would dissuade Federal Governments from the use of tariffs had proven incredibly naïve and was quickly forgotten.[287]

1902 would be a year marked by severe drought, economic depression and high unemployment. The drought, which had now lasted since the Reid administration, was a large factor in the economic woes but it was not the only factor. The new tariff also played its part in the retraction of business, as did a number of small scale industrial troubles caused by those who wanted to see what they could get out of the new Arbitration Court. A shrinking economy meant a shrinking stream of government revenue, a great problem for a Ministry that was committed to large scale spending. Were it not for this spending See should have been in a good place to deal with the problems he now faced. After all, federation had meant a decrease in the responsibilities of the State Government and an increase in its revenue via the tariff. Under normal circumstances this should have left a substantial kitty available to deal with both the drought and the decreasing revenue, but any extra money the Government received had vanished faster than it had appeared, and soon they would be relying on extensive borrowing to keep the ship afloat.

In these circumstances the economic acumen of Carruthers would come to the fore. He spent the long parliamentary recess focusing mainly on his private business, but he never left politics alone for too long. He took an active part in a public meeting calling for the reform of Parliament and reduction of expenditure, though his desire to make such issues a party question was opposed, leading to the creation of a People's Reform League that like its Kyabram Victorian equivalent was separate from the Liberal Party. He also led a campaign to have the Federal capital site question resolved as soon as possible. With regards to the drought, he urged the Federal Government to remove the duties on fodder and grain for the relief of those affected. These pleas fell on deaf ears, but they did put the still essentially Protectionist State Government in an awkward position. At one prominent meeting the Minister for Lands Paddy Crick was left completely isolated as Carruthers successfully moved a motion forming a committee to lobby the Minister for Customs on the issue.

When Parliament resumed, he followed up these efforts with a gloomy show of foresight during the debate over the address in reply. After pushing for a number of forms of drought relief, Carruthers predicted that:

So surely as the large industries of this country will be affected by this drought so will the state finances be affected, and so surely will the time come when our revenue will be diminished and we shall be called upon for an expenditure, not for carrying on any scheme of public works, but for the purpose of helping our settlers tide over the difficult time that will come. It is necessary, if there is any extravagance being carried on of any kind, that it should be stopped, not so as to extend and increase the destitution, but to put our finances in such order that when the time of trouble comes we shall be able to weather the storm with as little disaster and confusion as possible.[288]

He went on to show how the Government had increased the loan obligations of the State by £11,723,098 since coming into office, and argued that regardless of what proportion of that money had been wisely invested, the sheer liability left the State in a precarious position to deal with the emerging economic downturn. His solution was to call on the members of the House to fulfil the promises most of them had made with regards to retrenchment, economy and the diminution of taxation. He felt that the former would help the Government weather the coming storm, while the latter would relieve the people who were left to face it. These cuts in spending and taxation would have to be made carefully so as not to exacerbate the situation, but if done correctly Carruthers felt the problems the State faced could be mitigated.

The speech stole the show in the debate. Not only did Carruthers demonstrate a considerable grasp of the financial situation, arguably greater than that of either the Government or the official Opposition, but he also showed his reasonableness for on a number of counts he actually defended the policy of the Ministry against those who would condemn it in its entirety. It made an immediate impression amongst the press. Carruthers had styled himself as the arbiter of financial stability, and as the economy continued to deteriorate that image would become ever more resonant.

The debate placed even greater pressure on Lee who once again had been completely overshadowed. Still the member for Tenterfield refused to budge, even though his replacement seemed inevitable. He held onto his position tenaciously until September when fate intervened. Lee was struck down by an extended illness, and though he was still reluctant to go, his health forced him to resign from the leadership of the Liberal Party and thus the Opposition.

The transfer of power would be remarkably smooth, a stark contrast to the drama that surrounded the election of both Reid and Lee. It was widely presumed that Carruthers' ascension was inevitable, though the names of Ashton, Brunker and former *Evening News* editor James Hogue were also mentioned. Before the Party even met Ashton and Hogue came out in favour of Carruthers. Ashton said that though private business prevented him from standing it mattered little because Carruthers was a better candidate anyway. In the meeting a motion was passed regretting the retirement of Lee before Brunker took it upon himself to nominate Carruthers. No other names were even suggested, and he was thus elected unanimously. Upon emerging Brunker declared that it was the "most enthusiastic" caucus meeting he had attended in his 22 years in Parliament.[289]

Carruthers received a number of letters congratulations upon his election. Interestingly one of them was from Wise who attacked the "petty intriguers" who had denied his former colleague the position the year before.[290] The person who was most pleased with the Party's choice was George Reid, for the damage he had inadvertently done his friend had now been erased. He wrote that "my best wishes for your success will always go with you, and they are nourished by personal friendship as well as political appreciation".[291]

Though Carruthers had found his way out of the political wilderness, still greater challenges lay ahead. When Lee announced his retirement he hoped that it would "have the effect of binding the Party closer together".[292] In many ways that was what Carruthers' leadership would have to do in order to succeed. Though the days of the factional era had long passed, the Liberal Party still suffered from a messiah complex, a hangover from the titanic leadership of Parkes and Reid. The Party still needed a strong leader to define its identity, unite it behind that definition and lead it to success. Carruthers would provide not only that but he would provide more, for the direction he led the Party down proved to be more permanent than the fiscal path. As he had predicted, the age of realignment was coming and Carruthers would help to shape that realignment not only in New South Wales but in Australia as a whole. The anti-socialist campaign, the Federal fusion and ultimately the Liberal Party of Australia would all be directly impacted by events that took place in New South Wales over the next few years.

RIVAL SAINTS – ST. GEORGE AND ST. JOSEPH

G.H. Reid in a new role (Melbourne political gossip says that G.H. Reid hopes to find Premier Barton definitely committed to Imperialism so that he may woo the Labor Party on an Australian nationalist programme as regards a preferential tariff and the navy.)

N.S.W. Opposition Leader Joseph Carruthers has issued his manifesto. It says that he is Joseph and that he will abolish all political sin. That's all it says.

Two Opposition leaders each searching for an agenda. From the *Bulletin*.

CHAPTER TEN

The Art of Opposition

Carruthers' ascension to the Liberal Party leadership was narrowly preceded by the rise of the "Kyabram movement" in Victoria and the two events should be seen as part of a wider push for the "retrenchment and reform" of government post federation. The thrust of this "reform" movement was the reduction or at least the containment of the size and thus the burden of government. It emerged as a reaction to the increase in government caused by federation, and also the spending policies of a number of Labor supported State ministries who were in power at the time. The reform movement was thus a product of political circumstances, but it had deep ideological roots.

The phrase "retrenchment and reform" recalled an earlier British Liberal slogan of "peace, retrenchment and reform" and it had clear Gladstonian undertones. Gladstone had a broad ideology that had greatly influenced Australian liberalism, but the reform movement had a narrower focus which largely confined itself to financial issues. According to economist Joseph Schumpeter, Gladstone had three financial principles: the retrenchment and rationalisation of state expenditure, a system of taxation that would interfere as little as possible with industrial and commercial operations, and the production of balanced budgets with surpluses to allow for fiscal reforms and the reduction of national debt.[293] While the laissez-faire implications of this analysis have been questioned, the fact remains that the patriarch of British liberalism generally supported low taxation, low spending and low debt. The underlying belief was that large government spending increased the economic burden on the people and hindered commerce, hence the distribution as well as the level of taxation was important. While economic arguments were important, this push for small government also tapped into a belief that wherever possible people should be left free to follow their own pursuits unmolested by the state, and this included financially.

As is clear from this description Gladstonian liberalism had little in common with the interventionist "new liberalism" of Bernard Wise or Alfred Deakin. By British standards Gladstonian liberalism was in fact old and their Liberal Party was already on the path that would lead it to the "people's budget" of 1909. Australia was acting as a time capsule of an older classical liberalism and its small government beliefs, and this was embodied in the reform movement. Over the next decade "new liberals" would secure many victories, but enough of this older element would survive to ensure that Australian liberalism would sit to the right of its British counterpart, a result that was no doubt partly facilitated by the lack of a British-style Conservative Party in Australia.

As has already been shown in the federation debates, Carruthers was one of the earliest heralds of the reform movement, though his delay in obtaining the leadership contributed to the fact that events in Victoria proceeded more rapidly. The "Kyabram movement" was a political agitation that began in late 1901 in the rural Victorian township from whence it got its name. Its main aims were the reduction of expenditure, debt and the number of members in State Parliament. After an initial meeting in the town, its supporters set up a committee which sent circulars throughout the State asking people to join their movement, which was subsequently formalised as the National Citizens' Reform League. According to the movement's chronicler, it was received with "spontaneous sympathy and active assistance" of the people.[294] This sympathy included the sympathy of the press whose support was crucial in the rapid expansion of the movement. The NCRL soon boasted membership in the thousands, and was able to place tremendous pressure on the Labor supported Peacock Government. After the Premier was defeated in a no-confidence motion forcing the dissolution of Parliament, the NCRL helped William Irvine achieve a landslide election victory in September 1902. Irvine went on to carry out retrenchment and the reduction of members, with the latter increasing the power of the rural vote.

Irvine's victory had much in common with what Carruthers was about to achieve in New South Wales. There were however some important differences. Kyabram was a movement that emerged from the countryside and retained an element of rural populism that the city Liberal Reformers lacked. Federation had impacted on both States very differently, and while the shift from previously low tariffs meant that the Braddon clause increased revenue and the burden of taxation in New South Wales, in Victoria the fourth of tariff revenue that went to the Commonwealth represented a significant drop in the State's funds that added impetus to calls for retrenchment. The actions of the Melbourne based Protectionist Federal Government were inevitably less controversial in Victoria than they were to her near North; therefore they played a less significant role in her State politics. In many ways the New South Wales reform movement was also more Gladstonian, for Carruthers' ideology was more broadly "liberal" and his idea of Lower House reform involved an equalisation of electorates that was reminiscent of Gladstone's electoral reforms.

While these were mainly differences in context, the main difference in practice between Irvine and Carruthers was that the NCRL remained largely "independent" of party politics while the soon to be established Liberal and Reform Association embraced it. The idea that Kyabram had been a non-party movement of measures not men has been dismissed as a myth, but once the romanticism of Kyabram's non-party status is stripped away it is clear that there was still a fundamental philosophical and tactical difference between the NCRL and the LRA.[295] The latter was thoroughly integrated with a parliamentary party while the former retained a fundamental distrust of politicians which made it deliberately keep its distance from its parliamentary backers. In New South Wales the People's Reform League did try to follow the NCRL's example, but it would prove unsuccessful and ultimately had to take a backseat to its party counterpart. Led by Carruthers, the New South Wales Liberal Party would try and to a large extent succeed in taking ownership of the reform movement in the State. This gave the Party the clear partisan agenda it had lost with the fiscal issue and would help facilitate the emergence of the lines of cleavage.

The story of the Kyabram movement is more widely known than the story of Carruthers and the formation of the LRA. This is because

Kyabram was more ideologically pure and therefore easier to romanticise for those who believe in the reduction of government. However, Carruthers' soft but deft touch combined with the acceptance of the necessity of party would ultimately produce a more significant legacy than his Victorian counterpart. By interpreting reform through a pragmatic rather than doctrinaire lens, connecting it with an older liberal tradition and a pre-existing party and then playing it off against ideological opponents, Carruthers would be able to weave a web of lasting success that would influence developments at a national level. Meanwhile Kyabram would fail to bring about a genuine realignment in Victorian politics. Irvine came close to producing a Labor versus anti-Labor divide in the State but that process eventually stagnated.[296] Unlike New South Wales which precipitated the Federal realignment, Victoria would remain a political aberration and would not truly fall into line with the national Liberal/Country-Labor party system until the 1950s.[297]

In September 1902 Carruthers' main concern was finding his feet as Opposition Leader. He took to the role quickly. The position entitled him to a small office which fit a table, a lounge and a few chairs. Joseph truly inhabited the space, and was frequently there until late hours smoking his pipe and forming political strategies. His main companion was John Nobbs, the Opposition whip. Nobbs was "a tall, good-natured fellow, like an overgrown boy, full of energy, and bent always on making friends".[298] A fellow conveyancer with an eclectic range of interests, he was by all accounts a loyal servant and assiduously guarded access to his chief. Cluttering the already claustrophobic office were many piles of newspapers, giving visitors the impression of a "pressman's den". In an age when each country district had its own paper, while Sydney possessed morning, evening and sectarian competitors, keeping track of how Liberal stocks were holding up was a thankless task. Carruthers understood its importance however, and painstakingly catalogued which papers were favourably or unfavourably inclined. Friendly pressmen were sent extra copies of speeches and whatever the Party produced, while attackers were ostracised lest they be given any extra material with which to fire a shot.

Perhaps fittingly, one of Carruthers first parliamentary actions as Opposition leader was to launch an attack on Bernhard Wise. Wise had been moved to the Legislative Council to pilot his Arbitration Bill through that House and after his humiliation at the Federal election he had decided to stay there. Despite sitting in the un-elected Chamber, Wise was still serving as the Government's Attorney-General and it was in that capacity that he became involved in the "Friedman Case". A jury had unanimously found Moss Morris Friedman guilty of a number of charges brought against him by the Crown, but the judge had been unhappy with their verdict prompting Wise to intervene and use his ministerial position to let the man off. While there were a number of issues with Wise's actions, including the fact that the man was freed even before the Governor's approval had been received, Carruthers latched on to what he saw as a breach of the long established principle of trial by jury.

On 1 October the Opposition Leader moved a motion of censure against the Government, launching into a detailed history of the rights and liberties of the people from the signing of the Magna Carta onwards and arguing that Wise had trodden on those rights by abusing his prerogative. Carruthers used all his legalistic skill to try to prove his constitutional case, citing precedent and the opinions of numerous respected lawyers who opposed the idea that individual judicial opinion could override the considered judgement of a jury. The principle of trial by jury was an essential part of British law, and though judges were meant to be impartial and well qualified, it was easy to argue that without specific grounds for appeal the unanimous view of a group of Friedman's peers should have been respected.

Though the Opposition leader was able to develop a sound case, Parliament was not an impartial court and the motion would still be voted on according to party lines. It was rumoured that the Labor Party was deeply divided over the issue and that it took the vote of a sick member who was absent from caucus to determine the Party's internal majority, but in the end they decided to support the Government.[299] The fledgling Country Party, which had temporarily united a number of rural independents, came to the same decision after its own amendment to the motion was ruled out of order. The vote thus revealed that Carruthers' ascension had done little to disturb the balance of power.

While the censure motion failed, Carruthers claimed that it had been a "moral victory" for the Opposition. He was able to get considerable political leverage out of the affair, for the Friedman Case formed an excellent example for his wider argument that Government Ministers were abusing their positions and that "responsible government" needed to be restored. "Responsible government" was a catchcry frequently used during this time period. It no longer had a clear definition like in the 1850s, but instead connoted a critique of numerous alleged failings of electoral responsibility including but not limited to minority government, financial disarray and abuses of prerogative. For Carruthers "responsibility" meant not only economic responsibility but responsibility to a Lower House based upon fewer electorates which were more equal in terms of population. It required an end to patronage, something that the continued lack of local government and increased public works spending was allegedly allowing to thrive. Responsible government also implied an attack on Labor, who were said to exercise power without responsibility via their balance of power position. Supposed "sectional" abuse was also lamented, as it was alleged that particular groups were reaping the benefits of ministerial money and power at the expense of the community as a whole. All these insinuations were difficult to either prove or disprove, but a palpable sense of disillusion with the working of the political system was there for Carruthers and the Liberals to exploit.

By mid-October Carruthers was claiming that the lines of cleavage had finally revealed themselves, and that the division would be between the Liberals who proposed to govern for all people, and the Government and Labor who tried to represent particular sections and classes.[300] This was a double-edged attack that aimed to discredit both parties by virtue of their connection to the other. The discursive positioning of the Ministry as irrevocably attached to Labor was an important move in the deprecation of an independent Progressive ideology which would pay dividends at the next election. Allegations that a Ministry had been too generous in giving concessions to Labor had been frequently made before, including against the Reid Government. By arguing that the Progressives' connection to large rural landowners represented a sectional outlook comparable with Labor's profession to represent the working class, Carruthers was going beyond such charges and positioning the Progressives on the opposite side of the lines of cleavage. Such a position made them irrelevant as the very nature of the lines required that there only be one major party on either side. Though most of the Progressives rejected such a positioning, they would increasingly find themselves bystanders to a Liberal-Labor political debate that marginalised their centre position and made them seem less of a real "choice" to electors.

Conversely, by connecting Labor's working class and union outlook with older landed interests in Parliament, Carruthers was trying to portray them as the new conservatives and link the upcoming anti-socialist battle with earlier liberal fights against the squattocracy. Liberalism valued individualism so highly that the representation of a particular group in Parliament was viewed as inherently insidious regardless of that group's place in society. The privileged position of unions under the Arbitration Act and the fact that the Trades Hall was directly reaping the benefits of O'Sullivan's spending provided some evidence for the claim that Labor was using Parliament to entrench union interests.

In defining his "liberal" position Carruthers quoted William Gladstone's statement that liberalism was the principle of "trusting the people only relieved by prudence" as opposed to "trusting the people only relieved by fear". This quote eloquently sums up Carruthers' generally small government beliefs, for he tried to leave the people to their own devices except in rare circumstances where he thought it prudent to intervene. It is noteworthy that Carruthers was equally at home quoting Gladstone and Burke. As a man who was playing a central role in the development of Australian liberalism, he was already engaged in the balancing of liberal and conservative principles which has continued to play out on the non-Labor side of politics. Much of his electoral success as leader would be built on his ability to keep moderate conservatives, who were naturally drawn to reform and anti-socialism, onside while still projecting a liberal image to the electorate.

It is important to note that Carruthers' liberalism had an element of conservatism to it, for though he had been actively involved in the revolution of party-liberalism many of his beliefs still harked back to an earlier age. This was a "new" conservatism, for it was based on the fact that the old conservatism had been so resoundingly defeated that liberalism had become the mainstream and therefore something that needed conservation as much as expansion. When Carruthers used the term conservative he clearly referred to the older version, but with hindsight we can see how the political traditions of the Australian right were beginning to intertwine. Though a self-described liberal who should be viewed as such, Carruthers was most comfortable when his liberal and conservative beliefs were in accord, such as in the fight for Privy Council appeals or for low taxation and spending. When he went out on a limb to the left or the right, such as with industrial arbitration and women's suffrage, his arguments became more laboured and he was less able to win electoral popularity.

Balancing where to sit on the political spectrum was made more difficult by the agitations of some of those on the fringe of the reform movement. Carruthers had been pushing for a reduction in government expenditure since before he became Opposition Leader, and once in that position he used this campaign as a key tool in differentiating his party from the Ministry. Carruthers' Liberals were not the only ones to embrace reform however. In early 1902 two organisations, the People's Reform League and the Taxpayers' Union, had been formed to act as ideological pressure groups and fight for a reduction in the size of government. Founded in Camden in direct emulation of Kyabram, the PRL's motto was "security and freedom are all that industry requires". The TU, as its name implied, sought to represent itself as a defender of taxpayer interests against the rapacious tentacles of government.

Both these organisations constantly critiqued the Government, but they also spent a large amount of time and effort pressuring the Liberals to adopt a policy of large-scale public service retrenchment. They were lobbying on fertile ground, as in the circumstances of the depression public debt was becoming an increasingly central topic of political debate. The mainstream press, who were obsessed with the reckless extravagance of the Government and the much maligned "Owe" Sullivan, gave both organisations a considerable amount of coverage. This helped the PRL attract a reasonable membership. The TU was less popular, but it had powerful financial backers. The overlap in their beliefs and function would soon lead them to a merger, retaining the PRL's name.

Though he styled himself as a champion of reform and fiscal responsibility, the Opposition leader tried to keep some distance from these hard-line groups. He relentlessly attacked the Government's spending, gaining significant political capital in the process. However, Carruthers also argued that if extravagance were halted wholescale retrenchments could be avoided though if it continued retrenchment in public and private life would be inevitable. This position drew significant newspaper criticism from those like the *Sydney Morning Herald* who urged Carruthers to remember Kyabram.[301] His colleagues were forced to jump to the defence of their leader's reform credentials, reminding the public of his actions during federation and the fact that he had attended the meeting which led to the establishment of the PRL.

Carruthers was not so much soft on reform as he was aware of the practical limitations of politics. His frequent speeches made it clear that he was entirely committed to reducing government expenditure, but in a pragmatic and measured way. He did not support indiscriminately culling civil servants. Their service had proved valuable when he was a Minister, their numbers had not greatly increased, and such a move would only be popular with a small section of the electorate. Instead he wanted to contain any expansion in public service expenditure and focus his cuts on areas where the Progressives' budget had expanded rapidly, specifically in the building of unnecessary and wasteful public works and the use of highly paid boards for administration. Carruthers had no qualms about the size of Government under Reid, which after all had been relatively small, and provided reductions were made for the introduction of the Federal Government he did not support arbitrarily firing those Government employees who performed necessary services.

The PRL and TU were proving to be a thorn in the right side of the

Liberals just as the Single Taxers had been a thorn in the left side of the Free Traders. Still, apart from the occasional publicised outburst, Carruthers largely avoided attacking them. Instead he stressed the need for unity, and in the face of attacks from those who insisted that reform must be non-party, began to set in motion the establishment of a new extra-parliamentary party organisation. The anti-party dimension of the reform movement is an important phenomenon. It was an extension of an older colonial liberal idea that rejected parties for trampling on the independence of members but it also tapped into a wider hatred of politicians in general. It was the politicians who had created the financial situation which the reform movement objected to and, with regard to the reduction of members, the politicians could not be trusted to retrench themselves. There was an inherent tension between this sentiment and the fact that the reform movement needed to work through politicians to achieve its aims. This was clearly represented in the structure of the PRL, which retained the right to preselect candidates but then required those candidates to resign from the non-party League.[302] Such a system was anachronistic before it was even introduced and offered little hope of establishing an effective and lasting political force.

Joseph Carruthers formed the Liberal and Reform Association on 19 December 1902, barely two months after he obtained the leadership. The Opposition leader chaired the formative public meeting and left it to Ashton to move the motion establishing and naming the LRA. The name represented the blending of colonial and Gladstonian liberalism with the post federation reform agenda, the latter having evolved from the former. Carruthers was trying to take ownership of reform and, more importantly, consolidate his party's hold on the title "liberal", a claim that stretched back to the LPA. It was claimed that the organisation would espouse a liberal philosophy of government based on "trusting the people", and that all of its policies would be tied to this underlying principle.[303] Though he was unable to attend the meeting, Reid gave the LRA his full support by publishing a letter he wrote to Carruthers wishing him luck and reiterating the need for drastic economy.

The process of forming a workable organisation out of this initial meeting was something that would take several months and committees were soon formed to draft the Association's platform and rules. The LRA's structure as it emerged had many similarities to that of the defunct FTLA. Local branches were to control preselections through plebiscites, though the executive was to have the power to deal with disputes and veto selections when absolutely necessary. Each branch would have the right to elect delegates to a central conference and that conference would be able to change the platform. That platform would not be binding on politicians however, a recognition of the fact that Liberals still envisaged themselves as more free and independent than caucus Labor. Above the conference would be a central council to deal with executive matters. This was made up of 24 members of Parliament and 24 extra-parliamentary members, soon to be joined by 24 members of the pre-existing Women's Liberal League.[304] Despite this equal representation the Parliamentary Party retained the right to elect the Parliamentary Leader, who in practice became the Leader of the Party as a whole. In this way individual members were given enough power to encourage involvement while the politicians maintained enough control to prevent chaos.

Membership required a financial contribution so that the organisation would have a fighting fund, though this was quite low beginning at just 3 pennies per quarter. It was hoped that with this low fee, which was considerably smaller than the majority of union fees at the time, the Party would be able to attract members from all sections of society. Liberalism still had a large number of traditional working class supporters as well as a particular appeal to middle and lower middle class people, and the membership numbers the LRA was able to achieve attest that it attracted a very broad base. Supporters could look forward to the material benefits of economic stability and decreased taxation, but as the Party eschewed sectional politics it relied on an appeal to principles to entice members.

The LRA was formed with the intention of pursuing liberal legislative and administrative goals. In order to achieve these, the organisation was specifically designed to fight the partisan battles of party-politics. Carruthers declared that "party warfare required party organisation", and the new organisation soon set up a headquarters and an administration capable of coordinating campaigns. The organisation embraced the nuts and bolts of electioneering and the partisanship inherent in the concept of the "lines of cleavage". Though the Progressives remained the main party of government, Carruthers had already begun to outline that the real lines would ultimately be drawn between Liberals and Labor. The accuracy of this prophecy would soon be corroborated by the ascension of the Watson Federal Labor Government and moves within the Labor Party machine to adopt a more explicit "socialist objective" of mass nationalisations in their platform. This would prompt the LRA to gradually turn its attention towards Labor, making an already unpopular government rhetorically irrelevant by engaging in a debate about socialism and the role of the state.

In the process the LRA would propagate and ultimately institutionalise an idea of liberalism which positioned itself as being fundamentally opposed to Labor's alleged anti-individualism, sectionalism and socialism. This was a pragmatic and to some extent logical adaptation of long standing liberal beliefs to the political concerns of the day. Liberalism, or at least classical liberalism, was by its very individualist nature anti-socialist but by placing this concern front and centre Carruthers was able to give a modern relevance to beliefs that were as old as democracy in New South Wales. The LRA combined positive Gladstonian liberalism, emphasising individualism and opportunity, with incessant appeals to keep the socialists out of power. The duality of these offensive and defensive roles worked perfectly within the "us or them" nature of the lines of cleavage. In a two-party system if you were not in power your philosophical enemy would be, and this helped to foster unity in a party that despite Wise's absence continued to contain a "broad church" of ideas. The unity of antagonism would only go so far without a purpose however and this is what liberalism, interpreted into an achievable platform, provided.

In order to be a source of unity rather than division amongst its supporters, the LRA's platform would need to embody a broad rather than doctrinaire interpretation of liberalism. This was a task to which our pragmatic subject was particularly suited. He was the primary author of the document which reflected his individualist beliefs and the Liberals' positive offensive purpose. The platform's points were as follows:

- The principles of responsible government are to be re-established in their integrity.
- General legislation to be based upon sound, liberal and humane principles tending to the common good, and not upon class interests.
- Ministerial administration to be just, firm and impartial.
- Reduction of Parliament to an 84 member Legislative Assembly and a 42 member representative Legislative Council (The Legislative Assembly currently had 125 members while the Legislative Council had no set limit to its membership).
- Economy, restricted loan expenditure, establishment of a sinking fund for the redemption of public debt.
- Freeze public service appointments unless absolutely necessary, end patronage, sound civil service and police superannuation.
- Local Government.
- Prudent public works with special consideration for water conservation.
- Simplified land and mining laws.
- Closer settlement.
- Education reform.[305]

Supplementing these points was a fighting platform including responsible government, restoration of State finances and the reduction of members. While this platform clearly encapsulated a reform agenda, the fact that it did not call for retrenchment and had planks covering a wide range of issues shows that Carruthers was looking beyond Kyabram and trying to establish a broader following while retaining his core ideology.

The council of the LRA moved two amendments to Carruthers' platform. One allowed reform of the Legislative Council to be pursued down "the lines of least resistance". The other called for the reform of the liquor traffic. This was the only part of the platform that could be considered inherently Protestant, and the fact that it was not even an original plank suggests that the sectarian element within the LRA was not overwhelming. Carruthers was a long-time supporter of the so-called "local option" and agreed to the amendment with little fuss. Local option was a scheme which would give voters from a particular electorate or municipality control over the number of liquor licences issued in that area. It tapped into Carruthers' belief in decentralisation and local autonomy, even if the prospect of local prohibition loomed as an effrontery to individual liberty. This compromise reflected the priorities of the time, and since John Carruthers had been heavily involved in temperance leagues, Joseph had been brought up to think that liberalism could bend on this issue.

This extensive platform shows that while the LRA deliberately utilised defensive rhetoric it was not, in W.K. Hancock's famous description, a "party of resistance" as opposed to a Labor "party of progress".[306] The LRA was seeking its own version of progress through the reduction of members, extension of local government, the continued implementation of closer settlement, education reform, balanced budgets and economic growth. Some of these policies were openly "resisted" by their Labor opponents.

Rather than representing an inclination to resist progress, the LRA's defensive role as an anti-socialist party symbolised an acceptance of the binary nature of an emerging two-party system. This was something which was perhaps easier for the Labor Party who could simply paint their opponents as class enemies or representatives of the rich. For the Liberals it required defining what made their opponents "illiberal", a task which took and has continued to take considerably more contemplation to achieve. Carruthers' clearest formulation of the difference between himself and his opponents would not come until late in the 1904 election campaign, but at this early stage the LRA already encapsulated the duality of party warfare. The dual role had existed to some extent in the FTLA's opposition to the Protectionists, but with a deeper philosophical objection to its opponents the LRA was able to harness it in a new and innovative way. The incessant nature of the lines of cleavage helped to make the new entity permanent, for the perpetual political battle would both require and support continued organisation.

The establishment of the LRA is the establishment of the New South Wales Liberal Party, for the core structure and ideology endures in the modern entity. It would be Carruthers' crowning achievement, easily surpassing all its failed predecessors. Its success was a product not just of its well-designed structure and enduring rhetorical stance, but also the time, effort and skill Carruthers' invested in his organisation. The new entity was run with an efficiency that only experience could bring, and he took care to ensure that pamphlets, speaking tours and preselections were all carefully considered and coordinated. As leader of the Liberal Parliamentary Party, Carruthers embraced the LRA and fully integrated it with his following. This gave it an immediate advantage over the FTLA and FTRC, which had both been run by rivals to the Free Trade Party leadership and had thus been kept at a distance. Carruthers' long and occasionally vicious fight for party unity had also helped to curb the excesses of independence that had characterised the preceding century, giving the LRA a level of cohesion while still maintaining the nominal freedom of thought that the liberal ideology required.

All these advantages meant that the LRA was not only more success-ful than its New South Wales predecessors but also its interstate counter-parts. In Victoria in particular anti-party and non-party groups continued to dominate non-Labor politics, and while these existed in the Mother State, the LRA would prove far more powerful than them. While Ky-abram had predated the PRL, the LRA predated anything of its scope, success and permanence amongst the non-Labor Parties in Australia. It was Carruthers who would make the LRA a success, and in doing so he would set the organisational agenda for the rest of the country.

One of the main aims behind the establishment of the LRA was that it would help prevent vote splitting, and that function would be put to an early test in a by-election in Tamworth. The Progressive R. J. Walsh had been forced to resign his seat after declaring bankruptcy and in an age before polls the election was seen as a test of the Government's popular-ity halfway through its term. In these circumstances it was important for the Opposition that their candidate fared well, but the local PRL branch threatened to undermine the opportunity.

No LRA branch had yet been established in Tamworth, so the pre-selection fell to the PRL. That body rejected the LRA-backed John Garland, and instead chose the local mayor, a Mr. Nankervis, as their candidate. The fiscal issue may have played a part in this decision, for the former Free Trader Garland was rejected in favour of a Protectionist. Nankervis refused to commit himself to the LRA platform, prompting the LRA to threaten to send in its own candidate. Carruthers was able to mount considerable pressure on Nankervis, forcing him to withdraw for "private reasons" and Garland, who had not intended to oppose the selected candidate, was chosen in his place.[307] A split was avoided and Garland went onto win the seat, though debate over whether he had been elected as a representative of the Liberals or the PRL continued to rage. The episode had shown the necessity of establishing local LRA branches as soon as possible and a campaign to do just that was intensified.

With the establishment of the LRA and increasingly fierce battles over spending policies, New South Wales politics was quickly becoming more partisan. Despite this, the Government and the Opposition had been able to come together to enact some measures of drought relief. This cause for unity would soon evaporate as in 1903 the drought finally began to break. While a relief to farmers, the rains offered little immediate relief to the State budget as it became increasingly difficult for the Government to borrow money. In January O'Sullivan boasted that his spending had helped to save the State in hard times and that it should be continued. Carruthers took the opposite view, and suggested that O'Sullivan had made the situation worse. He argued that the more the Secretary for Public works:

> attempts to use the State as a means of providing employment for the people, and for wet-nursing them, the more he destroys the avenues of ordinary employment by private enterprise, and the longer this state of affairs continues the greater will be the injury to private employment and enterprise, and the greater correspond-

ing demand upon the State to go on in a progressive scale with the public expenditure.[308]

To back this up he pointed to figures showing that emigration had exceeded immigration by 8,000 people in the last year and suggested that this exodus proved that the spending had failed to improve things for working people. He also argued that despite the reduced population employment levels were no higher than under Reid who had also endured drought and depression but who had managed to maintain a balanced budget. He cited artesian bore works as an example of where State competition was killing private companies, and suggested that reducing government fees would be a far more effective way of producing employment.

Regardless of whether proto-Keynesianism was helping or hurting the New South Wales economy, the funds to support such a policy would soon run out. During this time period State governments were incredibly reliant on London financiers who provided most of the capital for public works spending and other required borrowing. This outward flow of capital fuelled the development of Britain's settler colonies, while providing investment returns and new markets for London's capitalists. This interdependence was one of the defining characteristics of the "British World" in which Carruthers lived and which he admired. Nevertheless, it also meant that colonial governments were open to the dictates of those they were borrowing from. London's financiers had their own culture which was inherently conservative and which formed assumptions aimed at minimising investment risk.[309] The community was particularly concerned that governments followed the Gladstonian budgetary model of controlled spending and low debt, while avoiding any public work which offered little hope of remuneration. Failure to follow these guidelines made lenders question whether a government would be able to pay back what they borrowed.

The See Government's exceptionally high borrowing and heavy use of relief works for the unemployed inevitably raised alarm bells in the financial community, and British Banks became less and less willing to lend the Government money. O'Sullivan's biographer largely blames the negativity of the London press for this development, condemning "that hectoring tone with which the City of London could then afford to address the rest of the world".[310] The press played an important role in shaping the opinions of London's financial community, but in this case it appears that it was simply reflecting back a wide-spread view of the perceived pitfalls of excessive borrowing. The fact that Barton, who could still be expected to defend his former National Federalist colleagues, was soon making a polite attack on the borrowing policies of State governments and warning that they could harm Australian credit, suggests that the problem ran deeper than a few acts of editorial bias.[311]

In the midst of this worsening situation the Treasurer dropped a bombshell while delivering a speech at Cowra. Blaming the drought and financial turmoil in Britain, Waddell confessed that spending and borrowing must be reduced or else the Government risked defaults and a deterioration of its credit. In order to combat this he flagged retrenchment in the civil service, and even proposed putting a limit on the old age pension scheme which had been the Government's signature policy. Despite protesting that the level of debt and spending had been exaggerated, he had effectively admitted that many of the claims of the Liberals and the wider reform movement were correct.

That movement met his speech with incredulity. The *Sydney Morning Herald* suggested that Waddell's profession that government was "a question of finance from beginning to end" was a truism and should have been realised earlier.[312] Carruthers was sceptical of the Treasurer's commitment, and argued that apart from old age pensions, new spending introduced by the Government should be eliminated before any civil servants were laid off. The reaction people were most interested in was that of the Premier, but he remained silent and refused to either defend or castigate his Treasurer. He justified his stance on the grounds that he did not want to give fuel to the press, but in effect he did the opposite for the latter took it as proof of a divided Cabinet.

Further divisions were revealed when O'Sullivan came out in support of striking Victorian railway workers, an interjection which prompted some of his Cabinet colleagues to try to force his resignation. The strike was caused by both pay cuts and the introduction of separate parliamentary representation for railway workers and public servants. These separate seats isolated the political influence of their constituents, strengthening the position of Irvine's supporters.

Up until this point Carruthers had generally supported the moves of the Irvine Government and he was still under pressure to do so, but sectional suffrage was not something that he could countenance. He made it clear that his Liberals would not be following suit, for the move involved dividing people into classes in a manner completely contradictory to his definition of liberalism as non-classist and non-sectional.[313] For the same reasons he rejected suggestions of a tax on absentee landlords, for he felt that was a tax on a class of people rather than on the land itself. The difference between the two leaders is significant, for a belief in classless politics has become one of the defining principles of Australian liberalism, far easier to pin down than economic beliefs which have been subject to the sway of historical trends. Carruthers was not necessarily the first to propagate this belief but he was drawing an important line in the sand for the limits of conservatism within post-federation liberalism. In doing so he was strengthening his credentials amongst swing voters, who were easily put off by reactionaries.

Parliament resumed in June amidst threats from See to introduce press regulation in response to frequent attacks from the Sydney papers. Blaming the press for the Government's misfortune was a common theme amongst Cabinet members. O'Sullivan's unpublished memoirs seldom discuss Carruthers but frequently rail against the "foul treatment" of the "party newspapers".[314] While it is true that the major newspapers generally supported the Opposition, O'Sullivan's own *Freemans' Journal* was equally subjective as was *The Worker* and the pro-PRL *Sunday Times*. Carruthers was more than happy to take up the opportunity given by See to style himself as the defender of a free press, and was soon indulgently quoting Thomas Jefferson and even Byron; "freedom's battle, once begun, though baffled oft, is ever won".[315] See's threats ultimately came to nothing, though he was tempted to turn the *Government Gazette* into a State owned newspaper.

The traditional censure over the address in reply revealed that the months of turmoil had damaged the Government. There were several defections to the Opposition, though the solidarity of the Labor Party ensured that See's position remained safe. Further censure motions also failed. One was over a Royal Commission which had strongly censured O'Sullivan for political interference in the administration of the Fitzroy Dock at Cockatoo Island. No charges were laid, but the finding was grist to the mill for those who felt the Secretary for Works had been engaging in patronage all along.

Another censure involved the leasing of premises for a Government Savings Bank from the Citizens' Life Assurance Society. Though See had a vested interest in this Society, Carruthers focused his censure on the fact that the lease involved an expenditure of at least £20,000 which had not received parliamentary approval. The impropriety was of a similar kind to that which brought down Reid, only that this time it involved a far greater sum of money. The Government retorted with its own accusation that Carruthers had been involved in a Building Society which owned land at Port Hacking that had its value increased by a government-built wharf in 1889. When it was revealed that the vast majority of that land had been sold in 1885 this "stinkpot" blew up in See's face.[316] The Government was left clearly embarrassed, but since Carruthers had promised never to accept minority government with Labor backing he was not in a position to topple the Ministry.

Due partly to the censure motions and partly to the fact that the Government was running out of steam, the session would prove to be highly unproductive. One of the few significant achievements was the passing of a Crown Lands Amendment Act which received bipartisan support and built on Carruthers' earlier Act by reducing interest and adding further flexibility to the system. The other significant act was the passing of a Bill submitting a referendum to the people on the reduction of members. While the reduction of members was a central pillar of the reform agenda, it was also something that several members of the Government had pledged themselves to before the last election. The referendum was an option that allowed Ministerialists to fulfil these pledges without antagonising Labor who opposed the reduction.

Carruthers was sceptical of the referendum partly because of the Labor influence and also because the time taken threatened to ensure that the reduction might not take place before the next election. His fears were partially realised when a Labor amendment removing the 80 member lowest option from the referendum was carried with the help of Government supporters. The member for St George was exasperated that the Government would vote to amend its own Bill and tried to get it recommitted to re-insert the excluded option, but the gag provisions were eventually used and the Bill passed as it stood.[317] Ever the pragmatist Carruthers set about leading the campaign for a 90 vote, which was now the lowest option. With the session over he gave a number of speeches preaching his case and even published a signed plea to the electors in several issues of the *Sydney Morning Herald*. For cost saving purposes the referendum was held on the same day as the Federal election. It is difficult to determine if either event affected the other result. Certainly there was still a significant crossover between reform supporters and Free Traders, and the 90 option received an overwhelming majority in the poll.

One might expect that the Government's direct involvement in the reduction of members may have taken the wind out of the sails of the reform movement, but it had quite the opposite effect. The circumstances of the referendum meant that the Progressives received little credit for its success while simultaneously the reformers could argue that it was their agitation that forced the Government's hand.

Success in the referendum was both preceded and succeeded by by-election victories. The large number of by-elections between the 1901 and 1904 election is quite astounding and most showed a significant drift away from the Government. Garland's election in Tamworth was followed by Liberal successes in Willoughby, Glen Innes, Armidale, Moree and the Illawarra. The Newcastle based seat of Waratah was retained by Labor while an independent Liberal won Ryde, but elsewhere the LRA either retained or gained power in every election during which the organisation had existed. An interesting trend was that the earlier by-elections were contested by Progressives, while the later ones were contested almost exclusively by the Labor Party. The incumbents had a large part to do with this, but as it became clear that the political tide was receding against the Government, only Labor had the organisational fortitude to put up candidates in seats where their party had little chance of winning.

It was this organisational fortitude that the LRA wanted to exceed for its goal was to do what Labor had not and win power in its own right. Its program of expansion had proceeded rapidly so that by March 1904 it could claim 15,000 members.[318] In May the previous year it was misreported that Carruthers claimed the organisation had 70,000 members. This figure has sometimes been quoted as some sort of gross exaggeration but in context it was clearly just an editorial mistake for in the same speech he said that the LRA had 70 branches with an average membership of 100 people, and later estimates showed a steady increase from a starting point of about 7,000 members.[319] The Association continued to grow rapidly from March, so by the time of the election in August more plausible claims of membership near or above 70,000 could be made. The large figure has been described as "credible, if unverifiable" when compared with the high participation rates recorded for Liberal preselections and it is certainly more credible when the rise necessary to match the claim is less meteoric.[320]

What is clear is that the LRA was able to appeal to a similar section of the population as the Kyabram movement, but unlike that movement it was bringing its members into something with a greater integration with the parliamentary party and which went beyond a simple protest over the political system. Ultimately it was bringing them into something more permanent than the already waning Kyabram movement, for when the reform was over the Liberal Party and its well-developed organisation could remain, free to find a fresh liberal agenda.

That future required success at the upcoming election so that the LRA could imprint itself on the political map in a way that the FTLA never had. All energies were focused on that goal as the organising, literary and finance committees of the Association prepared to cover all bases. Carruthers was mainly involved in the former and it was in that capacity that he oversaw the appointment of 26-year-old clerk Archdale Parkhill as general organiser of the LRA. Parkhill was a figure plucked from obscurity who would go on to become the "doyen of Australian political organisers and makers of politicians".[321] Considering his later importance it is remarkable how little has been written about him. What has been written amounts to a few honourable mentions and a short *Australian Dictionary of Biography* entry. Prior to his appointment his only real political experience was as the honourable secretary of the Waverley branch of the Australian Protestant Defence Association and as a nominee for the local council. It is difficult to know why Carruthers chose him, the militant Protestantism of the APDA was still something the Opposition leader was trying to keep at a distance, but Parkhill soon became his protégé and one to whom he imparted all his organisational and political experience and skill. Such was their relationship that in 1927 Parkhill, then Federal member for Warringah, could write to his aged mentor that "I have been in public life since I started with you in 1904, and the lines you suggested have been the lines that I have followed and intend to follow".[322] It was through Parkhill that much of Carruthers' lasting historical importance would be emitted. Not only did Parkhill make the LRA a success and keep it alive after his mentor's retirement, but he would take its structure and modus operandi and introduce it to the Federal sphere.

Parkhill's appointment took place in March, the same month as the Premier's wife died. Understandably See was thrown into a state of intense mourning and temporarily withdrew from the political sphere. In his absence Wise was made acting Premier. After a very short session in January which had given effect to the result of the referendum, Parliament would not sit for a number of months if it sat at all before the election, hence Wise's position was largely ceremonial. Nevertheless, he was quick to jump at the opportunity of leadership. Taking a page from the Opposition book, he began to preach the need for borrowing to end and for the introduction of local government, though he simultaneously maintained that the Opposition was exaggerating the financial situation and that the economy was on the rise. Borrowing and spending were controversial issues within the Government. The Treasurer had forced a considerable amount of retrenchment upon the public works department since his Cowra speech, though the Liberals did not think it very noticeable. Up until this point the split over economy had mainly been between Waddell and O'Sullivan, but now Wise was clearly making a claim to be in the reduction camp. Perhaps he sensed that that was what was popular amongst the majority of Ministerialists whom he would need to appease as he would soon make a bid for the leadership.

Wise's enemies took his new position as an about face typical of a man with his reputation for political inconsistency. Carruthers claimed that Wise was stealing the Liberal Party's clothes and that his local government scheme was as "cumbersome" and "burdensome" as those which had failed before it.[323] His main complaint was that the scheme was not sufficiently simple for use in underdeveloped country areas while in the city it proposed a degree of centralisation that he felt would be deeply unpopular.

It was these country areas to which he now turned his attention. The LRA had not emerged from the country in the way that Kyabram had, and while its city base had certain benefits it meant that the organisation had more work to do in order to win rural seats. The by-elections had shown that the rural vote was not as solidly Progressive as it once had been and in May Carruthers embarked on an extended tour to capitalise on this dissatisfaction.

The tour inevitably involved a large number of propagandistic speeches, but more importantly it allowed Carruthers to directly oversee preselections and try to ensure each seat had a Liberal candidate. He left Parkhill behind to maintain operations in Sydney, but he kept in close contact with his young protégé. Little of Parkhill's papers survive today, but of the handful of letters which remain two come from this tour. They reveal much about the methods of campaigning at the time and how Carruthers used every technique available to him to win votes. In the letters Carruthers' main theme was the failings of the literary committee, who led him to say in exasperation that "I'd give the man who would do this work [writing and distributing political pamphlets] well the pick of any seat in the Ministry so much do I think of its value".[324] He was insistent that copies of speeches and other literature be sent along with money in order to hire a man to distribute them. He maintained that this was a far more effective way of spending money than hiring halls and that candidates, rather than the LRA, should be made to pay for their own meetings. He also requested copies of diagrams comparing land settlement under Reid to the present administration. A less scrupulous technique was revealed when Carruthers requested that an upcoming public meeting in Redfern be stacked to ensure a positive crowd.

Carruthers was "dead dog tired with hard travelling" but his hands on approach was effective in mobilising the resources of the LRA and would pay considerable dividends at the election. The last major threat to the electoral chances of the LRA was vote splitting with the PRL. Several attempts had been made to come to a preselection agreement with the League but they had fallen down on Carruthers' insistence that he maintain the final say. In the end the successful expansion of the LRA forced the PRL to back down. An agreement was reached whereby preselection disputes would be resolved by an executive panel consisting of representatives of the Parliamentary Opposition, LRA, PRL, Women's Liberal League and other kindred associations. Carruthers, Want and the PRL-affiliated McMillan also had their own separate seats on this panel. The fact that the Opposition and LRA were represented separately gave them a numerical advantage over the PRL and left Carruthers in charge. This arrangement did not solve all of the problems of vote splitting but it would prove effective in containing the disruption.

The other groups that disturbed LRA preselections were sectarian and temperance organisations. Much has been made of their role in the election, particularly by J.D. Bollen who views it as a key moment in the firming of Protestant ties to the Liberal Party.[325] In many ways Henry Parkes' "Kiama ghost" was the natural political inheritance of the LRA. For a number of historical and cultural reasons Protestants had long been attracted to the Party and in an age of sectarianism the fringe elements of the LRA's membership dissuaded many Catholics from joining.

Sectarian and temperance groups were able to infiltrate a number of branches of the LRA, an inevitable downside of a participatory party that encouraged membership. Carruthers' attachment to local option helped to exaggerate this pre-existing Protestant-Liberal connection but at the same time that connection was never universal and it would be wrong to accuse him of openly courting the sectarian vote. Perhaps his position meant that he could take Protestant support for granted, nevertheless Carruthers' overwhelming focus was on financial and political issues.

While local option may have attracted some Protestant followers, it was perhaps more important in securing the votes of the newest section of the electorate; women. In a time when it was culturally unacceptable for women to frequent hotels, they enjoyed few of the benefits of an unrestricted liquor trade while they often had to deal with the negative effects of their husbands' drunkenness. For that reason temperance was an attractive female cause even amongst some Catholic households.

Carruthers' initial opposition to female suffrage did not put him as offside with women as one might expect. He embraced the Women's Liberal League and took pains to address as many female gatherings as possible. At the WLL's annual meeting he shrewdly linked liberalism's opposition to sectional politics to an underlying belief in "political equality".[326] Interestingly, he also told his audience not to focus too much on the personal qualities of a respective candidate, which were open to slander, but to vote based on underlying principles. Women felt the sting of the hard economic times as acutely, if not more acutely than men, and commentary after the election would suggest that the Liberals were able to attract a disproportionate number of their votes.

See returned in late May only to announce his retirement in early June on account of ill health. When See's impending retirement became known Wise sent him a letter insisting that only he had the qualifications to take the leadership and threatening that he would not serve under anyone else.[327] See told the Governor that he would prefer that Crick become Premier, but that Wise was his second choice. Sir Harry Rawson refused to have either. Crick had been "drinking to excess" at Executive

Council meetings, while Wise was still considered unreliable because of his role in the Friedman case. Thus rebuffed, the outgoing Premier advised the Governor that Waddell should be sent for. It is testament to how undeveloped the Progressive Party was that the leadership was still decided in this manner rather than by a vote. Such a method had been unthinkable within the Liberal Party since Reid's election in 1891 and in 1894 that party had even taken the step of nominally re-electing their leader before he assumed the Premiership. Wise and Crick refused to serve under Waddell; hence he was forced into making a considerable Cabinet reshuffle. O'Sullivan was shifted to Minister for Lands, allowing the Premier to pursue a policy of economy and retrenchment largely unmolested.

With high levels of debt and continued difficulty borrowing, economy was the main cry of the rapidly approaching election. Even the Labor Party's fighting platform placed "economic government" in second position.[328] The gathering consensus on all sides of politics that something must be done to reduce expenditure served only to strengthen Carruthers' position, for he had been beating that drum the longest and the loudest. Despite the fact that the Government was co-opting a number of his policies, Carruthers was succeeding in making the election about economic issues, a situation that ever since has tended to favour the Liberals.

He broadened the appeal of his anti-debt rhetoric by focusing on the amount of potential jobs that were being destroyed by the outflow of capital towards debt repayments. Jobs had been temporarily boomed by unsustainable spending, but in the process shackles were being placed on the future of the labour market.[329] Carruthers was trying to demonstrate to working men how the Government's lack of fiscal responsibility had a tangible effect on their lives. The appeal of this line of attack was inherently strengthened by the Progressives' withdrawal from public works spending; an action which proved, to their opponents at least, the fact their programs had always been a financial liability.

With reduction of members achieved, the LRA produced an updated fighting platform which elevated local government and closer settlement to new prominence. These issues also appeared on the Progressive and Labor platforms, but as an eternal advocate of local government and author of a successful Crown Lands Act, it was easy for Carruthers to claim that he was more sincere than those who had allegedly failed to do something about them after five years in office.

As the election campaign wore on it became increasingly clear that the Progressives were crumbling. With See, Wise and Crick either retired or detached, the Party had lost three of its main voices. Waddell and O'Sullivan were the only prominent members who remained and the two men stood aloof both personally and ideologically. What little was left of the PPA, which had functioned so successfully in 1901, did little to defend a Premier who was in near constant disagreement with that organisation's founder. Torn between selling Waddell's retrenchments and defending their record, the Progressives lacked fundamental ideological cohesion. Without it they were virtually unelectable, as voters were left confused about who or what the Party stood for.

In these circumstances Carruthers shrewdly continued to shift his attention towards the Labor Party, creating an election issue out of his clear lines of cleavage. This would serve to exacerbate the Government's increasing irrelevancy, as nothing highlighted the Progressives' lack of set ideology and cohesion more clearly than an ideological battle in which politicians were called to take sides. The fighting platforms of the Liberal and Labor Parties were still quite similar, so Carruthers focused on differences in the philosophical positions they claimed to represent. His main argument was that the Labor Party were the new Tories, the former fighting for union privileges as the latter fought for aristocratic privileges, and also attacking free parliament through use of the caucus solidarity. He lambasted his opponents for claiming to have improved things for working people when under their watch unemployment and the cost of living had both risen. Early-closing and old age pensions were "skin-deep" improvements as long as the jobs created by private enterprise were being sacrificed to government avarice.[330] The lines of cleavage were being refined, and in Carruthers' eyes they were liberalism and private enterprise against socialism, class prejudice and subjection to the State:

You will have to make a choice between a policy of extreme socialism, based on class prejudice, fomented by extremists, or the policy
of liberalism, which appeals to the higher and nobler instincts of
humanity. The issue is also for encouragement to honest endeavour in all classes, for individual enterprise, and for bedrock reforms
uplifting the people, and directing their energies and their capital
to the work of developing our resources, and building up a true
national prosperity. The issue is against the state persisting in its
endeavours to reduce the people to the condition of an army of
state employees, dependent upon political patronage for work, and
upon foreign money-lenders for loans to pay the wages.[331]

Here is the rhetorical philosophic stance of the modern Liberal Party,
articulated by the LRA leader before either Reid or Deakin had done so
either as coherently or with the express idea that liberalism was essentially opposed to the Labor Party for ideological reasons that ran deeper
than caucus solidarity. Others may have done so, but if so they generally
did it from a more reactionary perspective and they certainly did not do
so from a position of comparable leadership. With the members of Parliament reduced and retrenchment underway, Carruthers could see that
the reform movement would eventually run out of steam. In its place
he was trying to construct a liberal stance for the twentieth century, still
based on the common assumptions of colonial and Gladstonian liberalism, but with a new outlook and a new enemy. He was not doing so in
a bubble of State politics isolated from the rest of the country, but as
the leader of one of the most organised and largest (in terms of extra-
parliamentary membership) parties in Australia, hence his actions would
have lasting resonance particularly in the upcoming Federal anti-socialist
campaign. Much of the "socialism" he was specifically condemning was
actually the Labor supported policies of O'Sullivan, but at the same time
he was pre-empting the position of his opponents which would be given
more concrete policy expression over the coming years.

While offering a cause and a "philosophy of government", Carruthers was deliberately occupying broad ideological ground that would
allow him to attract support from a wide range of liberals and conserva-

tives. His liberal anti-socialism was not laissez faire and allowed room for "reforms uplifting the people", though there was a general if flexible belief in individualism and freedom that required the state stay limited in scope. This echoes Menzies' belief that the Liberals "were determined to be a progressive party, willing to make experiments, in no sense reactionary, but believing in the individual, his rights, and his enterprise, and rejecting the socialist panacea",[332] The latter clearly had a greater emphasis on government intervention than the former, but views on how much intervention is tolerable to freedom and individualism are something that have always varied among Australian Liberals. Like Menzies, Carruthers was trying to present himself as a unifying figure, while still staying true to the liberal (in Carruthers' case classical liberal) convictions that had underpinned his career.

Carruthers' focus on the Labor Party was a double-edged sword. As Michael Hogan has pointed out it succeeded in marginalising the Progressives but also helped to give Labor the increased prominence that would eventually lead to its governing in its own right.[333] Carruthers likely accepted this risk in order that in future there could be a straight out fight of the kind he had yearned for when tweedle-See and tweedle-Lee were in charge. It was not something he needed to do to achieve victory; all indications are that he could have coasted in on the reform issue alone. Nevertheless, in Carruthers' view it was something that was necessary, not only for the enduring relevance of the Liberal Party, but also for the functioning of a democracy freed from the blight of minority government and legislative paralysis, and where electors knew what they were voting for.

The emerging Liberal-Labor divide was solidified by O'Sullivan's efforts to make an electoral deal with Labor, cementing in many people's minds the idea that a vote for the Progressives was essentially the same as a vote for Labor. In the end the Ministerialists were squeezed out of the election. They held on to just 16 seats and worse still they only managed to contest half of the 90 electorates.[334] Several of the Progressives who did hold on had accepted a large part of the reform agenda and would soon gravitate towards the Liberal benches. The Liberals effectively won

45 seats while there was also an independent Liberal, 3 independents and 25 Labor supporters. Carruthers had a clear majority and for the first time the New South Wales Labor Party would be in outright and official Opposition. It was the dawning of a new era, the era of the modern party system that despite Liberal reformations, Labor splits and the emergence of the Country/National Party, has endured until the present day.

Carruthers with the Governor and Vice-Regal party. A perfect demonstration of our subject's stature. From the Mitchell Library, Sydney.

N.S.W.'S DEFENDER

Gladiator Carruthers : "Observe me tackle this ferocious animal, I made him myself."

Carruthers garnered a large amount of publicity for his fights with the Federal Government. From the *Bulletin*.

CHAPTER ELEVEN

The Clarity of Cleavage

Until the new Parliament met and it was revealed where the independents would sit and whether the Progressive rump would stay together, there was still some concern that the Liberal majority would be unworkably small. For this reason a number of people began to advocate that the abortive Liberal-Progressive coalition should be revived. Among these advocates were many, like the *Sydney Morning Herald*, who had been fiercely against a coalition just three years before. The impetus behind this backflip was not only that the Liberals would now dominate any such coalition, but also a growing distaste for the three-party system particularly now that Labor had a realistic possibility of achieving power.

The prospect of terms between the two old parties was scuttled by Waddell's refusal to resign the Premiership immediately. Though he tacitly admitted that he lacked a majority, he justified his stance on account of the urgent need to pass a temporary Supply Bill. This was required because the long gap since Parliament last sat meant that the previous ordinary Supply Bill threatened to expire if proceedings were delayed by the ministerial by-elections which would follow a change of government. There was also a constitutional issue for the Governor had taken an ill-timed trip and the Lieutenant-Governor had not been left with the power to commission governments. Though initially aggrieved at the Premier's obstinacy, Carruthers eventually agreed to help with the passage of supply.

With this object in view Parliament sat in late August. Though Carruthers was still technically the leader of the Opposition, he gave his support to the address in reply in order to bring swiftness to proceedings. McGowen objected that the ameliorative attitude went against both the role of an official Opposition and the integral notion that a government needed to have a majority. Soon to be leader of the Opposition himself, his objections seem to have been aimed at taking up that role early, for rather than attacking the Government he took aim at Carruthers for failing to fulfil his constitutional duty. Carruthers dismissed McGowen's critique on account of the "extremely novel" circumstances, and Waddell quickly achieved his aim in the face of an attempted Labor amendment. Labor's decision to oppose the expedient actions of the outgoing Government alienated it from some Progressives and may have hurt its ability to call on their votes in later censure motions. Despite the urging of some within Cabinet to test the strength of the House, Waddell resigned of his own accord and Carruthers was sent for.

In forming his Cabinet Carruthers repudiated a coalition, declaring that the Progressives must pick sides between the forces of Liberalism and the Labor socialists. He placed himself at the head of the Treasury where, he insisted, "the Premier always should be, with his fingers of the pulse of the country".[335] The first person he asked to join him was Ashton who was given the second most important post of Minister for Lands. This was hardly a surprising choice. Ashton not only had rural credentials but also a good reputation, even amongst the ever-critical writers of *The Catholic Press*. For a while now he had been Carruthers' right hand man, helping to engineer the former's rise to power and the formation of the LRA. The Ministry was rounded out with James Hogue as Colonial Secretary, Charles Lee as Secretary for Public Works, Charles Wade as Attorney General and Minister for Justice, Broughton O'Conor as Minister for Public Instruction, Labour and Industry, Samuel Moore as Secretary for Mines and Agriculture and John Hughes as Vice President of the Executive Council. In contrast to his immediate predecessors Carruthers limited himself to one Honorary Minister, William Dick. The Ministry was to be the first in New South Wales history in which all the members had been born in Australia and in his late forties the Premier was one of the youngest since the enactment of responsible government.

Despite his youth, and height, Carruthers comprehensively overshadowed his colleagues. His Ministry was notable for its relative lack of prior experience. As Free Traders and Liberals the Party had been out of government for five years and many of its senior members had gone into Federal politics. There was certainly some talent amongst those who remained. Wade had played rugby for England and as a practising lawyer towered above his opponents, using intimidation as much as skill to prove his points. Nevertheless Carruthers was their unquestioned leader. Having led the Party from electoral oblivion to Government in just three short years, his position was secure and, if needed, he could dictate to his colleagues on any important issue. On a day to day basis he followed a Reid style of Cabinet government based on consultation and amelioration, but the reason mutual respect flourished was because of the security of a lack of competition. *The Catholic Press* described a Premier who was, for the moment, in full control of men and events:

> Premier Carruthers looked very spruce and self-satisfied. Carruthers has a peculiar eye, twinkling with humour, like the eye of an old parrot which has watched the vicissitudes of a family, and seems to understand human life very well. The eye of Carruthers is not by any means a bad eye. The Premier is very clever, and very cunning, but his heart is not small, and as a matter of fact he has scarcely any personal enemies.[336]

After a delay caused by the by-elections, Parliament resumed in mid-September. Waddell and his rump took their seats on the Opposition crossbenches, though he and some of his more moderate followers had assured Carruthers of their general support.[337] Labor assumed the Opposition benches, but not without Crick raising a point of order declaring that precedent suggested that the outgoing Premier was still the official leader of the Opposition. Crick's grievance ignored the political reality of the lines of cleavage as they had emerged at the last election and the Speaker was able to find a precedent to justify the logical move. It was that political reality that Carruthers was now preparing to take advantage of. A large part of the justification for the lines of division was that a parliamentary democracy needed a clear two-party system in order to build stable government majorities capable of passing difficult legislation. Having achieved his desired realignment, the Premier now had to prove that the benefits would be tangible.

The first test of how stable the lines of cleavage were in the new Parliament would not be legislative but financial. Waddell's Supply Bill had only temporarily postponed the pressing issue of the budget and as the novelty of Labor's position wore off in the House, Carruthers began frantically preparing his financial statement. After his repeated attacks on the financial administration of the See-Waddell Government, Carruthers' entered the Treasury with great expectations that he would balance the budget and reduce the debt. He made early moves to fulfil that expectation, declaring that he would say "no, no, no" to those requesting government funds and putting an immediate freeze on public service appointments for twelve months.[338]

The financial statement delivered on 5 October was preceded by a disclaimer reminding the House of the limited time Carruthers had had to find savings and get to grips with the situation. His main problem was the large public debt his predecessors had left him. Though budget deficits had plagued the Lyne-See era, the vast majority of this debt was from public works spending. Most of this was treated separately from regular expenditure and paid for by loans, the majority of which were obtained from the Bank of England. In theory these loans paid for works that were meant to function as remunerative investments, but in practice many returned little of that investment. This problem had grown far worse under O'Sullivan's program of deliberate government employment, so that in many cases the returns needed to pay off the loans stagnated at 1899 levels despite the large subsequent increase in borrowing.[339] Meanwhile the debt continued to accrue interest of up to £3,000,000 a year, a staggering figure considering that ordinary revenue amounted to just £11,435,010.

In order to combat this Carruthers proposed to not only to reduce public works spending on top of major reductions already effected by Waddell, but also to create a sinking fund to pay off the debt, with two-thirds of the revenue from Crown land sales to go into the fund. Loan expenditure would thus be reduced to less than half of its average from the previous three years, from £4,103,000 to £1,926,000.[340] With regard to the budget itself, the Treasurer proceeded to outline a number of planned economies. Savings would be made by abolishing the position of Agent General, fitting civil servants into existing publicly-owned buildings and ending the practice of renting CBD office space at considerable expense, reducing the costs of the position of the Governor and removing publicly funded telephones from the homes of Ministers and civil servants. No civil servants were to be fired or have their salaries reduced, but a new system controlling pay rises was to be introduced to add to the savings made by the hiring freeze. Using these methods the ordinary expenditure would be reduced by approximately £109,000 on the three-yearly average. The yearly budget would thus be balanced, and by June 1905 a surplus of nearly £200,000 had been achieved with the help of improving seasons.

Carruthers' statement was met with a torrid backlash from both sides of politics. Those on the right of him argued that the cuts did not go nearly as deep as should be expected from a reform government, while some on the left bemoaned the treatment of civil servants in spite of Carruthers' careful insistence that none were to be fired. McGowen accused the Premier of limiting himself to "cheeseparing" and avoiding the difficult decision to increase taxation that the financial situation necessitated. The person who may have been happiest with the statement was Waddell, who took its mild reforms as a vindication of the emergency financial measures he had undertaken. Many drew the comparison with Waddell, though Ashton was quick to point out that Waddell had been forced into economies by circumstances which prevented further borrowing while Carruthers had freely chosen to be prudent with the public money.[341] Carruthers complained that those expecting the expenditure to be reduced more drastically had not read his campaign speeches and were imposing the unrealistic promises of others upon his head.

The main problem with the perception of the Treasurer's budget was that, apart from the continued pressures caused by the lack of a comprehensive system of local government, which Carruthers was planning to deal with, and the large interest accumulating debt, which the sinking fund and sustainable budget surpluses would bring under control, most of the problems with the finances were not structural but due to the "extravagant" style of the previous government. Considerable savings could be made by simply not instituting as many new public works projects as those that were reaching completion and by being more discerning in the giving out of endowments, which were budgetary gifts haphazardly and inefficiently given to organisations as diverse as shires, hospitals, universities and fire brigades. Such savings were not as visible as a "Black Wednesday" of mass government lay-offs but they were perhaps more effective in achieving Carruthers' financial goals.

Most of the attacks on the budget argued that Carruthers was not doing enough to reduce spending, but his attempt to do something with regard to tax imposition met with an even more negative reaction. The changes involved were relatively minor. The first would impose wharfage fees on New South Welshmen. Formerly these had just been levied on people from interstate, but the Federal Constitution made such differentiation illegal and Carruthers was left with the choice of either imposing them on his countrymen or giving up an important source of revenue when he was already having difficulty balancing the budget. The other involved amending the Stamp Duties Act in order to increase the penalty for not paying and reduce an exemption in probate duties from £50,000 to £30,000. Carruthers regarded this as a "closing of leakages" rather than a true increase in taxation.[342]

These Bills almost provoked a constitutional crisis. In the Legislative Council the Harbour Rates Bill was amended to remove a clause allowing wharfage charges to be levied on goods unloaded at private wharves while the Stamp Duties Bill was also heavily amended before being ruled a money bill by the Speaker. This incited a standoff, for the Westminster tradition implied that a nominee Upper Chamber should not have the power to amend money bills. This implication was controversial and there were many in the Legislative Council who claimed that the amendments made to the Stamp Duties Bill were aimed at removing ambiguities rather than restricting the Assembly's power to raise revenue.

In the end a compromise was reached and a new Stamp Duties Bill and a virtually unchanged Harbour Rates Bill were passed by the Legislative Council. After these initial skirmishes the Council was "less confrontational" and generally got on well with both the Carruthers and Wade Governments.[343] While the precedent of amelioration may have been one reason for the positive approach, another reason for the change in attitude was a strengthening of leadership. John Hughes represented the Government in the Upper Chamber in 1904 and while he had done an admirable job in difficult circumstances he would soon be supplemented by the presence of James Brunker as a member of the Executive Council without portfolio. Brunker's experience and loyalty would once again prove invaluable for Carruthers, as having the Government's position clearly and authoritatively articulated led to far fewer outright defeats.

Once the Council was subdued any talk of its constitutional reform faded away. Its ameliorative attitude made such reform less urgent, especially since career defining local government legislation was still to pass, but even after this had been achieved the issue was left alone. Perhaps Carruthers found it difficult to come up with a sound alternative to the nominee system, particularly as the Federal Senate was revealing problems of its own, or maybe he saw the Council as a brake on extremism in an age where socialism was becoming an ever more real question of political debate. No clear explanation was ever given for the change of heart and the issue was allowed to become one of Carruthers' very few unfulfilled electoral promises.

If Carruthers' relationship with the Legislative Council was productive, his relationship with the Governor was downright friendly. Sir Harry Rawson was a decorated Admiral who had been appointed to the State's vice-regal office in 1902. A large and imposing figure, he had an adventurous spirit and was not shy of offering his opinion on a variety of government matters. He and Carruthers got on marvellously. The Premier paid his Governor the deference due to his office, but they also developed quite a personal rapport. This was a time when a healthy relationship with the Governor was still very important. Not only was the post responsible for commissioning governments, calling elections and appointing Legislative Councillors, but in the imperial age Governors were also an essential go-between in discussions with the Mother Country. They expected to be well-informed of the internal happenings of the

Ministry, and Carruthers appears to have relished being able to vent to a trustworthy confidant.

Rawson was personally opposed to socialism and had had a difficult time juggling the dysfunctional end of the Progressive Government. He naturally appreciated the stability Carruthers gave him and the improved reputation the State quickly achieved in Britain. While they struck a common chord early, the two men's relationship was cemented after the tragic demise of Lady Rawson. When she first fell ill the Rawsons were away from the Colony, but after a brief period of improvement she died at sea on their way back to Sydney. Isolated in the antipodes as he dealt with his wife's death, Carruthers offered the Governor much needed emotional support. Joseph was after all no stranger to tragedy, and over a private cigar or a personal note he did what he could to lift Rawson's spirits. After this Rawson became, privately at least, a sure backer of the Premier and a source of more solid support than many ministerial backbenchers. While this may imply some bias possessed by the holder of a supposedly impartial office, it must be said that Carruthers seldom abused his privileged position. The Premier could have gotten anyone he liked appointed to the Legislative Council but suggested very few ascend to such a station. Rawson privately went in to bat for Carruthers in negotiations with the Council, pointing out to its members that ministerial setbacks would embolden Labor. Nevertheless, visible controversies were avoided. This was appreciated by both men but particularly Rawson, who became one of the most popular Governors in New South Wales history and eventually had his appointment extended by popular demand.

1905 would be marked by a return to economic prosperity and a subsequent lessening of press criticisms of the Government. The upturn was partly due to circumstances outside of the Government's control, but Carruthers could take some credit for a restoration in the confidence of the financial markets. The previous Ministry's spending policies had spooked not only lenders to the Government, but also the private British investors who remained essential to the New South Wales economy. A steady hand at the wheel now ensured the State got the maximum advantage out of the break in the drought.

The improved conditions would not bring an end to political controversy. One of the most ideological debates of the year was to wage over the manufacture of locomotives. The debate revolved around whether these should be constructed at home or overseas and whether they should be made by the government or private enterprise. It was the Railway Commissioners, in particular John Oliver, who found that it would be cheaper to produce the locomotives overseas. Due to the independent nature of the Commission, most of its members' actions were free from ministerial oversight but due to a quirk in the Act introduced by Henry Parkes ministerial approval was required to send these contracts abroad. Carruthers was hesitant to do so, arguing that the local economic benefits would offset the discrepancy in contract costs provided that discrepancy was not overwhelming. When the media got wind of these negotiations both the Labor and Progressive Parties came out against foreign manufacture no matter what the cost.

This coalescence of protectionist and socialist interests threatened to unite the Opposition and the cross-bench, but Carruthers largely ignored this threat and pursued his own liberal economic goals. Though he publicly pushed the benefits of local manufacture, he refused to commit to it at any price and held his nerve to bring forward cheaper offers from home. Once these were produced the Labor Party continued to argue that the locomotives should be built in State railway workshops, but with the protectionist issue now gone there was little hope of forcing the Government's hand. The tender went to Clyde Engineering with iron and steel to be supplied by William Sandford. The latter was a hardline Protectionist who had privately debated Carruthers on the merits of socialism.[344] His success in winning an important contract strongly suggests that the Treasurer avoided using his office as a means for political patronage.

The row over the locomotives contract serves as a good microcosm for the relative attitudes of each of the parties towards the role of the state. In this instance the Liberals could fiercely support private enterprise and to some extent even foreign enterprise without questioning the government's role in paying for the locomotives in the first place. Meanwhile the difference between Liberals and the fragmented Progressives is shown by the former's belief in budgetary prudence and a reverence for the money of the taxpayer, while the latter would have been willing to spend more to achieve their own philosophical and economic goals. For some Waddellite instincts towards balanced budgets and private enterprise tempered this desire for spending, while others continued to sympathise with Labor even after the foreign manufacture issue was settled, hence after the initial protectionist furore the Progressives continued to drift towards their relative sides of the emerging political divide. The episode demonstrates how the new lines of cleavage were to a large extent clear (and becoming clearer), even without the presence of a dogmatic laissez-faire position.

The fact that Carruthers was willing to act so nonchalantly when faced with the threat of a Labor-Progressive combination also shows the confidence he had in the political division and in his party's solidarity. There was good reason for this faith, as despite intense press criticisms of his financial policy the Liberals had been largely united in Parliament. This situation would continue, as in contrast to Parkes and even Reid, Carruthers was highly successful at keeping his troops in line even without the caucus pledge that his ideology denied him. This success is partly attributable to a hang-over from his battles for party discipline as Reid's attack dog and also to the fact that federation had thinned out the ranks of talented State parliamentarians. Perhaps it was the sight of the Labor Party occupying the Opposition benches that kept the Liberals from bickering, for the upshot of an emerging two-party system was the knowledge that if they were not in government their ideological opponents would be. The dual role previously discussed was thus a source of unity inside Parliament as well as out of it. Something had certainly changed since Carruthers had entered Parliament, and whatever subtle forces were acting upon them, liberals seem to have lost some of their voting independence by this point. It is noteworthy how many times Carruthers gave a free vote to his backbenchers, and while this may seem quite liberal, the fact that such freedom was now the "gift" of the Premier hints at firmer discipline. This restrained freedom was a pragmatic compromise between individualism and consistency which typifies Carruthers' long struggle to create a party that was solid whilst still being "liberal".

Party unity would prove even more important as the Carruthers Government faced the biggest controversy of its tenure, the land scandals. The corruption at the heart of these scandals took place during the life of the previous Government, when people had allegedly paid money to the Minister for Lands Paddy Crick and his close friend and fellow MP W.N. Willis for the consideration of Crown land leases, and frequently the reclassification of existing leases as improvement leases. These improvement leases were meant to be given out on land that was not yet suitable for closer settlement and under the clauses of Carruthers' 1895 Land Act they gave more generous terms than their closer settlement equivalents. Because of these terms, which included being able to acquire far more land under a 28-year lease and then be rewarded with permanent ownership for having improved it, people wanted to have their land reclassified no matter how suitable for closer settlement it already was and this is where the incentive for corruption came in. The scandal broke when a Mr. R.S. Sims was unsuccessful in his attempt to have his land reclassified and thus tried to recover the money that through an intermediary had been given to Willis.[345] Initially the Government was somewhat unresponsive to the allegations that were revealed during Sims' court case, but after a sustained press agitation a Royal Commission into the administration of the Lands Department was set up. This subsequently revealed cases where payments had been made for the consideration of leases, something that Crick defended as the equivalent of a barrister's fee.

Though the incidents occurred when he was in Opposition, Carruthers was dragged into the land scandals for several reasons. Firstly, he had been the Minister for Lands under Reid and any allegations of institutional corruption thus reflected badly on him. Secondly, his law firm had the misfortune of having acted for Willis in some of his legal proceedings and once this was revealed Carruthers retired from practising law until he was out of office. On both accounts he was exonerated. He appeared freely before the Commission, gave it all of his books and in the end the Commissioner, though he was not directly investigating the Premier, felt compelled to state that the evidence had shown no wrong-doing by Carruthers. Even Labor historian H.V. Evatt, who was no fan of the Premier, having looked closely at this period of history found that "there was no substance in the innuendoes against Carruthers".[346] The third reason Carruthers was dragged in however was the one he could not escape, and that was the Government's apparent lack of urgency in dealing with the scandals. People could point to the delay in appointing the Commission and then in extending its powers, the fact that Willis was allowed to escape to South Africa and the delay in retrieving him, and also the botched prosecutions that ensured most of the guilty parties got off, all to suggest that Carruthers did not want the matter sorted out and then insert their own scurrilous reason as to why.

In his biography of Labor member William Holman, one of the fiercest critics of the Government during the time of the scandals, Evatt seems to accept from his subject that something untoward must have gone on, but fails to give a clear reason as to why. What he does give is the subtle implication that Carruthers was trying to protect members of the former See-Waddell group who were drifting towards the Liberal benches.[347] He even goes so far as to assert that Norton, who attacked Holman in the Assembly and forced him into a distracting by-election, was trying to protect both Crick and Carruthers from Holman's critiques. Such assertions cannot be sustained against the weight of evidence from actions which we know far more about. As has been shown earlier, Carruthers and Norton held each other in such contempt from their previous libel battle that it is difficult to imagine them combining no matter what the circumstances. Rather than easing with the passing of time, the evidence actually suggests that their ill-feelings were as strong as ever, for after Carruthers retired for health reasons it was Norton who would suggest that he had done so to flee the indignity of the scandals.

As for Carruthers' needing to protect the former See-Waddell group in order to shore up his position in the Assembly, the Premier needed only some of the votes of that extremely fractured group to hold power.

These votes were specifically those of Waddell and his immediate followers. Waddell and Crick had a strained relationship; the latter had refused
to serve under the former and while that was about pride as much as
anything else Crick had later attacked Waddell during the 1904 election
campaign.[348] Since Crick had been part of the See but not the Waddell
Government, he could easily be thrown under the bus and that is what
Carruthers eventually did, kicking him out of Parliament and using him
as a stick with which to beat Labor who had kept him in power. As any
Opposition may be expected to do with anything, Labor tried to use the
handling of the scandals to attack the Government but their censure
motions failed.

If Carruthers was guilty of anything when it came to the land scandals it was of a severe misreading of public sentiment. The Premier felt
the matter needed to be dealt with through the courts and that any government interference in the process of trial by jury would be an intense
breach of office, equivalent at least to the Friedman affair. His papers
reveal that he was collecting and heavily influenced by intellectual justifi-
cations for the principle of trial by jury, particularly that of liberal writer
Alexis de Toqueville who had suggested that its introduction was a key
moment in humanity's ascent from barbarism. Inflamed by the prospect
of corruption in one of the State's most important departments and
fanned by a frenzied press, the public had no time for such legal niceties.
By the time Carruthers realised this and moved against Crick, the damage
to the Ministry's reputation had already been done.

Throughout the entire ordeal the Governor gave the Premier his full
support. Rawson had an intense dislike for the drunkard Crick, and had
refused to even contemplate commissioning him Premier after See had
resigned. He was outraged that his genuine friend should be dragged
through the mud based on the misdeeds of such a lowlife. He wrote to
Carruthers "I think it is shameful the way they [both the press and the
Opposition] have tried to drag you into it".[349] In public Rawson made it
subtly clear that his opinion of the Premier had not changed, a great help
in what were trying times.

Part of the reason why Carruthers appeared to lack urgency when dealing with the scandals and attempted to gag debate over them is that he did not want distractions while he attempted to push his signature pieces of legislation, the Local Government Bills, through the House. The first of these, the Local Government (Shires) Bill was introduced in June 1905. Its aim was to incorporate compulsorily all rural areas of the State into shires, with the exclusion of the far Western areas which did not yet have the population to support such administration. It was shortly followed by the introduction of the Local Government (Extension) Bill which dealt with the municipalities of more urbanised areas. The main difference between the two was the number of responsibilities each required the local government body to undertake. Both shires and municipalities would need to care for roads, bridges, wharves, regulation of traffic, lights at crossroads, bushfires, floods, kerbing, guttering, tree-planting, street lighting and management of public watering places.[350] A municipality would also be required to provide a sanitary service, deal with garbage, provide drains, sewers, simple water supplies, regulate and license public vehicles and hawkers, care for and manage parks, reserves and commons not under trustees, while a shire could choose to undertake these responsibilities. Further responsibilities could also be undertaken by application to the Local Government Commissioners. The State retained the right to declare any important work a national one and thereby assume responsibility over it. While arguably a necessary clause, if abused this left the door open for the continued presence of the "roads and bridges" member. It was hoped that the degree of flexibility present in the Bills would allow for the vast range of developmental stages present across New South Wales.

Determined that the new level of government should not result in a great increase in the overall burden of taxation as federation had, Carruthers gave local governments an endowment based on the number of responsibilities they had accepted and effectively handed over the land tax so that large new imposts were not required to fund them. This land tax now took the form of council rates of 1d in the £ on the unimproved value of land, which could be increased according to requirements. The average rate levied by shires immediately following the passing of the

Act was 1.08d and while the average for municipalities was higher their constituents had previously been paying both rates and the land tax.[351] At this level the rate was a tax hike only to the extent that the new rates lacked the exemptions of the old land tax and that Crown land leases would now become rateable. Carruthers justified this by arguing that the inefficiencies and abuses of the existing system were increasing the public debt and thus pushing up taxation. On top of these general rates, special rates could be levied on the improved or unimproved value of land but only by municipalities and only if approved by a poll.

While almost all the provisions of the two Bills were hotly debated, it was the proposed franchise that caused the most controversy. Though plural voting in any single Council was to be abolished, the Bills gave the vote only to those who paid rates, either directly or indirectly through rent, and allowed a ratepayer to vote in more than one Council. In this manner the franchise was much wider than that of the older Municipalities Act, but the Labor Party still objected to this provision as undemocratic. Carruthers brushed off their concerns, insisting that those who did not even contribute half a penny to the municipal coffers should not vote in elections that would ultimately determine how that money was spent. Though he likely believed in this ideological justification, it is probable that like Reid, Carruthers also felt that a compromise on the franchise would help to get the Bills through the Legislative Council.

Reid's Local Government Bill had been killed off by Labor concerns over the franchise, but Carruthers was now in a position to ignore them. In many ways the passing of the Local Government Bills was the legislative upshot of Carruthers' clear lines of cleavage. Beyond defining issues that helped to shape government majorities, previous Parliaments had often been able to overcome party divides and the staunch individuality of members to pass much through what amounted to consensus. Compulsory arbitration is an example of this, as despite loud critics on the fringes many in the three major Parties came together to pass what, for different reasons, they thought to be a beneficial Act. There were however limits to this consensus. Once a reform became too complex and too wide sweeping the cumulative adversaries of its individual clauses would ultimately defeat it. Local government had been the perennial victim of this. Despite near universal support, a failure to reach a consensus on details had meant that it had frequently been passed over. Meanwhile legislation on more divisive issues like the tariff had passed because its backers succeeded in making it a yes-no question. Now in an increasingly divided House with parties representing broad ideological positions rather than single issues, numerous questions became a matter of yes or no, for the clear lines of cleavage made every question that had a degree of importance a choice between Liberal and Labor. This in turn firmed up majorities meaning that ironically partisanship was able to break a deadlock which was more than a decade old. A number of amendments were made to the Local Government Bills before they were passed, and Liberals were given a largely free hand in the discussion of provisions but once it became a question of whether the Bills would succeed or fail the Liberal majority was enough to see them through.

Though in basic principle they had near universal approval, Carruthers' Local Government Bills were coloured by the ideological prism that defined his side of the political divide. In advocating the Shires Bill Carruthers pointed to the tiny proportion of the State that had been incorporated and argued that the lack of local government created an over-reliance on the State Government. He felt this centralisation had "destroyed the spirit of self-reliance in the people", dragged public servants away from the country and into the city and placed a great strain on the public purse.[352] Carruthers argued that without local government people had been more willing to push for greater local spending because the costs of that spending would be dissipated across the State, but with more direct responsibility they could be taught that government spending was "putting a burden on their own backs". To reinforce this he even put in a provision that required a municipality to gain the approval of the Local Government Commissioners and then its ratepayers at a poll before it could engage in any borrowing. Local government had long been thought of as a remedy to the insidious influence of the so-called "roads and bridges" member whose sole purpose was to secure spending for their area, but now Carruthers' liberal viewpoint had led him to the theory that decentralisation could be used to actively reduce the size of government.

One may question whether this theory has proven naïve. Voter apathy towards the lowest tier of government has arguably meant that electors pay less rather than more attention to spending at that level. Equally local government has not killed off the impulse that saw "roads and bridges" members seek spending on their electorates in the hope of being rewarded at the ballot-box. Even so, the fact that pieces of legislation that were not inherently ideological were becoming so offers a glimpse into the new political reality that was emerging at this time. The Local Government Bills, amalgamated as the Local Government Act 1906, were perhaps more successful in their simpler aims of giving people greater representation at a local level and facilitating the smooth administration of the State. Twenty years after Carruthers first sought election his promise on local government had been fulfilled and his Act would remain in place with little amendment for nearly 85 years.[353]

The other major piece of legislation introduced in 1905 was the Liquor (Amendment) Bill. Moved by Wade as a non-party measure, this instituted a number of regulations for the liquor industry, including restrictions on the sale of liquor to children, on Sundays and on election days. Its central and most controversial clause however was local option, which gave each electorate the ability to choose between continuing the sale of liquor at present levels, reducing the number of liquor licences or eliminating them entirely, based on a poll of its electors. As originally introduced a 50% participation rate and two-thirds majority would be required to completely eliminate licences but temperance lobbying saw this reduced to 30% participation and a three-fifths majority.

Almost as controversial as local option itself was the issue of whether or not the hoteliers who were robbed of their business by a vote should be entitled to compensation. Carruthers voted against compensation but suggested that hoteliers be given "reasonable" notice before being required to terminate their business.[354] This was a difficult position to maintain as in essence a property right was being unilaterally taken away by the Government without paying any respect to its value, a precedent that the business community and many ideological liberals did not want set. It had more than a modicum of socialism about it and for those without a deep seeded hatred of the industry could only be justified on budgetary grounds. Even for a government dedicated to reducing the debt these grounds were thin and the whole affair demonstrated that economically liberal goals did not necessarily suit socially conservative legislation.

There was another ideological tension inherent in the Liquor Bill, for the complete abolition of the liquor trade by vote was a "tyranny of the majority" that restricted the freedom of both individuals and businesses and was therefore arguably illiberal. One could contend that since each electorate could make up its own mind, State wide prohibition was extremely unlikely to eventuate and therefore the tyranny would be lessened, but Carruthers' long-standing position on this issue was still somewhat incongruous to his other beliefs. The incongruity can be attributed to Carruthers' pragmatism and flexibility that made him a classical liberal rather than a libertarian, and this biography has already suggested that his father's relationship with alcohol affected Joseph's attitude towards this issue.

Don Harwin has suggested that while Carruthers was "more than just a cynical exploiter of the temperance lobby for political purposes" he may have had an eye on working class Protestant votes which might be wooed by local option.[355] This view has some merit, and if this was the case Carruthers may have felt that *moderate* temperance legislation was a way to appease these voters without sacrificing too many principles or engaging in sectarianism. It is important to remember however that evidence of secret motivations eludes historians at the best of times, and after the passing of a century even more so. Publicly Carruthers would complain that temperance got in the way of a clear choice between liberalism and socialism, and the evidence suggests that he continued to view the lines of cleavage as his main vote winner. Later in life Carruthers would admit that license restriction polls only succeeded in those electorates where there was the least need for them, but he never intimated that the legislation should have therefore gone further in the way of prohibition.[356]

Similar to the Liquor Bill and maintaining some of its paternalism was the gambling legislation introduced in 1906. This restricted betting outside licensed race-courses. Some suggested that this was unfair as only the wealthy were able to attend race courses while the poor did their gambling in hotels and in the streets. It was soon amended so as to permit trots at agricultural shows. These were reasonably pervasive so that all but the most metropolitan poor could access some gambling throughout the year. There was some suggestion that this amendment may have been made as a sop to O'Sullivan, who had been uniting opposition to the Bill under the New South Wales Sporting League, but its main aim was undoubtedly to appease the rural voters who would be so vital come election time. The motivation behind the legislation itself seems to be more nuanced than the simpler wowserism behind local option. After all, gambling was still to be legally available and its restriction off-course could be justified on the grounds that it was impossible to regulate away from the track. The gambling legislation is perhaps best understood as a reaction to new technology, for it was the developments of the electronic age that had made off-track betting possible and it was the novelty of this possibility that helped to fuel an exaggerated fear of its social consequences.

This fear inevitably flourished amongst conservative Protestant groups and though most of these wanted the Government to take a far firmer stance on betting, on the whole the gambling legislation helped to strengthen the pre-existing sectarian affiliations of the two major parties. Interestingly Labor leader McGowen, who was not a Catholic, actually supported both the Liquor and Gaming Bills, though he was not very bellicose about it and, like the Liberals, his party was given a free hand to vote on the issues.

With the two Bills the Protestant-Liberal alliance, if it had ever consciously existed, had reached its peak and subtly both sides began to drift apart. For decades it would remain the case that Protestants were more likely to vote Liberal and Catholics more likely to vote Labor, but at the next election Protestant groups were less visibly active. These groups set about recovering a "middle position" that would allow them to have some influence over Labor.[357] For their part the Liberals were concerned that they might seem too Protestant and thereby alienate a significant part of the electorate. Carruthers received a private warning from one of his Cabinet colleagues that the APDA needed to be kept at arm's length for the good of the Party, and though the Liquor and Gaming Bills were hailed as reform achievements the Premier proposed no new wowser legislation at the next election.[358]

It was not this wowser legislation which met with the worst reaction from Catholic newspapers, but Carruthers' decision to use some of his accumulated surplus to make public schooling completely free by abolishing the residual threepence a week fee that was presently being charged for tuition. The *Catholic Press* vehemently denounced the fee abolition as a tax on Catholics who would be forced to pay even more for a public education system which they objected to using.[359] The Labor Party supported the Bill however, as did most of the Progressive rump, leaving Catholics nowhere to express electorally their indignation.

The introduction of free education was part of a wider program to reform education and increase spending on it now that the seasons had improved. During the time of the See Government an extensive Royal Commission into education had taken place, but few of its wide-sweeping recommendations had been implemented. Carruthers had played a prominent role in pushing for the commission, and now that he was in power he was determined to act upon its findings. In Minister for Public Instruction Broughton O'Conor, Carruthers had chosen a popular and adept ally to help him with the task. Before joining the Ministry O'Conor had been a National Federalist then an independent member, and his elevation was therefore based on his personal talents (and guaranteeing his vote), rather than partisan loyalty.

The central aspect of the education reforms was the appointment of a Director of Education to coordinate the public service effort that went behind the face-to-face teaching of students. With careful planning a new syllabus was laid down, placing a greater emphasis on science than ever before. A new program was introduced which saw itinerant teachers sent around rural schools to teach the technical subjects they had previously been missing out on. Teacher training was improved with the establishment of the long-delayed Teachers College at the University of Sydney. Teachers' wages were increased, as was the money spent on public school buildings. The Technical College in Ultimo, which Carruthers had propped up as Minister for Public Instruction, was given another boost with increased funding and a specialist super-intendent painstakingly sourced from England. Money was also set aside for the founding of university veterinary and agricultural schools.

A more personal reform was the introduction of Empire Day. Carruthers personally spearheaded the introduction of the celebration which would be held annually on the 24th of May, Queen Victoria's birthday. He convinced the other Premiers to join him in making the day one to inculcate students in patriotism and their duty to a wider British world. There is some suggestion that Carruthers saw imperialist-nationalism as a counter both to fledgling republicanism and socialism.[360] He had long viewed the British Empire as the embodiment of ideals including liberalism, democracy and freedom, and he felt that it would be beneficial to society if these ideals were reinforced from an early age. Celebrated with addresses, songs, flag-waving and occasional fireworks, Empire Day would become a calendar staple for decades.

Of particular concern to the historically minded Premier was the building of a library near Parliament. This was designed to house a collection of important documents and artefacts from the Colony's early history which had been bequeathed to the State by collector and philanthropist David Scott Mitchell. It was built in conspicuously grand style, especially considering that Carruthers had criticised the spending his predecessors had heaped on the even more ostentatious Central Station. He justified this extravagance by the value of Mitchell's collection, without which he claimed "the history of New South Wales could not be written" and also on Mitchell's insistence that his bequest was conditional on the collection being well housed.[361] Over time the wealth of the collection has been built upon with donations of other historical documents and the Mitchell Library has become one of the most important academic buildings in all of Australia. A plaque commemorating the lay-ing of a foundation stone by Carruthers still emblazons the magnificent building which now holds his own papers.

While Carruthers had taken great pains to stabilise the public works budget, he did not put a halt to infrastructure building during his Premiership. The most important construction begun while he was in office was the North Coast Railway which opened up the Mid-North Coast and Northern Rivers area of which his family had been pioneers.

The creation of a unified State Bank was one of the most controversial planks of Liberal's 1904 election platform. Towards the end of that year Carruthers had managed to get it passed by the Legislative Assembly, but it was promptly rejected by the Council as one of several Bills that prompted the Government's early standoff with that Chamber. One of the Council's main objections was that the Bill would allow the new bank to subsume the existing Barrack Street Savings Bank without its depositors' permission. In 1906 the Savings Bank Bill was reintroduced with a new clause that required the approval of a poll of these depositors before their savings could be absorbed into the new entity. Labor was largely dissatisfied with this concession but it appeased the now more ameliorative Upper House and this time they allowed the Bill's passage.

Though it was widely condemned as a foray into socialism, the Savings Bank Act did not introduce the concept of a State Bank into New South Wales, but amalgamated existing State Banks including the old Savings Bank, the Post Office Savings Bank and the Advances to Settlers Board, and transferred control of the new entity into the hands of three Commissioners. Its aim was to carry on the business of these establishments more efficiently. The new government bank possessed few powers not held by its predecessors, was still restricted to holding savings and giving advances to settlers, and could not undertake most of the business of an ordinary bank and thus compete with private institutions. Despite all these conditions its right-wing critics feared that centralisation would make the bank more powerful and they worried that a single bank would be easier for the Labor Party to use for socialistic ends. They took Labor objections to the Barrack Street poll as proof of disguised intentions that would not have been approved by depositors, and until that clause was introduced they had claimed that Carruthers' Bill was aimed at trying to cosy up to the Labor Party.

The fact that Carruthers was able to ignore these fears shows the security of his position within the lines of cleavage. He was able to accept the look of ideological inconsistency in order to improve the State's finances, which were partially reliant on the savings contained within the bank and would thus reap the benefits of increased efficiency. All the while he felt safe that, within certain limits, the Liberal-Labor dichotomy would help prevent the leaking of votes to the right for fear of putting his opponents into power. That is not to say that Carruthers' ignored the views of his right-wing critics, just that he artfully balanced how pragmatic he could be while keeping his diffuse supporters onside. A large amount of the campaign against the Bill was based on misinformation. Important party donors who had not even read the document threatened to withdraw their funds, while the organisers of the Women's Liberal League requested hundreds of copies of the Bill in order to assuage their members' fears. Once a methodical campaign of explanation was carried out however, few supporters were lost over the issue.

One of the cost-saving exercises Carruthers had proposed at the beginning of his Premiership was the abolition of the position of Agent-General in London, a post which might soon be superseded by the appointment of a Federal High Commissioner. He realised however that as long as the States continued to negotiate British loans independently, separate Agent-Generals would be required. To this end Carruthers had Timothy Coghlan perform the role of acting Agent-General before being given the official title, at a level of pay lower than his predecessor, in 1906. Coghlan was a long serving public servant with considerable financial acumen and free trade sympathies. He had been offered the position of Federal statistician by Deakin but had refused it under obscure circumstances. There is some suggestion that the New South Wales Government had to threaten his pension in order to corral him into the decision.[362]

Showing no signs of ill-feeling, Coghlan fought vigorously for the interests of New South Wales and her Government. With the State's economy going strong once again, he launched a campaign to attract suitable migrants to fuel New South Wales' expansion. Carruthers insisted that only those suited to hard work would be of benefit, while those with "English notions, wives and young families" were bound to fail. Coghlan's main focus was financial. By successfully selling Carruthers' economic reliability in contrast with his predecessors, he was able to float new loans at lower interest rates to pay off existing debts. In the process of doing so he controversially overlooked the Bank of England to pursue better terms from the London County and Westminster Bank. State governments had traditionally chosen between these two institutions when procuring loans, but prior to this New South Wales had paid extra for the more prestigious option. Carruthers also directed Coghlan to invest part of the budget surplus in England, where it could continue to grow for future use.[363]

It was this surplus that was proving to be an intractable political problem for the Treasurer. With controlled spending and a booming economy, the surplus was growing rapidly each year. In 1905 the excess of ordinary revenue over expenditure was approximately £200,000, in 1906 it was £900,000 and in 1907 it was £600,000.[364] This was a considerable proportion of the revenue when ordinary expenditure fluctuated between approximately £11,000,000 and £12,500,000. While much of this went to paying off inherited debt and funding public works that would have otherwise required new loans, people began complaining that the surpluses demonstrated that taxation was clearly too high. This discontent was reflected in the *Daily Telegraph* and in particular the *Sydney Morning Herald*, which began to turn on Carruthers. The latter demanded that the income tax be abolished since it had been introduced to fund free trade which no longer existed and since it was inquisitorial and unnecessarily probed into people's private affairs. The *Herald* also warned that even if Carruthers was investing the surplus wisely the temptation it offered governments would eventually breed extravagance. Their warning was not unfounded, for Carruthers' papers reveal that some of his own supporters, and even Bruce Smith, had begun to lobby him for increased spending.[365]

When reflecting on his financial administration in his memoirs Carruthers said that he followed the Gladstonian principle that the best way to restore the public finances and to fix unemployment was to leave money to "fructify" in people's pockets:

> I made the chief aim of my policy ... to strengthen the position of individual members of the community to earn more money to improve their financial position, to assure them more prosperity, more of the good things of life, feeling satisfied that if I succeeded in that purpose the unemployment problem would be solved and with it the problem of our financial difficulties.[366]

While it is true that the Treasurer avoided the temptation of trying to tax his way back into surplus, up until 1906 he had been more cautious than this bold statement implies. In that year his budget finally attempted to reduce the burden of government along his ideological lines. Even this was done in a more limited and calculated way than his critics would have liked. To encourage commerce railway rates were lowered and tolls on punts and ferries were abolished. Carruthers claimed that this succeeded in its aim to the extent that despite lower rates railway profits greatly rose through increased use, though he admitted that the luck of good seasons also helped. These reductions in indirect taxation were followed by a promise to abolish income tax for farmers who paid land tax, adding fuel to the agricultural boom that had followed the end of the drought.

This was not enough for those that once again began to cry that "reform" had not been carried into fruition. These hard-line reformers, many of whom continued to make their home in the PRL, were also concerned that Carruthers had not done anything about the Industrial Arbitration Act. Considering the number of labour deputations he saw who claimed that it was essentially broken and needed to be strengthened, this inaction was at least a position of neutrality rather than of sympathising with the Opposition but it was still a sticking point for many. Further adding to the Premier's difficulties was another scandal, this time more limited in scope, which involved the Railway Commissioners. An inquiry into their affairs found that they had mishandled the tendering of coal contracts and while by law the Commissioners had acted independently of the Government there was much handwringing over their replacement. Things became so bad that there were rumours of a secret caucus condemning the Premier's handling of the land scandals and of McMillan being brought in to Parliament and then the Liberal leadership to deliver a more hard line approach.[367] This was the only avenue open to critics to the right of Carruthers to whom a Labor Government was unthinkable, but party loyalty held and no coup eventuated.

Carruthers was the face of the land scandals and the finances so this negativity focused on him, but many of his Ministers were personally popular. Most surprisingly, this included Ashton, who though he was Minister for Lands seemed to stand above much of the ruckus. Before the scandals broke he had passed a Land Bill strengthening his office's powers to resume large estates by arrangement or if needed by compulsion with due oversight by a Closer Settlement Board of local and court representatives. This land would then be parcelled out as freehold, much to the ire of Labor who generally approved resumption but opposed the subsequent alienation of the land. Once the Bill was passed Ashton quietly went about utilising these powers so that by 1907 Carruthers could claim that a vast quantity of land had been made available and 5,652 new settlers had been placed upon it.[368] Ashton was also involved in the setting up of a large and innovative irrigation scheme with the erection of the Barren Jack (now Burrinjuck) reservoir. When the scandal hit he proposed to place the administration of the Lands Department in the hands of independent Commissioners to prevent further abuses, but a Bill on the matter was allowed to lapse. Sick of politics and frustrated by a number of accusations which had been hurled against him, he announced that he would not be standing at the next election.

Ashton was not the only one, for he would be joined by fellow Cabinet members O'Conor and William Dick. All three would soon be nominated for the Legislative Council where they would continue to prosecute liberal causes, but for the moment their exodus left a huge hole in the Ministry. To plug that hole, one final attempt was made to bring the

Progressives into the Liberal ranks. When writing two decades later Carruthers would justify this by saying "the line of cleavage was distinct enough to warrant the action I took".[369] Clearly he felt that liberal anti-socialism would have ultimately consumed the identity of the rudderless Progressives. The LRA gave Carruthers a free hand to negotiate, and meetings of both parliamentary parties agreed in principle to a coalition. What they could not agree on was the details of a union. The Liberals were prepared to offer a Cabinet position to Waddell immediately and after the election to reconsider offices based on merit rather than party affiliation. Despite their numerical inferiority, many Progressives resented this attempt to absorb their following and demanded a greater guarantee of representation in a more equal coalition. This demand was not ceded and in May 1907 a meeting of the Progressives voted against joining the Government by 7 votes to 5.[370]

At this result Waddell, who had led the "yes" vote, resigned from the Party and took up the post of Colonial Secretary. His decision shattered the rump and whatever semblance of a Progressive "Party" which remained soon evaporated. Several of its members followed Waddell's lead and became fully fledged Liberals, while others styled themselves as independents. O'Sullivan, who himself had led the "no" vote, set up a Democratic Party which adopted almost the entire Labor platform but rejected the pledge. It would not meet with electoral success.

When Waddell joined the Liberal Cabinet he did not have to undertake a ministerial by-election because the Government had passed a Parliamentary Elections Act finally removing this archaic necessity. The main aim of the Act was to bring the State's electoral laws into line with those of the Commonwealth. Most of its clauses were uncontroversial, but some fuss was stirred up over the decision to abolish electors' rights and to reintroduce candidates' deposits. The former was a form of documentation required to vote, which in theory was meant to prevent voter fraud. In practice many believed it had encouraged fraud, for the rights were allegedly collected and used to assume people's votes. In a time before compulsory voting the necessity to obtain such documentation also likely discouraged people from voting, an impediment for the Liberals who despite the LRA still felt themselves less able to mobilise their supporters than their unionised opponents.

The candidates' deposit was an old requirement that demanded those who decided to stand for election hand over a sum of money which would only be returned to them if they obtained a certain percentage of the vote. It was meant to discourage a multiplicity of candidates who had no hope of winning but could serve to complicate the electoral process. Thought undemocratic by some, the deposit requirement had been removed by a previous Act but the Elections Bill Hogue brought before Parliament proposed to reintroduce it at a lower sum. Both clauses were met with Labor objections, but the latter attracted far more opposition and it was dropped amidst newspaper howls that Carruthers was once again giving in to the socialists.[371]

For months Carruthers had to put up with relentless criticisms that he was letting the LRA fall behind in its organising efforts and that he had failed to articulate a new policy for the rapidly impending elections. When negotiations with the Progressives came to an end the Premier was finally free to articulate a fresh liberal agenda, safe in the knowledge that he would not have to appease a coalition partner. In an address to his constituents in Kogarah the Premier declared that through a combination of good seasons, reduced spending (which he claimed had gone down per head of population despite complaints that it was still too high), and good management, it was finally possible to reduce taxation greatly.[372] He promised to abolish the income tax on all incomes derived from personal exertion, and instead of leaving in place the expensive machinery of that taxation just to levy incomes derived from interest and investment he proposed to introduce a small automatic dividend duty which would entail none of the inquisitorial evils of the present system. His differentiation between money a man earned "by the sweat of his hands and brain" and money "earned for him while he slept" echoed the logic behind the old free trade belief in taxing only the unimproved value of land.

To go with the abolition of the income tax, the Premier also proposed to remove the stamp duty on receipts which discouraged business activity and to further reduce railway rates. All told there was to be £720,000 less taxation while still leaving a surplus for leaner years. Other policy proposals included removing the Conciliation and Arbitration Act and replacing it with wages boards which he claimed promoted harmony not hostility and had been far more successful in Victoria. There was to be a Workmen's Compensation Bill, the size of Parliament would be further reduced to 60 members and a greater Sydney body would be given control over those local government responsibilities in which centralisation was utterly necessary for cost effectiveness.

The policy outlined in the speech was one of the most radical and economically liberal ever put forward by an Australian Liberal leader and it suggests that Carruthers' earlier obstinacy towards his critics resulted not from ideological disagreement but from this shrewd and practical politician's desire to wait until both the economic and political situation was ripe. The distinguished historian Ronald Syme once wrote that "no statement of unrealised intentions is a safe guide to history, for it is unverifiable and therefore the most attractive form of misrepresentation".[373] It would seem that this sound piece of historiographical theory has been misused on Carruthers. Historians have repeatedly related how he did not live up to his reform agenda and that he was not as economically liberal as some of his followers, all the while largely ignoring the policy promises made in the lead up to the 1907 election.[374] Though he never got the opportunity to fulfil these it would be wrong to throw them away. After all, excepting Legislative Council reform Carruthers had a good track record of making good on those policy promises which he had given clear articulation, and most of his promises would be carried through by his immediate successor Charles Wade. These included the establishment of wages boards, the abolition of most forms of stamp duty and the abolition of income tax for earnings under £1000. The latter was a controversial compromise that eliminated the need for a dividend duty. The fact that Wade, a man not known for his political finesse, was able to achieve such radical reforms is further testament to the legislative effects of the lines of cleavage.

To ignore the proposals of 1907 is to misunderstand Carruthers and

269

inevitably place him further left on the political spectrum than he by rights should be. In many ways his Premiership proved to be the archetype of Liberal rule in the age of the lines of cleavage. The first term focused on conservative economic management, clearing up the mess Carruthers felt his predecessors had left him while also enacting the main policies that had helped to propel him to power. By the time of the next election the economic situation had improved to the point where the Liberals could offer tax reductions without increasing the debt or making drastic cuts to spending. Carruthers was setting a precedent that many Liberals, including at the Federal level, would come to follow even if they would not be conscious of doing so. Meanwhile the precedents of three-party chaos in the Federal sphere, and of hard line and reactive "reform" in Victoria, which were being set simultaneously, would not be followed in the same way. Establishing historical causation to the point of saying that post-war governments were directly influenced by Carruthers' example is difficult, but it is reasonable to say that as the Premier of the fledgling Commonwealth's largest State his actions helped to shape, to some extent, the political climate of the nation from which these future governments would emerge.

Carruthers' new small-government policy was met with a joyous reaction from the same pressmen who had often been baying for his political blood. The PRL-sympathising *Sunday Times* discussed the proposals under the heading "progress and prosperity" and admitted that the Government had "so far shown a disposition to carry out its pledges".[375] The *Sydney Morning Herald* was also reasonably happy, though it criticised the dividend duty as a tax on industry that would discourage investment. Labor papers were inevitably suspicious of the wages boards, but it looked as though Carruthers could be assured of the general support of much of the press during an election fought on these lines. These proposals would soon fall into the background however, as issues with the Federal Government that had nagged away throughout Premier's term finally blew up in an unprecedented manner.

CHAPTER TWELVE

On the National Stage

When Carruthers ascended to the Premiership in 1904 he received numerous congratulatory letters from across the State and indeed the country. Free Trade Senator Edward Millen warned the Premier that "it is no light task to wean the constituency from the lavish expenditure to which they have grown accustomed" but that "its successful accomplishment must lend to the permanent wellbeing of the State".[376] One supporter buoyed by the success of the election urged Carruthers to enter Federal politics, to which the exhausted campaigner replied "I shall reach no higher sphere of work until I get wings".[377] Bernhard Wise sent his old colleague a rather self-aggrandising letter emphasising the similarity between them and hinting, ever so slightly, that he felt it should have been him occupying the top job.[378] The most important letter however was that sent by George Reid, who beamed to his long-time friend that:

> to vanquish the Ministerial and Labor parties combined was a task of great magnitude, and that you have succeeded in doing that points to good leadership, good organisation, devoted services and an unmistakable rally to the cause of good government by the electors generally.[379]

Carruthers' time as Premier corresponded almost entirely with Reid's famed anti-socialist campaign and neither event can be fully understood without the other. That campaign lasted from late 1904 until the 1906 Federal election and its aim, apart from defeating nascent socialism, was to bring an end to the three-party turmoil in Federal politics, in the same way that Carruthers had ended it in New South Wales politics, by making the central political question a choice between Reid's liberal anti-socialism and what he argued was Labor's increasing socialism.

It was Carruthers' electoral success that helped to convince Reid that anti-socialism could be used as a tool to subdue not only Labor, but by making the fiscal issue redundant as it had become in New South Wales, the Protectionists as well. Reid "saw in an anti-socialist crusade the best, indeed the only means, of bringing about a [political] realignment", which was necessary for the functioning of responsible government based on stable majorities.[380] This was the exact same reasoning that Carruthers had elaborated in his lines of cleavage statement in 1901. The emphasis Reid's letter places on the "magnitude" of Carruthers' successful task highlights the extent to which he was impressed by the achievement of a stable majority and along with similarities in rhetoric, strategy and organisation, strongly suggests that the anti-socialist campaign was at least partly inspired by Carruthers' efforts.[381] At one point in the campaign Reid even used the term "line of cleavage" when elaborating on the difference between democracy and socialism.[382] This is a crucial historical point, for the campaign would play a key role in setting up the party-division in Federal politics in a manner which mirrored the situation in New South Wales.

Before discussing Carruthers' role in the anti-socialist campaign it is necessary to offer a brief background as to what was happening in Federal politics. As in New South Wales in the 1890s, early Federal politics was dominated by a battle between Free Traders, Protectionists and the Labor Party. Unlike the 1890s however, the Labor Party was no longer a minor player and by 1903 it held representation roughly equal to its fiscal rivals. This equality and the inability of any two of the three parties to form a stable coalition led to political instability which saw members from all three parties achieve the Prime Ministership in the second Parliament, only to be subsequently deposed.

It was Labor's turn at the top of this political ruckus which caused an important break. The sight of a Labor Prime Minister committed to a great expansion in the size and role of the Federal Government suggested that there were bigger issues to be fought over than the tariff. Despite the brevity of J.C. Watson's reign, it sufficiently scared the anti-socialist elements of the two Federal fiscal parties that they formed a coalition. In 1904 Reid formed a Ministry from a combination of his Free Traders (rapidly being restyled as the Anti-Socialist Party) and a number of

Protectionists. With the coalition necessitating a retirement of the fiscal issue, the new government needed a reason for its existence and found one readily in rallying round the anti-socialist flag. While that flag had not been entirely created by Carruthers, he had come up with the idea of using it to bring about a political realignment, and now it was being picked up by Reid with the hope off doing the same.

Anti-socialism centred on a rejection of some of the big government aspects of Labor ideology. While not laissez-faire and allowing for an important role for the state, it objected to how big some in the Labor Party wanted that role to be and generally supported private enterprise against those who wanted to see it partially or wholly usurped. It opposed proposals for union privileges which were seen as detrimental to freedom and sinisterly pushing the interests of a particular section of society. These privileges were given expression not only in the special place of unions in the Federal Arbitration Act, but also by the "union label" proposals that aimed to give benefits to manufacturers who employed only union labour.[383] Most of all, anti-socialism opposed what was known as the "socialist objective" in the Labor platform. Initially this had just proposed the nationalisation of monopolies, something that a significant number of liberals could agree to, but now there was a movement to expand this objective to include the "nationalisation of the means of production, distribution and exchange".[384] While successful in Queensland, nationally and in New South Wales this movement succeeded only in obtaining a plank for the "collective ownership of monopolies, and the extension of the industrial and economic functions of the State". Even this milder goal was objectionable to Carruthers, who not only supported the pervading capitalist system but also held a moral objection to the subjugation of individual freedom to a powerful state.

Perhaps at an earlier time the socialist objective would not have caused such uproar, for as long as Labor remained a small party, winning legislative concessions from its bigger cousins, it could not hope to achieve such a goal. In the early Federal period the growing prospect of a Labor Government, both nationally and in New South Wales, brought the objective to a new prominence for it began to seem like a genuine possibility. While both Reid and Carruthers had allied themselves with a small and therefore "harmless" Labor Party in colonial politics, they soon saw that the prospect of mass nationalisations was a far bigger threat to liberal principles and free commerce than protection had ever been. It was for this reason that Carruthers had fought for the division of politics based not on trivial single issues, but on a philosophical approach to the role of government.

Reid would also come round to this position, but in Federal politics where the fiscal issue was still alive, putting anti-socialism first would not be an easy move. Many Free Traders criticised Reid for what they considered to be an abandonment of their core principle, while his Protectionist counterpart Alfred Deakin was unwilling to join Reid in letting sleeping dogs lie. Deakin was an imposing figure in the first decade after federation. A lawyer and occasional journalist, he had an eclectic range of interests ranging from spiritualism to writing poetry. This romanticism bled naturally into political beliefs which emphasised the possibility of smoothing the rough edges of human nature through the intervention of a benevolent state. As a pupil of David Syme, Deakin had been schooled in protectionist theory and a new liberalism which was archetypically Victorian. Though he never won an election outright, he served as Prime Minister three times and found it far less compromising to call on Labor support than did Reid. His central policy proposal "new protection" tied high tariff barriers to government-enforced high wages in a way that was inherently attractive to the Labor Electoral Leagues. Nevertheless, he maintained individualist beliefs and an acceptance of some forms of private enterprise that made him sceptical of absolute socialism and particularly the caucus pledge.

In 1904, shortly after Labor's Chris Watson became Prime Minister, Carruthers penned a letter to Deakin impressing upon him the urgent need to unite with Reid against the socialists. He insisted that although he was a follower of Reid and a Free Trade sympathiser he had been extremely disappointed by the recent fall of the Deakin Government and urged an anti-Labor coalition under either fiscal leader.[385] He also related that he had written to Reid about the coalition and that the Free Trade leader had expressed his willingness to combine provided Deakin reciprocated.

How important Carruthers' behind the scenes involvement was in the formation of the anti-socialist coalition is difficult to tell. It is doubtful whether Deakin would have paid much attention to the opinions of the "little man" from Sydney. Indeed, Deakin's eventual decision not to join a Reid coalition Cabinet suggests that he listened more to Wise's insidious suggestion "not to make the error of treating him [Reid] as if he were a gentlemen".[386] What the letter does reveal is that Carruthers had been discussing political strategy with Reid who was far more likely to heed his views. The letter to Deakin was sent on 1 May, hence the prior discussion with Reid must have been held in late April, concurrently with Watson's ascension to the Prime Ministership. Carruthers was thus one of Reid's earliest consultants on the political situation. The absence of sources makes it difficult to draw too deep a conclusion, but the evidence of early and important strategic discussion reinforces the likelihood that the anti-socialist campaign was partly inspired by Carruthers.

In late 1904 Reid's coalition did one better than Watson by managing to face Parliament and survive. The political situation was far from settled however and in the parliamentary recess of 1905 it began to look like the coalition could collapse. Carruthers once again took it upon himself to intervene and wrote to Deakin desperately urging him to end his aloofness from the Government. Denouncing Labor proposals for union preference he claimed that "socialism – so called – is too good a term for the Labor platform, which aims at nothing more nor less than to grip with dirty hands men who in industrial life have succeeded by honest effort and pull them down in the hopes that by artificial legislation Unionists, bound hip and thigh by union rules and tradition, may work the system of government for their seeming advantage".[387]

In his next letter he argued that since New South Wales had sacrificed Free Trade for federation the least the Protectionists could do was to sacrifice even higher tariffs in order to combat the Labor-Socialists. He also insisted that he was not working in Reid's interest but that:

> If you were Premier I should urge Reid and others to support you and I may say that at present I am keeping back our State Liberal Party, which consists of Free-traders and protectionists alike, from joining in with the Federal Liberal Party until I see what you do, If you fall into line, not with Reid, but with the fight for a Liberal policy versus a Labor-Socialist Policy, then our State Party will go with the Federal Party too.[388]

Peter Loveday uses this letter to imply that there was some sort of tension between Carruthers and Reid, but such a reading seems misguided.[389] Carruthers' insistence that he was not working in Reid's interest should not be taken at face value. This sort of assurance would have been necessary to get Deakin onside and while it is clear that Carruthers genuinely believed that a strong Federal coalition would be desirable that does not proscribe the possibility that he discussed his letter with Reid in advance in a manner that has not survived to us. As for falling in line "not with Reid" that was also about tempering Deakin, and ultimately his argument was that while either one of them could have been Prime Minister now that Reid was Deakin should support him. The holding back of the State Liberal Party was more likely to have been about not aggravating the Progressives than waiting for Deakin's direction, and it did not preclude Carruthers from lending Reid his most valuable political weapon in the form of Archdale Parkhill, as will be discussed below. The greatest tell-tale sign that Carruthers actually agreed with most of what Reid was doing was the fact that he described the anti-socialists as the Federal Liberal Party, a clear indication that he believed Reid's anti-socialism to be a correct interpretation of liberalism.

None of Deakin's responses were very reassuring.[390] While insisting that he had no desire to kick his Protectionist coalition friends out of office, Deakin dismissed the idea that the fiscal issue needed to be laid aside. He sympathised with Carruthers' distrust of Labor, but argued that Watson was far more reasonable than his State counterparts. As far as Deakin was concerned the limited responsibilities of the Federal Government meant that socialism could only be carried out at a State level, hence the realignment necessary in New South Wales was irrelevant to the Commonwealth Parliament.

Two weeks later Deakin made these views public by delivering a speech at Ballarat in which he dismissed the logic that anti-socialism needed to be put ahead of the fiscal issue. That speech let off a chain reaction that quickly led to the fall of Reid and the emergence of a Deakin Government based on Labor support. Awash with anger, frustration and dismay Carruthers penned one more letter to the new Prime Minister:

> I am so disappointed at the turn of events that I cannot really express any opinion of them … You Federal people don't understand the problem [of the Labor Party] because you have no financial trouble, but we in the State Govt. know that in our financing we discover the real opinion of Australia and the causes which continue to hold her back. The Labor Party is a "bete noir" to the forces that control our affairs outside the States and although you and others may affect to have a good opinion of Watson and his clan God help us when the forces that have made them get the domination of Australia.[391]

This passage reveals that along with an ideological opposition to the socialist objective and union preference, Carruthers' anti-socialism was based on a fear of the practical financial consequences of Labor rule. The hint is that in his negotiations with London banks the Treasurer had discovered that the See Government's inability to borrow money towards the end of its life was based not only on its extravagance but on the perception in England that it was the unreliable Labor-Socialists who were dictating that extravagance. Carruthers held the fear that the double whammy of the negative economic impact of socialist policies combined with a withdrawal of British capital could bring Australia to its knees. It was this practical fear that gave urgency to Carruthers' deep-seated ideological opposition to socialism, and given that he undoubtedly related these concerns to Reid, may also explain the haste and passion of the Federal anti-socialist leader.

That passion was expressed in the form of a national speaking tour preaching the anti-socialist message. This began while Reid was Prime Minister with a probable eye towards an early election, but was continued in Opposition even to the detriment of his parliamentary attendance. In words that directly echoed Carruthers', Reid told his audiences that "the real choice is between socialism and liberalism, between force and freedom". He showed particular concern to ensure that his tour reached not only the smaller States but also regional centres, much like Carruthers' emphasis on speaking to country voters. This similarity was hardly surprising, as much of the anti-socialist touring was organised by Archdale Parkhill, who as Secretary of the Australian Liberal League was performing a similar role for Reid as he had for Carruthers.

Inspired by the LRA, this new league was Federal in structure and was to be based on extensive local branches "to be combined and coordinated at the State level by a central executive consisting of branch delegates, democratically selected".[392] Once the coalition fell apart the League was superseded by the Australian Democratic Union, which unlike its predecessor was outwardly affiliated with the LRA. The fact that Carruthers allowed this affiliation suggests both that he was punishing Deakin for failing to "fall into line" and that he had accepted that for the moment a union between the Federal fiscal parties was impossible. Parkhill was central to both organisations, and set up a Pitt Street office with its own telephone and stationery to facilitate the running of affairs.

Though more successful than its Protectionist counterparts the ADU would fail to become the permanent Federal party organisation its leaders had hoped for. Post fusion it would be succeeded in New South Wales by the Federal Liberal League. Many of the branches of the FLL were made up of those of the LRA, and the new organisation borrowed its method of branch preselection and endorsement by a central council.[393] Parkhill was once again central to the FLL, and also played an important role as the "national political organiser" of what was an otherwise federally divided Commonwealth Liberal Party.[394] In that role Carruthers' protégé would go on to provide a strong LRA influence in the organisational structure of Federal non-Labor. Crucially he would later take the only national position in the extra-parliamentary organisation of the Nationalist Party, the first Federal non-Labor Party to last more than a decade and the first to start to develop the sort of organisational size and permanence its predecessors had desired. Because of Parkhill's unrivalled position in the Nationalist Party it may be argued that the organisational structure of Federal non-Labor, which would eventually evolve into that of the United Australia Party and then the modern Liberal Party, grew more out of the LRA than any other single source.

Reid's anti-socialist campaign came to an end with the election on 12 December 1906. The day before, the *Daily Telegraph* printed a letter written by the Premier "to the Federal electors of New South Wales". In it Carruthers urged people to vote for Reid as the State's most powerful friend, before embarking on one last rhetorical tirade against socialism:

> The State's prosperity today is not owing to the laws of Parliament, but to the enterprise of the people … As a native-born Australian, and the son of a working man, and as one who has risen from the lowest rung of the ladder to almost the highest position in the land, I feel that the incentive to the exercise of ability and industry lies in the encouragement of individual merit under liberalism, rather than in the levelling down of men under socialism.[395]

Carruthers' letter reads as though it was written by a modern free-market liberal yet by the same token it makes an appeal to the same romanticised notion of the self-made man that he had expounded as Minister for Public Instruction. This shows that for men like Carruthers and Reid their position in the new lines of cleavage was a natural adaptation of their colonial liberalism. Politics had evolved greatly since Carruthers had entered Parliament in 1887 and he had been at the forefront of that evolution, yet the tales of Gladstone and Parkes that had inspired an earlier generation of Young Turks to enter politics were still informing the opinions of the men who were heralding a new political age in which their achievements would no longer be met with the same reverence.

It was individualism that was the uniting factor. Carruthers had a view of history as the product of the cumulative actions of great men and, given his thoughts on Queen Victoria, women as well. To him ideologies and structures, like socialism and the bound caucus, which restricted or discouraged the individual actions of people threatened not only freedom but the course of human progress. It was not so much that greed was good, but that ambition, incentive and inspiration were irreplaceable. The allegation that socialism "levelled down" men is particularly interesting for it dismisses one of socialism's fundamental attributes; equality. Carruthers believed that equality of outcomes could only be achieved by restricting people to the lowest common denominator in a manner that bound humanity by removing opportunity.

The 1906 election would prove to be the beginning of a new age at the Federal level. Reid failed to achieve his goal of emulating Carruthers' success in winning a majority, yet he came remarkably close to doing so. Senate results show that despite only picking up a couple of Lower House seats, the Anti-Socialists came closer than any party had before to achieving a full 50% of the vote.[396] Moreover the vote of the Protectionists had been crippled to the benefit of both Labor and the Anti-Socialists, pointing to the fact that the New South Wales lines of cleavage were beginning to emerge at a Federal level. Ironically the Protectionist Party was left with just 16 fully-committed Lower House members, the exact same number as the Progressive rump had emerged with in 1904. The Protectionists had actually received a lower proportion of the vote than the Progressives had, but electoral boundaries conspired to give them a greater share of the 75 member House of Representatives. Despite the electoral battering, Labor support allowed Deakin and the Protectionists to hold on to power tentatively in a humiliating situation that Carruthers suggested the Prime Minister could only accept on account of having not "any grit left in him".

Circumstances, including Deakin's stubbornness and the tariff, conspired so that the full effects of the election result would not be felt for a number of years, but by the time the Federal writs were next issued the Anti-Socialists and Protectionists had "fallen into line" as the new Commonwealth Liberal Party. The election results forced the hand of the Protectionists, who were left with the choice of joining the Anti-Socialists, joining Labor (which the caucus pledge made practically impossible), or facing annihilation. After securing further tariff increases and with Reid's gracious retirement smoothing the transition, they chose the former option.

The Carruthers-inspired anti-socialist campaign thus belatedly succeeded in transporting the lines of cleavage into the Federal sphere. As a product of that campaign, the CLP was set up to occupy the same rhetorical philosophic stance as the LRA, fighting for liberty against those who would allegedly entrust all power to the state. Because the CLP was created partly to kick out the Fisher Government it embodied the dual defensive and offensive roles that had been important to the LRA's success and like that organisation the CLP firmly embraced the idea of permanent political lines. Joseph Cook played a central role in the formation of the fusion party and its only election victory, and it is reasonable to assume that as a New South Welshman and Carruthers' old friend, he like Reid partly borrowed his anti-socialist emphasis from Carruthers.

Constrained by the environment created by the anti-socialist campaign, a reluctant Deakin also played a central part in the fusion. Judith Brett has argued that he did so not because of any economic opposition to Labor's "socialism" but because of a rejection of the caucus pledge.[397] Echoing Brett but from a different perspective, Gregory Melleuish has maintained that for six decades after the fusion Australian liberalism combined Deakinite statism, populism and conservatism to the virtual exclusion of classical liberalism.[398] Both are right about Deakin's big government emphasis, but it would be wrong to assume that this completely overwhelmed the liberal anti-socialist element within the CLP. After all, Deakin failed miserably at the 1910 election and the former Protectionists made up a disproportionate chunk of those who lost their seats.

It was only once Cook took up liberal anti-socialism and embraced the lines of cleavage he inherited from Carruthers and Reid that the Party met with success, however briefly. Though the economic and regulatory policy pursued by Liberals has been open to debate and change, the non-Labor side of the lines of cleavage has consistently defined itself by a belief in individual initiative and the benefits of private enterprise. This has been one of the crucial aspects dividing Australian politics, and even during its interventionist Keynesian phase the Liberal Party still believed that private business should be encouraged and was generally better than state enterprise. As leader of the CLP Deakin did cite a belief in "private enterprise" and "independent initiative" but his repeated downplaying of that belief throughout his career suggests that its continual centrality in the non-Labor tradition is due to the influence of others, including Carruthers and his original definition of the philosophical differences between the parties.[399] Combined with the individualism that saw even Deakin reject the caucus pledge, these economic and personal beliefs, however broad and inconsistent, have been perhaps the only permanent parts of Australian liberalism and it is no coincidence that Carruthers had constructed his party's ideological position around them.

Despite the considerable swing and the ultimate historic legacy, at the time Reid's election campaign was viewed by the media and the general public as a failure. The most disappointing aspect of the result was the fact that a number of New South Wales seats had been lost to Labor, losses which ate into impressive gains achieved elsewhere. This led to a great deal of finger pointing which took aim at the LRA for not lifting enough weight. Though Carruthers' letter to the electors had received considerable coverage and the Premier had attended a rally in support of his local Anti-Socialist candidate, the fact that New South Wales Parliament was sitting during the latter stages of the campaign impeded many prominent State members from helping out.

Tensions between State and Federal Liberals remained subdued until Carruthers made a rather unfortunate choice of words at a public meeting. At this meeting Carruthers claimed that the State Liberals were not "anti-anything", a statement that was interpreted as a swipe at Reid.[400] The latter responded by pointing to his 15 to 20 planks of positive policy, which he argued was the maximum amount the limited scope of Federal politics would allow, and by saying that at the next State election the ADU would not "wait to be asked" to help out. One may add that Carruthers' own 1904 campaign was at least as against debt and extravagance as it was pro anything else and that positive and negative are both entirely matters of perspective.

Carruthers claimed that his statement had been misconstrued as a sneer and after a series of angry letters the situation died down. It is likely that this public spat has informed the general historical view that Carruthers did not strongly support the anti-socialist campaign, but as has been shown he supported it publicly, privately and organisationally, efforts which should not be discounted because of ugly scenes born out of disappointment.[401] The spat proved to be an even greater sour note as it was one of the last significant public interactions between two friends whose political fortunes had been so intertwined. Reid would give up the leadership of the Anti-Socialists to make way for fusion and eventually take up the post of High Commissioner in London. Though the occasional surviving card attests that they remained friends until the end, Carruthers would see little of Reid from 1910 until his death in 1918, at which point he would lead the public mourning for Australia's fourth Prime Minister.

Though in hindsight a sombre event, the spat did have one positive effect for it sparked a flurry of activity which tried to unite the Federal and State Liberal Parties.[402] It is now taken for granted that Federal and State parties should mirror each other, but given that the Constitution separates their responsibilities the benefits of such a connection are not necessarily apparent. After all an unpopular and/or divisive Federal policy might unnecessarily encumber a State party and Carruthers had shown himself somewhat reluctant to attach himself too readily to his Federal counterpart for fear of the fiscal issue. It was the lesson of the 1906 poll, that all resources must be mustered in order to win an election, which convinced numerous important Liberals that the benefits of amalgamating State and Federal parties outweighed the negatives. Despite considerable negotiation this combination would not eventuate until the creation of the Commonwealth Liberal Party, and even then imperfectly, but it was the talks between Reid and Carruthers that set the ball rolling. Joseph Cook, who was also involved in these negotiations, would reap the benefits of this in 1913 when he was propelled to power on the back of a number of gains in a united and well organised New South Wales.[403]

The organisational, rhetorical and tactical precedents set in 1904 and followed through by Reid in the anti-socialist campaign are arguably Carruthers' most important national legacy, yet they are not his most remembered. If Carruthers is remembered today it is generally as one of the earliest and most ardent States' rights Premiers, and in this G. E. Sherington has argued, he set a precedent that future State leaders would continually follow in pursuit of easy votes.[404]

States' rights is a term that should be ascribed to Carruthers with caution. During the time of the Federal Conventions it was a term used to describe those delegates who favoured strengthening the powers of the States' House, something that the future New South Wales Premier ardently opposed. It was only after federation had been enacted that this term became synonymous with State autonomy, a cause that retrospectively Carruthers had always supported. This had been evident not only in his fight to keep the scope of the Federal Government limited and over the Murray waters question, but also in the ideology that led him to pursue local government vigorously. In many ways States' rights was a natural fit for the Liberal side of the lines of cleavage, as it had already expressed its opposition to big and centralised government. This connection was to some extent an anathema to Deakinite liberalism and it was only brought in to the wider Australian liberal tradition by people like Carruthers. Since his time Liberals and non-Labor in general have, while still exhibiting centralising tendencies, frequently shown more reverence for the role of the States under the Constitution than their opposition.[405]

Carruthers' role in the birth of this States' rights liberal tradition is unique. Not only did he lead the largest State in to near rebellion against the Federal Government in its earliest years, but he did so as a former active Federal delegate. This gave him some licence to cry that the Constitution was being misused, long before the more significant distortions of its intentions. Circumstances ensured that his belief in State autonomy became more vehement over time, but years later he could still express regret that he had been forced to "engage in a controversy little to my liking as one of the framers of the Constitution and as an ardent advocate of its acceptance by the people of the State".[406] The centrepiece of that controversy was the fight over the capital question, but it also involved the role of the States within the new Commonwealth and the financial relationship between the States and the Commonwealth.

Before embarking on a discussion of Carruthers' relationship with the Commonwealth Government some important background information is required to contextualise the issues involved. The most important contextual point is that the power relationship between the Federal Government and the States was entirely different to that of today. In its earliest years the Commonwealth's powers were kept almost entirely within the bounds of the Constitution, and while there were already those who hoped to extend those bounds, Reid could still justify only having 15-20 planks of policy on account of the Federal Government's only having that many responsibilities. Meanwhile the well-established State governments, who had built up a considerable role in their near 50 years of existence, were left all the responsibilities that were not explicitly taken from them. Such was the discrepancy in roles that in 1904-5 Commonwealth expenditure was approximately £4,300,000 while New South Wales expended approximately £11,200,000.[407] Thus the New South Wales Premier could think of himself as occupying, while not the most prestigious position in the country, perhaps still the most powerful. The relative importance of the tiers of government was also reflected in newspaper coverage, where far more attention was payed to State politics than has since been the case. In 1907 at the height of the New South Wales election and the battles over States' rights Carruthers would even come to dominate the pages of *The Bulletin*, the "national" newspaper of the day.

The confidence Carruthers had in the strength of his position is clearly seen in his relationship with the two Prime Ministers he had to deal with during his Premiership; Reid and Deakin. It is necessary to treat his relationship with each separately in order to gauge how personality clashes affected his dealings with the Commonwealth. Carruthers' friend held the top office for the early stages of his Premiership and though this period saw some conflict between the two, relative cordiality held the day. This was seen in negotiations over Dawes Point, a militarily important site which the Commonwealth was induced to relinquish its claim over in exchange for land at Darling Island. More remarkable was that the two were able to keep the peace whilst Carruthers tried to subvert the Commonwealth's control over foreign relations in a dispute over horses.

Reid's short stint in the top job corresponded with a short conflict to Australia's North. This was the Russo-Japanese war fought over conflicting interests in Manchuria. Britain had a treaty of alliance with Japan, but decided to adopt a position of outward neutrality towards the conflict that Australia, and therefore Reid, was bound to follow. Meanwhile Carruthers had been pursuing trade opportunities with Japan and Asia more generally through his "Commercial Agent in the East" J.B. Suttor. Based on the amount of correspondence that survives with Suttor, Carruthers saw Asia and Japan in particular as an area of economic interest for New South Wales second only to Britain herself.[408] Through his contacts Suttor was able to push contracts for the export of wool, frozen meat and wood into Japan, the Philippines and a number of other Asian markets. The war gave he and Carruthers a new opportunity to export horses, and it was arranged that 12,000 would be sent to Japan.

The question was whether the horses represented a violation of British neutrality. After discussions with Rawson, who beyond his official position was something of an expert on foreign relations, Carruthers came to the conclusion that it was not. According to his reasoning not only were horses not necessarily a war good, but since the transaction was not between the New South Wales and Japanese Governments but between two private companies, the Commonwealth had no right to intercede. Reid disagreed and the two men had a rather heated private discussion on the matter which was only ended when Carruthers threatened to make the dispute public, forcing Reid to give in to his friend.

This did not prove to be the end of the matter for in extraordinary circumstances Russian agents were sent up from Melbourne to try to sabotage the attempt to transport the horses from Sydney Harbour.[409] Their plot was discovered however and their train was stopped at Moss Vale where they were arrested. The Japanese Government offered Carruthers the Order of the Rising Sun (First Class) in gratitude for his role in foiling the plot. In order to receive such a foreign decoration he would need direct permission from the King. Rawson wrote earnestly to

ON THE NATIONAL STAGE

the Colonial Office requesting such permission but in the controversial circumstances it was readily declined.[410]

The event was remarkable for several reasons. Firstly, Carruthers had an interest in engaging in Australia's "near north" that was decades before its time and while it does appear that other State governments had agents in the "East" none were as active as Suttor and none seem to have been as willing to risk jeopardising Australian foreign policy in pursuit of their trade goals. While Carruthers was acutely aware of the importance of Britain as his State's greatest trading partner, the fact that he already saw the need to diversify trade relationships and give greater account to geographical necessities was incredibly prescient. Outside of the war Carruthers even hosted Japanese military officials and came away with an impression of "a very fine race of people, most honourable in carrying out their negotiations".[411] One wonders how different the history of the Pacific would have been if these bilateral trade relationships had been allowed to flourish rather than being squeezed out by protectionism and geopolitical concerns.

As remarkable as Carruthers' foresight is the fact that he would not only try but succeed in dictating his will to the Federal Government on such an important foreign relations issue. This may have just been a case of Carruthers being able to manipulate his friend, but nevertheless it still shows that the Commonwealth was weak and that the New South Wales leader was staking a claim to autonomy of action even in those areas where the Constitution gave the Commonwealth a clear prerogative.

The resolution to the incident contrasts strongly with a more minor one, again involving Suttor, which took place a few months later under Deakin. New South Welshman A.R. Weigall had been travelling through Korea with a survey party when the group were molested by a group of Japanese soldiers who thought they were Russian spies.[412] Weigall appealed to the British ambassador in Japan for protection and recompense, but upon receiving an unsatisfactory response approached Suttor to do something about it. Suttor referred the case to the State Government who got the Governor to send it directly to the British Colonial Office without reference to the Commonwealth. The incident formed part of a wider dispute between the States and the Commonwealth about how independently the former could deal with the British Government, and when Deakin heard about the "interception" of an appeal to the "Australian Government" he quickly descended into a long and bitter argument with the New South Wales Premier.

These arguments were frequent and numerous, partly because Carruthers was keen to do whatever he could to defend the autonomy that he felt had been built into a limited Constitution but also because the relationship between the two men had become utterly toxic. At one point they even bickered over an effort Carruthers made to send flour to relieve a famine in Japan, something that the Prime Minister felt was unconstitutional.[413] D.I. Wright once described Carruthers as "perhaps the only Premier who could make Deakin really angry".[414] On one occasion after receiving a particularly acrimonious letter, Deakin's secretary asked him what response to give, to which the normally affable Alfred replied "tell him to go to hell – three pages".

In order to understand this visceral dislike it is important to remember a few things. First and most importantly, Deakin was a Federalist-ultra who was willing to expand the role of what he saw as the higher level of government and therefore he approached each dispute from a completely different perspective to Carruthers. Another seldom mentioned issue however was the fact that Deakin re-ascended to the Prime Ministership in 1905 on the back of what was perceived to be a betrayal of Carruthers' friend and the anti-socialist cause. This poisoned their working relationship from the very beginning. In 1905 Deakin not only believed in protection, which was taking the more interventionist form of "new protection" in an even greater contrast to Carruthers' small-government beliefs, but he also rejected the notion of States' rights and the necessity of the clear lines of cleavage. Carruthers would potentially have had more in common with a Labor Prime Minister, for at least they could be expected to accept the latter point; hence he and Deakin were simply not on the same page.

Carruthers foreshadowed a cooling in their relationship, for in the same letter in which he expressed his disappointment at the fall of Reid the New South Wales leader warned his new Federal counterpart that "NSW is warm on subjects that naturally the Federal Govt. is cool upon and without any desire to embarrass you – we are bound to conflict soon on such questions".[415] One of these questions was the financial question. The Federal Conventions had entangled State and Federal finances not only through the Braddon clause but also through a provision allowing the Commonwealth to make grants to the States with attached conditions. The reliance of most States on tariff revenue meant that this entanglement was to some extent inevitable, and Carruthers had not been one of those people who "advocated that there should be no mixing up of the States and Commonwealth in any revenue collected by the latter".[416] Nevertheless, the provisions left the States financially "bound to the chariot wheels" of the Federal Government in a manner completely contrary to Carruthers' belief in autonomy that would become ever more apparent after he left office.

For the length of his Premiership the main financial issues between the tiers of government would be the transfer of State debts and the extension or replacement of the Braddon clause which was due to expire after ten years. The two parties could not come to an agreement, largely because the Federal Government wanted to expand its role through greater defence spending and old age pensions and was therefore unwilling to agree to give the States as much of the future tariff revenue as they desired. The transfer of State debts should have been easier to resolve, but since it was likely to decrease the amount of interest the States would have to pay, it was held over as a bargaining chip to get the States to agree to a lower percentage of tariff revenue. Carruthers, who had been quite successful in negotiating low interest in London, had grown dismissive of the idea that the Federal Government would automatically be able to do better and proposed that an adequate fixed sum be returned to the States after the expiry of the clause. This scheme initially had some support but it was eventually rejected as it would not allow for any growth in the revenue returnable to the States.

The issues would not be resolved until after Carruthers had retired and he would later regret that the Braddon clause had not just been made permanent in the first place. After all, the State's negotiating position deteriorated as time went on and the 1927 agreement reached around the time Carruthers was writing his memoirs left the States in a far weaker position than they had been in 1901. Arguably the States had always been in a weak position when negotiating with the Federal Government, but this was a fact that Carruthers essentially ignored in all his high-handed arguments with the Commonwealth. Partly this was because of his naivety and equally bravado, but the New South Wales Premier had an ace up his sleeve in the form of secession.

Secession had been explicitly outlawed by the Constitution, but in the event that the majority of States agreed to dissolution it was difficult to imagine that this would prove much of a lion in the path. The fierce debates over the financial arrangements, the Federal Government's obstinacy in paying compensation for its takeover of the profitable post and telegraph offices, fears of socialism and various individual grievances meant that in the early years of the Commonwealth such a majority seemed possible. Famously the West Australian Government passed a resolution on secession in 1906, while more privately Carruthers and Queensland Premier Arthur Morgan discussed secession as a real possibility.[417] If Tasmania could be convinced, there was little Victoria or South Australia could do.

The reason Carruthers was seriously considering secession, if only as a very distant possibility, was that the capital site issue remained unresolved. Though the Constitution specified that the capital must be within New South Wales, a gentlemen's agreement kept the temporary capital in Melbourne and therefore kept the Parliament supposedly under the sway of Melbourne's newspapers and Protectionist culture. To many New South Welshmen, and particularly Carruthers who had been the architect of the provision keeping the capital site in New South Wales and had kept out of Federal politics because of the tyranny of distance, this situation was intolerable. Though according to some legal opinion the position of Melbourne as the capital even temporarily was unconstitutional, the only real solution to the issue was to pick a permanent site. It was a question that many Victorians were happy to see go unresolved, and there was some talk of a deliberate delaying strategy whereby Victorian members in the House of Representatives voted for a different site to their Senate counterparts in order to create a deadlock arbitrarily.[418] Despite these obstacles, the deadlock was eventually resolved and during Watson's brief Prime Ministership Dalgety was chosen as the site.

As the newly elected Premier Carruthers was unhappy with this choice. Dalgety had a questionable climate, was so distant from any major centre that connecting it by rail would be exceedingly expensive and the Commonwealth Government was asking for more of New South Wales land than Carruthers was ready to give. Most importantly, Dalgety was well over the 100 mile minimum distance from Sydney stipulated by the Constitution and would offer the Mother Colony none of the advantages that having the capital site within its borders implied. Carruthers later claimed that he had been privately told that people voted for Dalgety because it was so unsuitable that it would keep the capital in Melbourne by default.[419]

He may have been forced to accept the Dalgety decision, were it not for the wording of the Constitution which said that the capital "shall be within the territory which shall have been granted to or acquired by the Commonwealth". Carruthers took this as meaning that the Federal Parliament had the right to choose the capital site within the territory granted by New South Wales, but that it was up to New South Wales to choose what territory it granted. If the State did not want the capital to be in Dalgety it would simply not grant any territory in the Dalgety area. Many people disagreed with Carruthers' interpretation but because the Federal Government never forced the issue by driving a survey peg into the ground, the matter was never heard by the High Court.

Instead Carruthers was left free to take the matter to the New South Wales Parliament which explicitly rejected Dalgety but left the options of Tumut, Lyndhurst and Yass. As Prime Minister, Reid was sent a resolution listing these three sites and also saying that New South Wales would be willing to offer 100-200 square miles rather than the 900 requested for Dalgety. Keen not to look too parochial as he prepared for a national election, Reid rejected this proposal and delegated the issue to Dugald

Thomson. The latter proceeded to launch into a public debate with Carruthers, which may have been one of the reasons the New South Wales Anti-Socialist vote suffered at the next election. Despite this bad blood, there may still have been room for Carruthers to come to an agreement with his friend as he had so many times before. Any such hope was extinguished with the reaccession of Deakin, who repeatedly refused to accept the prerogative of the New South Wales Parliament to exclude Dalgety, leading to a stalemate which was to last the length of Carruthers' Premiership. It was in an exasperated attempt to end that stalemate that Carruthers openly threatened secession, and in his 1907 policy speech in which he revealed his plans to abolish income tax the Premier also proposed a referendum on the capital site issue.

Though the furore and threats of secession garnered the most press attention, the New South Wales Government also took more practical steps towards securing a more favourable capital site. Federal politicians were shown around the various sites at the State's expense, while data and survey analyses were carried out both of which would contribute to the eventual selection of Canberra as the capital site.[420] That selection would take place during the term of Carruthers' successor Wade, who along with the unlikely partnership of Chris Watson and William Irvine, helped secure Canberra's success in the face of continued opposition from the Deakin Government.

The importance of Carruthers' role in the eventual selection of Canberra has been controversial. David Headon has suggested that he was "arguably the most influential participant in the capital site story", while both G.E. Sherington and D.I. Wright have argued that the selection of Canberra represented a compromise that was only really possible once Carruthers had gone.[421] Sherington cites Wade's acceptance of handing over 900 square miles of land and a sea port, both of which Carruthers had initially rejected, as evidence of this. What such a view fails to acknowledge is that while Carruthers was partial to bluffing his opponents with a hard line stance and even flights of Ciceronian rhetoric, when ground was given in an effort to compromise he was generally more than willing to reciprocate. This had been the case with the Federal Constitution, which Carruthers had been more willing to accept in its original form than Reid. It was an alliance of elements of the Labor Party with Anti-Socialists and the simultaneously protectionist and anti-socialist "Corner" which won the day for Canberra, and ironically the latter group was the product of the gradual transportation of Carruthers' lines of cleavage into Federal politics.

If one believes that Dalgety was not as utterly unsuitable as Carruthers made out then it is possible to accuse him of hypocrisy for refusing to accept it while simultaneously attacking the perceived delaying tactics of his Victorian opponents. By the same token it is impossible to deny that without Carruthers' stubbornness Canberra would likely not have been chosen, and the capital site would likely have been further from Sydney. A quarter of a century passed between the beginning of the Commonwealth and the relocation of Parliament. In that time a large Protectionist tariff was settled on in Melbourne and the invention of air travel began killing off the tyranny of distance. In a Canberra newspaper an aged Carruthers could claim his satisfaction at seeing one of his preferred capital sites chosen and express hope in "the best modern city of the future", but in his memoirs he bemoaned the capital as a "costly experiment that has yet to justify itself".[422] In his mind the greatest compromise was the fact that the capital was not Sydney.

Carruthers' intractability over the capital site issue and open use of threats of secession are two of the main reasons he is remembered as perhaps the fiercest of the early States' rights leaders, but they are not the only ones. Of even greater remark at the time was an incident known as the wire netting affair. This was the result of a clash of interests between the Federal Government, who despite their near defeat in the 1906 election pushed through an even higher tariff schedule in line with the implementation of "new protection", and the New South Wales Government who were having trouble dealing with a rabbit plague.

The rabbit plague had emerged not long after the breaking of the drought, and the agricultural destruction it wrought threatened to derail the State's economic recovery. Such was the State Government's concern that it led them to support controversial experiments on the use of a deliberately introduced disease for rabbit destruction. These were being conducted in the isolated environment of Broughton Island by French scientist Dr Jean Danysz, though fear of possible consequences meant there was considerable hesitation about the idea of introducing the microbe to the mainland. Even without these concerns the experiment would take time, so for the moment the only practicable solution was to attempt to fence the rabbits out. The issue was that the wire netting needed for such fencing had been added to the protective tariff schedule, at a rate of 30% for foreign manufacture and 25% for British manufacture.[423]

Carruthers was indignant at this move. He pointed out that there were no significant Australian private businesses producing wire netting, and that in fact the major manufacturer was the Victorian prison system.[424] To preference gaols over farmers was, in his opinion, quite absurd, particularly in a time of such crisis. The New South Wales Government had already been planning to import wire netting, but now with the rise in duties it was decided to use that direct importation in combination with section 114 of the Constitution, which prevented the Commonwealth Government from taxing the property of the States, to bypass the tariff. There was some controversy over whether this clause applied to goods imported by the States, but a 1903 New South Wales Supreme Court ruling had held that it did and though the Federal Government had lodged an appeal to the Privy Council the matter had been allowed to lapse by the appellant.

Confident of his constitutional position, when in August 1907 the steamer *Kent* arrived in Sydney with a shipment of wire netting, Carruthers got his officials to seize its cargo by force. After receiving approval from the Executive Council some public servants and a group of policemen were sent down to the Pyrmont Docks where they began surreptitiously unloading the ship and moving its contents to government storage facilities. All of this was done behind the backs of Federal customs officers, who legally had a bond over the goods until they had been cleared. Eventually the officers found out that a ship was being unloaded without their permission, and after telegramming Melbourne for instructions they tried to block the further transference of goods by sitting on them.

The incident provoked a storm the likes of which has seldom been seen in Australian politics. Members of the Federal Labor Party called for Carruthers' arrest, while Minister for Customs William Lyne sent the New South Wales Premier a provocative telegram.[425] The press was almost universally critical of the Premier's actions. The *Sydney Morning Herald* and *Daily Telegraph*, who normally supported Carruthers on States' rights issues, both took shots at him. The *Telegraph* described the actions of a "militant protestor" while the *Herald* lamented that the "ill-timed and ill-advised" stunt damaged Carruthers' strong argument on the tariff issue. *The Bulletin* claimed that the Premier's actions "might have been the beginning of civil war", while their cartoonist Hop drew Carruthers setting fire to the Federal Parliament.[426] The *Sunday Times* was practically alone when it rejoiced that the "tea" had been thrown "overboard" and that independence would surely follow.[427] A few Federal Free Traders even joined in the chorus of criticism, so that the greatest support Reid was able to give his friend was to say nothing at all. At the end of a speech to his supporters given a couple of days after the incident Reid joked that he had "forgotten" to say anything about it.

Despite the public negativity Carruthers received numerous personal letters of support, the appreciation he felt for which is shown by the fact that he kept them all. One of the least equivocal was from Rawson. In language formal enough to imply it was meant for posterity, he wrote:

> I entirely endorse your action in forcing the Federal Government to bring action against the State with reference to their illegal charge of duties on State goods since 1903, & though in doing it you had to do an illegal act, it was the only method to bring the matter to a crisis.[428]

The motivations behind Carruthers' actions are controversial. Sherington dismisses the idea that the Constitutional issue was central and suggests that it was "obvious" that the affair was "purely political" and designed to win country votes in the upcoming election.[429] Carruthers was a skilled politician who inevitably paid some attention to how the seizure would play to the electorate, but that does not mean his actions were as opportunistic as Sherington suggests. After all the seizure was a risky political move which put him offside with the influential Sydney papers. This was dangerous for urban areas were becoming increasingly important electoral trenches. The demise of the Progressives gave the Liberals some space in the country, and though it was important to consolidate these votes against a Labor Party that had several regional strongholds, it was equally important to minimise the loss of Sydney seats. Sherington seems to think that a throw of the dice was necessary for the Government to win the upcoming election given the negative impact of the land scandals, but it appears that by this time Carruthers had largely shaken off that setback and was reinvigorating the Party with his promise of income tax abolition backed up by sound economic management. By engaging in the stunt over wire netting he was jeopardising that political recovery by detracting from his central message and also risking aggravating Protectionist sympathies amongst his erstwhile Progressive supporters. Carruthers did not run away from these political dangers and he did make Federal issues central to his 1907 election campaign, but given the way that the wire netting affair captured the imagination of the press, to do otherwise would have been to push against an irresistible tide.

If one accepts that the Liberals stood to lose possibly as many votes as they gained through the wire netting affair, then it becomes clear that Carruthers was acting out of some sort of principle. Even if that principle was purely securing the best interests of New South Wales, then he was at least fulfilling his duty as Premier and Treasurer. Beyond this Carruthers was seeking to secure the autonomy of the States to pursue their goals without unnecessary hindrance from the Federal Government. For a man who had fought to keep the majority of Constitutional responsibilities in the hands of the States, this autonomy was necessary to the successful running of a Federal system. Just because Carruthers believed in what he was doing does not mean the wire netting affair was not a stunt. On the contrary, it was a deliberate stunt designed to bring a constitutional issue to a head. This was exactly what he had been urging the Federal Government to do with regards to planting a survey peg in the Dalgety site, except this time the power was in his hands. It has been pointed out that the Premier had paid tariff duty on the less politically charged importation of railway material, but the very nature of a constitutional test case such as this required that one issue be picked out, and it made sense that it would be the one which was most controversial.[430]

The wire netting affair succeeded in bringing about that test case, but it would not be heard in the Privy Council where the original appeal had been lodged. Instead it was heard in a High Court dominated by the ultra-Federalist and former Cabinet colleague of Deakin and Lyne, Edmund Barton. The Court found against the State Government, a decision Carruthers held with such enduring bitterness that it shows how deeply he cared about the issue:

> As to the decision of the High Court which was in favour of the Federal Government, one has to accept it as the final law. That does not prevent me from saying that there still lies in the archives of the Privy Council an appeal on the same matter by the Federal Government -- an appeal which from fear of an adverse decision to this day has been unprosecuted by the appellant, the Federal Government … The High Court and the Privy Council do not see quite eye to eye with each other in regard to the interpretation of the State and Federal Constitutions.[431]

The defeat in the High Court was representative of Carruthers' general defeat on States' rights matters. His only real victory over Deakin was on the capital site issue, and the delays and the passing of the protectionist tariff made that victory somewhat hollow. His belief that the smaller State Parliaments were inevitably more representative and flexible lost out to those that believed the highest tier of government had a special prerogative and that centralisation created efficiency. Just because Carruthers lost these battles however, does not mean they were not important. In the first decade of the Commonwealth the political situation and the operation of the Constitution were in a state of flux. Carruthers did more than any other Premier to have those questions left over by the conventions settled. Though they were not settled in the States' favour,

Carruthers' actions helped to ensure that by the end of the decade many of the fundamental questions had been resolved and the turmoil had died down. That does not mean that the relationship between the States and the Commonwealth has not subsequently been difficult, but arguably it has not been as difficult as in those early years.

Despite all his grievances, Carruthers never pulled the trigger on his secession threats. To do so may have destroyed the legacy of Parkes, Reid and ultimately himself. After Carruthers' time the threat of a secession backed by the majority of the States died out and provincial governments, though frequently remaining disgruntled, have become comparatively more passive. The victory of the ultra-Federalists, particularly once Isaac Isaacs took his place on the High Court benches, was near total and for better or worse the chariot wheels have dragged the States along.

The wire netting affair cast a shadow over the 1907 election for it superseded much of the debate about the Government's record. The campaign still saw some highlights. In 1906 Carruthers had taken an innovative motorcar tour of northern New South Wales. The trip was something of a novelty, with both horses and people frequently scared by the unfamiliar sight of an automobile. Despite dirt roads and high rainfall ensuring the car got bogged at least once a day, the adventure proved the value of automotive transport as a campaign facilitator. Carruthers organised the purchase of the first New South Wales government car and used it extensively throughout 1907. He insisted that since the car saved travel time it also saved travel expenses and was therefore a worthwhile investment even for a reform government.

Carruthers campaigned primarily on his record and on his battles with the Federal Government. He promised that if re-elected he would hold referendums on the capital site, the continuation of the Braddon clause and whether New South Wales should lobby for "a more just and liberal [Federal] constitution".[432] Banjo Paterson wrote the Liberals a campaign song, "the good old liberal flag", which emphasised the ideological link between Carruthers and some of the legends of New South Wales politics: Parkes, Wentworth and Dunmore Lang.[433] To the strains of that tune, Reid led a large rally of Liberals at the Sydney Town

Hall the night before the election. There he declared that he was whole-heartedly committed to "any fight which involved either political or com-mercial freedom in Australia" and gave a resounding endorsement to his old friend.[434]

The mixed appeal of the wire netting issue was reflected in the election results, for the Government lost ground in Sydney but gained ground in the country. Those results are difficult to interpret, for though there were more "Liberals" elected in 1907 than 1904 the destruction of the Progressives meant that there were also more Labor members, and the Government's working majority was thus reduced. How to classify the candidates is also difficult, as modern analysis lists 8 independent Liberals who generally supported Carruthers but whose connections to the LRA is suspect. If these are counted then the Liberals had a com-fortable majority of 53 out of 90 with 4 true independents.[435] If all the "independents" of any stripe are dismissed then the Liberals still had a solid lead of 45 seats to Labor's 32.

Carruthers boasted of a great victory, and vindication for all he had been pushing particularly in regards to the Federal Government. The election was definitely viewed as having Federal consequences, and how it was perceived interstate varied according to that State's view of federa-tion. The *Brisbane Courier* boasted of "Mr. Carruthers' triumph", while in Adelaide *The Advertiser* focused on the "heavy government losses" suf-fered in the inner city.[436] Michael Hogan has argued that "without the collapse of the Progressives" whose rural seats were generally picked up by the Government, the Liberals would have had "little to rejoice about".[437] The consequences of realignment were a two-way street how-ever, and the collapse of the Progressives helped to consolidate the anti-Government vote in the city, partly facilitating the Liberal losses. Admit-tedly most of the seats the Liberals lost in 1907 had not had Progressive candidates in 1904, but voter turnout was up from 59.31% to 66.72% suggesting that a two-party system had ended voter confusion and, given Carruthers' clashes with Deakin, it is likely that much of that upswing was Progressive/Protectionist voters coming out to vote for Labor in the city.

To assess whether the 1907 election victory was indeed a triumph, the achievement needs to be contextualised with a view to the political instability of the New South Wales Parliament up until this point. At a little over five years, George Reid had served as Premier for the longest continuous period in the Colony's history. His Premiership had started with a short term culminating in a snap election designed to pressure the Legislative Council. He then served one full term before being rewarded with a hung Parliament which soon brought him down. Reid was succeeded by a Protectionist/Progressive Government that went through three Premiers and won just one full term with little opposition from Charles Lee. In serving a full term and then winning a stable majority that would go on to serve another, Carruthers and the Liberals achieved something that was then unequalled in New South Wales political history. This was evidence of the tangible benefit the lines of cleavage had on the stability of the Legislative Assembly, a precedent that like so many others would soon be repeated in the House of Representatives.

The evasive second term had been won through both the strength of the economy and the popular appeal of Carruthers' anti-Federal rhetoric and proposed tax cuts, but he would not get the opportunity to break Reid's record. Not long after the election the Premier was forced to retire for health reasons. For years rumours circulated that this was a cover, that the indignity of the lands scandals and the difficulty of forming a Ministry with the new former-Progressive Liberals forced his hand.[438] Both suggestions were difficult to believe. Carruthers had been deeply hurt by the abuse he was exposed to as Premier. He cared too much about his reputation and how it reflected on his family not to be. He told Deakin that he hated the political life, and that he felt "like Hamilton that one stands with his back against the wall all the time fighting for his honour and his manhood, which, in the ordinary course of one's life in a profession or a business would never be assailed".[439] Despite such lamentations Carruthers remained drawn to public action. For twenty of his fifty years politics was all he had known. Though he had faced some considerable abuse, he had been practically exonerated by the commission into the lands scandals and none of the unfounded allegations were as bad of those of the old Norton libel case which he had managed to put behind him. The task of forming a Ministry cannot have been that difficult considering his less adept successor Charles Wade accomplished the task with little fuss, so that also should not have been an issue.

Finally Beverley Earnshaw found proof that Carruthers' story of ill-health had indeed been true, for his papers reveal evidence of a heart attack that cut his career short.[440] The delicate constitution that had seen him sent to Goulburn as a boy had finally caught up with him and combined with the excesses of a campaign that saw the stresses of the wire netting affair and an exhaustive regional tour, it had all proved too much for the "little" man's body. Rawson, who had witnessed a physical decline in the Premier's health, had frequently requested that he take rest but the message had not been heeded. Carruthers was so ill that he was not even able to write his own letter of resignation, instead dictating it to Alice. In what was quite a flagrant breach of Liberal Party precedent, Carruthers directly advised the Governor to ask Wade to form a government, rather than suggest that he wait for a leadership election. There were several frantic telephone calls between Cabinet members and the Carruthers residence, but the request for Wade still seems to have been a decision primarily made by the retiring Premier. Little fuss was raised over it. Parliament was already due to sit and the emergency of Carruthers' health necessitated a prompt response.

At around fifty years of age Carruthers retired conspicuously and, it must be said tragically, early. His Government had overseen a period of considerable economic growth that would continue under his successor. Fuelled by tax cuts and the confidence that stable governance gave markets, unemployment was down and incomes were up. Even in the face of protective tariffs aimed at propping up Victorian manufacturing, New South Wales had reasserted herself as the predominant State in Australia, and the benefits flowed to directly to her citizens. Money had fructified in people's pockets, and Carruthers could be confident that people from all classes were better off than they had been three years before.

Carruthers' heart would soon recover allowing him to take up a less stressful position in the Legislative Council that did not require the vigorous campaigning that had been such a pivotal part of his electoral success. From this vantage point he would see his lines of cleavage distorted by the First World War, the rise of the Country Party and other events. Still the flexibility of those lines ensured they never truly disappeared. By the end of his life they were already making a comeback, with Joseph Lyons' campaign against debt echoing his cries from an earlier age. Lyons and the United Australia Party owed much to Carruthers' successful demonising of debt in the public's mind. After the Second World War the lines would re-emerge, with nationalisation and communism giving a sharp relief to underlying political disputes which were decades old. As peace brought stability to the political arena, Australian politics would stabilise around the idea that despite their internal disputes "Liberals" were intrinsically different to "Labor" and vice versa. The lines of cleavage, or as one contemporary politician has described them the "battle-lines", continue to inform the political debate and function as a small dose of clarity to an otherwise confused state of political affairs.

WHAT HAPPENED.

An interview took place yesterday between the State Premier and Mr. G.H. Reid. Mr. Carruthers explained that a number of matters of interest were discussed, but not of public importance. - *News Item.*

GEORGE: | "DO YOU THINK I CAN MAKE THIS ANIMAL WORK?"
JOSEPH: |

Hop suggests that both Carruthers and Reid had concocted their enemies.
From the *Bulletin*, Sydney.

CHAPTER THIRTEEN
No Quiet Retirement

The heart attack forced Carruthers to retire from the Premiership, but for the moment he remained the member for St George. On 17 October he managed to drag himself to Parliament to take the oath of allegiance and sign on to the roll, though he did not stay to participate in the debates. He paired against the first censure motion directed at the Wade Government, which was comfortably defeated 52 to 34. Carruthers spent most of his time quietly recuperating at his "Ellesmere" home in Sans Souci. Meanwhile Wade quickly got on with implementing his predecessor's promises. His Ministry created an autonomous Department of Agriculture and Waddell swiftly brought in a Bill to abolish income tax below £1000.

Freed from the burden and stress of office, it did not take long for Carruthers' fifty-year-old body to recover. He was soon looking for work that offered more interest than the simple local advocacy of a back bencher, and it just so happened that an opportunity suited to his talents was about to arise. In 1908 the fourth modern Olympic Games were to take place in London. To coincide with the large influx of international visitors and celebrate the recent signing of the Entente Cordiale between Britain and France, it was organised that a great Franco-British Exhibition would be held in western London. This was a throw-back to the Great Exhibition of 1851, one of the defining spectacles of the Victorian age. The new event was to be even grander, covering a full 140 acres of fairground.

The exhibition gave the various members of the Empire the opportunity to show off their goods to the rest of the world and promote trade relations. For New South Wales, whose economy had relied on exports for a long time, the chance presented to them was particularly enticing. Some four hundred tonnes of various articles were earmarked for the Mother State's display, and the logistics of the task required that someone with considerable experience travel to England to oversee proceedings. Wade showed no hesitation in choosing Carruthers, who may have already been planning a trip to Britain, as the man for the job. The former Premier already had a close working relationship with the Agent-General Timothy Coghlan, and while in office he had shown a deep concern for trade issues.

The Premier offered Carruthers £1200 to meet all expenses incurred from the trip. He was also given two additional responsibilities; to renegotiate the loans of the State with the Bank of England and to inquire into the general scheme of immigration and working of the Agent-General's office. A public banquet was held at the Sydney Town Hall to send Carruthers off in style. He was farewelled with speeches from Reid and Wade and the hearty cheers of the dining guests. He then set sail in late March, leaving behind a letter of resignation with the chairman of his election committee Clement Lewis, to be handed to the Speaker. Had he been travelling to England in a personal capacity, Carruthers would have been able to keep his seat and simply miss parliamentary sittings, but in order to accept the fee he felt that he was morally obligated to give up his position as member for St George.

Leaving their children in the care of their maternal grandparents, Joseph and Alice travelled aboard the R.M.S. Asturias, a joint passenger and mail steamer said to have the most "luxurious passenger accommodation [that had] been seen in the waters of the island continent".[441] It was well that they were travelling in luxury. Unbeknownst to anyone, Alice was in fact in the early stages of pregnancy. She would carry "Peg", the family's final child, for the entirety of the trip before giving birth back in Australia. It would be a testing time for her. Both parents missed their children and wrote near constantly to update them on their journey, the things they saw and their health as well as inquiring about what was going on back at home. In this manner most of the children could be talked to directly, even if little Alice needed the Burnetts to read out the letters for her. Evelyn, who Joseph affectionately wrote of as "little curly hair", was too young even for this and her mother worried that by the time she came home her daughter would have forgotten her.

When the Carruthers arrived in England they were greeted by John Henniker Heaton, the Conservative Member for Canterbury, who treated them to dinner at the House of Commons. At this stage Joseph would perhaps still have been more comfortable mixing in Liberal circles, but Heaton had lived more than twenty years in New South Wales and was known colloquially as the "Member for Australia", so it was quite natural that he would be the one to show his distinguished guest around. Heaton had been the architect of the "penny post" that hoped to strengthen imperial ties by keeping communication throughout the Empire affordable. Carruthers was also intent on strengthening imperial relationships. During his trip he promoted British immigration to Australia, selling the continent to potential migrants not on its high wages but as a land of opportunity for the industrious man.[442] On Empire Day Carruthers gave a speech to the King's School of Canterbury, exchanging flag's on behalf of her Australian namesake and lauding the union jack as a symbol of liberty, national security and Empire.

Continuing on the theme, Carruthers took it upon himself to write to the Chancellor of the Exchequer Lloyd George with an elaborate scheme to promote imperial integration. He first introduced himself by bragging about his achievements regarding federation and Norfolk Island, and boasting that his LRA was "the largest party practically in the whole continent".[443] He then warned Lloyd George of the dangers of protectionism, and in response to a public call to use preferential trade to knit together the Empire, Carruthers proposed a tariff-free alternative. He suggested that the public debts of Australia and Britain should be pooled together to achieve a lower rate of interest, in a similar fashion to what the State and Federal Governments were trying to negotiate back home. Carruthers advised that the savings thus produced could be spent on imperial purposes like defence. There is little evidence that the Chancellor seriously considered the proposal.

The Franco-British Exhibition was opened by the Prince of Wales to a crowd that despite pouring rain numbered in the thousands. The New South Wales exhibit's central feature was a showcase of the various minerals and timbers extracted from the State. Furs and stuffed animals were displayed, while harvests of cereals, fruits and even eucalyptus oils were also brought over. A more delicate section included an art gallery and native Australian flowers frozen in ice. A bar was set up to advertise a variety of Australian wines, and Carruthers was not shy about expressing his high opinion of them. The highlight of the exhibition was a visit from both the British King and the President of France. The Lord Jersey personally introduced Carruthers to the King, though an attempt to guide His Majesty towards a full tour of the New South Wales exhibit proved less than successful.[444]

It was not the last contact Carruthers would have with royalty, for when the exhibition began to settle into a routine he and Alice's social engagements stepped up in pace. They attended functions at Windsor Castle, St James's and Buckingham Palace. The latter occasion was particularly special. As a lifelong monarchist, to be invited to an official engagement at the palace was a grand honour, and even someone with Joseph's long career behind him was more than a little bit nervous. He took the occasion very seriously. Sporting an uncharacteristic beard, he donned a ceremonial sword and an outfit of Georgian flair. Alice wore a grand flowing gown that she kept in pristine condition for the rest of her life.

Still more pageantry was to come. When the King released his Birthday Honours Joseph was informed that he was to be invested as a Knight Commander of the Order of St Michael and St George. On 21 July 1908 the Carruthers once again visited Buckingham Palace for the knighting ceremony. This then opened up further opportunities. Sir Joseph was invited to give an address to the Anglo-Saxon Club, and he used the opportunity to presciently draw attention to the rise of the nations of the East, warning of a time when Australia would have to pay the penalty for the mistakes of her past. He was given an honorary Doctorate of Laws from the University of St Andrews, where he gave a speech that supported the enfranchisement of women while expressing concerns over the "antics" of some in the British suffragette movement. He also spent a week in Paris, where he was perturbed to learn that most Parisians felt that war with Germany was inevitable.

Carruthers' time in Europe was not all spent attending balls and addressing social clubs. He wrote extensive reports on the Scottish fishing industry and how its methods could be reproduced in Australia, as well as one on the advertisement of New South Wales to potential immigrants which included a number of critiques of the adequacy of current methods. He was even keeping in touch with Archdale Parkhill, and playing a significant role in directing his protégé's preparations for the upcoming Federal and State elections from afar.[445] Perhaps Carruthers' most significant role overseas was his hard fought negotiations with the Bank of England. The numerous telegrams and letters discussing the issue with Wade, which survive in Carruthers' papers, offer ample evidence of the arduousness of the task. The results speak for themselves however, and Carruthers was able to reduce charges for the inscription and management of New South Wales accounts by 12.5%.[446]

Carruthers' victory over the loans was one of many victories the Wade Government secured in the first half of its term. Even the highly controversial wages boards legislation, despite fierce union opposition, was passed with enough assuaging amendments to somewhat subdue Labor leader James McGowen. The new Act replaced the existing cumbersome machinery for industrial arbitration with a system that was intended to be more efficient and ameliorative. It provided for industry-specific boards of adjudication that were to be run by an independent chairman with an equal number of union and employer representatives, created an Industrial Court to hear appeals from these boards, imposed harsh penalties against strikes and lock-outs, and maintained existing awards created by its predecessor until otherwise challenged.[447] Crucially, the new system gave less priority to unions over independent workers and therefore went some way to alleviating the near-compulsion to join a union that Carruthers had critiqued in Wise's Act. Though there would be significant industrial unrest for the next few years, the updated arbitration system Carruthers had promised in 1907 would prove to be largely successful and the concept of wages boards would eventually be expanded to cover almost every industry and trade.

Wade's successes were built around Carruthers' 1907 platform and the momentum that the clear election victory gave him. By late 1908 however, both of these were beginning to exhaust. Strikes led by militant unionists and socialist groups such as the Industrial Workers of the World were causing considerable problems and, despite the fact that even William Holman was denouncing the IWW, Wade was losing his grip on the situation. It was practically inevitable then, that when Carruthers arrived back in Australia replete with the prestige of his knighthood, he would be asked to bring a stabilising hand to the Parliament. So it was that in October a reinvigorated Sir Joseph ascended to the Legislative Council. There were rumours that Rawson had not even waited for Wade's advice to make the move.

It was clear almost immediately that Carruthers viewed his new role as a Councillor as being materially different to that he had fulfilled as a member of the Legislative Assembly. He took the view that, in order to have any productive place in the system of government, the unelected House had to truly be a place of moral, practical and logical review. As a liberal, Carruthers had long venerated an individual's right to their opinion, but now as a Legislative Councillor he felt that individual judgement must supersede all other imperatives. Partisanship was about winning elections and forming governments. It therefore had little place in the State's Upper House beyond letting members of the Executive Council guide the ministerial program through the debates. Sir Joseph's inherent liberal political outlook meant that on many issues his independence from his old party would not always be marked, and outside the House he remained a partisan supporter of the Liberal electoral machine. Nevertheless, his philosophical position would frequently surface in an individual stance over an eclectic range of issues and would play the central role in shaping his attitude towards attempts to reform the Council.

Carruthers' image of the Council was to some extent old fashioned. Premiers had long pressured Governors into making politicised appointments, and it was hoped that on key issues Councillors would vote to the benefit of those who had put them there.[448] As Premier Carruthers had largely refrained from such a course of action, and though his nominees like James Brunker were often liberal leaning, so few appointments were made that it is difficult to accuse him of politicising the Council. Wade and his Progressive predecessors showed less restraint, but as the Legislative Assembly became ever more partisan, the difference between the two tiers remained stark.

Sir Joseph embraced his new role as overseer, and in his first speech back in Parliament he was dissecting the minute details of legislation designed to stop the spread of contagious diseases amongst prisoners. He followed that up with practical attempts to improve the Defamation Amendment Bill, the Nurses Registration Bill and an amendment to the Crown Lands Act aimed at allowing leaseholders to convert their runs into limited freehold. He took a more controversial stance when he directly opposed the Government's Closer Settlement Bill. This proposed to give the Minister for Lands extraordinary powers to resume land that was already owned and to restrict the sale of land within 5 miles of a railway. Carruthers felt that such overt control would distort the market for land, thereby undermining its value as a commodity and hindering closer settlement.[449] As a Knight, former Premier, and Federal delegate, Sir Joseph's speeches garnered more attention than those of most of his new colleagues, but in a period of relative cordiality between the Houses the practical work of the House of review garnered little public comment.

It was as a commentator on a number of controversial issues, many of which never reached the Legislative Council, that Carruthers maintained public relevance. One of the key talking points during late 1909 and early 1910 was the twin-referendum on the financial relationship between the Commonwealth and the States. On 13 April the people would be asked to give the Commonwealth the power to make a population-based fixed payment to the States out of surplus revenue, following an agreement between the Commonwealth and the States that the former would pay the latter a fixed sum of 25s per person in lieu of the expiring Braddon Clause. A separate referendum question proposed to give the Commonwealth unrestricted power to take over State debts and thereby suggested a Federal monopoly of public borrowing.

Carruthers himself had once proposed a fixed payment, and expressed that he was unconcerned how the referendum on that issue would turn out. With regards to the transfer of debts however, Sir Joseph came out as one of the leading proponents of a no vote. He argued that the Commonwealth, who did not possess the tangible securities for loans that the States possessed in the form of railways and public amenities, would not be able to obtain cheaper interest rates than them.[450] He pointed out that railway companies had a long history of obtaining lower rates for loans from British Banks than national governments, and that New South Wales possessed the assets to lobby as a sort of hybrid of the two. The only security the Federal Government had to pay off the loans was the power to levy taxation, and Carruthers did not want to risk heaping extra taxation on people in order to pay off loans that the State Government could already afford. He also intimated that since borrowing was integral to the running of the States, power over State debts could give the Commonwealth ancillary power over the internal affairs of provincial governments.[451]

Having recently obtained a discount for his State from the Bank of England, Carruthers' opinion was received with considerable interest by the electorate. The *Sydney Morning Herald* dismissed his arguments and urged voters to vote for a double-yes or else risk a financial catastrophe that could lead to a breakup of the federation. Wade also rejected the intervention of his former chief, arguing that the High Court would see off any attempt to use the powers to control the running of the States. Despite this backlash, Sir Joseph's vocal opposition appears to have had a direct impact on the referendum vote. Against the wishes of her Premier, New South Wales would be the only State to vote no on the transfer of State debts. Nation-wide it was actually the fixed payment that was met with greater concern, and it was defeated after being rejected by New South Wales, Victoria and South Australia.

The referendums were held on the same day as the 1910 Federal election. That election would be the first test of the new Commonwealth Liberal Party, the product of a belated fusion of the Anti-Socialists and Protectionists that had propelled Deakin back to power after a brief period of Labor rule. Carruthers had remained a passionate advocate of fusion, and when the new party finally emerged Joseph Cook placed his former colleague on the Council of the New South Wales Federal Liberal League. In that capacity he continued to provide invaluable advice to Parkhill, who was doing the real grunt work of the organisation. There were many who wanted Carruthers to take a more active role by standing for Reid's vacated East Sydney seat or the Senate, but he continued to eschew the extra workload and travel.

The election was a disaster for the CLP, particularly in New South Wales where five seats were lost to Labor. The influence of Sir Joseph's attacks on the twin-referendum may have had something to do with the result, since they helped to undermine the agreement between State and Federal leaders that had been the Fusion Government's signature achievement. Perhaps a greater impetus behind the CLP's poor vote in New South Wales was a widespread distaste for Deakin as a man who embodied the State's grievances with a Melbourne-based Parliament, and a feeling that Reid, who had been forced into retirement to smooth over the deal between the old fiscal parties, had been short changed. Carruthers was the catalyst for much of this anti-Deakin sentiment, and his half-hearted endorsement of Deakin's policies, laced with the caveat that he was "no fervent admirer" of the Prime Minister, did little to quell the concerns of his supporters.[452]

Labor's Federal victory came as an ill-omen to a State Government that was already in considerable political strife. Through 1909-10 a large scale coal strike had progressively degenerated, prompting Wade to introduce amendments to the Industrial Disputes Act aimed at combatting some of the more sinister agitators behind the trouble. Colloquially dubbed the "Coercion Act", the most controversial amendment allowed retrospective imprisonment for inciting workers to strike. Many of the worst aspects of the strike were organised by militant unionists with little sympathy for the Labor Party, but Wade's heavy-handed legislation and the subsequent arrest of strike-leader Peter Bowling prompted a Labor backlash that quickly attracted public sympathy.

Carruthers was alarmed at the prospect of a Labor victory, and publicly warned of the dangers of block voting, the powerful of the liquor trade and the growing consensus amongst Catholics to vote for the Labor Party now that the Progressives had disappeared. This inevitably met with a backlash from the Catholic Press, serving only to exacerbate the problem. Sir Joseph's lamentations about the general trend of Catholic voting should not be seen as proof of harboured sectarian animosities. When the prospect of free higher education loomed on the political horizon, he supported an extensive system of scholarships that could be used to access religious schools, rather than stirring up the "embers of the fight of twenty to forty years ago" with an attempt to introduce institutionalised secular high schools.[453] This had echoes of Menzies' later olive branch to Catholic education, and suggests that Sir Joseph's comments on Catholic voting habits reflected a genuine feeling of regret rather than an attack.

The State election of 14 October 1910 did result in a Labor victory, but a much smaller one than some may have expected. Freed from the burden of the unpopular Deakin, the New South Wales Liberals were able to campaign on their record of reform and economic success to claw back many of the votes they had lost at the Federal election. With 46 seats, Labor won a slim majority over their LRA and independent Liberal opponents.[454] This would create an incredibly unstable Legislative Assembly, which would go through considerable turmoil over the coming years. With the Lower House in a raucous, and an untested party occupying the ministerial benches, the role of the House of review would be more important than ever. Carruthers, often in tandem with his old ministerial colleague James Ashton, would lead an effective inquisition on the Government's legislative program. Some have suggested that this bordered on reactionary wrecking, but a considerable amount was allowed through, at least until the dying days of McGowen's term.[455]

One Bill that Sir Joseph did fiercely oppose was the new Income Tax Bill. This Bill reduced Wade's £1000 exemption level back down to £300 and created a sliding scale of taxation that greatly increased the rate of taxation for those earning above certain thresholds and particularly targeted absentee landlords. Though Carruthers was wary of blocking what was essentially a money bill, he argued that the flaws of a Bill which was rushed through Parliament and that Labor had little mandate for, were so great that it was worth risking a fight for the Council's existence to stop it. Though he tacitly admitted that the democratic House should have the supremacy that he once fought for, he argued that since Labor had not put the income tax proposals before the people at the last election, they could not claim that they represented the democratic will. Putting his philosophical position plainly, Carruthers said "that if there is any warrant for the existence of a second chamber, it is that occasionally it may give to the people an opportunity of adjudicating on proposed legislation".[456] He thus envisaged the Council as a potential safeguard of democracy, which could protect the sovereignty of the people during the three-years between elections.

The decision he wanted placed in the hands of the people was over a massive increase in the burden of government, which he felt there was little justification for. Sir Joseph pointed out that a surplus of £13,000 had carried over from the last financial year, and that with prosperous times likely to continue there was little excuse for the tax grab. He claimed that the motivation for the changes was not necessity but ideology. That Labor, intent on getting after their philosophical enemies, wanted to treat people with money as criminals whilst disregarding the considerable philanthropic works many engaged in. He also warned that if the Government continued to take unnecessarily, they would drain the funds available for private investment and ultimately cost the State jobs. He particularly attacked a provision levelling a considerably higher rate of taxation on companies than individuals as discouraging the formation of companies and thus retracting business. Summing up his view of the centrality of unfettered individual enterprise in the success of an economy, he stated that "if prosperity comes to a country with modern self-governing institutions, very little of that prosperity is contributed by legislation and acts of Government, although I will admit that legislation and acts of Government can diminish its prosperity".

Many of his fellow Councillors shared Carruthers' concerns over the Income Tax Bill, but a number were either unconvinced by his justification for interfering with a money bill, or scared by the prospect of a full blown dispute with a party that was already committed to the abolition of the second Chamber. The second and third readings were passed by the Council, and the Bill was carried into law.

The Income Tax Bill would not be Carruthers' only defeat, as despite its tiny majority the McGowen Government went about dismantling many of the achievements of its predecessor. An amendment to the Industrial Arbitration Act was initially blocked by the Council, but a conference between the Houses reintroduced illiberal preferences to unionists with the small consolation that these could be cancelled if a union participated in or aided a strike. Sir Joseph lamented this as a denial of "equal rights to citizens who equally obey the laws of the country", and claimed that had the Constitution explicitly embodied a principle of equality, union preference would have been deemed illegal.[457] A Crown Lands Amendment emphasising leasehold over freehold was also passed, largely undoing Wade's efforts to give leaseholders the opportunity to take ownership of their land. Carruthers critiqued Labor's Bill, not so much for what it did to Wade's reforms, but as a threat to the incredibly successful system he had set up in 1895.

The McGowen Government was of a highly interventionist nature. It increased spending, both on public works and government programs, in an O'Sullivan-style way. Though some legislation failed to get through, regulations were multiplied and made more rigid for a variety of industries. Perhaps most controversially of all, McGowen introduced a number of state enterprises, particularly government-run coalmines. Other State enterprises either proposed or introduced included brickworks, steelworks, a housing company, a clothing factory and even a bakery. Some would compete with private enterprise while those intended to fulfil government contracts would cut out business altogether. They were justified as an effort to cut inflation and the costs of public works; however in many respects they ignored the basic laws of supply and demand. Their bureaucratic inefficiencies would soon become apparent, but they would be hidden by the centralising necessities of the First World War. As an instinctive liberal, Carruthers frequently critiqued many of these efforts, but he was generally willing to begrudgingly let them through.

He knew the distinction between legitimate criticism and obstructionism and he made an effort to stay clear of the latter.

On less ideological issues Carruthers was far more likely to side with the Government. He strongly supported the Bursary Endowment Act of 1912, which funded a large number of bursaries to help people access secondary and university education and set up a Bursary Endowment Board to oversee their administration. These were made available to children attending Catholic High Schools in a manner mirroring the proposals Sir Joseph had already publicly outlined. He also voted for the Parliamentary Allowances Bill which attempted to increase the wages of members of the Legislative Assembly. Carruthers did not agree in principle to lifting those wages, but thought the Legislative Council had no business rejecting a Bill that only pertained to the other House.

Outside of Parliament, it was new referendum proposals that were the focus of debate. Buoyed by their stunning election victory, in 1911 the new Federal Labor Government tried to centralise power in the hands of the Commonwealth in a manner that even Deakin was appalled by.[458] On 26 April Labor would ask the people to extend the Commonwealth's powers over trade, commerce, the control of corporations, labour and employment, and also to give power to the Commonwealth to nationalise monopolies. The result of both polls would be crucial if Labor were to fully implement "new protection". More sinisterly, the powers would give the Federal Government the ability to actually carry out the socialist objective.

This meant that the referendums would be fought over two main issues. One was a fight over the transference of power from the States to the Commonwealth and thus regional autonomy and the functioning of the federation. The other was over the potential use of the new powers in a deliberate attempt to increase the size and restrictiveness of government in a manner that ran directly counter to a classical liberal emphasis on individual freedom. The radical nature of the proposals even helped to galvanise the opposition of many "new liberals" who accepted a prominent role for the state, hence they brought the lines of cleavage in Australian politics into a stark relief that was only distorted by a State Labor backlash against encroaching prerogatives. As a leading Liberal, anti-socialist and proponent of States' rights, Sir Joseph would act as a significant figure in the no campaign. It is worth noting that that campaign was primarily organised by Parkhill, who directly oversaw proceedings not only in New South Wales, but also in Victoria, Tasmania and South Australia.[459]

In December 1910 Carruthers brought up the referendum proposals in the Legislative Council, calling for the State Parliament to debate a matter that was vital to its existence. Viciously attacking what he felt was a Federal vote of censure over how the States had handled the running of their autonomous affairs, Sir Joseph implored the New South Wales Government to take a firm stand on the issue that up until that point they had been avoiding:

> There can be no greater argument for the abolition of the Parlia-
> ment of New South Wales, if by its silence it concurs in a proce-
> dure of this character. If a man is on trial for his life, he sees that
> he has counsel to defend him. He will use every power within his
> reach, and make his voice heard to show cause. This Parliament is
> now on its trial.[460]

The speech was widely reported and contributed to a heaping of pressure on the Premier to make his position known. Such pressure would eventually lead to both McGowen and Holman publicly breaking ranks with their Federal counterparts in what was a significant blow to the yes campaign.

Sir Joseph's other significant contribution to the debate was a heavily publicised address given at Paddington Town Hall in March of 1911. Here he attacked what he considered to be an attempt at a backdoor unification of the States. He argued that not only was unification unsuitable for such a large country, but that the haphazard administration of existing Federal prerogatives such as the postal service and immigration showed that the Commonwealth Parliament's track record could not justify an increase in its responsibilities. He also critiqued the bureaucratic consequences of centralisation, ridiculing the prospect of a plumber

from Paddington having to go to the Federal Government to get a licence to ply his trade. Finally he warned that too much interference in
the trade of the country would act as a "dry-rot" that would eat away at
economic development.[461] The speech was more practical than some of
his rhetorical tirades of the past, but it achieved its simple aims.

Both referendums were soundly defeated, receiving less than 40% of
the popular vote and carrying only Western Australia. Still, the Federal
Labor Government was not discouraged and in 1913 it brought forward
more referendums asking for powers over trusts, trade and commerce,
industrial matters, corporations, railway disputes and the nationalisation
of monopolies. Most of these were the same questions asked in 1911,
only divided up so that there was a greater chance of at least some getting through.

Carruthers was indignant that the first vote had not been accepted as
the democratic will of the people. He wrote a long article for the *Sunday
Times* comparing the upcoming vote to the biblical story of Esau and
Jacob and urging the people of New South Wales not to sell their birth-
right of self-government, which had been won for them by heroes like
Parkes and Wentworth. He argued that while he had supported a federation based on the premise that some powers would be given up to the
Commonwealth, those had explicitly been things like tariffs and defence
which concerned Australia's interaction with the outside world. Now, at
the very moment that Britain was accepting that local autonomy was
more democratic and just in regards to Irish Home Rule, Australia was
asked to take the opposite course and betray the Federal spirit in favour
of "the domineering spirit of a power which seeks to usurp an authority
that of right belongs to another".[462]

Underlying this rhetoric was a philosophy of decentralisation that had
been vital to Carruthers' political career. As the architect of his State's
system of comprehensive local government, he genuinely believed that
the closer people were to directly looking after their own affairs, the better the outcomes that would be achieved. Liberalism itself was grounded
on individual autonomy, on the right of each person to control as much
as possible of their own life. If the political system required that some of

that autonomy be ceded, it followed that this should be done in gradual steps, each requiring further justification. In a local community with fewer voters, an individual's vote held greater value compared to a vote in the State. Once this reached a national level, so many voters were involved that a person's vote held little power, and they were thus left with little real control over the decisions of the National Parliament. For that reason, Carruthers believed that only those decisions that logic dictated had to be decided on a national level should be given to the Commonwealth, and for him the industrial powers the referendums asked for did not fall in to that category.

The 1913 referendums were held in conjunction with the Federal election and both resulted in narrow victories for the forces of liberalism. All the referendum proposals were defeated on the popular vote, though this time they were carried by three States. Joseph Cook won a narrow majority in the House of Representatives, though his failure to take the Senate would soon lead to a double dissolution over an attempt to remove union preference in government employment. In these circumstances and with the Liberals needing a Senate ticket twice its regular size, the calls for Sir Joseph to finally ascend to Federal politics became louder than ever. Parkhill personally begged his mentor to lead the New South Wales ticket, and when his first request was rebuffed he asked again.[463] Though Parkhill undoubtedly had some personal bias towards Carruthers, it is noteworthy that the Liberal's leading organiser still saw Sir Joseph as a vote winner. The persistence did not pay off, and Carruthers once again declined on account of his health but also the need to stay and fight for the Legislative Council.

That institution appeared to be in greater peril than ever before. Wade had failed to use his time in Opposition to construct a clear Liberal agenda, and while Labor's income tax and wild spending gave him the opportunity to utilise the defensive aspect of the lines of cleavage, without positive ballast he had made little headway. A policy of freehold, superannuation for public servants, extra technical schools, a domestic science college, improved care for the "feeble-minded" and legislation against clandestine marriage agencies failed to capture the public's imagination.[464] In rural areas a fight had broken out between a "Country Party Association" and what was essentially a Farmers and Settlers faction within the Liberal Party, and this added an unnecessary distraction to the 1913 election campaign. Only one CPA member would get up and the Party quickly disintegrated, but it still managed to hurt the Liberal cause.

Under the strong leadership of William Holman Labor won the election of 6 December comfortably. A barrister with a latent talent for advocacy, Holman was a strong believer in government intervention and the Labor cause. He had garnered particular fame for debating Reid during the Anti-Socialist campaign, where he had argued that Labor only wanted to extend the role of the state because it was necessary to secure for workers "the full results of their industry". Freed from the constraint of the previous perilous Assembly, there were many who felt that he would quickly use his majority to abolish the Legislative Council. Time would prove these predictions wrong, but liberals looked with apprehension upon the new Parliament and the inevitable push for still bigger and more intrusive government.

Sir Joseph would have to endure yet another one of his proud achievements being dismantled, as Labor reintroduced many of the stamp duties that his Government had repealed. As a money bill, he felt compelled to allow the passage of the stamp duties legislation, but he made his distaste for it clear to all who would listen. A dismayed Carruthers told the Council that stamp duties were a terrible form of taxation as they were so complicated that they could make innocent men guilty of evasion by simple mistake. He also critiqued their economic impact, claiming that "there are many easier ways of getting revenue than by putting shackles on the trade and enterprise of the community".[465]

Debates over taxation and the role of government, the bread and butter of the lines of cleavage, would soon fade into the background in the face of an event so cataclysmic that it would force a reorientation of the political divide. In August 1914, after a chain of unfortunate events, Germany invaded Belgium prompting Britain to declare war. As an integral part of the Empire, Australia was inevitably drawn into the fray. This prompted a party truce in the New South Wales Parliament, with

Holman promising to avoid contentious legislation and Wade offering the help of the Opposition in maintaining financial stability. Though unaffected by the push against partisanship, the role of the Legislative Council as a House of review was also impacted, for the thoroughness of legislative dissection would be constrained by a desire not to impede the urgent needs of the war effort.

Like a majority of Australians, Carruthers supported the war and felt that the country had an obligation to do her duty as a part of the British Empire. He saw the war as a battle for the continued existence, not so much of the United Kingdom which would likely survive defeat in a diminished fashion, but of the Empire itself. For a long time he had maintained an idealised image of the Empire as a font and defender of democracy and liberal freedoms. He believed that freedom was not something that was innate to politics, but something that had been won through the historical struggles of British history. Australia and the Empire were the recipients of a legacy that had to be defended against competing political systems. Germany was less democratic and more authoritarian than Britain, and her victory would inevitably promote the growth of such systems elsewhere. Based on this reasoning Sir Joseph now focused all his energy on saving that which he admired.

Like many, Carruthers thought that the war would be over quickly, though he took the sober view that even a short war would require many sacrifices and be costly for Australia. As Gallipoli began to reveal the extent of those sacrifices, Carruthers lent his voice to the recruiting campaign. At a grand rally held at the Sydney Exhibition Building in August 1915 he told the crowd:

> It is up to Australia to do her duty. For a hundred years we have lived in peace in these lands because we have lived under the protection of the flag which for a thousand years has braved the battle and the breeze, and the least we can do is to say to the old land: now we have been sharers in your every glory, and we must now be partakers in your burdens too.[466]

His sons were too young to enlist but Ida, the only surviving child of his first marriage, volunteered to join the Australian Army Nursing Service. She was sent to Egypt to tend to the victims of the Gallipoli campaign but after the evacuation of the peninsula she was transferred to France. There she witnessed and did her best to help the countless casualties of the Somme. Eventually her health broke down; she was ruled unfit for service and sent back home.[467]

Back in Australia, her father's day to day concern was the political logistics of the war. Carruthers gave the political truce his firm backing and called for the suspension of all partisan politics. He was quite indignant when the outbreak of war did not lead to the 1914 Federal election going uncontested, and the eventual Liberal defeat did little to soften that sentiment. In the Council he tried to offer his advice to the Government and improve the administration of the war effort wherever possible. He spent considerable time on the dry work of ensuring that the effort was fully funded. Wary of heaping too much taxation on an already struggling economy, our normally debt-averse subject called for the extensive use of war bonds that could be paid off in brighter days. Though he admitted that loans would also be necessary, he continued to push for economy so Australia would not be forced into competing for American loans needed by the British Government.

Sir Joseph vigorously and successfully opposed a land super tax that tried to raise revenue while achieving the ideological aim of breaking up large estates, pointing out that with most able bodied men already overseas there would not be enough people to cultivate new plots and that these might act as an incentive for would-be volunteers to stay home.[468] Other ideological legislation was also shot down as an unnecessary threat to the political truce. Carruthers attacked a new Superannuation Bill that would have diverted money from the war effort. He also lambasted a Trade Union Amendment Bill that would have allowed a secret vote at a union meeting to permit the use of union funds for political purposes, thereby indirectly compelling the members who supplied those funds to make political donations. Sir Joseph thought that the Labor Party were incredibly naive in pushing this, as it was likely to deter people from joining unions and thus hurt their cause.

Carruthers' attacks on ideological legislation were a two-way street, since in the circumstances of the war he frequently showed himself willing to bend on some of his liberal sensibilities. He very strongly supported restrictions on naturalised Germans who he felt raised a security risk. He was also willing to sacrifice individual freedoms when it came to the supreme issue of conscription. Australian law already enshrined compulsory military service, but this did not extend beyond the Commonwealth. In the midst of an external war and with volunteers dwindling, there was a push to extend this in order to fully mobilise the able-bodied manpower of the nation. Carruthers took an ends justify the means attitude towards this, arguing that the "old formulae of [limited] government" was insufficient when that which in peace could and should defend liberty faced a dire threat to its existence.[469] He even wrote a letter to the editor of the London *Times* urging Britain to lead the way on compulsory service. When that eventuated, Carruthers was insistent that Australia must follow.

Carruthers was not the only one who had to make a conscious philosophical choice over conscription, as members of the Labor Party divided over the issue. Arguably the submission of individual conscience to the will of the majority under conscription fit more smoothly into their collectivist ideology than it did into liberalism, but Labor as a whole were less sold on the merits of sacrificing all to save the Empire. Many of their Catholic supporters, laden with the historical memory of centuries of Irish oppression, were particularly cold on the idea of being forced to fight for England. Already psychologically committed to winning the war and familiar with the necessities revealed by the burden of office, Holman and the Prime Minister Billy Hughes came to the conclusion that compulsion was necessary. Hughes faced dissent from many within his own ranks, and fell back on the traditional Labor position of putting the issue to a referendum.

Carruthers viewed the referendum as an unnecessary delay, but once forced he campaigned for a yes vote. That campaign fell short as the referendum was rejected by three States and on the popular vote. Most unions had fought for a no vote, and it was clear that there would be repercussions for both Holman and Hughes for their perceived betrayal of the cause. Holman had already had considerable difficulties with his party and had temporarily lost his leadership only to regain it with a promise to force a referendum on the abolition of the Legislative Council. In 1916 the Executive Council had lobbied the Governor to grant this, but Carruthers successfully led a protest arguing that it would be unconstitutional to grant a referendum without first taking the matter through Parliament.[470] In the end the abolition effort went nowhere.

As a result of his role in the yes campaign, Holman's position now looked untenable. He would surely be rolled by his anti-conscription colleagues and in the process the war effort might be jeopardised. With this in mind, secret negotiations began with the aim of forming a new Ministry from a combination of the Labor conscriptionists, the Liberals and the "Progressive" Farmers and Settlers members. The process was not a smooth one. Many in the Liberal-leaning press discouraged the idea of rescuing a weakened Holman and instead wanted Wade to capitalise on the situation to seize power in his own right. As a fierce believer in the notion that partisan politics must be eliminated for the war effort, Carruthers did not agree. Long before Holman split with Labor, Sir Joseph was reported to be cosying up to the Premier. He took a central role in the negotiations to form a stable war coalition. In his autobiography he claimed to be personally responsible for the amalgamation of the Liberal Party with the remnants of the Holman Government, though unfortunately this was a tangent that he never elaborated on.[471]

The inevitable expulsion of Holman and his pro-conscription colleagues from the Labor Party took place just four days after the referendum. In his place Ernest Durack was elected temporary Labor leader, and he began preparing a vote of censure against the Ministry. This brought the matter to a head. Holman clearly had the numbers to defeat the censure, but there was some hand-wringing as to whether the Governor should withdraw the Premier's commission as it had been given to him as Labor leader. In the end the Colonial Office intervened to protect a valuable war ally, and Holman formed a new National Ministry. With the issue out in the open, Carruthers took pains to justify the compromise to the public.

Through both his private and public actions, Sir Joseph was ultimately sacrificing his cherished Liberal Party for the war effort. It was a decision he made because he genuinely felt that the external threats to the Empire jeopardised liberalism more than the big government tendencies of his new colleagues. With little more than a name change, his LRA would survive as the extra-parliamentary organisation of the soon to be formalised Nationalist Party. The Nationalists adopted the LRA's constitution, with only a few tweaks to the size of the Executive, and though Holman tried to bring some of his Labor discipline to the Party, it maintained the loose make up characteristic of its liberal origins.[472] A considerable amount of liberal ideology also survived in the New South Wales branch of the Party, particularly once the Labor "rats" gradually lost their seats. Still, with patriotism replacing liberty as the Party's explicit *raison d'être*, the lines of cleavage were inevitably blurred.

Carruthers addresses a wartime rally in Martin Place.
From the Mitchell Library, Sydney.

CHAPTER FOURTEEN

Gentleman Farmer

Though Carruthers had been instrumental in the creation of the Nationalist State Government, it soon became clear that he was far from an unquestioning Holmanite. He supported a push to delay State elections beyond the constitutional norm and thus allow the new Government to consolidate under the pretext of the war effort. Beyond this, Carruthers viewed attempts to use that same pretext to increase the scope of government more dubiously. He successfully amended a restrictive Liquor Bill to allow pubs to stay open after six o'clock to sell non-alcoholic drinks, and was consequently denounced by the temperance leaders of the NSW Alliance. He dismissed a Workmen's Compensation Bill as a derelict leftover of the old Labor Government, which would primarily benefit the same men whose highly divisive strikes were impeding the war effort. He also tried to amend a Bill imposing a tax on automobiles to ensure that it only lasted for the duration of the war, but this was rebuffed as an attempt to amend a money bill.

When the elections were eventually held, Sir Joseph wrote a public appeal urging people to vote Nationalist. Arguing that the survival of the Empire was a bigger issue than the old Liberal-Labor lines of cleavage, he believed that Labor could not be trusted to give full attention to the wartime imperative. He said that while he was sure of the loyalty of the new Labor leader John Storey, those behind him could not be trusted. He claimed that since the conscription referendum anarchists and disloyalists had been flocking to the Labor banner, and thus that those who enjoyed the benefits and stability of the Empire had an obligation to vote for the existing Government.[473] The whole Nationalist campaign was based on a similar mix of patriotic appeals and scaremongering, and the combination worked far more successfully than it had during the conscription fight. The Nationalists won 52 seats to Labor's 33, and the

Parliament was thus afforded a level of stability that it had not seen for several years.

That stability allowed Carruthers to focus less on legislation and more on pursuing public interests outside of the Legislative Council. Many of these revolved around the agricultural industry. Sir Joseph had purchased several rural properties including the large "Hiawatha" estate near Jindabyne. The estate had been purchased as a holiday retreat, with its pleasant air and genial climate expected to help Carruthers with his frail health. After his retirement gave him additional leisure time, its restless owner set it up as an experimental farm. The name "Hiawatha" meant the meeting of the waters, and the vast property sat near the intersection of the Snowy, Thredbo and Eucambe rivers. Though it had rich soil to complement plentiful irrigation, the area was prone to frost and it took careful planning to ensure that its crops survived the winter.

With several resident workers, the property operated as a large scale farm while maintaining the attractions of a holiday retreat. The Carruthers family used to take trips there, exposing the children to the rural lifestyle of Sir Joseph's own boyhood. During their stays the children were frequently taken to fish on the Snowy River, and their father saw to it personally that they treated the sport as an art-form. It was hoped that the rural stays might inculcate the boys in particular towards farming, and that the eldest, Joseph, would eventually take over. This did not eventuate. With a strong rebellious streak Joseph became for a time a tap-dance instructor before settling down as an accountant.[474] Wallace seems to have gleamed from the rural wilderness an adventurous spirit, and he left for Canada to be a railway conductor before returning to become a lawyer. Douglas became an ear, nose and throat specialist, perhaps wanting to help his father with his own condition. Following the social precepts of the day, the daughters' horizons were more limited and they gradually married off: Eve to naval officer Lieutenant-Commander Paul Hirst in 1929, Ida to Kenneth McIntyre in 1932, Alice to Dr Duncan Geoffrey Maitland in 1934 and Peg to Second-Lieutenant James Fleming in Scotland during the dark days of 1941. The "Hiawatha" property was sold in 1920 due to ongoing difficulties obtaining labour.

While in operation "Hiawatha" was quite innovative. Carruthers had long had an interest in agricultural experimentation which stretched back to his days at Sydney University. There he had studied agricultural chemistry under geology professor Archibald Liveridge. Liveridge brought a scientific approach to farming that was quite innovative for the time. It inspired Carruthers greatly, but he was at university to become a lawyer and diligently followed his father's choice of career-path. Once in the Legislative Council, Carruthers was finally able to put his long-dormant knowledge to work. He used Hiawatha's fertile land to grow numerous varieties of imported wheat and other grains, with the intent of determining which would succeed in Australian conditions. He would cultivate those that thrived and then sell or give the seed to other farmers in the hope of increasing Australia's agricultural output. He could get a boyish excitement out of the success of a new crop which offered a reward far greater than any financial proceeds. By 1917 he was having considerable success in this enterprise, and was consequently elected to the Council of the Royal Agricultural Society. From that point onwards, Carruthers became an advocate for rural industries and for the central role he felt that Australian wheat could play in both winning and then paying for the war.

His argument, which he publicly enunciated numerous times, was that unlike the European powers whose lands and manpower had been devastated by direct contact with the war, Australia possessed the natural and human resources to become the Allies' breadbasket. He even suggested that providing food may be more important to the overall war effort than Australia sending more troops. His argument was picked up by many anti-conscriptionists, and used as a key justification for the no campaign for the second conscription referendum. Carruthers himself continued to support conscription, but the numerous citations of his viewpoint played some role in ensuring that the second referendum was defeated more soundly than the first.[475]

While focused on the necessities of victory, Carruthers was also concerned that the cost of the war was getting out of hand and that Australia would be saddled with debt for decades to come. At a speech given at the Royal Easter Show he argued that there was only one way to pay off that debt once the war ended. Higher taxation would require numerous hardships and impede enterprise in a way that would be counterproductive to the cause. Hence the only viable solution to the problem was to grow production and thus increase revenue without increasing the burdens placed upon the people. As someone with firsthand experience of the potential yields of specialised crops, he believed that there was room to increase production in such a manner. He also believed that with European agriculture likely to take a long time to recover, there would be ample room in the export market to absorb the extra produce.[476]

There was a major problem with Carruthers' proposed solution to the problem of war debt. That was that rather than looking likely to increase, production was in danger of collapsing due to unprofitability. In the circumstances of the war the Government had imposed price fixation aimed at the cost of bread, and this had been set at such a low level that it destroyed the price of wheat and thus the incentive to grow it. Carruthers was a vocal critic of the fixed price, which he argued had been set against the interests of the producer.[477] He based his objection on the basic laws of supply and demand. According to this, the only sustainable way of decreasing the cost of bread would be to increase production and thus supply. The long term effect of price fixing was to reduce production, so that in the end it would inevitably drive up the price of wheat despite the Government's involvement. He had argued similarly against the Fair Rents Act that capped rents and thus hurt the market for housing, ensuring less were built and ultimately reducing the supply of rental properties.

While Carruthers gained a reputation for critiquing Holman's socialistic forays into heavy government intervention, it was an act of conservatism that garnered his most emotive denunciation. In 1918 the New South Wales Government introduced a Sedition Bill aimed at silencing some of the more militant opponents of the war by disqualifying them from engaging in State or local politics for a period of five years. It appears Holman may have been concerned with an Interstate Labor Conference that had indicated it might favour a negotiated peace in the face of the Ludendorff offensive, and a more general trend of far left activists openly attacking the war effort. In 1917 there had been a general strike which spread through many key industries, and while it was controversial enough that workers would be more concerned with pay and conditions than winning the war that their countrymen were risking their lives for, there was a genuine fear that the strike had been deliberately orchestrated. The strike had been defeated and in the circumstances of the war the participants had been firmly punished, but the fear remained that the same thing could happen again.

Sir Joseph felt that the Sedition Bill went beyond its express intention and struck at the heart of the freedom of speech necessary for a liberal democracy to function.[478] He pointed out that the men who had won reforms such as the Magna Carta and the Declaration of Rights had, at various points, engaged in sedition and that to clamp down heavily on critiques of the Government would be detrimental to both progress and transparent administration. He argued that while disloyalty should be attacked, sedition did not inherently equate to disloyalty, and most people criticising the Government did so in the hope of improving rather than undermining the nation. He was particularly vehement on the disqualification proposal that would rob a person of their vote and their right to sit in Parliament for breaking the law; something he felt completely undermined the central tenets of British democracy. He compared the Bill to the actions of the Bolsheviks and the Germans, and concluded that while some freedoms must be sacrificed for the war effort, self-government was not one of them. Finally he summed up by saying that a strong democracy had nothing to fear from a few stump orators in the Domain, and that they must be careful not to impose a remedy worse than the disease they hoped to cure.

Carruthers' speech on the issue was one of the longest he ever gave in the Legislative Council. It earned widespread attention, particularly in the Labor press. In the Council he received considerable support from Labor men such as McGowen and Richard Meagher, and their opposition led to the Bill being heavily amended. Its operation was restricted purely to acts of disloyal sedition aimed at compromising the war effort.

In that form it was read a third time, but the end of the war would prevent the legislation from ever passing into law.

Carruthers' fierce defence of the liberal right to free speech came at a time when his oldest liberal friend had just passed away. George Reid had been serving as the member for St George's, Hanover Square in the British Parliament, where his main action had been to fight for the vigorous prosecution of the war. Carruthers was still keenly interested in his old friend's exploits, and when Wade went to England in the aftermath of the formation of the Nationalist Government, one of the first things Sir Joseph had asked him was how Reid was doing.[479] He was surprised to hear that Reid had not been nearly as successful in Britain as he had in the antipodes, and perhaps because of this Reid had taken a break from Parliament to visit America and lobby for the war effort. Exhausted upon return, he appeared in Westminster a few more times before dying of cerebral thrombosis on 12 September 1918.

Carruthers was devastated to hear the news, and took the opportunity to pay tribute to the pervasive role his friend had played in his political life:

> He was perhaps more associated with my life than any man in the whole of Australia. I was extremely upset when I read of the death of my friend, because I never regarded George Reid except as a man so full of health and of life and of everything that goes to make life enjoyable that I never contemplated his death. It came to me as a very deep shock. It was like losing one of my own family. It was to me the losing of a loyal comrade, the losing of a big brother – because that is what George Reid was to me in my life … I knew him better than most men, and I knew from long experience what men can seldom say of those they know, that he was a soul of honour. I never knew Reid to do a dishonourable thing in his life, nor to do or tolerate a shady action. The public life of the country was, in his keeping, absolutely pure.[480]

A couple of years later, Carruthers would be shocked to discover that Reid's grave sat virtually unadorned. The British Empire League undertook to rectify the situation, and Sir Joseph was appointed honorary treasurer of the George Reid Memorial Fund. After several generous donations, including one from the Prince of Wales, he was able to ensure that his old friend was provided with a suitable headstone and a small memorial at Westminster.

Carruthers' mourning was cut short by news of the armistice of 11 November, and the knowledge that the goal he and Reid had been fighting for had been achieved. The Empire had been saved, and though the unsubdued Bolshevik menace still loomed large in Sir Joseph's mind, victory over the Germans was something worth celebrating. On the 13th, the President of the Legislative Council led its members in impromptu renditions of God Save the King and Rule Britannia. Sir Joseph rose to speak on a motion offering congratulations to the King, and boasted of a triumph of liberty, won at a terrible cost, that acted as "some recompense for all of the pain, anguish, and suffering one has gone through during the last four years".[481]

1919 would be a year of rebuilding, and Sir Joseph remained determined that agriculture must lead the way. In August he was elected President of the NSW Chamber of Agriculture and he seized upon a newly expanded role as a lobbyist. The main thing he was lobbying for was the rights of farmers that he felt had been compromised by wartime bureaucracy. During the war the Government had used the Wheat Acquisition Act of 1914 to commandeer grain in order to ensure that its sale and distribution could be centrally coordinated. The war threatened shipping lanes, and a large amount of grain that would normally be exported was stored in government wheat pools to be offloaded in more secure times. The farmers were meant to be paid for what they had given, but bookkeeping was unreliable and many had received as little as a third of the value for their crops. Administration at the sales end was also criticised, as backroom deals lead to sales that went untendered. While farmers saw little of what the Government owed them, a widespread drought created extra financial pressures that combined to drive many off their land. This threatened to undermine Australia's economic recovery, not to mention the old liberal goal of closer settlement.

In order to bring these grievances to a head, Carruthers moved for a select committee to investigate the actions of the NSW Wheat Board that had been responsible for the administration of the Acquisition Act. There were too many aggrieved persons for the Government to ignore this push, but it decided to appoint a Royal Commission instead. There was considerable controversy over who would be placed upon it. The Government was asking for Justice Pring, Colonel James Murdoch, and Thomas Campbell Murdoch, a prominent retail trader, was critiqued for having little knowledge of the farming industry while more alarmingly Campbell had acted as the secretary to Arthur Trethowan who was directly involved in the Wheat Board.[482] Carruthers pleaded with the Government to make more considered appointments, but he was ignored.

Despite its somewhat compromised membership, the Commission ultimately condemned the administration of the Wheat Board and thus vindicated Carruthers' critiques of it. Allegations of bribery and misappropriated funds were revealed, and though no one was convicted the responsible Minister was forced to resign.[483] Carruthers also called for a Royal Commission into the effects of the drought and increased railway rates, and while this was only met with the "consideration" of the Government, the public appeal helped to secure the release of £1,000,000 of funding for drought relief.

Sir Joseph also had to come to the defence of the agricultural sector when the Government attempted to introduce yet another Liquor Bill. The Bill created a board to carry out the reduction of licences, and also enabled a referendum on the liquor issue. A vote of no-licence at that referendum would ban not only the sale of alcohol, but also its possession, manufacture or export. There was a constitutional issue here as the State Government had no legal right to make laws on exports, but Carruthers was concerned with the flow on economic effects. As a long-time advocate of the Australian wine industry, he could see that the Bill threatened to destroy that industry in its entirety. He fought vigorously for the exemption of light wines from the effects of the Act, but his efforts were to no avail. The legislation passed, though luckily that aspect of the Act was never utilised as the liquor referendum, not held until 1928, was resoundingly defeated.

All told, Carruthers acted as a bit of a nuisance for the post-war Holman Government. He opposed their Sharefarming Bill because he felt that government controlled sharefarms would ultimately subsume the private ones that already existed. He was sceptical of their Superannuation Bill, suggesting that it imposed such heavy burdens on the people that no government would dare implement it in full while also arguing that a scheme limited to public servants was unfair, for it taxed poor private workers to pay for their government counterparts' pensions.[484] When the Child Maintenance Bill appeared before the Council, Carruthers combined with John Peden to remove a clause that would have usurped the Board of Trade's living wage. He was not a fan of the arbitrary imposition of a living wage, but he argued that now it was in place it should only be changed via an amendment to the relevant Act. Holman felt that the amendment fundamentally undermined the legislation, and the Bill was eventually dropped after some idle talk of swamping the Council.

The defeat over Child Maintenance and the revelations of the Royal Commission undermined the position of the Government with an election looming. Carruthers' position in that election was somewhat unclear. With the war now over, there was no great imperative to support the Nationalists particularly since Holman had been pursuing so much interventionist legislation. Sir Joseph was still nominally an extra-parliamentary member of that party, but his attachment was far from zealous. The increasingly well-organised country "Progressives" had some appeal, though their limited outlook stood somewhat at odds with Carruthers' liberal view of politics. In the end it was the knowledge that Labor represented an untethered version of Holman's vices that made up Carruthers' mind for him. He publicly called upon people to vote for the best men of either Nationalist or Progressive stripe, and thus to keep the socialists out at all costs.[485] Many Nationalists were perturbed that such an influential figure had not endorsed them far above their country rivals, but until their leadership changed to reflect their liberal heritage, Carruthers' primary political concern was defensive.

The 1920 election was the first fought under a new Electoral Act that reintroduced proportionally represented multi-member electorates.

It was intended that these would mitigate the problem of vote-splitting amongst non-Labor candidates by ensuring that more than one candidate could get up. Hopes that the new system would produce clarity were soon dashed however, as the election result produced a hung Parliament. Labor won 43 seats, the Nationalists 28 and the Progressives 15, while the remainder fell to independents of varying political stripe. In the resulting negotiations non Labor were hamstrung by the reluctance of many Progressives to risk subsuming their party in a coalition with the Nationalists. Labor soon gained the upper hand under the pragmatic leadership of John Storey, but in order for them to govern they needed to find a speaker that would not impact their parliamentary numbers. The widely popular Daniel Levy, who had held the position during the previous Government, was the obvious choice. He was reluctant to accept the position because he did not want to betray his party by helping Labor govern. In the end it took the intervention of Carruthers to convince him that as long as he resigned once the Opposition had the numbers to topple Labor, there was no harm in facilitating the functioning of responsible government in the meantime.[486] Now in his sixties, Sir Joseph had become a sort of grandfatherly figure to young parliamentarians, the custodian of the respectability of both Houses and the traditions of a bygone age.

Such continuity stood as an island amidst immense change, for the 1920 election was a watershed moment in the evolution of the New South Wales party system. Its central legacy was the creation of a permanent country party, after many stillborn attempts, and thus the imposition of a stable three-party system on the Legislative Assembly. Arguably one of the reasons a country party succeeded at this election was that Holman, and therefore the Nationalists, failed to embody either liberal or conservative values. The lines of cleavage had been sacrificed to the necessities of wartime, and in seventeen months of peace they had yet to be resurrected. The hung Parliament was a reflection of the fact that politics was no longer a clear choice between enterprise and socialism, or even over conscription, and that in the ensuing circumstances voters had wandered.

As is often the case, this low point created the opportunity for renewal. William Holman lost his seat at the election, and George Warburton Fuller was elected the new leader of the Nationalists. Fuller came from a proud Kiama family that Carruthers had a long connection to. He had served as a Free Trade backbencher in the 1890s, and while he was hardly a political titan, he was a direct product of the Parkes-Reid political school. Though he was perhaps more conservative than some of his predecessors, Fuller embodied some clear liberal beliefs and over time he would re-establish an agenda and an identity for the Nationalists. In doing so he would reforge the lines of cleavage, and drag the Progressives towards what became an inevitable coalition. In the background of all this, Carruthers would help to pull the strings. No longer just a simple critic, he became more of an advisor and the patriarch of liberal renewal.

For the moment, Carruthers' main priority was how to react to Labor's legislative program. In theory the Premier was quite restricted in what he could do, for a mere 43 seats offered him little mandate for wide sweeping change. Nevertheless, many of Storey's radical colleagues were keen to ensure that their ideology be put into effect as quickly as possible. This created considerable turmoil inside both the Labor Leagues and the Lower House. In the Upper House, the lack of a clear democratic majority gave the Councillors relatively free rein to amend and reject Bills as they pleased.

A toxic relationship soon developed between the Council and the Government. Things got so bad that the Governor was convinced to make 16 new Labor appointees to help pass legislation, but Carruthers avoided the temptation of acting as a wrecker. He certainly found much he objected to in the Labor program, but he kept up a policy of trying to improve rather than block legislation. This was the case when he successfully amended the Profiteering Prevention Bill to exempt primary producers, allowing them to store and sell their goods as they pleased on account of the vicissitudes of their trade.[487] Though even after this amendment he continued to dislike a Bill that inherently restricted the market and therefore hurt enterprise, he was willing to accept that the Government had some right to pass legislation that it had committed itself to during the election. Carruthers also reluctantly refused to block increases in stamp duties and the income tax that Labor pushed through in the hope of combating the ever-increasing public debt. He argued that, while increased taxation could have been avoided with judicious economy and the best way out of debt was to encourage people and businesses to earn, the Ministry in power needed to be able to control attempts to fix its finances.[488]

Independently from the Government, Carruthers organised a Select Committee of the Legislative Council to inquire into rural conditions. He was appointed chairman of what would be a massive undertaking involving 114 meetings, 371 submissions and lasting over fifteen months.[489] The committee revealed the extent of the drift of population from the country into the city, the poor state of closer settlement and the backwardness of Australian farming methods in comparison to the rest of the world. It suggested that improvements were needed in agricultural education, financing, the breaking up of estates, irrigation schemes, rural roads and bridges, pest eradication, cattle breeding, veterinary qualification, access to telephones and other amenities, and the expansion of bush-nursing. Such was the value of the highly technical report that it would be used as a textbook at the University of Sydney and in agricultural colleges.

While the report had many detailed and scientific findings, its ultimate (and somewhat speculative) conclusion was that if these improvements were made and more producers were placed on the land the flow on effects would create not only greater crop yields and therefore greater export opportunities, but also a greater demand for labour and a larger market for local goods. This idea would eventually be refined into the simple notion that the economic impact of each additional farmer would support employment for two and a half other Australians, suggesting possibilities for population and economic growth that would fascinate politicians and obsess Sir Joseph for years to come.[490]

Inspired by the Committee's report, in July 1921 Carruthers delivered an address at the Nationalist Club announcing the advent of the "Million Farms Campaign". The aim of the campaign was the settling of a million new farmers on a million new farms through a combination of intense immigration, the opening up of new lands and the subdivision of existing estates. It was argued that the vast majority of Australia's land remained undeveloped, and though much of that land was unsuitable for farming, large tracks remained ripe for closer settlement provided they could secure new railways, irrigation works and other amenities. The campaign proposed a centrally coordinated scheme in which the Federal Government would work in tandem with the States to provide these pre-requisites. British capital would be used to fund the scheme, and Britain would provide immigrants that would help to relieve its vast post-war un-employment problem. This capital would be obtained at a reduced cost because Britain would be keen to unload its surplus population but also because a more highly populated Australia would strengthen the Empire while requiring less of Britain's defensive resources.

Much was made of the fact that an increased population would de-crease the individual burden of Australia's war debt, but the defensive motive was the central imperative behind the scheme. The war had spooked Australia, making her more aware than ever of her isolation from Europe. During the First World War this had proved a blessing, but in future wars it was likely to prove a curse. Carruthers was very grateful for the security Britain had provided since 1788, but he felt it was naïve to rely upon it forever. In future wars it seemed likely that the Royal Navy might be caught up in other engagements while Australia faced her own threat, and the only way she could ever hope to defend herself in such a scenario was to have the population to do so. The Million Farms would provide this, not just directly but also indirectly through the two and a half principle. To emphasize this defensive push Carruthers sug-gested concluding public meetings with the statement "Australia must be saved" in emulation of Cato's famous phrase about the destruction of Carthage.[491]

The Million Farms Campaign was inherently tied to White Australia, for one of the main reasons Australians feared the possibility of invasion was because of their cultural and racial difference from their neighbours. The Campaign would frequently use appeals to White Australia in its propaganda. For the moment Carruthers remained committed to that principle, though he was far from zealous about it. He still respected the Japanese and personally toasted Admiral Saito at a function held when the latter visited Sydney. He was also open to bringing in non-Anglo-Saxon Europeans to fill up his Million Farms, particularly Italians who were controversial in conservative circles not only because of their ethnicity but also because of their strong Catholicism.

The "Million Farms Campaign" received national press attention and quickly won over a large number of supporters. New Settlers Leagues were set up in most States to lay the groundwork for increased immigration, while a Million Farms Committee was formed to sell the message. It adopted innovative marketing techniques including posters full of visually demonstrated statistics and moving pictures showcasing the idyllic fertility of rural Australia. The pictures, much like the campaign itself, were pretty over-optimistic. Australia's post-war debt was already extremely high, and though the increased production promised to relieve that burden, many were reluctant to take a gamble. Carruthers deliberately downplayed the cost of the scheme, quoting a figure of £30,000,000 that he later admitted would only be the starting point.

As acting Prime Minister Joseph Cook responded to the campaign with cautious support, but when Billy Hughes returned from a trip to England he embraced the Million Farms and agreed to what he could to encourage immigration and land development. Carruthers was so reinvigorated by his enthusiasm for the scheme that for the first time he seriously contemplated entering the Senate so that he could push the agenda. He even wrote to Hughes about it, but events in the New South Wales Parliament soon drew him back in.[492]

The Select Committee and the initial announcement of the Million Farms Campaign took place in a period of relative cordiality between Carruthers and the Labor Party. Some of its members supported the Campaign which was sold as being non-party, though the Labor press was concerned that immigrants would be given priority over local unemployed workers. Carruthers' pragmatic attitude was typical of much of his time in the Legislative Council, but one of the reasons for his amelioration may have been his friendship with John Storey. Despite the ideological chasm that existed between them, the two men were quite close and even during Storey's Premiership they used to go on fishing trips together. Storey would use these as an opportunity to confidentially vent about Labor's internal wrangles to a man with no small experience of party strife.[493] By 1921 those wrangles had become intense and when combined with a journey to England, they contributed to a steep breakdown in Storey's health and ultimately his death in early October of nephritis.

Storey was replaced by James Dooley, a man who lacked the popularity of his predecessor. There were rumours that one or two Labor members might cross the floor against him, and so the trigger arranged between Levy and Carruthers was finally pulled. Levy resigned from the speakership, destroying Labor's majority. Dooley asked the Governor for dissolution but he was denied and forced to resign from the Premiership. Meanwhile Fuller was trying to arrange a coalition between the Nationalists and the Progressives to form an alternate Government. The Progressives agreed to support Fuller in the House, but on the issue of the coalition they split, with many members fearing that it would lead to their party being subsumed.[494] Fuller formed a Ministry out of his supporters and the coalition Progressives, and Carruthers accepted the post of Vice President of the Executive Council. He had frequently refused to take on similar roles in the past, and it seems that he only agreed because of his special relationship with Fuller. The botched coalition negotiations meant that when the Ministry faced the House it had little hope of inducing any Labor members to cross the floor. In the event a Nationalist split and offered himself up for speaker. He was refused and Levy took up his old post while Dooley formed a new Ministry pledged to an early election.

The coalition negotiations showed the Nationals that if they were going to win the next election they needed to cultivate rural support and Progressive sympathy. This was a period of heightened tensions between the city and the country, with many rural people so frustrated with Sydney-based government that they wanted to set up New States to replace it. Carruthers had a hard time convincing country people that his schemes would bring more alleviation to rural concerns than the setting up of new governments, but his highly visible role in working for country development meant that he would still be a key tool in bridging the gap between the Nationalists and the Progressives. It has even been suggested that the Nationalists deliberately resurrected Carruthers' career with this goal in mind, but that is to ignore the important role he had already been playing and the numerous positions he had previously been offered but deliberately turned down.[495]

Carruthers was appointed the coalition Campaign Director in what was a significant innovation for the time. The Liberal/Nationalist Party had traditionally appointed a committee to fulfil such a role, so Sir Joseph's position implied a greater personal responsibility for the result of the election than most who came before him. More importantly, the idea that the campaign would be conducted as a coalition was quite groundbreaking. Despite the absence of the non-coalition "True Blue" Progressives, this would pose significant problems in terms of both preselection and balancing competing ideological interests. Carruthers' main emphasis was unsurprisingly on unity, and he urged against opposing sitting non-Labor members regardless of whether they had supported the coalition.

In the midst of an economic downturn which had followed the war, Sir Joseph framed the election battle in terms of finance. Labor's solution to wartime and post-war inflation had been to increase spending and hope that arbitrary price controls could overcome economic imperatives. In the end the recession burst the bubble of rising prices, but public works failed to curb a rising unemployment rate. With revenue falling, Labor could only fund its spending through increases to debt and taxation. Carruthers denounced the economic consequences of this, declaring:

> I have no faith in heavy taxation, nor in high charges for everything. What can it avail a man if wages are high and work is scarce, and the costs of living are prohibitive? Any fool can spend money. It takes a wise man to make it and to use it so as to get full value for it.[496]

Sir Joseph laid a solid groundwork for electoral organisation, but eventually the competing interests became too much for him. He resigned his Campaign Directorship and was replaced by a committee. He told Hughes he had resigned because he could not "endure the interference of those who don't understand politics and think they know what we have had years of learning from experience".[497]

Carruthers' role in the campaign did not end with his resignation and he continued to push hard for a coalition victory. Needing a cause to woo country voters, Fuller picked up the Million Farms scheme and gave many of its proposals a prominent place in his policy speech. "True Blue" leader Michael Bruxner also emphasised the need for land development, but Carruthers' presence gave the Nationals some much needed legitimacy over this issue. It provided the offensive agenda to go with the defensive agenda Labor's financial mismanagement had gifted the coalition. Unemployment was sitting at 9.5%, and the coalition won a relatively comfortable victory with 41 seats to Labor's 36, while there were also 9 "True Blue" Progressives.[498] Elsewhere the various Country Parties had threatened to side with Labor, but Bruxner was a headstrong anti-socialist so there was never much doubt over his general support.

Fuller formed a Cabinet and the coalition Progressives were soon absorbed into the Nationalist fold. Carruthers took up the position of Vice President of the Executive Council, and would play a central role in the Ministry. The Fuller Government was a return to a Liberal style of governance after the compromised days of Holman. Its central emphasis was on balanced budgets and reducing taxation where possible. The Treasurer Arthur Cox even managed to produce budget surpluses while decreasing the income tax. Significant investment in public works was maintained, but increased scrutiny was applied in determining whether works would be productive and necessary.

The Government would also be notable for abolishing a number of state-run businesses including a trawling company, timber yard, bakery, sawmill and a power station. Many of these socialistic forays were unprofitable, but much has been made of the fact that some were shut down despite the fact that they were making money. This has been painted as the impractical result of stubborn ideology.[499] Such a view ignores the fact that men like Carruthers saw economic growth as the path out of war-debt, hence they felt that if private businesses were allowed to flourish in the place of those of the State, the returns would find their way back to the Treasury eventually anyway. The Government also removed public servants from the jurisdiction of the Arbitration Court. This had less to do with the sectional outlook of Irvinism, and more to do with maintaining some government control over wage-rates and thus the spending of taxpayers' money.

Carruthers would be a powerful figure in Cabinet, so much so that there were complaints that he was dictating affairs. In a debate in the Legislative Assembly the Nationalist member for North Sydney Reginald Weaver denounced him as the "Czar" of the State.[500] Meanwhile the *Australian Worker* produced a cartoon depicting Carruthers as the ventriloquist controlling both Fuller and coalition deputy-leader Walter Wearne.[501] Much of this tension resulted from Carruthers' emphasis on rural spending which perturbed some Sydney members, but he also clashed with some of the more militant sectarians in Cabinet. Chief amongst these was Thomas Ley, architect of the "Ne Temere" Bill. This Bill was a reaction against a papal decree which insisted that Catholics must be married by a priest. Some Protestants viewed this as a threat to civil marriage and tried to change the law to make it illegal to suggest that the lawfully married were not truly and sufficiently so. As the representative of the Government, Carruthers supported the Bill in the Council, but he put up little fight against an amendment that ultimately wrecked the legislation. On temperance too, he frustrated the militant Protestants. He fought for a delay in the referendum mandated by the 1919 Liquor Act and he also backed the deletion of a clause in the Liquor Bill that would have empowered the License Reduction Board to shut down the wine industry even before a vote for prohibition.[502]

Carruthers' role in the Legislative Council was an invaluable one for the Government, but it was extremely taxing. Since the Council remained unelected, Governments were reluctant to appoint extra Ministers to it, hence two men were left to do the work of ten in the Assembly. Sir Joseph had to directly guide almost every piece of Government legislation through the Upper House in an effort that had the aging man working thirteen hours a day. The recent addition of many Labor members meant that he had to see off attacks from both the left and right and navigate the fractured ideological makeup of the Council. Nevertheless he had several triumphs. One was the passing of the Sydney Harbour Bridge Bill which had to be defended against rural members upset at the massive outlay being spent in the city and dismayed that the bridge was designed to open up North Sydney in a way that would only exacerbate the drift towards the city. Another was the passing of the Monopolies Bill designed to stop the manipulation of the market by combines. This was vigorously opposed by James Ashton in a free-market manner that Carruthers would normally be sympathetic to, but the latter swallowed his pride and fought hard for the Government's policy. He justified his position by pointing to the increased costs combines were heaping on the State Government, thereby flipping the argument and making it one about saving taxpayer money.[503]

The main reason that Carruthers had taken a spot in the Ministry was to pursue his goal of land development. A Cabinet sub-committee was set up to push this forward, and Sir Joseph took a prominent role in directing its efforts. The committee quickly focused in on the lands of the Murray-Darling basin as the most ripe for settlement. Despite being relatively fertile, little of the Western half of the New South Wales side of the Murray had been settled. This was largely due to provincialism. Geography required that anything produced in this area be exported via Melbourne, hence New South Wales had been reluctant to spend the money to open up these lands when they would not be the primary beneficiary of the effort. Federation had done little to alleviate these prejudices, and Carruthers faced an uphill battle getting his colleagues on board. He soon found himself faced with several Cabinet leaks that suggested the fertile area of the Murray was smaller than the Government had been making out.[504] Worse still, it appeared that this information had been deliberately hidden from the public. Carruthers' role in these cover-ups is debateable, and as someone who had spent considerable time surveying the area he insisted that the negative reports were unnecessarily pessimistic. Still, as the face of the Murray scheme Carruthers' reputation was inevitably tarnished.

The fact that he allowed this to happen is symptomatic of the deep emotional investment he had placed in his Million Farms. In many ways they were to him what federation had been to Parkes; the opportunity to cap off a long career with a lasting national legacy. For that reason he showed a naivety towards the possibilities of land settlement that was uncharacteristic of a man whose career had revolved around pragmatism. The leaks ruined the chances of an extensive Murray Scheme. Some money was still spent, an agreement was negotiated with the Commonwealth to further facilitate the construction of the Hume Dam and the 1922 Border Railways Acts began the long overdue process of integrating Riverina transportation. The results, while substantial, never quite lived up to the grand expectations that had been raised.

Opening up lands was only half of the problem that the Million Farms faced; the other was finding people to settle on them. Despite earlier talk about relieving England of her unemployment problem, it was soon realised that not just any old rabble would be suitable for farming. British people were inevitably unaccustomed to Australian conditions, and it became apparent that they would need to be trained in order to be successful. Carruthers wanted the British Government to provide funds for that training and for the public works necessary to open up the land. After long negotiations a deal was hammered out whereby Britain would provide loan of up to £6,000,000 to the New South Wales Government at a third of the regular interest, provided they could settle 6,000 immigrants within a period of five years.[505] Fewer immigrants could be settled for a reduced loan, maintaining a ratio of £1,000 per immigrant. This deal soon began to unravel as it became apparent new lands could not be opened up for the requisite price while Britain was unwilling to provide the type of settler, namely returned soldiers with some capital, that New South Wales wanted. Advertising campaigns in Britain brought in a significant number of immigrants to New South Wales independently, but none were ever settled under the terms of the scheme.

At a Federal level outcomes were slightly more positive for the Million Farms Campaign. The 1922 election produced a hung Parliament, and Billy Hughes was forced out of the Prime Ministership to make way for a coalition government lead by Stanley Melbourne Bruce and Earl Page. Carruthers was quite perturbed at the fall of Hughes, for he had been making significant headway in lobbying for an immigration and closer settlement scheme. The ascendance of Bruce meant that Sir Joseph had to start the whole process over again, only now with a Victorian with whom he was unfamiliar. The public appetite for immigration whipped up by the Million Farms Campaign remained strong however, and Bruce picked up what was a popular national issue. Over his time as Prime Minister he secured £34,000,000 worth of loans for the settlement of immigrants and he also established the Development and Migration Commission to oversee the whole process of assisted immigration.[506]

There were two main reasons why so many of the schemes resulting from the Million Farms Campaign fell short. One was that, despite Carruthers' bold predictions, the post-war international market for agricultural products remained depressed and there were simply not the economic opportunities to expand agriculture in the way he desired. In 1925 the prices for wool and wheat would finally start to rise, but this was after Carruthers' initial push had exhausted itself.[507] The second reason was that the schemes were too reliant on a large outlay of capital which the Fuller Government was reluctant to spend.

Carruthers was also naturally spending averse, and though he felt that the defence of Australia was a task worthy of the cost, he soon began looking for cheaper alternatives. In justifying this shift he explained that "in leaning on the Government you might as well lean on your own shadow. The Government is, after all, only the shadow of yourselves".[508] The argument was that the main way the Government could obtain money was to skim off the productive capacity of individuals through taxation, something that acted as a drain on the community. Therefore, the most effective way of achieving a monumental task like closer settlement would not be through public spending alone but through directly releasing the individual efforts of the people.

The scheme Carruthers proposed to do this was the Community Settlements and Rural Credit Bill. Announced at the end of the 1922 parliamentary session, the Bill proposed to enable community members to form settlement associations that could pool together resources and borrow money for the buying back of large estates. The members would benefit through the subsequent sale of that land as smaller plots, and also through the boon to the community resulting from an increase in population. It was hoped that large land owners would be more willing to sell to community members and that the communities directly participating in closer settlement would be able to help new settlers succeed in a way that governments could not. To help with this the Bill also introduced registration and tax breaks for rural co-operatives which were intended to foster this spirit of mutual self-help.

The Bill was announced at the end of session to allow time for an expansive discussion over its clauses before it was made into law. To facilitate this, a large number of community conferences were held throughout the State. These soon revealed that many people were less interested in the community settlement provisions and more in the possible benefits of tax incentivised co-operatives. A Co-Operatives Bill had been a long time coming. Not only had many of these associations existed for decades without government backing, but most of the Empire had already instituted legislation giving co-operatives legal status. Carruthers' Bill was based on a report on India's system, which was the most recently instituted and therefore seen as the most modern and effective. That report had initially been given to the previous Labor Government, leading several of its members to claim that Carruthers was stealing their policy, but they had not acted on it while in office.

After the conferences and under the direction of respected Legislative Councillor Professor John Peden, the Bill was expanded to cover non-rural co-operatives and thereby step beyond the bounds of a closer settlement policy. The shift was unpopular with many Nationalists, as urban co-operatives now stood to be given tax and other advantages over individual businesses. As a representative of the Chamber of Commerce Parkhill personally lobbied his mentor over the unfairness of this privilege, but Carruthers retorted that the tax breaks were small and that registration mandated a limited profitability that would prevent direct competition with businesses anyway.[509] It has been argued that co-operatives legislation stood as an ideological outlier, forced on governments by what was happening overseas, but ultimately incompatible with both individualistic capitalism and state based socialism.[510] This may well have been the case, but Sir Joseph was still able to justify creating a government-free path to ascend the early steps of the economic ladder on the grounds of anti-socialism. A program of specially dedicated tax breaks may not have been laissez-faire, but it did offer an appealing way to lessen unemployment and thus the push for state welfare.

Passed as the Co-operation, Community Settlement, and Credit Act 1923, the main thrust of Carruthers' amended legislation was to allow individuals to pool financial resources and thereby obtain equipment, overcome economies of scale and access credit. The point was to allow people with little means a way of accessing what was necessary to increase their economic production by relying on each other. Societies covered by the Act included those formed on the basis of rural agriculture, trading, community settlement, community advancement, rural and urban credit, investment and building. Registration required a society to follow strict rules, dividends were limited and reserve funds were mandated to ensure long-term economic stability. The Act would prove a tremendous success and not be replaced until 1992. Its legacy can be seen in the continued existence not only of rural co-operatives, but also building societies and credit unions. Ironically, the community settlement provisions that were initially the centre piece of the legislation proved to be some of the least utilised. Some associations were formed and may have had some mild successes, but even Carruthers' own attempt to form a community settlement in the Monaro District ultimately fell apart due to lack of community interest.

The Fuller Government faced the 1925 election with a substantial record. Though the recession had endured in the early years of the administration, economic times were beginning to improve, tentatively fostered by the Government's financial management. Socialism had been wound back, and some lasting pieces of legislation had also been passed. Despite this, the Nationalists still faced several electoral problems. The removal of public servants from the Arbitration Court had alienated what was an increasingly large proportion of the electorate. Sectarian excursions had angered Catholics, while the efforts of Carruthers and others to block them had also hurt the Government's reputation amongst militant Protestants. Most damaging of all however was the Government's failure to live up to the grand expectations it had raised concerning rural development. A large amount had been achieved but more had been promised and this gave the True Blue Progressives, free from the responsibilities of office, great ammunition to critique the Ministry in the hope of securing more seats.

In the end this split in the right would prove costly. Many preferences failed to flow directly between the two anti-socialist parties and Labor was able to sneak in with 46 seats despite receiving a significantly smaller percentage of the vote than the combined total of the Nationalists and Progressives.[511] Jack Lang would use his serendipitous position to pursue the most extensive Labor program in the history of the State, thus teaching his opponents a valuable lesson about what electoral disunity had cost them. In the aftermath the True Blues would rename themselves the Country Party, and begrudgingly accept that coalition was a necessity.

The election loss propelled Carruthers out of the Ministry for the last time. His task as Vice President had been an exhausting one. Two of his recent predecessors had practically died in the job, and in 1923 Carruthers had faced a bout of influenza that had almost seen him off. The Nationalists would be back in power by 1927 but without Fuller as leader Carruthers would be unwilling to put himself through the same strain. It mattered little for his task had been completed. Million Farms had failed to live up to expectations, but the New South Wales Nationalist Party was in all but name a Liberal Party again. Holmanism had been vanquished, and with the Empire safe Carruthers had shrewdly and successfully utilised Fuller to retrieve his political legacy.

CHAPTER FIFTEEN

A Man of the Pacific and a Councillor Until the End

One of Carruthers' last acts as a member of the Fuller Government was to represent New South Wales at the Pan-Pacific Food Conservation Conference held in Hawaii in 1924. He paid for his own ticket to avoid any political controversy for undertaking what was as much a labour of love as it was a governmental priority. The conference was notable for the wide range of Pacific nations that attended, and while it was largely ceremonial Sir Joseph was able to pick up important information on Pacific fishing industries and the canning of pineapples. He was also able to negotiate the lifting of an embargo that had prevented Australian fruit from entering the islands for fear of spreading pests.

Carruthers' time in Hawaii proved to be a considerable culture shock. He found his new American friends knew very little about Australia, but they were keen to learn and he was asked to give a number of addresses describing the island continent. He had been sent a film to advertise Australia, but after one showing he had it pulled after being appalled by its mushy love story and lack of real information. Carruthers was equally intrigued about his hosts. For a number of years he had loosely ascribed to the white Australia policy, less from a belief in the supposed inferiority of non-whites than from a serious fear of ethnic tensions. What he found in Hawaii was a multicultural society functioning not only harmoniously but also prosperously. Americans, native Hawaiians, Japanese people and Filipinos were all living and working alongside each other in a manner that made Carruthers question his previous assumptions. He came away from his trip claiming that he no longer feared an influx of Asians into the British dominions.[512] He was particularly impressed by the high wages all ethnic groups received, and cited a Filipino strike to try to dismiss the common Australian assumption that non-white immigrants would undercut wages.

Carruthers felt one of the keys to the harmony Hawaii experienced was the economic prosperity it enjoyed thanks to its free access to the American and Philippine markets.[513] Combined with advanced techniques for the preservation and transportation of tropical fruits, this allowed Hawaiian companies to make considerable profits on what were essentially domestic exports. Ever the free trader, Sir Joseph wanted the British nations of the Pacific to emulate this success. Over the next few years he would lobby for the removal of tariffs from goods imported from the Polynesian Islands, particularly Fiji. His efforts would sadly be to no avail. Arguments for the mutual benefits that would be derived from encouraging economic growth in the region were cast aside in favour of protecting the market for Queensland crops.

One of the reasons Carruthers was so enthusiastic about visiting Hawaii was because of his fascination with Captain Cook, who had been killed there. Sir Joseph had long been obsessed with the man who took Australia for the British Empire, and had fought for his veneration. He saw the lowly-born navigator as a great self-made man to be held up as example for all Australians to emulate. He took it as "an augury of the future of these great lands [that] our very founder was one who fought his way to success by unaided efforts, by industry and by patient but persevering labour".[514] He also saw him as a man of science, whose map making had done invaluable service for the growth of trade and immigration.

As Minister for Lands under Reid, Carruthers had acquired land at the site of Cook's landing at Kurnell for the Government and set it up as a national memorial. Ever after he was a regular attendant and speaker at the annual ceremony held at Kurnell to mark the anniversary of the Endeavour's famous disembarkation. When visiting Britain in 1908 Carruthers was shocked to find that the heart of the Empire had no significant memorial to its most prominent explorer, and he subsequently lobbied successfully for the erection of a statue of Cook in London.

Carruthers' surprise at Britain's callous attitude paled in comparison to the jolting revelation that Hawaiians viewed the navigator with open hostility. Many felt that Cook had abused the hospitality of the native

Hawaiians and that his untimely death was not undeserved. Sir Joseph was quick to try to change the minds of any he heard expressing that opinion, but he soon decided that that would not be enough. Instead he put plans into motion to redeem and foster the memory of Cook in Hawaii, and also to fight the historical battle of discovering what really led to his demise. This work and research would require Carruthers to spend a considerable amount of time in the Pacific, and he made it a yearly ritual to visit Hawaii, several other islands and on one occasion California to browse historical documents.

His first goal was to improve access to the memorial where Captain Cook had died. This had been erected in 1874 before the United States had taken control of the islands, but most of the land around it was now privately owned by Japanese settlers. Carruthers was able to secure the help of the Japanese Consul to transfer the land to the American administration in order to enable the setting up of a park around the memorial.[515] He also won Commonwealth funding to improve the jetty at Kealakekua Bay leading on to the monument.

The memorial would form the centre-piece of a massive celebration planned for the sesquicentenary of Cook's death in 1928. This was Carruthers' brainchild though he found a strong backer in Hawaiian Governor Wallace Farrington. The event would be an exercise in expressing the strong ties between the Pacific nations of the British Empire and the United States. Held over several days, it involved a naval display featuring the HMAS Brisbane, the HMS Cornwall from Britain, the HMS Dunedin from New Zealand and the USS Pennsylvania. The latter carried the US Secretary of War Dwight F. Davis. In the main ceremony a new bronze tablet was unveiled at the place of Cook's death while the warships fired a salute while anchored side by side with native canoes. Carruthers gave the main address proclaiming that Australia, New Zealand and even Canada were the real monuments to Captain Cook, before the last post was played in what was an emotional scene:

> The blue waters of the Pacific Ocean on one side of us were just rippled by the softest breath of wind; the sky over our heads was a canopy of unfeckled blue; on the shore-side towered the craggy

cliffs of the Kona, honeycombed with the burial caves of the old Hawaiian feudal chiefs. The bugle notes were softly re-echoed from these cliffs, and when the last drawn-out tones of the call were sounded – "Come to rest; Come to rest; Come to rest;" – the echo repeated them very slowly and softly as though a spirit were responding. It seemed to many of us as if the spirit of Cook might have been there listening and answering the call.[516]

Carruthers continued with the sesquicentenary theme for the title of his book, *Captain James Cook R.N., 150 Years After*. The culmination of years of research, the book was very much a historian's work, unconstrained by narrative and focused on argument. The author admitted he possessed a certain bias but claimed that he would try to act impartially when adjudicating on a number of historical points. The first of which was that Captain Cook deliberately set out to annex Australia. The author dismissed the argument about the discovery of the continent, citing the fact that Cook already possessed maps locating New Holland. Instead he pointed to "secret instructions" recently discovered in the Bolckow collection of Cook's papers bought by the Australian Government, to suggest that the taking of Australia was "of set design". He also discussed the ill-fated voyage of French Captain La Perouse in order to establish that there was a real competition between the European powers over the taking of the southern continent, and thus that if Cook had not succeeded another European nation would have.

The second point was to prove that Captain Cook had died through a series of misunderstandings and not due to the fact that Cook had disrespected or abused the natives. He argued that the negative image of Cook's actions came from the account given by John Ledyard, an American who later defected from the royal navy and lived out his days in his homeland. In post-revolutionary war United States, it was far more profitable to abuse a British hero than to defend him and Carruthers pointed to the other, less damning, accounts of Cook's final days to suggest that Ledyard was fundamentally unreliable. The author admitted that some of Cook's men had gotten out of line, as had some natives who had stolen a cutter, and suggested that it was these men rather than Cook or the Hawaiian King that were responsible for how events panned out.

The final point the book set out to prove was the one most revealing of the author's character. That was that the Hawaiian's were not, nor had been cannibals and that they in fact possessed a sophisticated and moral culture. He took pains to defend the social structure of what he described as "a very fine race, whose culture goes back to a period when the inhabitants of the British Isles were in a state of semi-barbarism". He even showed understanding towards allegations that could not be dismissed as easily as the cannibalism charges. He suggested that the several instances of thieving experienced by Cook were symptomatic of the Hawaiians' different understanding of property under their feudal system, while he also claimed criticism of promiscuity was anachronistic for a pre-Christian society.

Carruthers had grand plans for his book, and even hoped that it might be adapted to become a school textbook to teach Australian children about their founder. This would have taken a large amount of work, for as noted the book was not a biography and more a series of loosely connected historiographical debates. David Drummond, the Minister for Education in the Bavin Ministry, politely declined the suggestion that an abridged version of the book be made essential reading for school children.[517] Despite this setback, the book was published simultaneously in Australia, Britain and America, and seems to have sold reasonably well in the face of the depression.

Over the years Carruthers spent in the Pacific researching for his book he developed a love for the area. He was a regular attendee of meetings of the Pan-Pacific Union in Honolulu. Set up in 1911 by American businessman Alexander Hume Ford, the PPU brought together philanthropists, politicians and pioneers from across the region to promote peace, brotherhood and a number of both scientific and charitable works. Carruthers became a passionate advocate of closer ties between Pacific nations and help for those that were only just beginning to develop. His island hopping trips became such a habit that he continued them even after his book was completed. Sometimes Lady Carruthers would accompany him, sometimes one of his now adult children would come to keep a watchful eye on him, but from 1924 Sir Joseph would never spend another full winter in Sydney.

The extensive time Carruthers spent in the Pacific exposed him to the unrest then being experienced in Western Samoa. That territory had been in the possession of Germany, but the allies captured it during the war, and the League of Nations ultimately mandated that it become the responsibility of New Zealand. On visiting the island, Sir Joseph was shocked to discover the authoritarian way that that responsibility was being discharged. The administrator Sir George Richardson had surrounded himself with a government of sympathetic appointees and was putting down any opposition with arbitrary exercises of power. Carruthers learned of chiefs with nationalist or democratic leanings being banished and deprived of hereditary titles, all without trial. He wrote several letters to the *Sydney Morning Herald* denouncing these "Moscow methods" and suggesting that they imperilled peace on the island.[518] His central argument was that it was a betrayal of basic British principles to deny legal and democratic justice to the Samoan people, and that ultimately the New Zealand Government was bringing the whole Empire into disrepute with its actions.[519]

This last sentiment was too much for many, and it led to Carruthers being vigorously attacked in the New Zealand Parliament. The Government's response was to pass legislation retrospectively endorsing the actions of the administrator and to belatedly launch an inquiry into the administration of Western Samoa. Carruthers felt that the terms of reference the inquiry was given were too narrow and when it ultimately exonerated the leadership he held it up as a farce. In essence it determined that the actions of the administrator were legal while side-stepping the issue of whether or not they were morally or even logically sound. Carruthers was particularly aggrieved that when Samoan businessman and independence campaigner Olaf Nelson had gone to New Zealand to give evidence in favour of the persecuted natives, his associates were harassed and deprived of their right to trade. Sir Joseph was in close contact with Nelson, who seems to have informed many of his liberal views on the situation. Carruthers concluded that New Zealand was clearly failing to live up to the terms of its mandate which dictated to "promote to the utmost the material and moral well-being and social progress of the inhabitants of the territory" and that consequently the administration might be handed over to the Samoan people or at least the United States.[520] The latter had been overseeing the governance of the Eastern half of Samoa under more democratic terms and had seen far fewer incidents of unrest.

The success of the United Party in the 1928 New Zealand election led to a change of government that promised to defuse the situation. Carruthers was sent a letter from the office of the new Prime Minister Sir Joseph Ward promising to take his views on the necessity of administrative reform into account.[521] This hope of renewal proved short-lived however. In 1929 an initially peaceful demonstration of the Mau independence movement was mishandled and put down with violence. 11 protestors died, and in the aftermath a New Zealand cruiser was sent to the island as a show of force against the alleged sedition. In response Sir Joseph strengthened his campaign for Samoan justice and engaged in some particularly vicious debates with Nationalist MLA and fellow Pacific traveller Thomas Henley, but ultimately it was to no avail. Samoa would not receive its independence until 1962, long after Carruthers' efforts had been forgotten. He ultimately found himself frustrated that the mistakes of Tasmania's treatment of Aborigines were being repeated, and that the union jack, a symbol of "Liberty, Freedom and Justice" was being muddied in the process.[522]

When not island hopping, Sir Joseph spent most of his final years in the Eastern Suburbs of Sydney. When he and Lady Carruthers returned from England they had not moved back into their grand "Ellesmere" property at Sans Souci and in 1911 they relocated to the more convenient "Highbury" in Waverley. Still a keen sportsman, Sir Joseph paid for the construction of a cricket pitch at the local Marist Brothers Catholic School nearby his house.[523] He himself was no longer up to the exertion of cricket, but he became an avid lawn-bowler holding memberships for both the City and Rose Bay Bowling Clubs. He even "represented"

New South Wales at bowling tournaments in the Pacific, though this was because he was already there rather than because of his skills of which there are mixed reports. At one tournament in Suva Carruthers had to be rescued after the coral arch the green had been built on collapsed in on itself.

The more central location made it easier for Carruthers to attend sittings of the Legislative Council. Despite his advancing age he continued to act as one of the main players in that arena. As a younger man Carruthers had opposed the nominee Council as an undemocratic barrier to responsible government. In the subsequent period he had grown to view it as an indispensable part of the well-functioning democratic system New South Wales enjoyed. Following precedents set by the emasculation of the British House of Lords, the Council had arguably softened since the 1890s and it was now less likely to directly block legislation that the Government had a clear mandate for. Instead, according to its backers, it now focused more on performing the subtle role of improving bills and only blocking those excursions for which the Government lacked a mandate. The Sedition Bill, Ne Temere and dozens of other pieces of legislation had proven to many the value of the Upper House in performing this role.

It was a role that was becoming ever more important as the Legislative Assembly descended into fiercer partisan struggles that allowed for less and less cool headed scrutiny at a Lower House level. This was a problem that would reach new depths in the midst of the Great Depression. In contrast, it was argued that the Council's nominee composition kept it sheltered from the blinkers of partisanship and allowed it to act as a fair House of review. By this point party support was virtually essential to getting elected, so it was feared that if the Council were reformed on an elective basis it would imbue party machinations as had occurred in the Federal Senate. Die-hard supporters of the Council thus argued that if the Council's role was to be maintained it must be defended not only against abolitionists but also against the reformers who claimed to be trying to save it.

Somewhat ironically considering his position as the Father of the

Liberal Party and Godfather of the Nationalists, Carruthers led the chorus of critics of expanding machine politics. There was an element of nostalgia in this, for when Carruthers had entered Parliament nearly four decades before party ties were looser and the quality of legislation had allegedly been better because of this. He could accept that strong parties were necessary in the Assembly where governments were formed, but he desperately wanted to defend the independence of the reviewing Chamber. He viewed the Council as the last bastion of old-style liberalism, as it preserved "liberty and freedom of conscience" amongst its membership.[524] It must be admitted that this liberty was frequently exercised against the wishes of the Labor Party, but Sir Joseph also practised what he preached against his friends. As a Minister in the Fuller Government Carruthers had been forced to act as a party Nationalist, but Wade, Holman, Thomas Bavin and Bertram Stevens all felt the heat of his free conscience.

Part of the reason for Carruthers' deep attachment to the role of the Legislative Council was his familial connection to William Charles Wentworth. A nominee Upper House that would bend, gradually and thoughtfully, to the will of popular opinion was perhaps the defining feature of Wentworth's constitution. Wentworth was in many ways a conservative, one of a flexible colonial bent, but still fearful of completely unfettered democracy. Carruthers seems to have been deliberately selective in remembering both Wentworth and Parkes as liberal titans when in the 1850s they had both clashed fiercely over the Council. While he was not alone in viewing New South Wales' founding father through rose-tinted glasses, John's connection to Wentworth and Joseph's obsession with historical continuity exaggerated this effect. In 1873 Joseph had attended Wentworth's ceremonial funeral and the event seems to have been a formative experience for him. Wentworth had died in England during the previous year and his body had been painstakingly shipped to Sydney for what was to be the Colony's first state funeral. Up to 70,000 people lined the streets as a glass-sided carriage, pulled by four plumed horses, led a procession involving the Governor, the Premier and just about every other prominent citizen. Newspapers reported footpaths so clogged with people that it was impossible to navigate them, as boys climbed tree-tops and gateposts to try to get a glimpse of the ceremony. The procession ended in Vaucluse as Wentworth's body was sealed away in its own mausoleum and a solemn eulogy delivered. For one teenage boy who witnessed it, this was his first taste of the grandness of his Colony and an outward display of her great destiny. Carruthers was left with the impression that Wentworth *was* New South Wales and that the Constitution he had written for the Mother State was, in many respects, a sacred document.

New Premier Jack Lang was a man that appeared to have little belief in the role of the Council. An imposing and populist firebrand, Lang had climbed his way up the ladder of the Labor Leagues through a mixture of determination and manipulation. As Premier he was concerned with enacting the Labor platform, and viewed virtually any amendment to his legislation as an obstacle rather than an improvement. A remarkably strong willed individual, he was also unlikely to heed to any obstruction calling for a direct mandate. Bede Nairn has argued that despite appearances Lang fundamentally accepted the existence of the Council and attacked it largely to distract members of his own party who frequently caused him trouble.[525] With hindsight this may have been partly true, but to his contemporaries Lang was the arch-enemy of the Upper House and Carruthers would dedicate the last years of his life to saving the Council from the Labor Leader, as well as Nationalist reformers.

Lang certainly wasted no time in testing the limits of the Council's discretion. Upon his election legislation was rushed through imposing a 44 hour work week, abolishing high school fees and placing public servants back under the jurisdiction of the Arbitration Court. Other bills proposed to amend the Local Government Act to remove Carruthers' requirement that voters made a contribution as direct or indirect ratepayers, to abolish capital punishment and to force compulsory unionism into the Arbitration Act. On many issues Lang's mandate was questionable, not only because he had received less votes than his opponents at the last election, but also because many reforms had not received a prominent place in his election policy speech. They were quickly met with intense dissection and though only a couple were blocked, many were amended to cushion their effects.

Carruthers missed the early part of the session and by the time he returned the Government was already promoting the idea of swamping the Council with new Labor members to overcome its alleged intransigence. Sensing this, Sir Joseph began publicly constructing the case against new appointments. Lang's argument in favour centred on the idea that Labor interests were not adequately represented in the Council, and that in essence it was a body made up of his opponents. In response, Carruthers did the sums to suggest that there were now 39 of 70 active MLCs who had been appointed under Labor Premiers, and that therefore the claim that Labor lacked representation was unsustainable.[526] The accuracy of this count is debatable, but Lang retorted that the only figure that mattered was that a mere 17 MLCs remained pledged to the Labor platform. This argument held little weight for his opponents. To believers in a deliberative Legislative Council it was an aberration that any members, excepting perhaps Ministers, be pledged and if formerly Labor MLCs had been voting against the Government's legislation this provided proof that it had been flawed and justified the Council's negativity. The debate thus stagnated on a fundamental philosophical disagreement.

The Governor, Sir Dudley de Chair, seems to have been sympathetic to Carruthers' argument, but considerable pressure was mounted on him to agree to the swamping. Such pressure had not been uncommon for previous Governors to experience, but Lang's demands and his persistence went beyond normal precedent.[527] He wanted numbers large enough not to simply coax out a compromise like Reid had done, but to push through whatever he wanted. This threatened to fundamentally change the nature of the Chamber, and the role it had played since the advent of responsible government. Despite his initial hesitation, de Chair eventually capitulated, accepting a record 25 appointments adding to 3 already made, based on Lang's assurance that the Government was not considering using the numbers to abolish the Council.[528] This would not give Lang an absolute majority of pledged members, but with numerous other Labor members and attendances erratic, the Premier could be assured of forcing his will on most matters.

Sir Joseph responded with an elaborate protest. When the Council met to swear in the new members amidst an atmosphere of palpable tension, Carruthers moved an adjournment motion hoping to delay the appointments. His supporting speech went over the arguments against the swamping in emotive detail. He pointed out that the appointment of so many members during the session was unprecedented and that there had been no attempt to overcome the disagreement between the Houses through the traditional method of a joint conference. He argued that increasing the Council to 99 members was a constitutional aberration, for the precedent suggested that counter swampings might follow each change of government quickly increasing the membership to untenable levels. Abolition would be preferable to this indirect destruction, but a Government that had received 25,000 less votes than the Nationalists and Country Party had no mandate for it.[529] He summed up by insisting that the Council had acted as a defender of the will and liberties of the people against the arbitrary excesses of government, and that if it were abolished that the people would insist on its replacement as soon as their views were allowed to be heard.

Carruthers' rhetoric was only exceeded by Ashton, who met the Council's seemingly imminent demise with the Roman gladiatorial epithet "we, who are about to die, salute".[530] The adjournment motion was eventually withdrawn, but the soapbox proved effective in conveying the Councillors' message.

As many had predicted during the adjournment debate, the Government soon reneged on Lang's suggestion that he would not use his new Upper House numbers in an attempt to vote that body out of existence. In January 1926 the Government introduced the Constitution Amendment Bill proposing the abolition of the Legislative Council. While present in the Labor platform, this policy had not been given an airing in the recent election campaign. To his enemies Lang was thus simultaneously breaking a promise with the Governor and attempting to radically change the constitution without a direct mandate from the people.

Labor won a preliminary victory, forcing the Bill to be read in the

Legislative Council by a vote of 45 to 43. The fierce debate quickly turned against the Government however, as critics were able to successfully point out that the Labor platform espoused a belief in the referendum yet that mechanism was being deliberately avoided in this instance. Moreover, the introduction of a formalised process of "initiative and referendum", often proposed by Labor members as a replacement check on the government of the day, was being put off to some indeterminate future. This gave pledged members a way to justify abandoning the legislation while still being able to claim they had upheld their democratic principles.

Carruthers insisted that the Government was running scared from the result of the recent Federal election, which had been a landslide victory for the Coalition, and that it did not dare to put the issue before the people because the result would be a forgone conclusion.[531] He also dismissed any promises of a theoretical replacement down the track as an unreliable distraction from the issue at hand. Sensing the tide of opinion slipping away from them, the Government successfully adjourned the debate against the wishes of Sir Joseph, who had miscalculated that he had the numbers to block them.

Parliament was then prorogued to give Labor a chance to regroup. In the meantime Carruthers organised a "memorial" to be sent to the King to urge him against assenting to the abolition legislation until the issue had been put before the people. 46 MLCs were convinced to sign the document, which de Chair controversially sent to the Dominions office without seeking government approval.[532] Any alleged impropriety ultimately mattered little, for the delay failed to achieve its intended goal. An attempt to reintroduce the Bill was defeated by 47 to 41. Seven pledged Labor members either crossed the floor or abstained. Labor MLC Patrick McGirr called for the defectors to be shot, but the Party settled for expulsion.

In the aftermath the Premier tried to have de Chair agree to a second swamping, but having already stretched the limits of precedent the Governor this time held his ground. Labor sent a tokenistic appeal to the British Secretary of State to intervene, but as he remained opposed to going to the people, Lang accepted that Carruthers and his fellow die-hards had won this round. The victory had been earned on several fronts. Public opinion had been swayed over; at least enough to scare Lang off a poll. Pressure to counter that of Lang had been put on the Governor, helping to fight off the second swamping. Most importantly a number of Labor members had been convinced to switch sides.

The propensity of Labor MLCs to abandon the dictates of their party once they entered the Upper House is an interesting phenomenon. The traditional explanation is that they enjoyed the comfort and prestige of the Chamber so had little motivation to vote themselves back in to obscurity. This is certainly an important factor, but the ability of political titans like Ashton, Peden and Carruthers to woo them through intellectual force and personal friendship should not be overlooked. Sir Joseph was a man who had gone on fishing trips with Labor Premiers and remained close with Bernhard Wise despite accumulating enough political bad blood to earn a lesser man an eternal enmity. His affability and the lure of his genuine belief in the benefits of a free political conscience and individual liberty tangibly affected the outcome of events. Carruthers was a constant presence in the parliamentary chambers, always willing to have a chat or play a game of billiards in a spirit of healthy competition. He had become particularly close to Ernest Farrar, a formerly Labor MLC who had left his party over conscription. At one time a shearer then a saddle maker, Farrar still considered himself a union man and along with Carruthers he acted as a valuable conduit in convincing further Labor MLCs to break the shackles of the pledge and embrace the house of review. Sir Joseph once told the Chamber that many Labor members "came here, perhaps to curse, but remained to pray", and if belief in the Legislative Council was a religion, Carruthers was the chief apostle.[533]

Though the Council was safe for the moment, the swamping had affected its ability to act as a check on legislation. With so many pledged Labor members, any amendment or negative vote would now require convincing almost all the unpledged of its merits. This consensus of free conscience would be difficult to achieve, but Carruthers scored an early victory over the Government's Parliamentary Electorates and Elections

Bill. This proposed to abolish the system of proportional representation and reinstitute single member electorates. Many were happy to see the experimental system go as it had encouraged close elections and thereby political turmoil, but the decision to replace it with first past the post voting was highly divisive. It was clear that without preferences Labor's unity would give it an electoral advantage, as the Nationalists and Country Party would once again be faced with the problem of a split vote. An amendment allowing preferences passed the Council by a single vote, and when the Assembly asked for an explanation Carruthers chaired the select committee created to formulate a response. That response was accepted by the Council, whose amendment made its way in to the final Act. A further amendment making voting compulsory failed to achieve the necessary support.

On many other issues Carruthers was able to do little more than register a protest. He attacked an amendment to the Arbitration Act that reinstated unions which had actively undermined the war effort while destroying the "loyalist" unions that had replaced them. Lang's various interventionist excursions were also critiqued for the heavy financial burden they would put on business and the destructive effect they would have on the economy. These included the expanded Workmens' Compensation Act and the Family Endowment Act. The latter introduced a weekly family payment of 5s per child, provided a family did not exceed a generous income threshold that was tied to the living wage.[534] It also set up an endowment fund to be paid for by employer contributions and the Government. Carruthers was highly concerned that the Act established the radical precedent of essentially giving employees different wages for the same work, and argued that it would ultimately drive down wages in favour of what was essentially a "state dole" that could only be funded through further taxation.[535]

When it came to Lang's most controversial proposal, to introduce a tax on newspapers, Sir Joseph was constrained by his deep belief in the specified role of the Legislative Council. Though he was unenthusiastic about increasing the cost of accessing information, Carruthers voted for the Bill under the pretence that the Government had a right to control its finances and that he would not offer Lang any constitutional issue on which to campaign for abolition.

Lang's Premiership was dogged by internal Labor Party struggles, somewhat ironically considering Storey had frequently complained to Carruthers about Lang's own machinations.[536] Eventually these issues reached a head with a leadership challenge that ended in a tie. Lang was able to hold on to his job, but the solidarity of his parliamentary majority soon seemed to be in jeopardy. When a censure motion inevitably came Lang had to use the promise of an early election to prevent three of his supporters from crossing the floor. The Premier also used the promise of an election to secure the passage of four months' supply and the continued confidence of the Governor. All this was soon abandoned however, as Lang negotiated agreement with two of the rebellious trio and then eschewed all of his promises in favour of calling back Parliament to shove through more of his ambitious legislative program.

This prompted Carruthers to move a motion of protest. He argued that the summoning of Parliament before the end of its prorogation, outside of an emergency, was both unprecedented and unconstitutional.[537] He attacked Lang's dishonourable breaking of his promise of an early election. This promise was a matter of public record, for the Premier had clearly articulated it in a speech he had given to Parliament. Carruthers also denounced the shady intrigues that had allowed Lang to re-establish his majority. The protest was backed by a vote of 41 to 39.

Lang's callous treatment of Parliament did much to increase the hatred with which the non-Labor community viewed him, but in a further twist internal Labor strife soon had the Premier back seeking an election. He secured this against the wishes of some of his fellow party members by resigning and then being recommissioned to the Premiership. Carruthers relished the opportunity of an election campaign and was heavily involved in speaking appearances for the Nationalist cause. His main emphasis was that the Legislative Council had been doing invaluable work in protecting the people and that only the defeat of the Government could preserve it. The Premier's erratic behaviour, divisive legislation and party wrangling virtually assured that defeat. When it came in the form of a 46-40 victory for the Nationalist and Country Parties, Carruthers was simultaneously relieved and disappointed that the opportunities gifted to the Opposition had not been further capitalised on.

Most of the seats gained by the new Coalition Government were picked up by the Country Party, a fact that did not reflect well on the new Premier Thomas Bavin. Bavin, a lawyer and former political staffer, was somewhat estranged from the New South Wales liberal tradition that Sir Joseph embodied. As the private secretary of both Barton and Deakin, Bavin had been schooled in the interventionist and somewhat aristo-cratic liberalism of these Prime Ministers, rather than the Gladstonian liberty emphasised by the Free Traders.[538] While certainly an ideological improvement on Holman, Carruthers would never be as close to Bavin as he had been to his predecessors. Age had something to do with this, but so too did political disagreements that would end up dominating their relationship.

Like Carruthers two decades before, Bavin took the reins of the Gov-ernment at a time when the State's finances were in a disastrous state. Lang had greatly increased the role of government and while taxation had increased, ordinary revenue had not matched the rise in spending. Inflated budgets and mismanaged railways combined with new welfare programs to create both a short term crisis and a long term structur-al short-fall. Many Nationalists were happy to keep the new widows' pension, but Bavin had controversially promised to retain almost all of Lang's legislation and was now left with the task of finding the money to keep it going while simultaneously bringing debt under control.

To Carruthers' chagrin, the Premier's solution was not to emulate his example of reducing spending in other areas and leaving people un-molested to fructify the economy, but to tackle the financial situation through the introduction of a graduated income and company tax. This tax proposed to create tax brackets and increase the rate of taxation for higher income earners, reduce the exemption level for all, and to com-bine the income of husband and wife and then tax the couple accord-ingly. Through these methods large swathes of the State's earners would be forced to pay more in order to fund the programs of an ex-Premier who as of yet had never clearly won an election.

Unsurprisingly, many politicians and commentators with longstanding liberal sympathies met Bavin's proposals with abhorrence. When the Bill reached the Legislative Council Carruthers unleashed upon it. He admitted that Lang's financial mismanagement and accumulated deficit had left the present Government with a disastrous situation, but argued that it should be met with a temporary supertax and reduced spending. Against the new institutionalised system of increased taxation Carruthers rallied all the rhetorical arguments against bloated government and bureaucracy. Money taken by the government was money that could no longer go to increased wages and other productive purposes, while it was an acknowledged fact that the government was a far less efficient spender than private individuals. Graduated taxation attacked success and effort, but when applied to businesses, whose size was usually reflective of the number of people involved, it also attacked efficiency. The mechanics of the new system were also criticised for being so overcomplicated that they would practically force private individuals into hiring accountants lest they risk breaking the law. It was a fallacy to tax married couples with twin incomes more, particularly while leaving de facto couples living "in adultery" free from this.[539] Carruthers concluded that the Government would be better off burning all the taxation Bills that had ever been passed in New South Wales, and starting from scratch with a goal of simplicity.

When looked at in total many of Carruthers' criticisms revolved around not just the increase in taxation, but the flow on consequences of trying to tax people based on their circumstances. An exemption level was one thing, but once the government started drawing intricate and arbitrary lines in the sand not only did the machinery of taxation become unnecessarily complicated, requiring a large bureaucracy to administer and reducing efficiency, but the system itself became unfair. Those who earned more already naturally paid more tax through simple multiplication. Some graduation may have been necessary to cover the increased burden of government, but legislation could not possibly account for the

myriad of circumstances experienced by individuals, families and companies, and by suggesting that it could the Government was introducing
a false pretence. The consequences of this pretence would not only discourage enterprise and thereby hurt the economy, but also alienate those
experiencing hardships that could not be accounted for. Carruthers ultimately acknowledged that the Bill and some level of graduation had to
be accepted, but he was hopeful that some of these inherent problems
could be mitigated.

The fact that the taxation proposals were introduced by a Nationalist Government put many Legislative Councillors in a bind. With Labor
supporting the proposals, there was no point in delaying the legislation
in the hope of a change of government. Moreover, if they attacked the
proposals too heavily they risked jeopardising Bavin's position, leading
to the return of Lang and even greater increases in taxation and spending. When giving his speech Carruthers repeatedly related how much he
respected the Premier, though his multiple objections quickly drowned
out these formalities. Most liberal Councillors similarly chose principle
over partisanship when it came to giving their honest opinions. Ashton
pointed out that the highest rate of taxation would now be twenty times
higher than under Reid, though he gloomily concluded that even that
would not be enough if the trend towards increased expenditure was not
halted immediately.[540] The Council ultimately proposed a large number
of amendments trying to eliminate many of the contradictions present
in the complex document and hold the increase in taxation to as low a
level as possible. These were taken to a conference between the Houses
where Bavin was ultimately able to assert his will. Even the reduction
in the exemption level from £300 to £250, which Carruthers was sure
would cost the Government votes, was ultimately forced through despite
a snap Legislative Assembly defeat over this issue.

The introduction of the graduated income tax was one of the few
times the Bavin Government made a radical change. Another was when
the Premier signed up the Commonwealth-State financial agreement that
created the Loans Council. This was a sacrifice of State autonomy that
Carruthers was naturally cold on. In other areas the Government largely

left things as they were as they tried to foster a feeling of stability that was lacking during the Lang era. This frustrated many supporters who were unhappy to accept what Lang had left. Sir Joseph lobbied hard to convince Bavin to reverse or amend his predecessor's changes to the local government franchise. He even proposed a mixed franchise that would give everyone a vote on planning issues but leave spending questions to those who provided the funds. The scheme was met with little enthusiasm.

In the aftermath of the Lang administration it was clear that if the Nationalists wanted the Legislative Council to survive, they needed to introduce safeguards to protect it. Bavin planned on doing this in two ways. Firstly, by changing the State's Constitution to ensure that the Council could only be abolished or have its powers or composition changed with a successful referendum vote. Secondly, the Council would be reformed to make it more democratic, thereby removing its critics' main rhetorical weapon. Carruthers was enthusiastic about the former proposal. His friend John Peden crafted a new passage of the Constitution to be known as section 7a. This craftily required a referendum not only to abolish or change the Council, but also to remove or change the new constitutional section itself.[541] There was some question as to whether binding the actions of future Parliaments through this restriction was legal, but even legal challenges would act as an impediment to any unilateral abolition Labor might be contemplating.

Section 7a received considerable support in Nationalist circles and passed through both Houses of Parliament despite Labor objections. Any attempt to democratise the Council would inevitably face more thorough conservative scrutiny. Carruthers' son Joseph was then working as a private secretary to Attorney-General Francis Boyce, and Sir Joseph would be heavily involved in lobbying the Government to pursue limited changes. During the time of the Fuller Government Boyce, Bavin and Carruthers had been involved in a Cabinet sub-committee investigating Council reform.[542] It had concluded that it would be desirable to place an upper limit on members to prevent partisan swampings that destroyed the function of the Council. Without swamping, a new solution would be required to resolve deadlocks, and this might involve both a joint sitting and a referendum. On the crucial issue of an elected Legislative Council the committee remained silent. This was likely because of Carruthers' hesitance towards it.

In 1927 he remained dismissive of the idea of an Upper House elected on the same franchise as the Lower, suggesting that the same party would likely end up in power in both Houses removing any genuine check on legislation:

> the only hope of appeal from Phillip drunk will be to the same Phillip in the same state in each House, since they will be elected on the same party cries of the same majority and with the backing of the same party machine.[543]

In private Carruthers had speculated on having a Council elected by ratepayers, but property qualifications were always going to be difficult to sell to the electorate. The Bavin Government came up with a compromise solution that would democratise the Council while hopefully ensuring that its composition remained distinct from that of the Assembly. The Bill Boyce introduced in September 1929 kept the former committee's limitation of member numbers and also the deadlock provisions allowing for a joint sitting, with the possibility of a referendum or dissolution if that failed. More radically, it proposed that the Council be elected by members of both Houses, nine year terms with a third of members retiring every three years, and an age qualification of thirty years.

Carruthers was indignant at the central premise of these proposals, election by members of Parliament. Many of his criticisms of an elected Council had revolved around a fear of its transformation into a party house. The new system proposed to give power over the choice of Council members directly to party caucuses with little reference to the electors, and it thus threatened to make the Council even more of a party house than the Assembly. Sir Joseph dubbed it a "house of political marionettes" and warned that the ambitious could use donations to a political party to buy their way in to the Chamber.[544]

Carruthers' outrage was not shared by all of his fellow Councillors.

Ashton had come to the conclusion that an elected Upper House was a historical inevitability, and was willing to accept Boyce's voting system provided he could secure a few minor amendments. With this support the Bill passed its second reading and moved into committee discussion. There Carruthers proposed the rather novel suggestion of separating the general changes to the functioning of the Council, such as limiting members and introducing deadlock provisions, and the change in how the Council's membership was to be composed.[545] He thus hoped to achieve the reforms he thought desirable while giving the people a separate choice at a referendum to decide whether the Council should be elected. Labor member Joseph Coates then seized on this suggestion and proposed that if the people were to be asked two referendum questions they might as well be asked a third on abolition. This wrecked the proposal, and Sir Joseph was left in the unenviable position of having to vote with the abolitionists against the third reading of the Bill.

The Bill then went to the Assembly where it was amended in such a manner as to almost completely remove any Legislative Council powers over money bills. Initially the Bill had restricted the Council from amending appropriation or taxation bills, but left it able to reject these and to suggest amendments to them. Now the Bill proposed not only to deny the Council the power to amend these bills, but it also allowed appropriation bills and bills imposing taxation for ordinary annual services to be presented for assent even if rejected by the Upper House.[546] Other bills imposing taxation could only be delayed.

The emasculation of the Council thus proposed was too much for Carruthers. He accepted that the Assembly had a right to supremacy over matters of finance, and pointed to the fact that he had been heavily involved in the greatest financial conflict the two Houses had ever experienced, that which took place during the Reid administration.[547] However, he argued that the Council had always had powers over the management and machinery of taxation, and that these should be preserved as management provisions were particularly complex and therefore benefitted from review. Carruthers was also aggrieved that Peden, the President of the Council since February, had helped to draft the provisions despite occupying a position that implied some level of objectivity. He was able to attract considerable support for his position and secured a narrow defeat of the provisions by a vote of 25-24. Sir Joseph wrote the select committee's report justifying this rejection and was ultimately able to secure a compromise whereby the Council was not excluded from touching bills dealing with the regulation of taxation.

Carruthers continued to publicly denounce the elected Council in anticipation of a referendum vote, but the vote never came. Wall Street crashed in October 1929, and the Government was quickly consumed by the pressures of the Great Depression. In the circumstances constitutional issues and the cost of a public vote seemed low priorities, and Bavin ultimately let the issue lapse.

The depression forced the Premier to finally start rolling back some of Lang's welfare legislation. The widows' pension was means tested, first children were excluded from the family endowment payment and the working week was lifted back to 48 hours.[548] Other spending cuts included reductions in public service salaries and reduced contributions to superannuation. Had Carruthers been in power he would have been able to justify and sell these changes on account of his liberal beliefs and economic acumen, but it was clear that the Deakinite Bavin had been forced into them with the utmost reluctance. Worse still, his critics were able to point to the fact that he had allowed spending to run at record high levels and already increased taxation, suggesting that he had left the State completely unprepared for any economic downturn. The financial reputation of the Nationalists, which should have been their greatest strength, was thus turned into an electoral liability.

An election was due in late 1930, timing that allowed the full force of the crash to reach New South Wales just as the State went to the polls. Under the lead of Lang, the Labor Party fought a campaign of naïve optimism, promising to reverse many of the cuts and renegotiate and raise loans to cover expenses. The non-Labor press naturally denounced the Opposition's irresponsibility suggesting that the priority should be to stabilise existing liabilities, rather than create new ones which could only be obtained at very high rates of interest. Carruthers joined in the fray. He argued that it was essential that New South Wales prioritise paying off her loans to ensure her reputation as a borrower, protecting the system of loan financing that had long been essential to the State's prosperity and basic solvency.[549] On another occasion he reiterated his long-held belief that you cannot tax yourself into prosperity. This was a minor swipe at Bavin who had introduced an employment relief tax, but it also emphasised the necessity of enterprise in leading the country out of the hole it was in.

Lang won the 1930 election in a landslide. Bavin's tactic of presenting budgetary retraction as his sober duty made little traction as he was overwhelmed by the populism of his opponent. Despite the pressures of the depression, one of Lang's first acts back in government was to push through a Council Abolition Bill. His opponents quickly denounced this as an unnecessary distraction, but they let the Bill through in the hope that section 7a would block it for them. There followed a series of legal disputes and appeals, before both the High Court and the Privy Council upheld 7a. The Council was thus saved from abolition, in what was a great victory and vindication for all of Sir Joseph's efforts.

His die-hard position would not rule the day however. It fell to Bertram Stevens to resurrect and pass the Bavin proposals for a Council elected by both Houses of Parliament. The Constitution Amendment (Legislative Council) Act 1933 restricted the Council from touching appropriation bills but not the regulation of taxation, and it thus embodied the amendment Carruthers had won in 1929. With this additional legacy, Sir Joseph had materially affected the constitutional composition of all three tiers of government.

In February 1930 Carruthers told the *Sydney Morning Herald* that "as one whose term of public service is nearing its end, I intend to be true to the interests of the people of this State right up to the end".[550] As the twentieth century entered its fourth decade Sir Joseph knew that he was not long for this world, but he was determined to go out fighting. His last years would be spent in an era of intense instability. The Great Depression brought unprecedented unemployment, social unrest and human misery. This turmoil created immense polarisation in politics.

The Communist Party and other fringe-left groups expanded rapidly as desperate people sought a way out of what, despite a high level of state involvement in the Australian economy, was often seen as a failure of capitalism. Partly-inspired by the rise European fascism, radical right-wing groups like the old and new guards threatened to impose stability through force.

In the circumstances Carruthers longed for earlier days of moderation and liberalism. He denounced those who preached the language of class conflict for exacerbating rather than curing society's ills. He also lamented the increasing militancy of the trade union movement during the difficult time period. In his memoirs he sensed a transformation:

> My father always was a trade-unionist, and so was my working brother. But the unions then were not out to make trouble: their aim was to end or to lessen trouble. The unionist was a comrade - not a comrade in arms but a comrade in work, and a friend in need, a friend, indeed, one to the other. Then someone started to preach discontent. [551]

He wanted to rekindle the community spirit that had been a defining part of the Australian colonial experience to help the young nation endure the present crisis. This meant practical help for those in distress, he and Alice were actively involved in a number of benevolent enterprises during this time period, but it also meant that those out of work must avoid becoming destructive in their despair.

In 1931 Carruthers unveiled a portrait of Reid to be hung in the Nationalist Club next to those of both Parkes and John Robertson.[552] The timing and the ostentatious size of the portrait (it was significantly bigger than its counterparts), said much. Reid had led the State through another period of severe economic downturn both as an Opposition leader willing to compromise and a Premier and Treasurer who promoted business while ameliorating the working class.

This record contrasted starkly with the policies being pursued by Lang, who was repudiating attempts at compromise. Australia was particularly vulnerable to the depression as it had a large public debt, relied heavily on overseas loans and was susceptible to movements in agricultural export prices. Its economy had been trending downwards even before Wall Street crashed, and when the latter occurred it hit hard. The Scullin Federal Labor Government immediately began negotiating with the Bank of England about how best to meet its loan obligations, and as a result Bank Director Otto Niemeyer was sent over to inquire into Australia's financial situation. His efforts culminated in the Melbourne Agreement, which called on all governments to rein in spending and pay off their debts to ensure the financial stability of the country and create conditions in which local markets could recover.

Lang rejected the orthodox economics that lay behind the agreement. He wanted keep spending high, force a reduction in the interest accruing on existing loans and raise new loans, something that the State's position within the Loans Council prevented. He also supported currency inflation, though his ability to put this into practise was restricted by the Federal system, and the construction of new public works to provide employment. Lang's proposals may seem proto-Keynesian, but this idea has been deconstructed by David Clark who points to the fact that Lang raised taxes and ultimately hoped for a balanced budget, to suggest that the Premier was pursuing sectional rather than economic ends.[553] Lang's actions had much in common with what O'Sullivan had done nearly three decades before. Both men pursued their government-provided employment goals with little regard for financial limitations, for the necessities of the private sector and for Australia's utter reliance on British Banks to remain viable. Lang was far more powerful than O'Sullivan however, and he was therefore able to pursue this course of action unfettered by a Waddell-equivalent, to a far more destructive conclusion.

In the Council Carruthers and his counterparts did whatever they could to curb Lang's radical plans and keep the State on the steady path of debt repayment they felt was essential for its financial survival. One of the main fights was over the Reduction of Interest Bill. This proposed to fix interest ceilings for hire-purchase agreements, mortgages, bank deposits, and, crucially, for government borrowing. It would limit interest and payments due to the holders of government bonds and savings bank

Investors, thereby reducing government costs at the expense of those individuals who, in good faith, had put their money into what was presumed to be the most reliable investment in the State.

Carruthers led the attack on what he dubbed the policy of a political "Jack Cade".[554] He thought that enforcing reduction of interest through the power of Parliament was debt repudiation through legislation and that it betrayed the sanctity of contracts. This latter principle, that a deal once struck could not retrospectively be undone without the permission of all of the parties to it, was fundamental to the functioning of society. "An Englishman's man word is his bond", and the honour and reputation of the State as a creditor was more important, both philosophically and in the long-term financially, than the money the Government hoped to save. He also suggested that the Bill violated New South Wales' obligation to pay its interest as part of the Loans Council and was therefore unconstitutional. Carruthers was able to galvanise the support of the unpledged Councillors, successfully moving a motion differing the reading of the Bill for six months before it was ultimately dropped.

If the Reduction of Interest Bill was a backhanded attempt at a repudiation of government debt, then it was just the first step in a wider attempt by the Government to shirk its financial responsibilities. Lang increased the unemployment relief tax, but used the cash to pay for his expansionist policies, rather than paying off the State's obligations. The Premier also let the State Savings Bank slide towards collapse. Carruthers had supported rushing through legislation to prop up this important institution but it was to no avail.

As circumstances continued to deteriorate, Lang tried to build the case for the suspension of interest payments to British bondholders. He pointed to the fact that some other countries had received reduced interest rates and argued that Australia needed to put her own interests first. These arguments were dismissed by his opponents who continued to argue that the nation's interests lay in maintaining its reputation as a borrower. In April 1931 Lang crossed the Rubicon by defaulting on the State's loan obligations for the first time.

Lang's actions greatly aggravated the Scullin Federal Government which was left with little choice but to foot the bill. In an unprecedented move, the New South Wales branch of the Labor Party was expelled from the Federal organisation. This was only the tip of Labor's iceberg of internal divisions. At the national level Treasurer Edward Theodore was leading a rebellion against the economic orthodoxy. Theodore had read Keynes and supported inflationary budgetary measures, though not the repudiation of Lang who he had a deep enmity for.[555] Mainstream opinion remained firmly against inflation. Not only were people wary of the hyperinflation they had seen in post-war Germany, but it was felt that inflation punished those who had prudently saved their money and thus encouraged reckless financing. Corruption allegations had forced Theodore to withdraw from his position as Treasurer, but in January 1931 he was reinstated. This prompted Joseph Lyons, the stand-in Treasurer and a fierce believer in prioritising debt repayment, to break away from Labor.

Lyons had already achieved hero-status amongst liberal circles for a campaign he had run to convert a massive government loan in order to pay the bondholders and maintain Australia's financial reputation. It encouraged individuals to buy into pre-existing government debts, at low rates of interest, for the good of the nation. Emphasising the sacrifices of ordinary people, the loan conversion was linked to earlier campaigns to sell war-bonds, and stressed the necessity of maintaining Australia's stability and honour. Despite the financial pressures individuals were experiencing, they bought into the loan conversion on mass, and the loan was over-subscribed.

The loan conversion fed into the establishment of "All for Australia Leagues" which continued to emphasise the need for sacrifice and stability. Sceptical of both Labor and the Nationalists, the AAL was a critique of contemporary governance that shared anti-party similarities with the PRL and Kyabram movement, though its philosophy was more centrist than either.[556] It attracted a vast number of followers, again akin to Kyabram, but Carruthers was sceptical of it. While he firmly supported the loan conversion campaign, Carruthers felt that the formalised AAL embodied a "chauvinistic spirit" and lacked the insight to see that the

Empire needed to work together to lift its constituent parts out of their economic doldrums.[557]

In May 1931 Lyons replaced John Latham as the official Opposition leader, and subsequently a United Australia Party was formed from a combination of the Nationalists and AAL. For a long time the New South Wales Nationalist Party remained mutually antagonistic towards the State's AAL. It was only after the two organisations were forced to fight a Federal election cooperatively in December 1931 that they fell in together. The election forced unity, and UAP victory exhausted much of the AAL's momentum as a protest movement. In the aftermath the old New South Wales Nationalists were able to set up a UAP division mirroring their previous organisation, and though it adopted a constitution which was more complex than its predecessor, its additional clauses were still built on the skeleton of 1902.[558] As a disciplined party rather than a popular movement, United Australia was more respectable, and Carruthers seems to have been enthusiastic about the idea of a party which put financial necessities first. Sound finance may not have been as complex or evocative a *raison d'être* as a broad liberalism in which financial management was only one aspect of the partisan agenda, but the UAP's focus certainly echoed the LRA's more closely than the Nationalist's had.

Lyons won the 1931 election in a landslide, and Lang, whose Federal supporters had prompted the poll by crossing the floor to censure Theodore with factional motivations, was more isolated than ever. He continued to repudiate his loan obligations as the new Prime Minister prepared legislation to recoup the money that the Federal Government was being forced to provide on New South Wales' behalf. In the Legislative Council the Government was having limited success in forcing its agenda through, and Lang was able to convince a reluctant Governor to agree to a swamping of 25 new MLCs. The State's financial position was dire, and as public servants began to miss paycheques, the Government searched desperately for any new sources of revenue.

In May 1932 it introduced a Mortgages Taxation Bill requiring mortgagees to pay 10% of the value of their mortgage to the State treasury. Carruthers suggested that since roughly nine out of ten homeowners had a mortgage, this was a tax directly attacking anyone in the community who had the audacity to own a home. He argued that to risk driving men off their properties was the worst thing a government could do in the face of an economic depression, because private property was essential to private economic activity. The greatest bank ever established in Australia was the "Bank of Nature" and without secure access to land the coffers of all other banks would remain empty.[559] Intermixed with this fiery rhetoric lay the sympathy of an old man who saw that people were suffering, but who was dismayed that they could be taken in by a false prophet whose extravagance, he felt, was fuelling rather than fixing unemployment.

The speech on the Mortgages Taxation Bill would be Carruthers' last opportunity to attack Lang in the Council. Lyons' legislation seizing New South Wales' assets in lieu of debt payments had been upheld by the High Court, and the Premier released a circular ordering his public servants to directly disobey the Federal law and refuse to hand over money. This prompted the Governor, after careful consideration, to dismiss Lang for engaging in illegal actions. The dismissal was and is controversial. Many have argued that it should have been left to the courts to decide whether the Premier's circular was illegal. Carruthers was convinced that the decision was the correct one. He believed "that when anyone openly refuses to obey the law of the land and defiantly incites public servants and citizens to do likewise there is a clear case of rebellion manifested" and the Governor must act to maintain law and order.[560] In response to those suggesting that the courts should have decided Lang's fate, Carruthers argued that Lang would get his trial at the election.

The poll of 11 June 1932 would be the last Carruthers would witness. The UAP forces were led by Bertram Stevens, a former Treasury official who had lost his job during Lang's first term as Premier. Stevens was a steady hand who embodied the UAP's mantra of putting financial management first. An aged Carruthers was no longer up to appearances on the hustings, but he could take pride in the resounding UAP victory and subsequent stabilisation of the existing order.

Sir Joseph's experience with the Stevens Government was brief and heated. Stevens placed a priority on reforming the Council, a proposal given urgency by the distorting effects Lang's final swamping had on the membership. Carruthers continued to protest that the unelected Chamber had proved its worth during the Lang years, and when his arguments were ignored he vowed not to lower himself to election by members of Parliament:

> Never in my life have I been defeated in an election by the people … I do not fear an election by the popular vote, but I certainly will not on bended knees ask the politicians of this State, by means of a secret ballot, to elect me to this House. I shall not demean myself by appealing to such a body.[561]

Carruthers would not be asked to test this commitment. In September his older brother, the Reverend Dr John Carruthers, died. John's long career had paralleled Joseph's, and the latter made his way to Mosman Methodist Church to attend what was a crowded funeral service. It would be one of his last outings. He was soon taken ill and spent much of November bed bound. Not wanting to fall behind in his work he had his eldest son act as his secretary, handling correspondence and taking dictated letters. One such letter was written to the *Sydney Morning Herald*, as even in his sick state Sir Joseph refused to let a statement that Parkes had believed in secular education go uncorrected. By the end of the month there were rumours that his health was finally improving. Council colleague J.W. Percival wrote to him with tragic optimism:

> Dear Sir Joseph,
>
> I was awfully pleased to learn from Mr Farrar that you are on the improve, and I sincerely trust it will not be long before you are seen at the House table as full of fight as of yore. The place does not seem the same without you and poor old genial "Billy" Dick out of it, and the place is full of strange faces. I am looking forward to giving you a good "licking" at billiards, a thrashing you will remember for a long time, so please hurry up and get real well. Surely you are not going to be so mean as to deprive me of the opportunity of trouncing a Knight of the Realm?
>
> Yours very truly, J.W. Percival.[562]

Two weeks later, on 10 December 1932, Carruthers was gone. He died at home with Alice by his side. His funeral was held at All Saints Anglican Church in Woollahra and he was buried in South Head Cemetery overlooking the ocean. In the words of Earnest Farrar, "he was laid to rest where the waves will murmur at his feet and the ozone of the Pacific Ocean will pass over him from the beautiful islands he loved so much and soothe him in his slumber".[563]

Carruthers died as he had lived; a fighter. The fire of his beliefs and the passion of his rhetoric left a mark on whoever saw him. He knew the political game inside and out and boasted achievements and a longevity of relevance that only someone with his innate and acquired skills could have. He had masterminded election victories, internal coups, desirable referendum results and unlikely parliamentary votes. All of this had been at the service of underlying liberal beliefs that while avoiding the absolutism of laissez-faire saw freedom of conscience, speech and enterprise as essential to human progress. Australia was a testament to that progress. The War and the Depression cast a shadow over what had otherwise been a great expansion in population, wealth and access to the good things in life. Some felt that the latter had been secured through government intervention, but for Carruthers it had always been underpinned by economic growth and the efforts of individuals to improve their lot. He had certainly improved his. The son of a convict, he had managed to acquire an education, start a business, purchase a home and raise a family. It was on the back of these simple achievements that the ambitious politician had built his career. His inner humanity and effortless conviviality had always been his greatest strengths.

BIBLIOGRAPHY

Primary Sources

Manuscripts

Barton, Sir Edmund. Papers, National Library of Australia, Canberra.

Carruthers, Sir Joseph Hector McNeil. Papers, Mitchell Library, Sydney.

Carruthers, Sir Joseph. *The Autobiography of Sir Joseph Hector McNeil Carruthers, K.C.M.G. Joey Yarns* ed. Willcox, Bill. (unpublished).

Deakin, Alfred. Papers, National Library of Australia, Canberra.

Garland, John. Papers, Mitchell Library, Sydney.

Hogue, James. Papers, Mitchell Library, Sydney.

"Immigration Encouragement. Million Farms Campaign", National Archives Australia, A457 1400/5.

McMillan, Sir William. Papers, Mitchell Library, Sydney.

O'Sullivan, Edward William. *From Colony to Commonwealth* (unpublished), housed in Mitchell Library Sydney.

Parkes, Sir Henry. Papers, Mitchell Library, Sydney.

Parkhill, Robert Archdale. Papers, National Library, Canberra.

Reid, Sir George. Papers, National Library of Australia, Canberra.

See, Sir John. Papers, Mitchell Library, Sydney.

Wise, Bernhard. Papers, Mitchell Library, Sydney.

Books/Reports

Carruthers, Sir Joseph. *A Lifetime in Conservative Politics: Political Memoirs of Sir Joseph Carruthers* ed. Hogan, Michael. (Sydney: UNSW Press Ltd. 2005).

Carruthers, Sir Joseph. *Captain James Cook, R.N. : One Hundred and Fifty Years After* (London: J. Murray, 1930).

Commonwealth Parliamentary Debates.

George, Henry. *Progress and Poverty: An Inquiry into the Cause of Industrial Depressions and of Increase of Want with Increase of Wealth: The Remedy* (New York: Doubleday, Page & Co. 1879).

Hughes, Colin. & Graham, B.D. *A Handbook of Australian Government and Politics 1890-1964* (Canberra: Australian National University Press 1968).

Hughes, Colin. & Graham, B.D. *Voting for the Australian House of Representatives 1901-1964* (Canberra: Australian National University Press 1968).

New South Wales Parliamentary Debates (NSWPD), Sydney.

New South Wales Parliamentary Papers, Sydney.

Nelson, H.L. *The Voice of the People* (Melbourne: Arbuckle, Waddell & Fawckner, 1902).

Official Report of the National Australian Convention Debates (Adelaide: Adelaide Government Printer, 1897).

Piddington, A.B. *Worshipful Masters* (Sydney: Angus & Robertson, 1929).

Reid, George. *Five Free Trade Essays* (Melbourne: Gordon & Gotch, 1875).

Reid, Sir George. *My Reminiscences* (London: Cassell & Co. Ltd. 1917).

Report of the Proceedings and Public Meetings of the First Annual Conference of the Free Trade and Liberal Association of New South Wales (Sydney: Gibbs, Shallard & Co. 1889).

Smith, Bruce. *Liberty and Liberalism: a protest against the growing tendency toward undue interference by the State with individual liberty, private enterprise, and the rights of property* (Melbourne: G. Robertson, 1887).

Starr, Graeme. *The Liberal Party of Australia: A Documentary History* (Richmond: Heinemann Educational Australia Pty. Ltd. 1980).

Wise, Bernhard. *The Making of the Australian Commonwealth, 1889-1900* (London: Longman, Green & Co. 1913).

Newspapers

The Advertiser, Adelaide.

The Age, Melbourne.

The Argus, Melbourne.

Australian Town and Country Journal, Sydney.

The Brisbane Courier, Brisbane.

The Bulletin, Sydney.

The Canberra Times, Canberra.

The Daily Telegraph, Sydney.

The Evening News, Sydney.

Freeman's Journal, Sydney.

Illawarra Mercury, Wollongong.

The Sunday Times, Sydney.

The Sydney Morning Herald, Sydney.

Secondary Sources

Books/Theses

Belich, James. *Replenishing the Earth: the Settler Revolution and the Rise of the Anglo-World, 1783-1919* (Oxford: Oxford University Press, 2009).

Biagini, Eugenio. *Liberty, Retrenchment and Reform: Popular Liberalism in the Age of Gladstone, 1860-1880* (Cambridge: Cambridge University Press, 2004).

Bollen, J.D. *Protestantism and Social Reform in New South Wales 1890-1910* (Melbourne: Melbourne University Press, 1972).

Bolton, Geoffrey. *Edmund Barton* (St Leonards: Allen & Unwin, 2000).

Brett, Judith. *Australian Liberals and the Moral Middle Class* (Melbourne: Cambridge University press, 2003).

Bridge, Carl. & Fedorowich, Kent. *The British World: diaspora, culture, and identity* (London: Frank Cass, 2003).

Broome, Richard. *Treasure in Earthen Vessels: Protestant Christianity in New South Wales Society, 1900-1914* (St. Lucia: University of Queensland Press, 1980).

Clune, David. & Turner, Ken. *The Governors of New South Wales 1788-2010* (Sydney: the Federation Press, 2009).

Clune, David. & Turner, Ken. *The Premiers of New South Wales 1856-2005* (Sydney: the Federation Press, 2006).

Clune, David. & Griffith, Gareth. *Decision and Deliberation: The Parliament of New South Wales 1856-2003* (Sydney: The Federation Press, 2006).

Cowling, Maurice. *The Impact of Labour, 1920-1924: the Beginning of Modern British Politics* (London: Cambridge University Press, 1971).

Cowling, Maurice. *The Nature and Limits of Political Science* (Cambridge: Cambridge University Press, 1963).

Crisp, L.F. *Federation Fathers* (Melbourne: Melbourne University Press, 1990).

Crisp, L.F. *George Houstoun Reid: Federation Father. Federal Failure?* (Canberra: SOCPAC printery, 1979).

Curran, James. *The Power of Speech: Australian Prime Ministers defining the national image* (Carlton: Melbourne University Press, 2004).

Davey, Paul. *The Nationals: The Progressive, Country and National Party in New South Wales 1919 to 2006* (Sydney: Federation Press, 2006).

Dickey, Brian. *Problems in Australian History: Politics in New South Wales 1856-1900* (North Melbourne: Cassell Australia Ltd. 1969).

Dilley, Andrew. *Finance, Politics, and Imperialism: Australia, Canada, and the City of London, c.1896-1914* (Houndmills: Palgrave Macmillan, 2012).

Earnshaw, Beverley. *One Flag, One Hope, One Destiny: Sir Joseph Carruthers and Australian Federation* (Sydney: The Kogarah Historical Society Inc. 2000).

Eggleston, F.W. *Reflections of an Australian Liberal* (Melbourne: F.W. Chesire, 1953).

Evatt, H.V. *Australian Labour Leader: The story of W. A. Holman and the Labour movement* (Sydney: Angus & Robertson, 1940).

Evatt, H.V. *Liberalism in Australia: An historical sketch of Australian politics down to the year 1915* (Sydney: the Law Book Co. of Australia Ltd. 1918).

Ferguson, Niall. *Empire: the rise and demise of the British world order and the lessons for global power* (New York: Basic Books, 2004).

Fitzherbert, Margaret. *Liberal Women: Federation – 1949* (Sydney: The Federation Press, 2004).

Freudenberg, G. *Cause for Power, the Official History of the New South Wales Branch of the Australian Labor Party* (Sydney: Pluto Press, 1991).

Golder, Hilary. *Politics, Patronage and Public Works: the Administration of New South Wales Volume 1 1842-1900* (Sydney: UNSW Press, 2005).

Gorman, Zachary. *Debating a Tiger Cub: The Anti-Socialist Campaign*, BA Honours Thesis, the University of Sydney, 2012.

Gorman, Zachary. "George Reid's Anti-Socialist Campaign in the Evolution of Australian Liberalism" in Gregory Melleuish, *Liberalism and Conservatism* (Ballarat: Connor Court Publishing, 2015).

Grassby, Al. & Ordonez, Silvia. *The Man Time Forgot: The Life and Times of John Christian Watson, Australia's first Labor Prime Minister* (Annandale: Pluto Press Australia Ltd. 1999).

Grattan, Michelle. *Australian Prime Ministers* (Sydney: New Holland Publishers, 2000).

Gunnar, Peter. *Good Iron Mac: The Life of Australian Federation Father Sir William McMillan* (Sydney: Federation Press, 1995).

Hagan, Jim & Turner, Ken. *A History of the Labor Party in New South Wales 1891-1991* (Melbourne: Longman Chesire, 1991).

Hancock, Ian. *National and Permanent?: The Federal Organisation of the Liberal Party of Australia, 1944-1965* (Melbourne: Melbourne University Press, 2000).

Hancock, Ian. *The Liberals: a history of the NSW Division of the Liberal Party of Australia, 1945-2000* (Annandale: Federation Press, 2007).

Hancock, W.K. *Australia* (London: Ernest Ben, 1930).

Harwin, Don. "Joseph(later Sir Joseph) Hector Carruthers" in David Clune & Ken Turner, *The Premiers of New South Wales 1856-2005, Volume 2 1901-2005* (Sydney: the Federation Press, 2006).

Hazlehurst, Cameron. *Australian Conservatism: Essays in twentieth century political history* (Canberra: ANU Press, 1979).

Henry, K.H. *From Plough to Premiership: The Career of Sir John See 1845-1907* (M.A. Thesis Macquarie University, 1974).

Hogan, Michael & Clune, David. *The People's Choice: Electoral Politics in 20th Century New South Wales Volume 1 1901-1927* (Sydney: Parliament of New South Wales and the University of Sydney, 2001).

Hogan, Michael. Muir, Lesley. & Golder, Hilary. *The People's Choice: Electoral Politics in Colonial New South Wales* (Sydney: Federation Press, 2007).

Kwan, Elizabeth. *Flag and Nation: Australians and their national flags since 1901* (Sydney: UNSW Press, 2006).

La Nauze, J.A. *Alfred Deakin: A Biography* (Melbourne: Angus & Robertson Publishers, 1979).

La Nauze, J.A. *The Making of the Australian Constitution* (Melbourne: Melbourne University Publishers, 1972).

Larcombe, F.A. *A History of Local Government in New South Wales Vol. 2: The Stabilization of Local Government in New South Wales 1858-1906* (Sydney: Sydney University Press, 1976).

Lee, David. *Stanley Melbourne Bruce: Australian Internationalist* (London: Continuum, 2010).

Loveday, P. Martin, A.W. & Parker, R.S. *The Emergence of the Australian Party System* (Sydney: Hale & Iremonger, 1977).

Loveday, P. & Martin, A. *Parliament, Factions and Parties: The First Thirty Years of Responsible Government in New South Wales 1856-1889* (Melbourne: Melbourne University Press, 1966).

Magee, Gary. & Thompson, Andrew. *Empire and Globalisation: networks of people, goods and capital in the British world, c.1850-1914* (Cambridge: Cambridge University Press, 2010)

Mansfield, Bruce. *Australian Democrat: the Career of Edward William O'Sullivan* (Sydney: Sydney University Press, 1965).

Martin, A. W. *Henry Parkes: A Biography* (Melbourne: Melbourne University Press, 1980).

Martin, A. W. *Robert Menzies: a life* (Carlton: Melbourne University Press, 1993).

McMinn, W.G. *George Reid* (Melbourne: Melbourne University Press, 1989).

McMullin, Ross. *The Light On The Hill: The Australian Labor Party 1891-1991* (Melbourne: Oxford university Press, 1991).

Melleuish, Gregory. *A Short History of Australian Liberalism* (St. Leonards: Centre for Independent Studies Ltd. 2001).

Murdoch, John. *Sir Joe: A Political Biography of Sir Joseph Cook* (London: Minerva Press, 1996).

Nairn, Bede. *Civilising Capitalism: the Labor Movement in New South Wales 1870-1900* (Canberra: ANU Press, 1973).

Nairn, Bede. *The Big Fella: Jack Lang and the Australian Labor Party 1891-1949* (Melbourne: Melbourne University Press, 1986).

Nethercote, John. *Liberalism and the Australian Federation* (Sydney: the Federation Press, 2001).

Pearl, Cyril. *The Wild Men of Sydney* (Melbourne: Cheshire-Lansdowne, 1958).

Pietsch, T. *Empire of Scholars: Universities, Networks and the British Academic World, 1850-1939* (Manchester: Manchester University Press, 2013).

Potter, Simon. *News and the British World: The Emergence of an Imperial Press system 1876-1922* (Oxford: Oxford University Press, 2003).

Pugh, Martin. *The Tories and the People, 1880-1935* (Oxford: B. Blackwell, 1985).

Quick, J. & Garran, R. *The Annotated Constitution of the Australian Commonwealth* (Sydney: Angus & Robertson, 1901).

Radi, Heather & Spearritt, Peter. *Jack Lang* (Marrickville: Hale & Iremonger, 1977)

Reynolds, John. *Edmund Barton* (Sydney: Angus & Robertson, 1948).

Rickard, John. *Class and Politics: New South Wales, Victoria and the early Commonwealth 1890-1910* (Canberra: ANU Press, 1976).

Roberts, S. *History of Australian Land Settlement 1788-1920* (Melbourne: MacMillan and Co. Ltd. 1924).

Roe, Michael. *Nine Australian Progressives: vitalism in bourgeois social thought, 1890-1960* (St Lucia: Queensland University Press, 1984).

Roe, Michael. *Quest for Authority in Eastern Australia, 1835-1851* (Melbourne: Melbourne University Press, 1965).

Ryan, J. A. *B. R. Wise: An Oxford Liberal in the Freetrade Party of New South Wales* (MA Thesis University of Sydney 1965).

Rydon, Joan. & Spann, Richard. *New South Wales Politics 1901-1910* (Melbourne: F.W. Chesire Pty. Ltd. 1962).

Souter, Gavin. *Lion and Kangaroo: the Initiation of Australia, 1901-1919* (Sydney: Collins, 1976).

St. John, Ian. *Gladstone and the Logic of Victorian Politics* (London: Anthem Press, 2010).

Strangio, Paul. & Dyrenfurth, Nick. *Confusion: The making of the Australian two-party system* (Melbourne: Melbourne University Press, 2009).

Ward, John. *Colonial Liberalism and its Aftermath 1867-1917* (Sydney: John Ferguson, 1980).

Ward, John. *The State and the People: Australian Federation and Nation Making, 1870-1901* (Sydney: the Federation press, 2001).

Wright, D. *Shadow of Dispute: Aspects of Commonwealth-State Relations, 1901-1910* (Canberra: ANU Press, 1970).

Journal Articles

Brown, Douglas. "New South Wales Family Endowment Act, 1927", *The Quarterly Journal of Economics*, Vol. 42, No. 3, May 1928, pp. 501-3.

Churchward, L.G. "The American Influence on the Australian Labour Movement", *Historical Studies, Australia and New Zealand*, Vol. 5, No. 19, November 1952, pp. 258-77.

Gorman, Zachary. "A Contested Contest: George Reid's election to the leadership of the New South Wales Free Trade Party", *Journal of Australian Colonial History*, Vol. 18, July 2016, pp. 182-197.

Headon, David. "Apple of Discord: Joseph Carruthers and his Canberra Story", *Canberra Historical Journal*, No. 61, December 2008, pp. 17-23.

Hearn, Mark. "Examined suspiciously: Alfred Deakin, Eleanor Cameron and Australian liberal discourse in the 1911 referendum", *History Australia*, Vol. 2, No. 3, Dec 2005: 87.1-87.20.

Lewis, Gary. "Million Farms Campaign, NSW 1919-25", *Labour History*, No.47, November 1984, pp. 55-72.

Loveday, P. "The Federal Convention: An Analysis of the Voting", *Australian Journal of Politics & History*, Vol. 18, Issue 2, August 1972, pp. 169-88.

Martin, A.W. "Free Trade and Protectionist Parties in New South Wales", *Historical Studies*, Vol. 6, issue 23, November 1954, pp. 315-23.

Martin, A.W. "William McMillan: A Merchant in Politics", *Journal of the Royal Australian Historical Society*, Vol. 40, 1954.

Murdoch, J. "The Western Australian Party in the 1906 Federal Elections: A comment on early Federal feeling in the West", *Australian Journal of Politics and History*, Vol. 32, issue 2, August 1967, pp. 247-50.

Nairn, Bede. "The Political Mastery of Sir Henry Parkes: New South Wales Politics 1871-1891", *Journal of the Royal Australian Historical Society*, Vol. 53, 1967, pp. 1-51.

Orr, Kirsten. "Eloquent in speech: Joseph Hector McNeil Carruthers, NSW minister of public instruction (1889-1891)", *Journal of Australian Colonial History*, Vol. 18, July 2016, pp. 161-181.

Ryan, J. A. "Bernhard Ringrose Wise", *Journal of the Royal Australian Historical Society*, Vol. 81, No. 1, June 1995, pp. 71-84.

Robinson, Geoffrey. "The all for Australia league in New South Wales: a study in political entrepreneurship and hegemony", *Australian Historical Studies*, 2008, Vol. 39, No. 1, pp. 36-52.

Sherington, G.E. "The Politics of 'State Rights': Carruthers and the New South Wales State Election of 1907", *Journal of the Royal Australian Historical Society*, Vol. 62, part 3, December 1976, pp. 179-88.

Sherington, G.E. "The Selection of Canberra as Australia's National Capital", *Journal of the Royal Australian Historical Society*, Vol. 56, part 2, June 1970, pp. 134-147.

Weller, P.M. "Preselection and Local Support: An Explanation of the Methods and Development of Early Non-Labor Parties in New South Wales", *Australian Journal of Politics & History*, Vol. 21. issue 1, April 1975, pp. 22-30.

Wood, Greg. "Founding Fathers: Mapping Canberra's DNA", *Canberra Historical Journal*, No.61, December 2008, pp. 24-9.

Wright, D. "The Politics of Federal Finance", *Historical Studies*, Vol. 13, No. 52, April 1969, pp. 460-76.

Compendiums

Australian Dictionary of Biography, National Centre of Biography, Australian National University Canberra.

ENDNOTES

Introduction

1 To a large extent, see Ian Hancock, *The Liberals: The NSW Division 1945-2000.*

Chapter One

2 Joseph Carruthers, *A Lifetime in Conservative Politics,* p. 14.

3 Beverley Earnshaw, *One Flag, One Hope, One Destiny: Sir Joseph Carruthers and Australian Federation,* pp. 9-13.

4 James Belich, *Replenishing the Earth: the Settler Revolution and the Rise of the Anglo-World, 1783-1919,* p. 206.

5 Michael Roe, *Quest for Authority in Eastern Australia, 1835-1851,* p. 6.

6 "St Mary's Cathedral Building Fund", *Freeman's Journal,* Thursday, 27/10/1927, p. 26.

7 Judith Brett, *Australian Liberals and the Moral Middle Class,* p. 55.

8 Joseph Carruthers, *The Autobiography of Sir Joseph Hector McNeil Carruthers, K.C.M.G. "Joey Yarns"* ed. Bill Willcox, p. 12.

9 George Metcalfe, "The Premier's Minority and Education", *The Sydney Mail,* Wednesday, 18/9/1907, p. 742.

10 Joseph Carruthers, "Random reflections and reminiscences" circa. 1927. ML MSS 1638/77 item 3, p. 8.

11 Joseph Carruthers, "Sir Henry Parkes", 1923, ML MSS 1638/75, p. 87.

12 Michael Roe, *Nine Australian Progressives,* pp. 1-22.

13 This is admittedly a quote from a much older Carruthers, but it reflects a view of the limitations of government that he was already starting to develop, Joseph Carruthers, "Random reflections and reminiscences", p. 74.

14 A.B. Piddington, *Worshipful Masters,* p. 9.

15 Joseph Carruthers, "Sir George Reid", 1918, ML MSS 1638/79, p. 168.

16 Michael Hogan, *A Lifetime in Conservative Politics,* p. 103.

17 "Politicians as they should be", *Evening News,* Saturday, 16/12/1905, p. 11.

18 Ian St. John, *Gladstone and the Logic of Victorian Politics,* pp. 254-262.

19 Eugenio Biagini, *Liberty, Retrenchment and Reform: Popular Liberalism in the Age of Gladstone, 1860-1880,* p. 108.

20 Joseph Carruthers, *Joey Yarns,* p. 61.

Chapter Two

21 Bede Nairn, "The Political Mastery of Sir Henry Parkes: New South Wales Politics 1871-1891", *Journal of the Royal Australian Historical Society*, Vol. 53, 1967, p. 19.

22 "National Protection Association", *Sydney Morning Herald*, Saturday, 18/9/1886, p. 9.

23 P. Loveday, A.W. Martin & P. Weller, "New South Wales" in *The emergence of the Australian party system* ed. P. Loveday, A.W. Martin, & R.S. Parker, p. 172.

24 Joseph Carruthers, *A Lifetime in Conservative Politics*, p. 65.

25 Ruth Teale, "Hammond, Mark John (1844–1908)", *Australian Dictionary of Biography*, 1972.

26 "Canterbury Electorate", *Sydney Morning Herald*, Wednesday, 2/2/1887, p. 7.

27 "Nominations Canterbury", *Sydney Morning Herald*, Wednesday, 9/2/1887, p. 5.

28 "Canterbury Electorate", *Sydney Morning Herald*, Wednesday, 2/2/1887, p. 7.

29 *Sydney Morning Herald*, Monday 7/2/1887, p. 7.

30 P. Loveday & A.W. Martin, *Parliament, Factions and Parties: The First Thirty Years of Responsible Government in New South Wales 1856-1889*, pp. 140-1.

31 J.A. Ryan, "Bernhard Ringrose Wise", *Journal of the Royal Australian Historical Society*, Vol. 81, No. 1, June 1995, p. 75.

32 *NSWPD*, 22/3/1887, p. 302.

33 Joseph Carruthers, *A Lifetime in Conservative Politics*, p. 73.

34 *NSWPD*, 17/4/1888, p. 4019.

35 Joseph Carruthers, *A Lifetime in Conservative Politics*, p. 17.

36 "Legislative Assembly", *Sydney Morning Herald*, Wednesday, 14/11/1888, p. 5.

37 *NSWPD*, 27/11/1888, p. 663.

38 *NSWPD*, 16/1/1889, p. 1587.

39 "Mr. J.H. Carruthers at St Peters", *Sydney Morning Herald*, Tuesday, 22/1/1889, pp. 4-5.

40 W.G. McMinn, *George Reid*, p. 44.

41 Joseph Carruthers, *A Lifetime in Conservative Politics*, p. 82.

42 "Canterbury Electorate", *Sydney Morning Herald*, Monday, 4/2/1889, p. 8.

43 Michael Hogan, "1889" in *The People's Choice: Electoral Politics in Colonial New South Wales*, p. 314.

44 A.W. Martin, *Henry Parkes: A Biography*, p. 375.

45 Joseph Carruthers, *A Lifetime in Conservative Politics*, p. 87.

Chapter Three

46 "Liberal Political Association", *Sydney Morning Herald*, Thursday, 28/3/1889, p. 5.

47 Peter Gunnar, *op. cit.*, pp. 41-2.

48 Joseph Carruthers, *Report of the Proceedings and Public Meetings of the First Annual Conference of the Free Trade and Liberal Association of New South Wales*, p. 51.

49 Henry George, *Progress and Poverty: An Inquiry into the Cause of Industrial Depressions and of Increase of Want with Increase of Wealth: The Remedy.*

50 L.G. Churchward, "The American Influence on the Australian Labour Movement", *Historical Studies, Australia and New Zealand*, Vol. 5, No. 19, November 1952, pp. 258-77.

51 "Marrickville Free Trade & Liberal Association", *Sydney Morning Herald*, Friday, 25/4/1890, p. 7.

52 W.G. McMinn, *George Reid*, p. 56.

53 Peter Gunnar, *op. cit.*, p. 43.

54 Joseph Carruthers, *A Lifetime in Conservative Politics*, pp. 88-9.

55 *NSWPD*, 20/6/1889, p. 2354.

56 *NSWPD*, 23/7/1889, p. 3316.

57 "Legislative Assembly", *Sydney Morning Herald*, Friday, 13/9/1889, p. 3.

58 Don Harwin, "Joseph(later Sir Joseph) Hector Carruthers" in David Clune & Ken Turner, *The Premiers of New South Wales 1856-2005, Volume 2 1901-2005*, p. 50.

59 Bruce Smith to Carruthers, 29/4/1891 & McMillan to Carruthers, 8/5/1891, Carruthers Papers, ML MSS 1638/20, pp. 413-5 & p. 449.

60 Kirsten Orr, "Eloquent in speech: Joseph Hector McNeil Carruthers, NSW minister of public instruction (1889-1891)", *Journal of Australian Colonial History*, Vol.18, July 2016, p. 164.

61 "The Minister of Public Instruction on technical education", *Sydney Morning Herald*, Tuesday 1/4/1890, p. 5.

62 "The Cadet Encampment", *Sydney Morning Herald*, Monday, 25/8/1890, p. 9.

63 "Arbour Day in Schools", *The Maitland Mercury*, Saturday, 7/6/1890, p. 7.

64 Reid to Carruthers, 17/7/1890, Carruthers Papers, ML MSS 1638/20, pp. 405-8.

65 P. Loveday, A.W. Martin & P. Weller, "New South Wales", pp. 182.

66 Michael Hogan & Ken Turner, "1891" in *The People's Choice: Electoral Politics in Colonial New South Wales*, p. 324.

Chapter Four

67 "Lecture by Mr. Carruthers", *Sydney Morning Herald,* Tuesday, 22/4/1890, p.,8.

68 Joseph Carruthers, *A Lifetime in Conservative Politics,* pp. 93-4.

69 "Mr. Carruthers at Ashfield", *Evening News,* Saturday, 11/4/1891, p. 4.

70 A.W. Martin, *Henry Parkes: A Biography,* p. 398.

71 Joseph Carruthers, *A Lifetime in Conservative Politics,* p. 92.

72 A.W. Martin, *Henry Parkes: A Biography,* p. 386.

73 Bede Nairn, "The Political Mastery of Sir Henry Parkes: New South Wales Politics 1871-1891", p. 4.

74 "Free Trade at Burwood", *Sydney Morning Herald,* Tuesday, 22/10/1889, p. 5.

75 "The Federation Question", *Sydney Morning Herald,* Saturday, 9/11/1889, p. 8.

76 W.G. McMinn, *George Reid,* pp. 64-5.

77 "A Split in the Cabinet", *Newcastle Morning Herald & Miners" Advocate,* Wednesday, 15/4/1891, p. 5. "NSW Ministry", *Evening News,* Thursday, 7/5/1891, p. 5.

78 Sir Henry Parkes, Diary, 22/4/1891, ML A 1018, p. 132.

79 "Mr. Carruthers", *Evening News,* Thursday, 14/5/1891, p. 2.

80 Peter Gunnar, *op. cit.,* p. 88.

81 Michael Hogan & Ken Turner, "1891", p. 330.

82 Bruce Smith to Carruthers, March 1891, Carruthers Papers, ML MSS 1638/20, p. 315.

83 "The Federation Question", *Sydney Morning Herald,* Saturday, 6/6/1891, p. 8.

84 "The FreeTrade Bunch for Camden", *Bowral Free Press,* Wednesday, 17/6/1891, p. 2.

85 Michael Hogan & Ken Turner, "1891", p. 346.

86 Carruthers to Carrington, 17/9/1891, quoted in A.W. Martin, *Henry Parkes: A Biography,* p. 406.

87 Bede Nairn, *Civilising Capitalism: the Labor Movement in New South Wales 1870-1900,* p. 7.

88 Joseph Carruthers, "Random reflections and reminiscences", p. 74.

89 Sir Henry Parkes, Diary, 7/7/1891, ML A 1018, p. 210.

90 Carruthers to Parkes, 19/4/1891, Parkes Papers, ML A877, pp. 477-80.

91 *NSWPD,* 12/8/1891, p. 823.

92 A.W. Martin, *Henry Parkes: A Biography,* p. 407.

93 Carruthers to Parkes, 26/10/1891, Parkes Papers, ML A877, p. 494.

94 "The Making of Premier Reid", *The Catholic Press,* Saturday 25/12/1897, p. 16.

95 Sir Henry Parkes, Diary, 17/11/1891, ML A 1018, p. 343.

96 Bernhard Wise, *The Making of the Australian Commonwealth, 1889-1900*, p. 173.

97 "Mr. Reid's Election as Opposition Leader", *Daily Telegraph*, Monday 10/1/1898, p. 4.

98 Joseph Carruthers, *A Lifetime in Conservative Politics*, p. 119.

99 Peter Gunnar, *op. cit.*, p.99. & *Sydney Morning Herald*, Friday 20/11/1891, p. 5.

100 Sir Henry Parkes, Diary, 1/11/1891, ML A 1018, p. 327.

101 This is somewhat speculative and less clear than Carruthers' role in shunting Parkes that, as has been said, was in and of itself an act in support of Reid.

102 Reid to Carruthers, 10/4/-, Carruthers Papers, ML MSS 1638/23, CY 3153, pp. 57-64.

103 "The Making of Premier Reid", *The Catholic Press*, Saturday 25/12/1897, p. 16. See also Wise to Carruthers 26/10/1889, Carruthers Papers, ML MSS1638/20, p. 449. For Wise warning Carruthers about Tories within the Party

104 W.G. McMinn, *George Reid*, p. 70.

105 Sir Henry Parkes, Diary, 6/1/1892, ML A 1018, p. 11.

Chapter Five

106 Joseph Carruthers, *A Lifetime in Conservative Politics*, p. 119.

107 J.A. Ryan, *B. R. Wise: An Oxford Liberal in the Freetrade Party of New South Wales*, p. 222.

108 "Canterbury Electorate", *Sydney Morning Herald*, Wednesday 6/1/1892, p. 6.

109 W.G. McMinn, *George Reid*, pp. 72-3.

110 *NSWPD*, 9/12/1891, p. 3461.

111 Bede Nairn, *Civilising Capitalism: the Labor Movement in New South Wales 1870-1900*, p. 77.

112 W.G. McMinn, *George Reid*, p. 74.

113 "Canterbury Electorate", *Sydney Morning Herald*, Wednesday 6/1/1892, p. 6.

114 "Capricious Carruthers", *Newcastle Morning Herald and Miners' Advocate*, Monday 11/1/1892, p. 5.

115 "An Afternoon with a Cabinet Minister", *The Catholic Press* Saturday 7/8/1897 p. 5.

116 *NSWPD*, 9/12/1891, p. 3473.

117 *NSWPD*, 19/1/1892, p. 4335.

118 *NSWPD*, 15/3/1892, p. 6464.

119 "Industrial Evolution", *Sydney Morning Herald*, Tuesday 31/5/1892, p. 6.

120 *NSWPD*, 31/8/1892, p. 87.

121 *NSWPD*, 22/9/1892, pp. 567-8.

122 "Mr. J. H. Carruthers M.L.A. on Social and Labour Problems", *Sydney Morning Herald*, Wednesday 16/3/1892, p. 7.

123 "South Sydney Free Trade and Liberal Association", *Sydney Morning Herald*, Tuesday 1/10/1889, p. 3.

124 *Sydney Morning Herald*, Thursday 15/12/1893, p. 6.

125 *NSWPD*, 14/12/1892, p. 2718.

126 *NSWPD*, 2/2/1893, p. 3671.

127 *NSWPD*, 16/2/1893, p. 4328.

128 *NSWPD*, 27/4/1893, p. 6511.

129 *NSWPD*, 28/11/1893, pp. 1413-5.

130 Carruthers to McMillan, 21/9/1893, McMillan Papers, ML MSS1884/2-4, CY1502, p. 271.

131 Wise to Carruthers, 26/10/[1893?], Carruthers Papers, ML MSS16319/20, p. 451.

132 Geoffrey Bolton, *Edmund Barton*, p. 115.

133 Carruthers to McMillan, 20/6/1893, McMillan Papers, ML MSS1884/2-4, CY1502, pp. 246-7.

134 Joseph Carruthers circa 1917-18, Carruthers Papers, ML MSS1638/38, p. 85.

135 "Freetraders at Hurstville", *Evening News,* Thursday, 24/8/1893, p. 3.

136 H.V. Evatt, *William Holman: Australian Labour Leader,* p. 118.

137 Joseph Carruthers, 22/7/1895, Carruthers Papers, ML 1638/78, CY3152, p. 10.

138 Wise to Parkes, 23/12/1893 & 4/12/1894, Parkes Papers, ML A912, p. 272 & 267.

139 George Reid. *My Reminiscences,* p. 91.

140 Carruthers to Parkes, 15/1/1894 & 15/6/1894, Parkes Papers, ML A877, pp. 511-4.

141 "Political Address", *Sydney Morning Herald*, Tuesday, 3/10/1893, p. 5.

142 Michael Hogan & Ken Turner "1894" in *The People's Choice: Electoral Politics in Colonial New South Wales,* p. 365.

143 *NSWPD*, 26/9/1893, p. 13.

144 "The Political Campaign", *Sydney Morning Herald,* Tuesday, 9/1/1894, p. 3.

145 W.G. McMinn, *George Reid,* p. 89.

146 Carruthers to Parkes, 15/1/1894, Parkes Papers, ML A877, pp. 513-4.

147 "Forthcoming General Elections", *Sydney Morning Herald,* Saturday 2/6/1894, p. 7.

148 Carruthers to Parkes, 15/6/1894, Parkes Papers, ML A877, pp. 511-2.

149 Reid to Carruthers, 8/6/1894, Carruthers Papers, ML MSS1638/20, pp. 645-6.

150 W.G. McMinn, *George Reid*, p. 89.

151 Michael Hogan & Ken Turner, "1894", p. 363.

152 "Canterbury Electorate", *Sydney Morning Herald*, Monday 25/6/1894, p. 6.

153 "Candidates and the Arbitration", *Sydney Morning Herald*, Thursday 12/7/1894, p. 7.

154 J.A. Ryan, B. R. *Wise: An Oxford Liberal in the Freetrade Party of New South Wales*, p. 315.

155 "Political Meetings", *Sydney Morning Herald*, Tuesday 16/1/1894, p. 6.

156 "Mr. Carruthers at the School of Arts", *National Advocate*, Saturday 7/7/1894, p. 2.

157 Michael Hogan & Ken Turner, "1894", p. 376.

158 P. Loveday, A.W. Martin & P. Weller, "New South Wales", p. 197.

159 Bernhard Wise, *The Making of the Australian Commonwealth, 1889-1900*, p. 216.

Chapter Six

160 P. Loveday, A.W. Martin & P. Weller, "New South Wales", p. 197.

161 "Mr. Wise's Speech", *Goulburn Evening Penny Post*, Thursday 2/8/1894, p. 4.

162 Description attributed to Parkes, "An Afternoon with a Cabinet Minister", *The Catholic Press*, Saturday 7/8/1897, p. 5.

163 "The Political Situation", *Sydney Morning Herald*, Saturday 4/8/1894, p. 9.

164 "Probable Opposition to New Ministers", *Sydney Morning Herald*, Thursday, 2/8/1894, p. 5.

165 "Mr. J H Carruthers at Kogarah", *Sydney Morning Herald*, Thursday 9/8/1894, p. 6.

166 "Banquet Mr. J H Carruthers", *Sydney Morning Herald*, Tuesday 4/9/1894, p. 6.

167 "Interview with Sir Henry Parkes", *Goulburn Evening Penny Post*, Thursday 9/8/1894, p. 4.

168 Reid to Carruthers, 8/6/1894, Carruthers Papers, ML MSS1638/20, pp. 645-6.

169 Carruthers Papers, ML MSS1638/2.

170 "An Interview with a Cabinet Minister", *The Catholic Press*, Saturday 7/8/1897, p. 5.

171 *NSWPD*, 28/8/1894, p. 9.

172 *NSWPD*, 13/9/1894, p. 435.

173 H.V. Evatt, *Liberalism in Australia: An Historical Sketch of Australian Politics Down to the year 1915*, pp. 24-34.

174 John Ward, *Colonial Liberalism and its Aftermath 1867-1917*, p. 12.

175 *NSWPD*, 13/9/1894, p. 436.

176 Stephen Roberts, *History of Australian Land Settlement 1788-1920*, p. 293.

177 *NSWPD*, 12/9/1894, pp. 400-1.

178 *NSWPD*, 7/11/1894, p. 2146.

179 *NSWPD*, 21/11/1894, p. 2560.

180 *NSWPD*, 4/4/1895, p. 5115.

181 *NSWPD*, 30/4/1895, p. 5757.

182 *NSWPD*, 21/5/1895, p. 6185.

183 "Mr. Carruthers' Opinion", *Sydney Morning Herald*, Tuesday, 14/5/1895, p. 5.

184 "Attitude of Sir H. Parkes", *Evening News,* Tuesday, 14/5/1895, p. 5.

185 "St George Electorate", *Sydney Morning Herald*, Wednesday, 10/7/1895, p. 6.

186 Purify quote from John M. Ward, "Carruthers, Sir Joseph Hector McNeil (1856-1932)", *Australian Dictionary of Biography*, 1979.

187 "A Timely Testimonial", *Bathurst Free Press & Mining Journal,* Tuesday, 23/7/1895, p. 2.

188 Joseph Carruthers, 22/7/1895, Carruthers Papers, ML MSS1638/78, CY3152, p. 18.

189 *Ibid.*, p. 22.

190 Michael Hogan & Ken Turner "1895" in *The People's Choice: Electoral Politics in Colonial New South Wales* p. 394. "Interview with Mr. Carruthers", *Sydney Morning Herald*, Friday 26/7/1895, p. 6. & W.G. McMinn, *George Reid,* p. 115.

191 Bede Nairn, *Civilising Capitalism: the Labor Movement in New South Wales 1870-1900*, p. 134.

192 *NSWPD*, 11/9/1895, p. 725.

193 For use of the terms see John Ward, *Colonial Liberalism and its Aftermath 1867-1917* & John Ward, *The State and the People: Australian Federation and Nation Making, 1870-1901.*

194 "The New Taxation", *Sydney Morning Herald,* Wednesday 4/12/1895, p. 5.

195 W.G. McMinn, *George Reid,* p. 119.

196 "Land and Labour", *Sydney Morning Herald,* Tuesday 19/11/1895, p. 6.

197 Carruthers to Parkes, 1889-1891, Parkes Papers, ML A877.

198 *NSWPD*, 11/6/1896, Vol. 82, p. 781.

199 *The Bulletin*, Saturday 9/11/1889, p. 4.

200 A.B. Piddington, *op. cit.,* p. 34.

Chapter Seven

201 Alfred Deakin, *The Federal Story: The Inner History of the Federal Cause 1880-1900* ed. J. A. La Nauze, p. 66.

202 Joseph Carruthers, *A Lifetime in Conservative Politics,* p. 118.

203 W.G. McMinn, *George Reid*, p. 128.

204 "The Ministry and the Late Sir Henry Parkes", *Sydney Morning Herald*, Saturday, 30/1/1897, p. 10.

205 "The Hon J H Carruthers at Kogarah", *Sydney Morning Herald*, Friday, 5/2/1897, p. 5.

206 "The Cardinal's Candidature", *Sydney Morning Herald*, Wednesday, 17/2/1897, p. 8.

207 "The Hon J H Carruthers at Kogarah", *Sydney Morning Herald*, Friday, 5/2/1897, p. 6.

208 Alfred Deakin, *The Federal Story*, p.86. & P. Loveday, "The Federal Convention: An Analysis of the Voting", *Australian Journal of Politics & History*, Vol. 18, issue 2, August 1972, p. 175.

209 Joseph Carruthers, 25/3/1897, *Official Report of the National Australasian Convention Debates First Session*, 23/3/1897, p. 86.

210 "The Impressions of Mr. Carruthers", *Sydney Morning Herald*, Saturday, 24/4/1897, p. 67.

211 Joseph Carruthers, *Commonwealth of Australia (Draft Constitution Bill): Report of Debates in the Legislative Assembly and Legislative Council*, 15/5/1897, p.8.

212 Bernhard Wise, *Official Report of the National Australasian Convention Debates Second Session*, 9/9/1897, p. 276.

213 Joseph Carruthers, *Ibid.*, 9/9/1897, p. 276.

214 Joseph Carruthers, *Ibid.*, 20/9/1897, p. 858.

215 L.F. Crisp, *Federation Fathers*, p. 21.

216 J. Quick & R. Garran, *The Annotated Constitution of the Australian Commonwealth*, pp. 192-3.

217 Michael Cannon, "Norton, John (1858–1916)", *Australian Dictionary of Biography*, 1988.

218 "The Proposed Municipality of Kogarah", *Sydney Morning Herald*, Saturday, 7/11/1885, p. 10.

219 J.A. La Nauze, *The Making of the Australian Constitution*, p. 221.

220 Joseph Carruthers, *Official Report of the National Australasian Convention Debates Third Session*, 31/1/1898, p. 322.

221 *Ibid.*, p. 2536.

222 Joseph Carruthers, *Official Report of the National Australasian Convention Debates Third Session*, 21/1/1898, p. 53.

223 W.G. McMinn, *George Reid*, p. 148.

224 "Successful meeting at Rockdale", *Sydney Morning Herald*, Saturday, 2/4/1898, p. 9.

225 Bernhard Wise, *The Making of the Australian Commonwealth*, p. 270.

226 Joseph Carruthers, 1918, Carruthers Papers, ML MSS1638/79, p. 155.

227 J. Quick & R. Garran, *op. cit.*, p. 209.

228 "General Elections", *Evening News,* Tuesday, 12/7/1898, p. 5.

Chapter Eight

229 *NSWPD,* 23/8/1898, p. 142.

230 J. Quick & R. Garran, *op. cit.,* pp. 216-7.

231 Reid to Carruthers, 2/2/1899, Carruthers Papers, ML MSS 1638/20, pp. 693-5.

232 *NSWPD,* 7/3/1899, p. 403.

233 W.G. McMinn, *George Reid,* p. 170.

234 John Rickard, *op. cit.,* p. 143.

235 *NSWPD,* 26/7/1899, p. 350.

236 *NSWPD,* 16/8/1899, p. 776.

237 Bernhard Wise, *The Making of the Australian Commonwealth,* p. 326.

238 *NSWPD,* 31/8/1899, p. 1084.

239 H.V. Evatt, *William Holman: Australian Labour Leader,* pp. 84-5. & T.A. Coghlan, *Labour and Industry in Australia: From the First Settlement in 1788 to the Establishment of the Commonwealth in 1901,* p. 2211.

240 Bede Nairn, *Civilising Capitalism: the Labor Movement in New South Wales 1870-1900,* p.220, George Reid, *My Reminiscences,* p.186. & "The Solid Six", *Sydney Morning Herald,* Thursday 26/11/1914, p. 8.

241 L.F. Fitzhardinge, *William Morris Hughes: A Political Biography,* p. 75.

242 Bede Nairn, *Civilising Capitalism: the Labor Movement in New South Wales 1870-1900,* p. 221.

243 *NSWPD,* 7/9/1899, p. 1273.

244 Reid to Carruthers, 14/9/1899, Carruthers Papers, ML CY 3153, pp. 60-1.

245 "A Meeting at Summer Hill", *Sydney Morning Herald,* Tuesday, 26/9/1899, p. 6.

246 "A Few Remarks", *The Worker,* Saturday, 4/11/1899, p. 4.

247 *NSWPD,* 8/12/1899, p. 3115.

248 *NSWPD,* 4/10/1900, p. 3605.

249 *NSWPD,* 8/11/1899, p. 2127.

250 *NSWPD,* 19/12/1899, p. 3509.

251 *NSWPD,* 25/7/1900, p. 1278.

252 "Views of Mr. Carruthers, M.L.A." *Sydney Morning Herald,* Friday 6/4/1900, p. 7.

253 "Federal Banquet at Bathurst", *Sydney Morning Herald,* Monday 26/11/1900, p. 3.

254 "Third Day's Sitting", *Sydney Morning Herald,* Saturday, 17/2/1900, p. 5.

255 "A Great Freetrade Demonstration", *Sydney Morning Herald,* Tuesday, 11/12/1900, p. 6.

256 "Selected Freetrade Candidates", *Sydney Morning Herald,* Friday, 22/2/1901, p. 5.

257 Beverley Earnshaw, *op. cit.,* p. 89.

258 Carruthers to Barton, 26/12/1900, Barton Papers, NLA Series 1, item 748.

259 A.B. Piddington, *Ibid.,* p. 44.

Chapter Nine

260 K.H. Henry, *From Plough to Premiership: The Career of Sir John See 1845-1907,* p. 1.

261 "Mr. Carruthers on the Situation", *Sydney Morning Herald,* Thursday, 18/4/1901, p. 5.

262 *Ibid.*

263 "Mr. J.H. Carruthers M.L.A. at Rockdale", *Sydney Morning Herald,* Friday, 26/4/1901, p. 8.

264 "East Maitland", *Newcastle Morning Herald and Miners" Advocate,* Thursday, 20/6/1901, p. 5.

265 Reid to Carruthers, 10/4/1901, Carruthers Papers, ML CY 3153, pp. 157-64.

266 "Leadership of the Opposition", *Sydney Morning Herald,* Wednesday, 17/4/1901, p. 7.

267 "The Political Situation", *Freeman's Journal,* Saturday, 20/4/1901, p. 13.

268 Joseph Carruthers, *A Lifetime in Conservative Politics,* p. 160.

269 Bruce Mansfield, *Australian Democrat: The Career of Edward William O"Sullivan 1846-1910,* pp. 165-6, & *NSWPD,* 30/7/1901, p. 127.

270 John Rickard, *op. cit.,* p. 176.

271 Bruce E. Mansfield, "O'Sullivan, Edward William (1846–1910)", *Australian Dictionary of Biography,* 1988.

272 "Mr. J.H. Carruthers M.L.A. at Rockdale", *Sydney Morning Herald,* Friday, 26/4/1901, p. 8.

273 "Interview with Mr. C.A. Lee", *Sydney Morning Herald,* Saturday, 27/4/1901, p. 10.

274 "The Liberal Party Manifesto", *Sydney Morning Herald,* Friday, 17/5/1901, p. 3.

275 Bruce Mansfield, *Australian Democrat,* p. 169.

276 Figures given from Michael Hogan, "1901" in *The People's Choice: Electoral Politics in 20th Century New South Wales,* p. 23.

277 "Mr. Carruthers' Opinion", *Sydney Morning Herald,* Friday 5/7/1901, p. 8.

278 *NSWPD*, 30/7/1901, p. 126.

279 *NSWPD*, 27/8/1901, p. 781.

280 Bruce Mansfield, *Australian Democrat*, p. 175.

281 *NSWPD*, 29/8/1901, p. 922.

282 Joseph Carruthers, *A Lifetime in Conservative Politics*, p. 159.

283 *NSWPD*, 21/8/1901, p. 679.

284 Carruthers Papers, ML 1638/10, pp. 165-70.

285 "The Federal Tariff", *Sydney Morning Herald*, Tuesday, 29/10/1901, p. 5.

286 "Statement by Mr. Carruthers", *Sydney Morning Herald*, Friday, 18/10/1901, p. 7.

287 "Meeting at Ashfield", *Sydney Morning Herald*, Monday, 4/11/1901, p. 8.

288 *NSWPD*, 4/6/1902, p. 148.

289 "Mr. Brunker's Views", *Sydney Morning Herald*, Friday, 19/9/1902, p. 7.

290 Wise to Carruthers, 21/9/1902, Carruthers Papers, ML CY 3153, pp. 124-5.

291 Reid to Carruthers, 19/9/1902, Carruthers Papers, ML CY 3153, pp. 129-30.

292 "Retirement of Mr. Lee", *Sydney Morning Herald*, Wednesday, 17/9/1902, p. 7.

Chapter Ten

293 Schumpeter as described in Eugenio Biagini, *op. cit.*, p. 103.

294 H.L. Nielson, *The Voice of the People*, p. 1.

295 John Rickard, *op. cit.*, p. 180.

296 Paul Strangio, "An intensity of feeling such as I had never witnessed: Fusion in Victoria", pp. 134-61.

297 D.W. Rawson, *op. cit.*, p. 45.

298 "Mr. Carruthers Talks", *The Catholic Press*, Thursday, 27/11/1902, p. 19.

299 "Interview with Mr. J.H. Carruthers", *Sydney Morning Herald*, Saturday, 4/10/1902, p. 11.

300 "Meeting at Paddington Town Hall", *Sydney Morning Herald*, Tuesday, 14/10/1902, p. 5.

301 "Liberalism and Reform", *Sydney Morning Herald*, Thursday, 23/10/1902, p. 6.

302 "State Politics", *Sydney Morning Herald*, Monday, 10/8/1903, p. 5.

303 "State Politics", *Sydney Morning Herald*, Saturday, 20/12/1902, p. 12.

304 P. Loveday, A.W. Martin & P. Weller, "New South Wales", p. 227.

305 "Liberal and Reform Association", *Sydney Morning Herald*, Tuesday, 10/3/1903, p. 5.

306 W.K. Hancock, *Australia*, pp. 238.

307 "The Clique Candidate", *The Worker*, Saturday, 28/3/1903, p. 4.

308 "The Public Works Expenditure", *Sydney Morning Herald*, Tuesday, 6/1/1903, p. 3.

309 Andrew Dilley, *Finance, Politics, and Imperialism*, pp. 67-84.

310 Bruce Mansfield, *Australian Democrat*, p. 189.

311 "Sir Edmund Barton's Tour", *Evening News*, Wednesday, 22/4/1903, p. 2.

312 "Mr. Waddell and the Minister", *Sydney Morning Herald*, Thursday, 9/4/1903, p. 7.

313 "The Position in Sydney", *The Advertiser (Adelaide)*, Wednesday, 13/5/1903, p.,6.

314 Edward O"Sullivan, *op. cit.*, p. 303.

315 "A Pre-Sessional Dinner", *Sydney Morning Herald*, Tuesday, 16/6/1903, p. 5.

316 "Essence of Parliament", *Evening News*, Wednesday, 11/11/1903, p. 6.

317 *NSWPD*, 18/11/1903, pp. 4320-4341.

318 "Work of the Week", *Evening News*, Monday, 28/3/1904, p. 7.

319 "Mr. Carruthers Speaks Out", *Sydney Morning Herald*, Saturday, 30/5/1903, p. 10.

320 Ian Hancock, *op. cit.*, p. 15.

321 P. Loveday, A.W. Martin & P. Weller, "New South Wales", p. 229.

322 Parkhill to Carruthers, 15/8/1927, Carruthers Papers, ML MSS 1638/7, p. 179.

323 "Interview with Mr. Carruthers", *Sydney Morning Herald*, Wednesday, 27/4/1904, p. 12.

324 Carruthers to Parkhill, "Sunday" May 1904, Parkhill Papers, NLA MS 4742, Folder 1.

325 J.D. Bollen, *Protestantism and Social Reform in New South Wales 1890-1910*, pp. 145-8.

326 "State Politics", *Sydney Morning Herald*, Saturday, 5/3/1904, p. 12.

327 Wise to See, 10/6/1904, See Papers, ML CY3590, pp. 182-3.

328 J. Rydon & R. Spann, *New South Wales Politics 1901-1910*, p. 48.

329 Andrew Dilley, *op. cit.*, p. 150.

330 "State Elections", *Sydney Morning Herald*, Thursday, 28/7/1904, p. 10.

331 "Appeal from the Liberal Leader", *Sydney Morning Herald*, Friday, 5/8/1904, p. 7.

332 Robert Menzies, *Afternoon Light: Some Memories of Men and Events*, p. 286.

333 Michael Hogan, "1904", p. 46.

334 Statistics from Michael Hogan, "1904", p. 52.

Chapter Eleven

335 "Mr. Waddell Resigns", *Sunday Times*, Sunday, 28/8/1904, p. 5.

336 "Sketches in the House", *The Catholic Press*, Thursday, 15/6/1905, p. 19.

337 "Interview with Mr. Carruthers", *Sydney Morning Herald*, Monday 29/8/1904, p. 7.

338 "The Premier at Rockdale", *Sydney Morning Herald,* Tuesday, 6/9/1904, p. 5.

339 Carruthers cited the railways as an example of this where he hoped returns could be increased, though he also condemned "wasteful" relief works that gave "less relief than if we disbursed the money as free gifts" *NSWPD,* 5/10/1904, pp. 521-30.

340 *NSWPD,* 12/10/1904, p. 701.

341 *NSWPD,* 13/10/1904, p. 738.

342 *NSWPD,* 5/10/1904, p. 517.

343 David Clune & Gareth Griffith, *Decision and Deliberation,* p. 199.

344 Carruthers to Sandford, 9/4/1907, Carruthers Papers, ML MSS 1638/51, p. 120.

345 For a more detailed account see Cyril Pearl, *The Wild Men of Sydney,* p.179. onwards, though note that Pearl's negative image of Carruthers is based heavily on Evatt who is dealt with below.

346 H.V. Evatt, *William Holman: Australian Labour Leader,* p. 181.

347 Evatt mentions this shortly before discussing the land scandals and even suggests Crick had been deliberately "accommodated". *Ibid.,* p. 169.

348 "A Free Lance", *Evening News,* Friday 19/8/1904, p. 4.

349 Rawson to Carruthers, 22/9/1905, Carruthers Papers, ML MSS 1638/6, p. 501.

350 "Local Government", *Sydney Morning Herald,* Friday, 21/7/1905, p. 5.

351 F.A. Larcombe, *A History of Local Government in New South Wales Vol. 2: The Stabilization of Local Government in New South Wales 1858-1906,* p. 284.

352 *NSWPD,* 27/7/1905, p. 1102.

353 Don Harwin, *op. cit.,* p. 61.

354 *NSWPD,* 10/8/1905, p. 1399.

355 Don Harwin, *op. cit.,* p. 62.

356 Joseph Carruthers, *A Lifetime in Conservative Politics,* p. 189.

357 J. Rydon & R. Spann, *op. cit.,* p.83. & J.D. Bollen, *op. cit.,* p. 168.

358 Waddell to Carruthers, 26/8/1907, Carruthers Papers, ML MSS 1638/34, pp. 277-80.

359 "Mr. Carruthers to Tax Catholics", *The Catholic Press,* Thursday, 21/6/1906, p. 18.

360 Elizabeth Kwan, *Flag and Nation: Australians and their national flags since 1901* (Sydney: UNSW Press, 2006) pp. 34-36.

361 "Mitchell Library", *Sydney Morning Herald,* Wednesday, 12/9/1906, p. 9.

362 Neville Hicks, "Coghlan, Sir Timothy Augustine (1855–1926)", *Australian Dictionary of Biography,* 1981.

363 Carruthers to Coghlan, 29/3/1906, Carruthers Papers, ML MSS 1638/35, p. 367.

364 Statistics from the NSW Government Bureau of Statistics presented in Joseph Carruthers, *Joey Yarns,* p. 55. Note that these figures are far more conservative than those given at the time.

365 Thomas Henley to Carruthers, 1906, Carruthers Papers, ML MSS 1638/26, pp. 79-83. & Bruce Smith to Carruthers, 3/5/1906, Carruthers Papers, ML MSS 1638/26, p. 335.

366 Joseph Carruthers, *A Lifetime in Conservative Politics,* pp. 167-9.

367 "State Politics", *Sydney Morning Herald,* Thursday, 17/1/1907, p. 7.

368 "The Elections", *Sunday Times,* 8/9/1907, p. 7.

369 Joseph Carruthers, *A Lifetime in Conservative Politics,* p. 186.

370 "No Coalition", *Sydney Morning Herald,* Wednesday, 8/5/1907, p. 9.

371 "Jump Jim Crow", *Sydney Morning Herald,* Thursday, 8/11/1906, p. 6.

372 "The Premier's Address", *Sydney Morning Herald,* Friday, 10/5/1907, pp. 7-8.

373 Ronald Syme, *The Roman Revolution,* p. 53.

374 Particularly Michael Hogan who claims simply that "Carruthers did not deliver" on his small-government reform promises, Michael Hogan ,"1907" in *The People's Choice: Electoral Politics in 20ᵗʰ Century New South Wales,* p. 60.

375 "Progress and Prosperity", *Sunday Times,* 12/5/1907, p. 6.

Chapter Twelve

376 Edward Millen to Carruthers, 8/9/1904, Carruthers Papers, ML MSS 1638/53, pp. 25-6.

377 E Roberts to Carruthers, 29/8/1904, Carruthers Papers, ML MSS 1638/53, p. 103.

378 Wise to Carruthers, 30/8/1904, Wise Papers, ML A2646 CY 1215, pp. 240-2.

379 Reid to Carruthers, 8/8/1904, Carruthers Papers, ML MSS 1638/23, CY 3153, p. 243.

380 W.G. McMinn, *George Reid,* p. 204.

381 Zachary Gorman, *Debating a Tiger Cub: The Anti-Socialist Campaign,* pp. 12-13.

382 "Federal Politics", *The Advertiser* (Adelaide), Tuesday, 7/8/1906, p. 7.

383 Zachary Gorman, "George Reid's Anti-Socialist Campaign in the Evolution of Australian Liberalism" in Gregory Melleuish, *Liberalism and Conservatism,* p. 29.

384 Ross McMullin, *The Light On The Hill: The Australian Labor Party 1891-1991,* p. 55.

385 Carruthers to Deakin, 1/5/1904, Deakin Papers, NLA MS 1540, 16/21.

386 Wise to Deakin, 1/5/1904, Deakin Papers, NLA MS 1540, 16/22.

387 Carruthers to Deakin, 7/6/1905, Deakin Papers, NLA MS 1540, 16/323-5.

388 Carruthers to Deakin, 13/6/1905, Deakin Papers, NLA MS 1540, 16/342-4.

389 P. Loveday, "The Federal Parties", p. 418.

390 Deakin to Carruthers, 8/6/1905, 19/6/1905, 20/7/1905, Carruthers Papers, ML MSS 1638/6, pp. 169-187.

391 Carruthers to Deakin, 18/7/1905, Deakin Papers, NLA MS 1540, 15/416.

392 P. Loveday, "The Federal Parties", p. 418. Based on an honours thesis by an undergraduate thesis by R.B. Scotton 1955 which is no longer retrievable

393 P. Loveday, "The Federal Parties", p. 447.

394 Michael Hogan, "So manifestly unreal and irrelevant: Confusion in New South Wales", p. 127.

395 Newspaper clipping, *Daily Telegraph*, 11/12/1906.

396 C.A. Hughes & B.D. Graham, *A Handbook of Australian Government and Politics 1890-1964*, p. 297. Carruthers actually pointed to senate results to emphasise Reid's success: newspaper clipping, *Daily Telegraph*, 14/12/1906.

397 Judith Brett, *op. cit.*, p. 25.

398 Gregory Melleuish, "Australian Liberalism" in J.R. Nethercote, *Liberalism and the Australian Federation*, p. 35.

399 Alfred Deakin, *Commonwealth Parliamentary Debates*, 21/6/1912, Vol.64, p. 101.

400 "Federal Politics", *Sydney Morning Herald*, Friday 1/2/1907, p. 7.

401 For examples of that view see Loveday as discussed earlier & also J. Rydon & R. Spann, *op. cit.*, p. 72.

402 Reid to Carruthers, 11/2/1907, Carruthers Papers, ML MSS 1638/31, p. 123. & Reid to Carruthers, 7/5/1907, Carruthers Papers, ML MSS 1638/31, p. 125.

403 The Liberals gained 6 seats in New South Wales between 1910 & 1913, C.A. Hughes & B.D. Graham, *op. cit.*, pp. 302-6.

404 G.E. Sherington, "The Politics of "State Rights": Carruthers and the New South Wales State Election of 1907", p. 187.

405 See Campbell Sharman, "Federalism and the Liberal Party" in J.R. Nethercote, *Liberalism and the Australian Federation*, p. 287.

406 "How Canberra came to be the National Capital", *The Canberra Times*, Monday 9/5/1927, p. 3.

407 "Points From The Budget", *Sydney Morning Herald*, Wednesday, 23/8/1905 p. 6. & "Budget Notes", *Sydney Morning Herald*, Wednesday, 13/9/1905, p. 6.

408 For examples see Suttor to Carruthers, Carruthers Papers, ML MSS 1638/51, pp. 74-94.

409 Joseph Carruthers, *A Lifetime in Conservative Politics,* p. 199.

410 Rawson to Carruthers, 16/2/1906, Carruthers Papers, ML MSS 1638/6.

411 Joseph Carruthers, *A Lifetime in Conservative Politics,* p. 201.

412 Account from D.I. Wright, *Shadow of Dispute,* pp. 26-7.

413 "The Japanese Famine", *Sydney Morning Herald,* Saturday, 17/2/1906, p. 13.

414 D.I. Wright, *Shadow of Dispute,* p. 27.

415 Carruthers to Deakin, 18/7/1905, Deakin Papers, NLA MS 1540, 15/416.

416 Joseph Carruthers, *A Lifetime in Conservative Politics,* p. 147.

417 Morgan to Carruthers, 29/3/1906, Carruthers Papers, ML MSS 1638/55, pp. 155-9. & Carruthers to Morgan, 16/11/1905, Carruthers Papers, ML MSS 1638/55, pp. 161-5.

418 It was Paddy Glynn suggested this was a strong possibility, D.I. Wright, *Shadow of Dispute,* p. 56.

419 "How Canberra came to be the National Capital", *The Canberra Times,* Monday, 9/5/1927, p. 4.

420 Greg Wood, "Founding Fathers: Mapping Canberra's DNA", *Canberra Historical Journal,* No.61, December 2008, pp. 26-7.

421 David Headon, . "Apple of Discord: Joseph Carruthers and his Canberra Story", *Canberra Historical Journal,* No.61, December 2008, p. 18. G.E. Sherington, "The Politics of "State Rights": Carruthers and the New South Wales State Election of 1907", p. 186. & D.I. Wright, *Shadow of Dispute,* p. 68.

422 "How Canberra came to be the National Capital", *The Canberra Times,* Monday, 9/5/1927, p. 7. & Joseph Carruthers, *A Lifetime in Conservative Politics,* p. 130.

423 G.E. Sherington, "The Politics of "State Rights": Carruthers and the New South Wales State Election of 1907", p 182.

424 "Duty on Wire Netting", *Sydney Morning Herald,* Wednesday, 14/8/1907, p. 9.

425 "Premier Defies Duties", *Sydney Morning Herald,* Thursday, 22/8/1907, p. 7.

426 "The Incendiary" & "The Founding of the NSW State Indent Department", *The Bulletin,* Thursday, 29/8/1907, p.1 & p. 6.

427 "The Federal Fetters", *Sunday Times,* 25/8/1907, p. 6.

428 Rawson to Carruthers, 27/8/1907, Carruthers Papers, ML MSS 1638/6, p. 644.

429 G.E. Sherington, "The Politics of "State Rights": Carruthers and the New South Wales State Election of 1907", p. 183.

430 *Ibid.*

431 Joseph Carruthers, "Random reflections and reminiscences", pp. 61-2.

432 J. Rydon & R. Spann, *op. cit.,* p. 87.

433 Beverley Earnshaw, *op. cit.,* p. 134.

434 "Liberal Rally", *Sydney Morning Herald,* Tuesday, 10/7/1907, p. 7.

435 C.A. Hughes & B.D. Graham, *op. cit.,* p. 438.

436 "Mr. Carruthers' Triumph", *Brisbane Courier,* Thursday, 12/9/1907, p. 4. & "Heavy Government Losses", *The Advertiser* (Adelaide), Wednesday, 11/9/1907, p. 9.

437 Michael Hogan "1907", p. 85.

438 E.g. G. Freudenberg, *Cause for Power, the Official History of the New South Wales Branch of the Australian Labor Party,* p.81. & Michael Hogan, "1907", p. 89.

439 Carruthers to Deakin, 13/6/1905, Deakin Papers, NLA MS 1540, 16/343.

440 Beverley Earnshaw, *op. cit.,* p. 137.

Chapter Thirteen

441 "The R.M.S. Asturias", *Western Mail,* Saturday, 7/3/1908, p. 14.

442 Carruthers Papers, ML MSS1638/12, p. 323.

443 Carruthers to Lloyd George, 1/8/1908, Carruthers Papers, ML MSS1638/12, pp. 285-7.

444 "The Week in London", *Sydney Morning Herald,* Tuesday, 30/6/1908, p. 4.

445 Parkhill related extensive organisational details to Carruthers and told him that "we shall want your guidance at both the Federal and state campaigns if we are to win", Parkhill to Carruthers, 29/6/1908, Carruthers Papers, ML MSS1638/11, pp. 329-30.

446 "Loan Charges", *Sydney Morning Herald,* Wednesday, 22/7/1908, p. 9.

447 David Clune, "Charles(late Sir Charles) Gregory Wade", in David Clune & Ken Turner, *The Premiers of New South Wales 1856-2005, Volume 2 1901-2005,* p. 83.

448 These hopes were not always realised, as once appointed MLC"s could prove unpredictable: David Clune & Gareth Griffith, *Decision and Deliberation,* p. 208.

449 *NSWPD*, 10/11/1909, pp. 3363-4.

450 "State Debts", *Sydney Morning Herald,* Thursday, 7/4/1910, p. 9.

451 "Constitutional Law", *Sydney Morning Herald,* Monday, 14/3/1910, p. 9.

452 "State Debts", *Sydney Morning Herald,* Thursday, 7/4/1910, p. 9.

453 "The State and Secondary Education", *Freeman's Journal,* Thursday, 14/7/1910, p. 37.

454 Michael Hogan, "1910" in *The People's Choice: Electoral Politics in 20th Century New South Wales,* p. 115.

455 Clune & Griffith have critiqued the traditional Labor view that in 1912-13 the Government was met with "outright hostility" from the Council: David Clune & Gareth

Griffith, *Decision and Deliberation,* pp. 254-5.

456 *NSWPD,* 13/12/1911, p. 2701.

457 *NSWPD,* 28/2/1912, p. 3232.

458 Mark Hearn, "Examined suspiciously: Alfred Deakin, Eleanor Cameron and Australian liberal discourse in the 1911 referendum", *History Australia,* Vol. 2, No. 3, Dec 2005: 87.1-87.20.

459 "The Referendum", *Sydney Morning Herald,* Thursday, 29/12/1910, p. 7.

460 *NSWPD,* 15/12/1910, p. 973.

461 "The Referendum", *Sydney Morning Herald,* Thursday, 30/3/1911, p. 10.

462 "Shadow for Substance", *Sunday Times,* 18/5/1913, p. 9.

463 Parkhill to Carruthers, 1/5/1914, Carruthers Papers, ML MSS1638/21, pp. 289-299.

464 Michael Hogan, "1913", p. 140.

465 *NSWPD,* 6/4/1914, p. 1104.

466 "Path of Duty", *Sydney Morning Herald,* Monday, 2/8/1915, p. 9.

467 Beverley Earnshaw, *op. cit.,* p. 160.

468 *NSWPD,* 14/3/1916, p. 5278.

469 "God Help the Empire", *Sunday Times,* 3/10/1915, p. 19.

470 *NSWPD,* 24/8/1916, pp. 1099-1103.

471 Joseph Carruthers, Autobiography, Unpublished Version, ML MSS2914, p. 88.

472 Ian Hancock, *op. cit.* pp. 21-6.

Chapter Fourteen

473 "Appeal by Sir Joseph Carruthers", *Sydney Morning Herald,* Wednesday 21/3/1917, p. 12.

474 Beverley Earnshaw, *op. cit.,* p. 154.

475 E.g. "Fighting Conscription", *The Sun,* Thursday, 8/11/1917, p. 5; "Why No Won", *The Sun,* Thursday, 27/12/1917, p. 5.

476 "General", *The Land,* Friday, 5/4/1918, p. 9.

477 In November 1918 he successfully moved a motion at the RAS conference opposing price fixing, "A Strangled Industry", *The Farmer and Settler,* Friday, 29/11/1918, p. 7.

478 *NSWPD,* 24/10/1918, pp. 2302-16.

479 Wade to Carruthers, 1/3/1918, Carruthers Papers, ML MSS1638/21, pp. 347-53.

480 *NSWPD,* 25/9/1918, p. 1754.

481 *NSWPD,* 13/11/1918, p. 2711.

482 *NSWPD*, 11/9/1919, pp. 699-711.

483 W.G. McMinn, "Pring, Robert Darlow (1853–1922)", *Australian Dictionary of Biography*, 1988.

484 *NSWPD*, 3/12/1919, p. 3339.

485 "The Progressives", *The Farmer and Settler,* Tuesday, 2/3/1920, p. 3.

486 Joseph Carruthers, Autobiography, Unpublished Version, ML MSS2914, p. 672.

487 *NSWPD*, 10/12/1920, p. 3519.

488 *NSWPD*, 14/12/1920, p. 3534.

489 "Select Committee to Report on the Conditions and Prospects of the Agricultural Industry and Methods of Improving the Same", *NSW Parliamentary Papers*, 23/9/1920, Vol. 1.

490 2.5 figure from "The Million Farms Objective", 1921, in "Immigration Encouragement. Million Farms Campaign", NAA A457 1400/5 pt.2. p. 115.

491 "Rome and Australia", *The Sun,* Wednesday, 19/10/1921, p. 7.

492 Carruthers to Hughes, 1/2/1922 in "Immigration Encouragement. Million Farms Campaign", NAA A457 1400/5 pt.2. p. 23.

493 Joseph Carruthers, Autobiography, Unpublished Version, ML MSS2914, p. 301.

494 Paul Davey, *The Nationals: The Progressive, Country and National Party in New South Wales 1919 to 2006* (Sydney: Federation Press, 2006) pp. 22-23..

495 Gary Lewis, "Million Farms Campaign, N.S.W. 1919-25", *Labour History*, No. 47. November 1984, pp. 56-7.

496 "Sir Joseph Carruthers", *Sydney Morning Herald,* Friday, 13/1/1922, p. 10.

497 Carruthers to Hughes, 1/2/1922 in "Immigration Encouragement. Million Farms Campaign", NAA A457 1400/5 pt.2. p. 23.

498 Michael Hogan, "1922", pp. 236-262.

499 Michael Hogan, "1925", pp. 273-4.

500 *NSWPD*, 13/7/1922, p. 313.

501 "The Carruthers Puppet Show", *The Australian Worker,* Wednesday, 10/5/1922, p. 10.

502 *NSWPD*, 18/12/1923, p. 3544.

503 *NSWPD*, 20/12/1923, p. 3749.

504 "Another Suppressed Report", *Evening News,* Tuesday, 25/7/1922, p. 4.

505 "Land Settlement", *Sydney Morning Herald,* Monday, 30/7/1923, p. 10.

506 David Lee, *Stanley Melbourne Bruce: Australian Internationalist*, p. 38.

507 Michael Hogan, "1925", p. 271.

508 Joseph Carruthers, 16/5/1923, Carruthers Papers, ML MSS1638/70, Item 3, pp. 7-8

509 Carruthers to Fuller, 29/11/1923, Carruthers Papers, ML MSS1638/68, pp. 189-91.

510 Gary Lewis, *op. cit.,* p. 67.

511 Michael Hogan, "1925", p. 321.

Chapter Fifteen

512 "Hawaii", *Sydney Morning Herald*, Tuesday, 16/9/1924, p. 9.

513 "Matters of Moment", *the Farmer and Settler*, Friday, 13/11/1925 p. 9.

514 Carruthers Papers, ML MSS 1638/42, p. 181.

515 "Where Cook Fell", *Sydney Morning Herald*, Tuesday, 25/10/1925, p. 9.

516 Joseph Carruthers, *Captain James Cook R.N., 150 Years After*, p. 219.

517 Drummond to Carruthers, 10/12/1929, Carruthers Papers, ML MSS 1638/44, p. 221.

518 "Samoan Unrest", *Sydney Morning Herald*, Tuesday, 19/7/1927, p. 11.

519 "Unrest in Samoa", *Sydney Morning Herald*, Monday, 25/7/1927, p. 10.

520 "Samoan Affairs", *Sydney Morning Herald*, Saturday, 3/9/1927, p. 8.

521 Ward to Carruthers, 12/1/1929, Carruthers Papers, ML MSS 1638/17, p. 217.

522 Carruthers Papers, ML MSS 1638/63, Item 1.

523 "Bondi's Oldest Building", *The Catholic Press*, Thursday, 3/5/1928, p. 22.

524 Carruthers Papers, ML MSS 1638/76, p. 431.

525 Bede Nairn, *The Big Fella: Jack Lang and the Australian Labor Party 1891-1949*, p. 97.

526 "No Mandate", *Sydney Morning Herald*, Tuesday 20/10/1925, p. 9.

527 Anne Twomey, "Sir Dudley Rawson Stratford de Chair" in *The Governors of New South Wales 1788-2006*, p. 463.

528 David Clune & Gareth Griffith, *Decision and Deliberation*, p. 281.

529 *NSWPD*, 21/12/1925, p. 3701.

530 *Ibid.,* p. 3710.

531 *NSWPD*, 20/1/1926, p. 4185.

532 David Clune & Gareth Griffith, *Decision and Deliberation*, p. 284.

533 *NSWPD*, 6/9/1923, p. 713.

534 Douglas Brown, "New South Wales Family Endowment Act, 1927", *The Quarterly Journal of Economics*, Vol. 42, No. 3, May 1928, pp. 501-3.

535 *NSWPD*, 22/3/1927, p. 2294.

536 Joseph Carruthers, Autobiography, Unpublished Version, ML MSS2914, p. 301.

537 *NSWPD*, 23/12/1926, p. 122.

538 John McCarthy, "Bavin, Sir Thomas Rainsford (Tom) (1874-1941)", *Australian Dictionary of Biography*, 1979.

539 *NSWPD*, 13/11/1928, p. 1760.

540 *NSWPD*, 13/11/1928, p. 1762.

541 David Clune & Gareth Griffith, *Decision and Deliberation*, p. 288.

542 Heather Radi, "Lang's Legislative Councillors" in *Jack Lang* (Marrickville: Hale & Iremonger, 1977) p. 112.

543 "Legislative Council", *Sydney Morning Herald*, Wednesday, 6/4/1927, p. 10.

544 Carruthers Papers, ML MSS1638/76, p. 131 & *NSWPD*, 15/10/1929, pp. 443.

545 *NSWPD*, 15/10/1929, pp. 440-1.

546 David Clune & Gareth Griffith, *Decision and Deliberation*, p. 291.

547 *NSWPD*, 26/11/1929, pp. 1665-6.

548 J.B. Paul, "Thomas (later Sir Thomas) Rainsford Bavin" in David Clune & Ken Turner, *The Premiers of New South Wales 1856-2005, Volume 2 1901-2005*, p. 211.

549 "Nationalist Victory", *Sydney Morning Herald*, Friday, 24/10/1930, p. 12.

550 "Letters", *Sydney Morning Herald*, Monday 3/2/1930, p. 5.

551 Joseph Carruthers, *Joey Yarns,* p. 52.

552 "Nationalist Club Honours", *Sydney Morning Herald*, Thursday, 26/2/1931, p. 12.

553 David Clark, "Was Lang right?" in *Jack Lang*, p. 157.

554 *NSWPD*, 25/3/1931, p. 2150.

555 A.W. Martin, *Robert Menzies: a life*, Vol. 1, p. 79.

556 See Geoffrey Robinson, "The all for Australia league in New South Wales: a study in political entrepreneurship and hegemony", *Australian Historical Studies*, 2008, Vol. 39, No. 1, pp. 36-52.

557 *NSWPD*, 25/3/1931, p. 2152.

558 Ian Hancock, *op. cit.,* pp. 28-31.

559 *NSWPD*, 12/5/1932, p. 9363.

560 "Judge Piddington and the Governor", *Sydney Morning Herald*, Monday, 23/5/1932, p. 8.

561 *NSWPD*, 20/9/1932, p. 292.

562 Percival to Carruthers, 24/11/1932, Carruthers Papers, ML MSS1638/22, p. 423.

563 *NSWPD*, 13/12/1932, p. 2792.

INDEX

retrenchment and reform
movements, 16, 27, 132, 206,
209-11, 216-7, 221, 226, 232,
235, 237

sectarianism, 7, 51, 141, 232-4, 258-
60, 311-2, 338, 342, 348

See, John, 82, 92-3, 186-7, 189-95,
202-3, 205, 225, 227-8, 231, 234

single tax, 46-7, 68, 99, 179

Smith, Bruce, 28, 35, 37, 40, 51, 59,
61-2, 65, 69, 74, 76-8, 81, 86, 91,
98, 110, 130, 135, 142-3, 156, 158,
178, 180, 264

tax reform, 26-7, 33, 43-4, 46-7, 52,
93-5, 99-100, 108, 111, 119, 123,
125, 128, 131, 168-70, 203, 227,
246, 254-5, 260, 264-5, 268-70,

292, 296, 300-1, 303, 312-4, 318,
321, 325, 336, 346-7, 363, 365-7,
372, 378

Waddell, Thomas, 10, 189, 191, 226,
232, 235-6, 241-5, 250, 252-3,
267, 303, 374

Wade, Charles, 242-3, 247, 257, 301,
303-4, 307-11, 318, 320, 323, 330

Wentworth, William, 2, 11, 90, 93,
124, 298, 317, 357-8

Wise, Bernhard, 23, 28-30, 35, 40, 44,
62, 74-8, 86, 92, 96, 98-100, 103-4,
106, 108, 110, 119-21, 123, 126-7,
129-30, 137, 142-3, 146, 148, 155,
157-8, 162, 167, 169, 172, 178, 180,
185, 194, 202-3, 207, 210, 213,
231-2, 234-6, 271, 340, 362

www.ingramcontent.com/pod-product-compliance
Lightning Source LLC
Chambersburg PA
CBHW071008140426
42814CB00004BA/160